George Younger

A Life Well Lived

BY THE SAME AUTHOR

The Scottish Secretaries

GEORGE YOUNGER

A Life Well Lived

David Torrance

BIRLINN

The Publisher acknowledges the generous support of
Diana, Viscountess Younger of Leckie, towards
the publication of this book

First published in 2008 by
Birlinn Limited
West Newington House
10 Newington Road
Edinburgh
EH9 1QS

www.birlinn.co.uk

ISBN 13: 978 1 84158 686 1
ISBN 10: 1 84158 686 2

British Library Cataloguing-in-Publication Data
A catalogue record for this book is available from the British Library

Typeset by Iolaire Typesetting, Newtonmore
Printed and bound by The Cromwell Press, Trowbridge

Contents

ILLUSTRATIONS

1st Viscount Younger of Leckie by Sir William Orpen, c.1920s (*Lady Younger*).

Teddy and Evelyn Younger, c.1960s (*Lady Younger*).

George with friend, c.1930s (*Lady Younger*).

George playing his French horn, c.1940s (*Lady Younger*).

George and friends in Korea, 1951 (*Lady Younger*).

The Younger brothers in TA gear, c.1950s (*Lady Younger*).

George and Diana Younger, a wedding photograph, 1954 (*Lady Younger*).

George's campaign poster from the 1959 general election (*Lady Younger*).

Diana and George campaigning in Ayr, c.1964 (*Lady Younger*).

Edward Heath visits George in Ayr, c.1969 (*Lady Younger*).

George visiting an air force base in the United States, 1968 (*Lady Younger*).

George with his hosts in South Africa, 1969 (*Lady Younger*).

The under-secretary for development with Scottish Secretary Gordon Campbell and Lady Tweedsmuir, c.1970 (*Lady Younger*).

George jets off to attract German investment to Scotland, 1971 (*Lady Younger*).

George with the Young Turks, 1975 (*Lady Younger*).

George with Andrew and Charlie at Winchester, 1981 (*Lady Younger*).

George and his son Andrew during the 1979 general election campaign (*Lady Younger*).

The Younger family in Bute House, 1979 (*Lady Younger*).

George, Willie Whitelaw and Margaret Thatcher at a Cabinet meeting, 1985 (*Lady Younger*).

Diana and George with Willie Whitelaw en route to the Royal Wedding, 1981 (*Lady Younger*)

George sees off Gorbachev at Edinburgh Airport, 1984 (*The Scotsman Publications*).

George being presented with a miniature bed of nails, 1985 (*Lady Younger*).

George wearing his Defence Council cap badge, 1987 (*Lady Younger*).

ACKNOWLEDGEMENTS

'NOBODY CAN WRITE the life of a man,' Dr Johnson remarked, 'but those who have ate and drunk and lived in social intercourse with him.' Alas, I never met George Younger and saw him in person only once, when he was Lord High Commissioner to the General Assembly of the Church of Scotland in 2002. He was by then terminally ill, although that fact had not yet been publicly revealed.

I had considered contacting Viscount Younger, as he then was, to interview him for a book I was researching on the Scottish Office. When news of his cancer emerged later that year I decided it would be churlish to do so but happily, three years later, I met Joanna Davidson – George's only daughter – to discuss her father's career for that book, which became *The Scottish Secretaries*. Joanna mentioned that the Younger family was looking for someone to edit a book of biographical essays on her father; I rather shamelessly offered my services.

Another year passed and the book's format gradually evolved. A cursory glance around the garage at Leckie – the Younger family home near Gargunnock in Stirlingshire – convinced me there was more than enough material for a full-length biography. Scottish politicians are sadly under-represented in biographical terms; I relished the opportunity to rectify that deficit in my own modest way.

The political biographer D. R. Thorpe said 'people, places and papers' were the three essential components of political biography and indeed, all three have proved invaluable. People first. I would like to record my thanks to the following, all of whom spoke to me either in person, by telephone or in writing (email or by hand): Sir Ian Andrews; Jeffrey Archer; John Berridge; Janet Buchanan-Smith; Frank Carlucci; Andrew Dunlop; John Findlay; Sir William Kerr Fraser; Lord Freeman; Robin Gill; Robert Gordon; John Graham; Ann Green; Lord Hamilton; Brian Hawtin; Ann Hay; Barry Henderson; Lord Heseltine; Sir Michael Hirst; Lord Home; John Howe; Matthew Hudson; Quintin Jardine; Bob

Kernohan; Iain Lawson; Lord Lee; Lord Levene; Lord Mackay of Clashfern; Peter Mackay; Kenneth MacKenzie; Sir Donald Maclean; Alan MacPherson; Sir George Mathewson; Professor John Mavor; Dr Gavin McCrone; Ian McIntyre; the Very Rev John Miller; Alasdair Milne; Sir Richard Mottram; Mike Murray; Sir Gerry Neale; Sir Michael Neubert; Ian Penman; Lord Powell; Lord Prior; Sir Michael Quinlan; Sir Malcolm Rifkind MP; Godfrey Robson; Sir Muir Russell; Sir Timothy Sainsbury; Lord Sanderson; David Scott; Eleanor Seditas; Lord Sewel; Sir Stephen Sherbourne; Lord Stewartby; Bill Taylor; Sir Teddy Taylor; Lord Trefgarne; Sir David Trippier; Lord Vallance; Geoffrey Warner; Sir Clive Whitmore.

Many of them commented on the draft manuscript, while individual chapters were also read by Ian Donnachie, Ranald Leask, Douglas Pattullo, D. R. Thorpe and my brother, Michael Torrance. Professor James Mitchell of Strathclyde University kindly read the whole manuscript and offered numerous invaluable insights, suggestions for additional sources and structural tips. Alex Neil MSP, Colin Faulkner and Andrew Kerr also read the entire manuscript. Although they have all saved me from several howlers and instigated many improvements, any remaining errors of fact or interpretation are entirely my responsibility. Thanks must also go to Judge Leonard Stark, who kindly provided an interview transcript from his own political research; Neil Freshwater, who helped with Napier University contacts; Mike Edwards, my colleague at STV, who was an invaluable reference tool on all things TA; my friend James Douse, who diligently tracked down contact details and sources, and offered endless encouragement; and David Rees, who took the flattering author picture which adorns the dustwrapper of this book. My parents also provided their usual silent encouragement.

Now for places. Nick Mackinnon, the housemaster at Hawkins, George's old house at Winchester College, kindly showed me around that beautiful school; my university friend Philip Atkinson drove me to Leeds to see the Royal Armouries of which Younger was chairman. I saw for myself Parliament, St Andrew's House, Dover House, New College, Oxford and, of course, Leckie, all of which enabled me to put the man in both domestic and professional context.

As for papers, by far the richest source was what is referred to in the text as 'GYP', or the George Younger Papers, which I have had the pleasure of examining and sorting over the past two years. Otherwise, Sheridan Westlake kindly gave permission to look at the Conservative Party Archive at the Bodleian Library; Peter Duncan, the former chairman of the Scottish Conservative Party, granted access to the Scottish Conservative and Unionist Association Papers at the National Library of Scotland; Nick

Mackinnon produced Hawkins' house records at Winchester College, while the Margaret Thatcher Foundation website – www.margaretthatcher.org – provided an excellent source of material covering the period 1975 to 1979. The British Library in London proved a conducive environment in which to work and check secondary sources, as did the London Library and the National Library of Scotland in Edinburgh. Corie Chambers at the House of Commons Library was, as ever, unknowingly helpful.

Hugh Andrew at Birlinn was as enthusiastic a publisher as ever, as were his excellent production team, particularly Jim Hutcheson, Kenny Redpath and Andrew Simmons. Philip Hillyer was also a diligent and sympathetic copy-editor. For help with the pictures, I must thank – among others – the *Scotsman* picture library and the *Herald*'s photograph archive at the Mitchell Library in Glasgow. Most of the illustrations, however, come from a formidable collection at Leckie.

The extraordinary hospitality afforded me by Diana, Viscountess Younger of Leckie, and the rest of the Younger clan, allowed me to fulfill at least part of Dr Johnson's requirement of a biographer. Joanna Davidson was encouraging throughout while her three brothers, James, Charlie and Andrew, all gave willingly of their time and memories. Bobby Younger, George's younger brother, furnished me with details of the family tree while his cousin, Sam Younger, took time out from chairing the Electoral Commission to talk about his father Kenneth Younger. A second cousin, the Scottish Tory MEP John Purvis, was also hugely helpful. During frequent visits to Leckie I was treated like one of the family; fed, watered, generally mothered and, most enjoyably of all, allowed to rummage at will through boxes of letters, diaries, papers and ephemera associated with Younger's long career in public life. At no point did Diana attempt to interfere with my research or my eventual interpretations, and her tirelessness in checking the text and recalling long-forgotten incidents was invaluable. It became very clear to me just how close the 50-year marriage of George and Diana had been. I hope this biography does George's life – as the title says, 'a life well lived' – justice.

David Torrance
August 2008
Edinburgh

Younger Family Tree

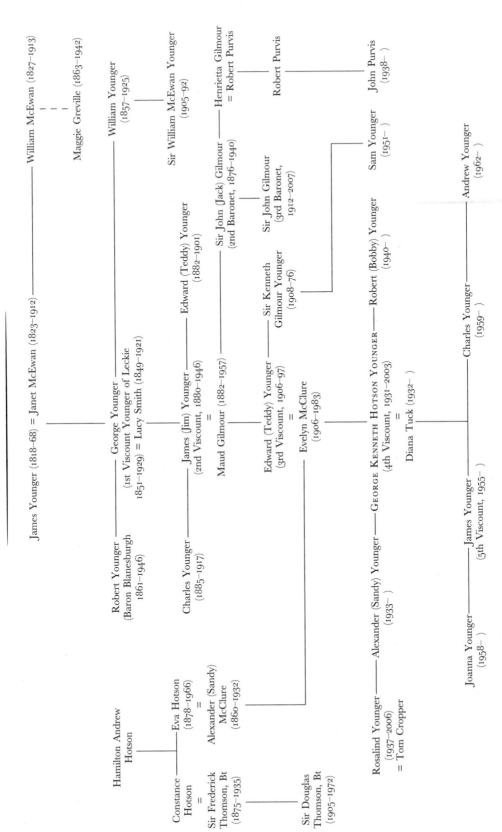

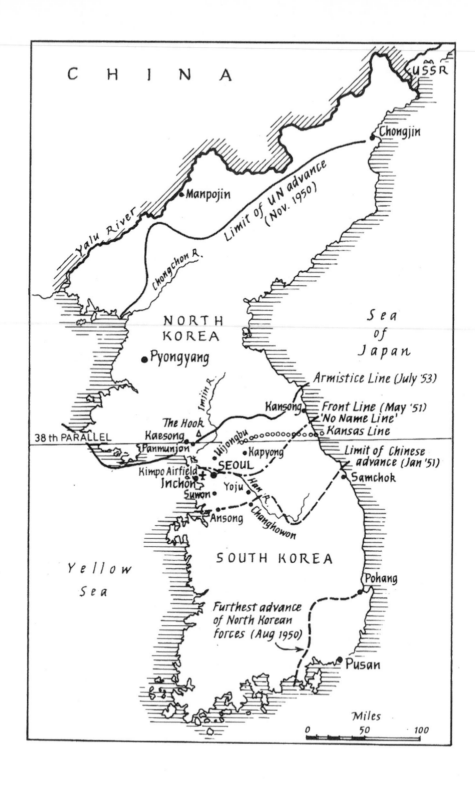

CHINA

USSR

Chongjin

Manpojin

Yalu River

Limit of UN advance (Nov. 1950)

Chongchon R.

NORTH KOREA

Sea of Japan

Pyongyang

Tmjin R.

Armistice Line (July '53)

Kansong

Front Line (May '51) 'No Name Line'

38th PARALLEL

The Hook

Kaesong

Kansas Line

Panmunjon

Wijongbu

Kapyong

Limit of Chinese advance (Jan '51)

SEOUL

Kimpo Airfield

Inchon

Yoju

Han R.

Samchok

Suwon

Ansong

Changhowon

Yellow Sea

SOUTH KOREA

Pohang

Furthest advance of North Korean forces (Aug 1950)

Pusan

Miles

0   50   100

FOREWORD

IT HAS BEEN GIVEN to few to play important parts in so many spheres of activity. George Younger was Secretary of State for Defence as the Cold War drew to a close; Warden of his *alma mater*, Winchester College, which provided him with an important role in the world of education; and chairman of the Royal Bank of Scotland, which became a very notable part of the United Kingdom financial sector thanks to the acquisition of NatWest in 2000, a takeover in which George played a major part.

These were significant achievements, but George's record in his native Scotland was equally remarkable. His first UK Cabinet posting was as Secretary of State for Scotland; he became an important officer in the Queen's Bodyguard for Scotland; a Knight of the Thistle; Lord High Commissioner to the General Assembly of the Church of Scotland on two occasions; and a doughty defender of the Argyll and Sutherland Highlanders in which he had served, most notably during the Korean War. David Torrance gives a fascinating account of all these and much more in this comprehensive and eminently readable book.

I first met George Younger when Margaret Thatcher invited me to become Lord Advocate in 1979. George had just been appointed Scottish Secretary and he welcomed me warmly, making it clear that he fully understood that the Scottish law officers were not part of the Scottish Office team but had their own autonomous responsibilities. Nevertheless, he afforded us any help we wished from the Scottish Office, for example the department's press office and staff. As a complete novice in politics, I found this immensely helpful.

George also invited us to attend the Scottish Office ministerial meetings over which he presided. His style of chairmanship was relaxed but imbued with great qualities of leadership and the ability to secure agreement on the way forward without being in the least dictatorial. The Scottish political scene of that time was far from calm. Some government policies were by no means acceptable to many Scots and occasionally otherwise loyal supporters gave public voice to their opposition. George's attitude was that no one ever progressed by cutting off the branch on which he was sitting, believing the correct course was to engage in rational argument in order to exercise some influence over the policy in question.

I have always felt that a law officer's role in government is very exposed and from time to time we experienced stormy waters. At such times George was a tremendous support. Without in any way becoming involved in our decision-making he gave us encouragement to hope that the storms would soon pass. Usually they did.

After I had been Lord Advocate for five years a vacancy occurred on the Bench of the Scottish Supreme Courts. It had been the practice for the Lord Advocate to nominate the candidate to fill such a vacancy to the Secretary of State, which was then passed on to Her Majesty for approval. In the circumstances, I felt reluctant to nominate myself and suggested to George that he should look into it and make the nomination without any intervention from me if he felt I was suitable. After a diplomatic period of time, he asked me if I would like to take it.

As a result my close relationship with George on a day-to-day basis came to an end. We were to become colleagues again three years later when I joined the Cabinet as Lord Chancellor and he was Secretary of State for Defence, which gave me an opportunity to observe his calm, courteous but powerfully persuasive manner in action for the benefit of a very different government department.

Later, after George had joined the Royal Bank of Scotland, I heard him speak in the House of Lords where he deployed the same qualities to a rather quieter audience. My wife Bett and I were privileged to be guests at the Banqueting House in Whitehall at a magnificent occasion to mark his retirement from the chairmanship of RBS at which it was clear he enjoyed great respect from his former colleagues. We were also guests of George and his lovely wife Diana when he became Lord High Commissioner two months later, the duties of which he carried out with such grace and distinction.

Sadly, George was taken from us much too soon. His was certainly a life well lived, not only in public life but also through private passions such as sailing and music. That rich life is accurately captured – through all of its different facets – in this carefully researched biography.

LORD MACKAY OF CLASHFERN
Lord Advocate 1979–84
Lord Chancellor 1987–97

Abbreviations

ABS   Alick Buchanan-Smith
ADH   Sir Alec Douglas-Home (Lord Home)
DY   Diana Younger
FCCG   Freddie C. C. Graham
GY   George Younger
GYP   George Younger Papers
LLY   Lord and Lady Younger
MT   Margaret Thatcher
MTF   Margaret Thatcher Foundation
TT   Teddy Taylor
WW   Willie Whitelaw

A note on the text: Mainly, the biography is in chronological order but in Chapters 9, 10, 12 and 13 it was necessary to group sections thematically. Sub-headings identify each theme.

PRELUDE

GEORGE KENNETH HOTSON YOUNGER was born on 22 September 1931 at Garfield House, a Victorian townhouse in Stirling. A child of the depression and the inter-war 'age of illusion', his life began amid one of the most turbulent periods in British politics. Ramsay MacDonald had recently split the Labour Party by forming a National Government comprising Conservatives, Liberals and the few Socialists who remained loyal to the first Labour prime minister. Just hours before George was born at shortly after 2 a.m., MacDonald's fledgling administration had been forced to abandon the Gold Standard. A general election was also imminent. The Youngers' motto was *Celer et Audax*, or 'Swift and Bold', both of which were useful attributes in the context of the early 1930s.

Despite the bleak economic climate, George Younger had been born to relative affluence and an assured position in society. As the eldest son of a viscount with a family brewery, he had no reason to doubt his prospects or question his role in the world. In this sense, the story of George Younger bears many similarities to the lives of Sir Alec Douglas-Home and Willie Whitelaw, both Scots and products of an age in which public service took precedence over personal and political gain.

The Younger family had a long history of public service. At the end of 1931, when George was born, his grandfather James, the 2nd Viscount Younger of Leckie, sat in the House of Lords as a crossbencher, while his brother-in-law, the former Secretary of State for Scotland, Sir John Gilmour, had just been appointed Minister of Agriculture in the new National Government. Sir John's sister, Maud Gilmour,[1] had married the 2nd Viscount in 1906. They had two daughters and two sons: Edward

[1] Another of Sir John's sisters, Henrietta Gilmour, married a Robert Purvis, whose grandson John (a second cousin of Younger's) served as a Conservative Member of the European Parliament from 1979 to 1984 and from 1999 to 2009.

(always known as Teddy) – the future 3rd Viscount and father of George – and Kenneth – later a Labour MP and minister – who had recently graduated from New College, Oxford.

That Teddy's eldest son, George, should pursue a career in politics may therefore appear to have been inevitable. Yet his path to Parliament was far from assured. Younger fought and lost a hopeless constituency (North Lanarkshire) like any other aspiring MP; stood aside in a far from hopeless seat (Kinross and West Perthshire) so that a prime minister could complete his transition from Earl to commoner; and, when George finally made it to the House of Commons, he fought like any other MP to retain a periodically marginal constituency.

Even years later George had his share of setbacks. As a junior Scottish Office minister in the early 1970s he was passed over for promotion despite a confident performance in the development brief; although elevated to the Conservative front bench as Shadow Defence Secretary in 1975 he was sacked without warning just a year later; and, after more than six years as Scottish Secretary in the 1980s, Younger often thought he would never make it to his only other coveted position of Defence Secretary.

Each time, a combination of good luck and unostentatious ability ensured that events soon turned in George's favour. Although he belonged in some ways to the old political era – when the eldest son of a viscount could reasonably assume that the worlds of business and politics would welcome him with open arms – Younger effectively constituted a bridge to the new. His Ayr seat was far from safe; he worked hard, both there and in the House; his progressive outlook on constitutional and domestic policy marked him out from the so-called 'knights of the shire' (a label which Sir John Gilmour,[2] George's cousin and a fellow Tory MP, often attracted) who took little interest in ideology. The Hon. George K. H. Younger – as he styled himself before dropping the prefix and middle initials – also had a flair for political presentation which not only rooted him firmly in the new political generation, but also pointed towards today's media-centric orthodoxy.

So the life of George Younger is undoubtedly an interesting one. Alas, he was almost alone in not producing a volume of memoirs following his departure from front-line politics in 1989. Although George drafted a synopsis and met with a publisher in 1991, the project came to nothing. Instead, he wrote three autobiographical features for *Scotland on Sunday*, which ran in October 1993 under the banner: 'Thatcher: The Inside

---

[2] Sir John (the 3rd baronet) was the eldest son of the former Scottish Secretary.

Story'. The former prime minister had just published her memoirs, something Younger considered 'a little premature'.[3]

The engaging but insubstantial articles shed little light on Younger's Cabinet career or his relationship with Margaret Thatcher. Always at the back of George's mind, however, was the intention to keep what he referred to in a radio interview as the 'Younger Diaries'. 'The Diaries will have two sides to them,' he elaborated on BBC Radio Scotland in 1985. 'I think that the most amusing . . . side of it will be the way in which the relationship between all the parts of the set-up in Scotland have clubbed together behind the scenes – and this is why it's only coming out in the diaries; it's not coming out now – to fix things in Scotland's favour.' He continued:

> I've had meetings, clandestine meetings, with trade unionists, with local authority people, with people in other parties – all sorts of people – and we have . . . shut the door, shut the window, and then put down our pens and said right, how do we sort this out, and there are some very amusing stories to be told about that. And the other end of things of course, much the most interesting side of the Younger Diaries – if they ever see the light of day – will be the Whitehall end in this sense; that one finds out within a few months of joining a team where the main helpers and supporters are going to be, and we have a number of very effective helpers and supporters in Whitehall who have never failed me yet and they'll have an honoured place in the Younger Diaries, but whether they'll be pleased – or their ghosts will be pleased – to see it I don't know.[4]

They never did, and although Younger did keep a diary sporadically from the late 1950s – when he first embarked upon a political career – until the end of the 1970s, the last entry is dated 26 July 1979, just three months after he joined Mrs Thatcher's Cabinet as Scottish Secretary. George had neither the inclination nor the time to be as prolific as Tony Benn, although the few dozen or so days he did record provide a valuable insight into both the politician and the man.

When the *Scotsman* asked Younger about his successful battle to reprieve the Ravenscraig steelworks in the early 1980s, he simply replied: 'That's memoirs stuff.' 'When he does cross that bridge and start his memoirs,' observed the resulting article, 'he will be able to assess whether his style of Scottish Secretaryship is still in vogue – and perhaps confirm what many quietly believe: that he in fact is a Tory Wet with a strong sense of Scottish identity.'[5]

[3] *Scotland on Sunday* 17/10/1993.
[4] *Playing the Scottish Card* II (BBC Radio Scotland) 16/9/1985.
[5] *Scotsman Magazine* 7/1985.

Younger undoubtedly had a strong sense of Scottish identity, but he was much more than just a 'Tory Wet'. There was also much more to George than just politics. Like Denis Healey, he had a vast 'political hinterland'; a range of outside interests into which happy retreat was always possible. Chiefly, that retreat was musical, thus the title of this brief preface. Continuing the theme, George's legacy is assessed in a coda at the end of this book. But first, it is useful to put him in historical and genealogical context by examining the Youngers of Leckie.

Chapter 1

THE YOUNGERS OF LECKIE

FOR MOST OF THE last three centuries the Youngers of Leckie were in
fact the Youngers of Alloa. The Younger family originally came from
Culross in Fife, where they owned saltpans, but moved to Alloa where
George Younger was born in 1722. Kirk records for 1745 describe him
simply as a 'brewer', and in 1762 he established George Younger & Sons
at the Meadow Brewery on Alloa's Bank Street. Although George
Younger died in 1788, the business continued to trade under his name
– handed down from father to son – for the next 175 years. In 1897 it
became a limited company, by which time George Younger & Sons was
among the largest breweries in Scotland with substantial export trade.

Situated on the north bank of the Forth Estuary, a few miles down
river from Stirling, Alloa had come into prominence as a manufacturing
town in the latter half of the eighteenth century. It was also well situated to
meet a related increase in demand for ale, being blessed with a supply
of pure water from the nearby Ochil Hills along with good-quality barley
from neighbouring Fife. By the turn of the twentieth century Alloa was
second only to Edinburgh as a brewing centre in Scotland. There, one
of the largest breweries was William Younger & Co. of Leith which,
despite the shared surname, had no proven connection with its Alloa
namesake, although Robert Younger – a direct descendant of the Youngers
of Alloa – had also begun brewing in the capital in the mid nineteenth
century.

Another Edinburgh connection was William McEwan & Co., established in 1856 and based at the Fountain Brewery[1] near the eastern
terminus of the Union Canal. William McEwan's sister Janet had married
James Younger (1818–68) – the fourth generation to run George Younger
& Sons – in 1850. Not only was McEwan's Fountain Brewery remarkably

---

[1] The Fountain Brewery closed in June 2005 when Scottish & Newcastle transferred production of
McEwan's and (William) Younger's beers to the Caledonian Brewery in Slateford.

successful, but in 1886 he entered Parliament as the Gladstonian Liberal MP for Edinburgh Central. A notable philanthropist, he funded the construction of Edinburgh's McEwan Hall, now familiar to generations of students as a graduation venue, and died in 1913 with a fortune valued at £1.5 million.[2]

Of James and Janet Younger's six children, three sons became notable in different fields. William (1857–1925) flourished as a brewer and became managing director of his uncle's firm, William McEwan & Co.,[3] while Robert (1861–1946, not the Edinburgh brewer), became a respected judge and – as Baron Blanesburgh – an influential lord of appeal and ultimately a law lord. But it was the eldest son, George, who transformed the family from the Youngers of Alloa into the Youngers of Leckie.

Born in 1851, George Younger took control of George Younger & Sons when he was not yet 17. Like his uncle, William McEwan, he thereafter mixed beer with politics, eventually being elected the Unionist MP for Ayr Burghs in 1906. A relatively small man with sparkling eyes and a great sense of fun, Younger was recognised as a capable debater in the House of Commons, particularly in opposing the 'people's budget' of 1909 (he reputedly collapsed during one debate, remarking 'Tell Lloyd George I'm no deid yet'[4] in his strong Scots accent). On demands for Scottish home rule, he declared: 'I do not find any strongly expressed sentiment in favour of this change in Scotland.'[5] He thought that administrative, rather than constitutional, reform was the answer, an argument his great-grandson would later use as Scottish Secretary.

But it was as a party organiser that Younger secured his place in Conservative Party history. Awarded a baronetcy in 1911, he rose steadily through the ranks, becoming Scottish Unionist Whip and, in 1917, party chairman. Sir George knocked into shape a party machine seriously weakened by the First World War, and although he initially saw the wartime coalition (led by the Liberal Lloyd George) as a necessary evil to keep Labour out of government, by 1919 he was determined that the Unionists should withdraw.

Matters came to a head in January 1922. Although Sir George had asked to be relieved as party chairman after the death of his wife Lucy (a talented pianist) in 1921, the new Unionist leader, Austen Chamberlain,

[2] His heiress was Margaret Anderson, later better known as the noted society hostess Dame Maggie Greville, who was probably McEwan's illegitimate daughter.
[3] William's son, Sir William McEwan Younger (1905–92), also worked at William McEwan & Co. and was George's predecessor as chairman of the Scottish Conservative Party from 1971 to 1974 (see p. 116).
[4] Slaven, *Dictionary of Scottish Business Biography*, 74.
[5] Marr, *The Battle for Scotland*, 237.

persuaded him to stay on. Nevertheless, Chamberlain treated his chairman rather coolly. The pair repeatedly clashed over tactics and, above all, continuing Unionist support for the coalition. Sir George acted as the main liaison between fellow rebels like Stanley Baldwin and Andrew Bonar Law, whom he was trying to persuade to lead the revolt. Younger urged Bonar Law to attend a decisive meeting of the Unionist Parliamentary party at the Carlton Club on 19 October 1922, and the future prime minister's speech proved crucial in the successful vote to jettison the coalition.

The leading Conservative coalitionist, Lord Birkenhead (F. E. Smith), famously denounced Younger as a presumptuous 'cabin boy' who aspired to run the ship,[6] but in the election that followed Sir George was vindicated as the Unionists were returned to office with a landslide majority. His reward was to become Viscount Younger of Leckie and Conservative Party treasurer.[7] Younger's great-grandson, also George, was understandably fascinated by his illustrious forebear, and his ghost was never far away throughout his life; whether he was working at the family brewery in the 1950s; representing Ayr in the Commons from the 1960s; pulling Conservative Party strings in the 1970s and 1980s; or chairing the Royal Bank of Scotland in the 1990s.[8] Wags could not resist comparisons. The 1st Viscount had been responsible for the resignation of Lloyd George; as Margaret Thatcher's campaign manager in 1990 the future 4th Viscount unwittingly played a part in the demise of another prime minister.

In 1931, when George was born, family life revolved around Leckie, the nineteenth-century Stirlingshire pile acquired by his great-grandfather in 1906. The 1st Viscount had died of a heart attack in 1929, but lives on to this day at Leckie in two oil paintings, one depicting him as a young brewer, and another – by the celebrated portrait painter Sir William Orpen – much later in life as a Conservative grandee.[9] His great-grandson used to cycle along the vast corridors in the basement of the sprawling building, which also provided opportunities for vigorous exercise. 'One of my uncles told me when I was small that I should always

---

[6] Birkenhead also remarked: 'Since the day when the proverbial frog swelled itself up in rivalry with the bull until it burst, no frog ever has been in such grave physical danger as Sir George Younger' (Birkenhead, *The Life of F. E. Smith*, 454).

[7] The 1st Viscount wanted to be styled 'Viscount Younger of Alloa', but the Earl of Mar and Kellie already possessed a subsidiary title of the same name. Similarly, his great-grandson wanted his life peerage to be 'Lord Younger of Ayr', but an existing title meant he instead chose Prestwick.

[8] The 1st Viscount was a director of the National Bank of Scotland and Lloyds Bank.

[9] A copy of Orpen's portrait hung at the Carlton Club until an IRA explosion damaged it beyond restoration in the early 1990s.

run up stairs,' George later recalled, 'so I run up stairs whenever possible; it keeps you fit.'[10]

The year of George's birth also saw the creation of Scottish Brewers Ltd, when the rival brewing firms of William Younger & Co. (the Leith brewery, no relationship established) and William McEwan & Co. (founded by the 1st Viscount's uncle) pooled certain financial and technical resources while continuing to compete fiercely for trade. George Younger & Sons was still trading in Alloa, where George's grandfather James, the 2nd Viscount Younger of Leckie, was a director. Born in 1880, James was the first of the family to attend Winchester and New College, Oxford, which thereafter became the norm for many of the Younger clan.[11] Both his brothers – Edward (or Teddy) and Charles – were killed in action (Teddy in the Boer War and Charles in the First World War), and James was himself severely injured in France when he was caught in an explosion towards the end of the Great War.

Jim, as he was known, had four children – two sons and two daughters – of which Edward (again known as Teddy) was the eldest. He was born on 21 November 1906, the year of the great Liberal landslide and the year in which his grandfather, George Younger, entered Parliament as the MP for Ayr Burghs. But unlike his grandfather, or indeed his brother Kenneth (from 1945 the Labour MP for Grimsby), Teddy did not seek a political career despite having studied PPE (Politics, Philosophy and Economics) at Oxford.

A natural Keynesian when it came to economic management, Teddy instead concentrated on farming and forestry – the latter of which became a great passion – on becoming the 3rd Viscount in 1946. Death duties hit the family hard, and his determination to maintain an estate staff despite the harsh realities of the post-war economy, together with extensive replanting, severely depleted his finances. He married Evelyn McClure, said to have been one of the most beautiful girls in Edinburgh, in 1930. Unlike her husband Evelyn was a staunch Tory, although Teddy would later veto her attempts to cover their car with Conservative stickers during an election campaign as he was the politically neutral Lord Lieutenant of Stirling. With a right-wing wife and a left-wing brother, Teddy sympathised in part with both, and although interested in affairs of state, spoke only occasionally in the House of Lords where he always sat on the non-party crossbenches.

Evelyn McClure's father was Alexander (known as Sandy) Logan McClure, an advocate from Greenock who married Eva Hotson in

---

[10] *Business a.m.* 15/2/2002.
[11] James, now the 5th Viscount, instead attended St Andrews University after leaving Winchester.

1905 despite being 19 years her senior. Evelyn's son George took not only one of his middle names from his maternal family (Hotson, the other was Kenneth[12]), but also many – or so his family believe – of his characteristics. Jessie Evelyn Ramsay Hotson, always known as Eva, was a stern but wonderful grandmother to George, and later supported him by sending copies of the *Sunday Post* to the Argylls in Korea. She was always at South Lodge (where the Youngers moved when George was three) for Christmas, while George and his family were also frequent visitors to Eva's home at Eglinton Crescent in Edinburgh. Fittingly for a future chairman of the Royal Bank of Scotland, George's great-grandfather (Eva's father), Hamilton Andrew Hotson, was a music-loving former general manager of the British Linen Bank. Equally fittingly, there were two political connections via Eva's sister Constance, or Connie. Her husband, Sir Frederick Thomson Bt, was the MP for South Aberdeen and served as Solicitor-General for Scotland and Scottish Whip for the Unionist Party, a post George would also hold in 1965. Sir Frederick's son, Douglas, inherited both his baronetcy and his parliamentary constituency, and was a first cousin as well as a great friend of George's mother Evelyn.

Evelyn diligently recorded George's early childhood in 'The Progress Book', a charming record complete with photographs, statistics and even a lock of his hair. Evelyn noticed that George had an ear for music (as did both his parents) when he was just two years old, singing the Tin Pan Alley classic 'Did you ever see a dream walking?' By the time of his fourth birthday he was able to play, as his mother recorded, 'several tunes with perfectly good rhythm'. Much later George would play reels on the piano by ear to entertain friends at parties.

Family holidays until 1938 were spent at Leckie ('Cook got scarlet fever,' Evelyn recorded on one such vacation, 'so we moved!'), his maternal grandparents' house at 16 Heriot Row in Edinburgh, as well as Elie, Earlsferry, Speyside, Greenock and Ossian House at Kincraig. George had been a healthy baby but always rather pale, and in May 1934 he lost a bit of blood after having his tonsils and adenoids removed. The Progress Book also recorded pointers to his future interests. Not only was he 'rather interested in maps', but 'fascinated by soldiers & bagpipes' despite being 'extremely frightened of them' – his mother recorded in June 1934 – '& gets into a dreadful state of panic if they come near him or march past him in the street'.

George had deep blue eyes, sharp eyesight, acute hearing and was also 'quite decided about what he likes'. He lacked a sweet tooth, and indeed

---

[12] This was probably in honour of his uncle, Kenneth Gilmour Younger, who later asked George to be his son Sam's godfather. Sam Younger later became chairman of the Electoral Commission.

never gained one. His 'hereditary peculiarities' (as recorded by Evelyn) included being 'very jumpy', although he was 'extremely quick at picking up things – very intelligent & clever'. Evelyn also noted that he was a 'very good mimic but [had] only average imagination & initiative', while possessing a 'most astonishingly good memory' which would later serve him well as a politician. At the end of his seventh year George was 'naturally clean & tidy. Very intelligent. Thinks everything out.'[13] The year was 1938, in which the Munich crisis and the declaration of war with Germany the following year turned George's, and his family's, lives upside down.

By the outbreak of war, George had a younger brother called Sandy, born in 1933, and a sister called Rosalind. Another brother, Robert (known as Bobby) followed in 1940. Younger's father had joined the 7th Battalion Argyll and Sutherland Highlanders in 1926 and by the outbreak of war had reached the rank of captain. When the Argylls received instructions to move to Bordon, near Aldershot, the Younger family moved south with them. Experiencing life outside Scotland for the first time had a profound impact on the eight-year-old George who remembered it being 'quite amazing . . . to discover how people spoke differently and [that] it was different in England'. He later recalled struggling to comprehend the local Hampshire accent while being fascinated by Army life. 'I remember the mass Beating of Retreat by the Bands of the Highland Division on one of the big parade grounds at Aldershot,' he said. 'That was a wonderful spectacle . . . I remember it being enormously impressive when I saw it first as the age of seven [sic].'

The countryside around Fleet, where the Youngers stayed, was littered with Bren-gun carriers and military equipment, and surrounded by deep trenches. George enjoyed learning how to drain them when they filled with rain-water, and also got to grips with the Bren-gun carriers, often riding on them. 'I even had the chance to drive one a few yards once,' he remembered, 'but it was far too difficult for a seven-year-old boy [but] I felt I had become, practically, a full scale fully trained soldier by the time I had done that.' He also remembered being entertained by small-scale infantry operations during his afternoon walks, his first direct experience of the 'Thin Red Line' (a reference to the Argylls' distinctive caps) which would run through the rest of his life. There was then a 'splendid . . . sort of pre-battle Christmas' before the so-called phoney war ended and the whole of the 51st Highland Division, of which the Argylls were an important component, was summoned to France to join the British Expeditionary Force.

---

[13] 'The Progress Book', GYP.

The Youngers returned to Scotland in January 1940. It was a cold winter with several feet of snow which blocked trains heading north. 'They couldn't get through from the South up to Beattock', remembered George, 'so we had a very adventurous journey through snowdrifts and all of that. So ended my first adventure abroad i.e. out of Scotland, and we were ready now for whatever 1940 had to bring for us.' He recalled a feeling of 'suppressed excitement' in the period that his father was abroad,[14] and indeed the war proved to be Teddy's finest hour, becoming a superb staff officer in 154 Brigade which contained the 7th and 8th Battalions of the Argylls. When his regiment was cut off by Panzers west of Dieppe, Teddy happened to be taking a message by motor-cycle to brigade headquarters and therefore escaped capture and imprisonment during the heavy fighting of 5–6 June 1940. He also helped organise the exit of the Arc Force (the rearguard action force of the British Army) from Le Havre during Dunkirk, which earned him an OBE later that year. His family awaited his return anxiously in Stirlingshire, and George recalled that 'the first we heard from him after he came back from Dunkirk was when he rang us from a telephone box in Troon'.[15]

Meanwhile, the family also turned its attention to George's education. Until then he had been mostly educated at home, and in 1940 a lady called Mrs Chapman appeared to teach him Latin until September that year, when winter term started at Cargilfield, a prep school on the outskirts of Edinburgh. Later Younger recalled going to R&W Forsyth, the outfitters in Edinburgh, which was to kit out the new scholar. Cargilfield, it seems, was quite demanding sartorially. Not only did George have to be fitted for a kilt and all of its associated accessories, but also a myriad of shirt studs which he found 'quite fascinating'. Inevitably, George became bored and was shunted outside while his harassed mother secured the remaining accessories. She was then heavily pregnant with Bobby (he was born on 25 September), so it fell to Evelyn's cousin Christine McClure – who shared George's interest in ships – to present him at Cargilfield. George spent the next few months in Edinburgh, but in 1941 was sent – along with the rest of the school – to Lawers in Perthshire.[16]

George was fascinated by the war, and would later tell people that it had interrupted his childhood, although in a positive rather than negative sense. 'It convinced me that soldiering was an important and fascinating activity,'[17] he later recalled. He followed war news closely, the dramatic

---

[14] Autobiographical notes, GYP.
[15] *Sunday Express* 29/6/1986.
[16] Younger later became a director of Cargilfield from 1970 to 1984.
[17] *Director* 7/1993.

sinking of HMS *Hood* making a particular impression. Otherwise, his was a fairly ordered existence. When Teddy was at home he worked about ten miles away at the family brewery and returned home every evening while Evelyn was active in the Girl Guides (George was, naturally, in the local Boy Scouts) and later the Women's Voluntary Service. Despite the international situation there was little political discussion at home, while George grew closer to his mother and grandfather during his father's long absences.

After returning from Dunkirk, Teddy was posted to help reform the Highland Division under Major-General Douglas Wimberley. He also attended the staff college at Camberley where he performed so effectively that he was called back as an instructor for several courses at Brasenose College, Oxford. Teddy sustained for several months a seriously poisoned foot, meaning he was desk-bound and encased in plaster of Paris. Again, this proved fortunate for had he been posted to join the 2nd Battalion in Malaya, Teddy would quickly have ended up in Changi prison. His last posting of the war was as chief of staff Northern Ireland under, at first, General Sir Alan Cunningham, and later General Bucknall.

In spite of the war, there was still scope for what George remembered fondly as 'wartime holidays' and also lots of time to indulge in reading (he read *War and Peace* in his early teens) and sporting activities. Unfortunately, the latter also gave rise to a serious accident. 'It was entirely my own fault,' said George later, remembering a pheasant shoot with his grandfather when he was 13. 'I was climbing over a wall and didn't unload my gun. Something you should always do.' In fact, he had used his 4/10 hammer gun to lean on as he did so, putting his left hand over the barrel. It went off and hit Younger's hand underneath his index finger, which was later removed at Stirling Infirmary. 'It must have nearly killed my grandfather.'[18] Surprisingly, very few people ever noticed that he had only three fingers (and a thumb) on one hand. As a result George – who said he could still feel the finger long after it was removed – had to stop playing the piano seriously and instead switched to the French horn.[19] Otherwise, and entirely typically, George just carried on as normal.

'I was educated half in Scotland and half in England,' Younger recalled when he was Scottish Secretary. 'So I am a bit of a half breed, I

---

[18] *Sunday Express* 29/6/1986.
[19] As it was Younger's left hand which was missing a finger, the French horn allowed him to use his three remaining fingers to control the horn's three valves, while his right hand sat inside the horn to control its tone.

suppose.'[20] He arrived at Winchester College in Hampshire ('delayed thro. shooting accident'[21] records the house register) in what was known as Cloister Time (the other terms were Short Half and Common Time), shortly after VE Day.[22] 'That was the biggest formative influence in my life',[23] he later recalled of the school. Whereas George – a third-generation Wykehamist – had enjoyed Cargilfield, he came to love Winchester.

Like many public schools, Winchester had many traditions which to the outside world must have seemed both quaint and baffling. Notions, that is 'any word, custom, person or place peculiar to Wykehamists', was one such convention, a language-within-a-language quickly assimilated by Wykehamists but meaningless to anyone else. A 'Commoner' was a boy who was not in College itself, where only the elite Scholars resided. 'Go down' meant dispersing for the holidays; a 'jig' was a clever man, and a 'thick' was a stupid person, a notion Younger used throughout his life, although never in a nasty way.[24] Even forty years after leaving Winchester, civil servants recall Younger indulging in Old Wykehamist banter while at the Ministry of Defence.

Younger's house had been founded by the Reverend C. H. Hawkins, whose nickname had been 'the Chawker' and George, therefore, was a proud Chawkerite. His housemaster was a gentlemanly but somewhat laconic man called G. W. (Gerry) Dicker. Winchester was renowned for its rigorous academic and intellectual standards, but although Younger – who studied the usual classics – was bright, he had no aspirations to intellectualism at school, unlike his contemporary Alasdair Milne, a College Scholar and future director-general of the BBC.

Above all, the school was very liberal in its attitudes. 'Anything is acceptable,' recalled Younger, 'you can be an intellectual, or a sportsman, and be respected for it. It made me extremely open-minded on all sorts of issues, because we were not taught any politics at all but we were taught to question everything.'[25] The school actively encouraged eccentric hobbies. 'Even then, when games were everything in schools, you could be a butterfly fancier at Winchester and hold your head up high.'[26] Younger

[20] *Scottish Portrait Magazine* 8/1983.
[21] Annals of Southgate House. Younger's house was known to the Post Office as Southgate House until 1940, when it was restyled Hawkins', but Wykehamists have always called it Chawker's.
[22] At a dinner on VE Day night, George impressed his family by declaring: 'No one is a winner in a war like this one.'
[23] *House Magazine* 7/6/1985.
[24] *Winchester College Notions* (c 1940).
[25] *House Magazine* 7/6/1985.
[26] *Director* 7/1993.

disciplined himself to concentrate in the noisy atmosphere of the 'mugging' hall, while in the holidays he devoured *Jane's Fighting Ships*, made models and learned by heart the location of every naval vessel sunk during the war.

Alasdair Milne remembered George, even though he was a Commoner, as 'just a nice guy who knew his place and how to make it'. He added, 'At school he was, as he was throughout his life, charming and unassuming. No kind of side or pride, or arrogance. Always smiling, always happy; he was remarkably consistent in that sense.'[27] George wrote to his parents at length every Sunday evening. Once, having failed to receive a letter, they dispatched a telegram which the housemaster pinned on the Chawker's message board. It asked simply: 'Are you dead?' It became a family joke and George thereafter sought to avoid receiving another telegram.

Conditions for boarders at Winchester were, as Milne recalled, 'frankly medieval'. Both Commoners and Scholars were forced to bathe each morning at 7 a.m., even in the freezing cold winter of 1947, although there was fun to be had by flooding the washing area and using the tin baths as makeshift boats. The food was also basic; rationing was still in place and meals often consisted of rather unusual fish. Discipline could be severe, and beatings were not unknown. The headmaster was Spencer Leeson, later Bishop of Peterborough, who presided over the return of many teachers from war service. The result was a rigorous and stimulating education, which gave Younger an invaluable preparation for life.

The first general election in nearly ten years took place a few months after VE Day, culminating in a dramatic landslide for the Labour Party. The election was the first Younger had been aware of, and although he was 'thrilled' by the result he could not understand why his parents were so upset by it. His outlook soon shifted. 'During the most formative years – between 14 and 20 – by the time I got to university, my views had changed,' he said later. 'I identified with anything that was not socialism.'[28] In the critical years that followed, he explained, 'the Labour Government got into more and more difficulties and so my first political impressions were of [the] Labour Government not working . . . coal shortages and rationing'.

Despite the uncertainty of his political allegiance, Younger's interest in politics had been roused. There were visits from the King and Queen, and war figures like Field Marshal Lord Wavell. The dashing Scottish Conservative MP and writer Fitzroy Maclean also came to speak to pupils

---

[27] Interview with Alasdair Milne, 23/1/2007.
[28] Roy, *Conversations in a Small Country*, 180.

at Winchester (he was still in the Commons when Younger became an MP in 1964), while George could 'well remember, for instance, Dick Crossman coming down to the debating society'.[29] But Winchester was not renowned, unlike Eton, for producing top-tier politicians. 'Put [Lord] Addington, our last Prime Minister, by the side of the elder Pitt, Gladstone or Balfour,' observed an earlier historian of the school, and 'the poor man vanishes into instant oblivion.'[30]

Younger enjoyed team sports but did not particularly excel at any, being content as an all-rounder and heavily committed to other activities, not least his music. He did, however, take part in all the usual Winchester games. In addition to running in Senior Steeplechase (cross-country), he much enjoyed playing Winchester football, a distinctive game peculiar to the school in which the skills of rugby and football were essentially combined. These matches were (and still are) hotly contested within the school between the house groups: Old Tutor Houses (OTH), Commoners and College. Younger also played cricket for the Toye and Eldon pots (or cups), football in the Ellis pot, and came sixteenth in the Junior Steeplechase during Short Half in 1946, for which he was awarded his house socks. Younger also won a prize for shooting, a sport he enjoyed throughout his life despite his earlier accident. On leaving Winchester, he quickly progressed from rifles to shotguns.

Younger's main extracurricular preoccupation, however, was music. He played French horn in the school orchestra and also sang in the school's choral society, known as Glee Club. The young musician Dennis Brain was Younger's main influence when it came to the French horn, and he perhaps even visited the school during his time there, while Isobel Baillie, the Scottish soprano, was a particular favourite among the singers he listened to on shellac 78 discs. George played at a recital on 27 November 1949 just weeks before he left Winchester. The College magazine noted that 'the fact that this performance of Beethoven's notoriously difficult wind quartet was not entirely successful should not discourage the wind players from attempting other equally difficult works'. However, the review added diplomatically, 'It should be noted that the four wind players appeared in every item on the programme, either singing or playing.'[31]

It was at Winchester that Younger learned to love music, and such was the influence of Henry Havergal (Winchester's music don) on Younger that when he invited several former pupils to come and 'make music' for

[29] *House Magazine* 7/6/1985.
[30] D'e Firth, *Winchester*, 85.
[31] *Wykehamist* 19/12/1949.

his eightieth birthday, George took time out from the Scottish Office and turned up at the Royal Academy of Music in London with his French horn and performed, unrehearsed, Bach's *Mass in B minor* and Parry's *At a Solemn Music*.

The ethos of Winchester was very much based around religion and daily chapel, where George was involved as a singer (tenor) in his own 'small way'. He also listened closely to the wisdom of George Macleod (a product, like Younger, of both Cargilfield and Winchester), and the entertaining sermons of Ronnie Selby Wright. 'These early impressions were compounded by the enormous influence which our magnificent Church Music had upon me,' he recalled towards the end of his life. 'I served for several years in the Chapel Choir at Winchester College which . . . covered much of the best of the traditional repertoire'.[32] Sunday communion at St Michael's Church (known notionally as 'Mikla') was also a fixture, at which it was customary for the vicar to drink up all the left-over communion wine. One Sunday, Younger was part of a group of boys who press-ganged as many people as possible to attend Mikla. The pews were full to bursting, but by pre-arrangement very few went up to communion. The unsuspecting vicar felt compelled to drink pints of wine while mischievous Wykehamists stifled their giggles.

Winchester also gave Younger his first opportunity to follow in his father's – and grandfather's – footsteps by becoming involved in military life. He joined the College Combined Cadet Force (CCF) and attended its annual camps at Aldershot, an area he knew from his father's first wartime posting. There were also holidays in France, and Younger enjoyed a range of low-grade sporting activities like tennis, swimming (at Gunners Hole) and sailing, which became a lifelong passion. He also enjoyed drama, taking part in a house performance of George Bernard Shaw's play *Androcles and the Lion* in June 1946. Younger was a popular pupil and became a house prefect during his last year, quickly moving up a notch to be a school prefect or Co. Prae. Thoughts soon turned to the next stage of his education, although National Service was inevitably going to delay it. In December 1949 Younger left his house along with four other boys. He was fulfilled, happy and fully prepared by his experience at Winchester to face whatever life held in store.

Fittingly for Younger's future career in public life, Budge D'e Firth in his history of the College observed that Winchester had 'not set great store on "honours" or "success". If these come – well and good, provided that they are carried with modesty; if they do not come, it is of little importance

---

[32] Speech as Lord High Commissioner, 20/5/2001, GYP.

provided that faithful service has been done . . . Nor do we require, even of our ablest sons, that they shall take a prominent place, except if duty demands it, in great affairs.'[33]

It was an entirely appropriate summary of Younger's general outlook on life, while Winchester's famous motto, 'Manners makyth man', also struck many of his future political and business colleagues as almost crafted with him in mind. As with the Argylls, Younger carefully retained links with his *alma mater* throughout his life. As an MP he arranged a Chawker's centenary dinner at the House of Commons, spoke regularly at OW events – including an annual parliamentary lunch – and also took a keen interest in proposals to abolish compulsory morning chapel, something which directly affected his eldest son James, who started at Winchester in the late 1960s. Younger even wrote to the headmaster, J. L. Thorn, to protest formally. Morning chapel, he wrote, gave the boys 'the habit of daily worship as a foundation of a Christian life', adding that he personally found 'the memory of daily worship at Winchester to be a most important part of my life, although I cannot claim to be a model churchgoer.' What was more, he argued, it emphasised that Winchester was basically a Christian institution. 'Those who are not Christians and who object to this have no need whatever to go to Winchester,' wrote Younger, 'and it seems to me rather sad that the Christian majority have their wishes threatened for the benefit of the non-Christian minority.'[34]

Although universal morning chapel at Winchester did not survive, nothing gave Younger more pleasure than becoming first, a Fellow in 1992, and then, in 1997, Warden, the highest aspiration for a Wykehamist and a position he held until his death six years later. 'It gave me a wonderful feeling of belonging to something I greatly admired and wanted to live up to,' he later said of his schooldays, 'a feeling that I'd been given a really liberal attitude to life, issues and people because it was such a liberal place.'[35] Just as that fine old school had prepared him thoroughly for life, it provided a familiar and comforting context for the end of that life.

---

[33] D'e Firth, *Winchester*, 87.
[34] GY to J. L. Thorn, 14/12/1969, GYP.
[35] *Director* 7/1993.

Chapter 2

COMING OF AGE

To understand a man, Napoleon once said, one has to know what was happening in the world when he was 20. In Younger's 20th year he was struggling to keep warm close to the border between North and South Korea as the Cold War made the world an increasingly dangerous place. The experience had a profound influence. 'It was on a Korean hillside on a dark, dank, cold night in 1951 that I really came of age,' he later reflected. 'I realised that my platoon of Jocks of the Argyll and Sutherland Highlanders was in a perilous position, and that I as a 19-year-old was responsible for their lives, as well as my own. Somehow we were lucky. The Korean and Chinese force did not locate us, and we survived. After that, I saw life in perspective.'[1]

Younger had been called up for his National Service in January 1950, a little buff envelope containing instructions having told him to report to Fort George near Inverness. Shortly after arriving, George was assessed by the Personnel Selection Officer. 'He calmly told me that owing to my hand I was not good enough medically for the infantry and asked me what was my preference of: Engineers . . . etc. – all the worst regiments,' he recounted to his parents in his weekly letter. 'I told him that . . . I had no desire to go into any of them, and said I would see my Company Commander and come back to him. I went at once to see [Glen] Kelway-Bamber & he was very nice and got the doctor to change the figures of my medical grading quietly so as to make it all right.'[2]

Younger had arrived at Fort George to find his kit laid out on his bed, prepared by a great childhood friend called James Stirling.[3] 'It was very,

---

[1] *Independent* 27/1/2003.
[2] GY to LLY, 30/1/1950, GYP. Younger used to tell people that Kelway-Bamber said: 'Come on doc, just change it.'
[3] Stirling later became Lord Lieutenant of Stirling. His son, Archie Stirling, also served with the Argylls.

very cold', George recalled, 'and it was a very tough experience for somebody who had just come from school in that army discipline was very rough at that time.' Fort George was run by the 1st Highland Light Infantry and was the training ground for all the Highland regiments. Younger went straight into the Argylls. 'There was no hot water,' he said, 'but on the other hand we learnt a lot.'

George was now '22329223 Pte. Younger G.' and shared a hut with 15 others, including a Welsh barrow-boy, a rivet-heater and an illiterate Glaswegian. Younger longed to get to Inverness for a day's leave, and on one visit was amused to be plied with Younger's Heavy Export Ale in a local pub. Basic training lasted about three months, although George was delayed by a couple of weeks which he spent recovering from a poisoned hand at a military hospital in Yorkshire.

Finally, in the spring, Younger passed out from Fort George and transferred to Eaton Hall Officer Cadet School in England. 'That was a very different kettle of fish,' he remembered. 'It was in the Duke of Westminster's former home, which was let to the army. Beautifully kept grounds, rather like a sort of school I suppose.' Younger met officer cadets from infantry units all over the UK, including a few he knew already from Fort George. There were intensive exercises where Younger would have to endure three days and three nights 'on the trot', including some in Wales, but it was a thorough and satisfying four months' training. The routine was a little more relaxed and he managed frequent trips to Winchester and Liverpool, where he saw plays at the Royal Court Theatre and concerts at the Philharmonic Hall, and visits to an aunt who lived in the Wirral.

Younger had arrived at Winchester soon after VE Day; now he passed out of Eaton Hall on the very day the Korean War began. 'I was already posted to the 1st Argylls in Hong Kong,' he remembered, 'but within a day or two of the Korean War breaking out the Argylls were sent straight to Korea and I was informed that I could no longer go to Korea because I was under nineteen.'[4]

The Korean War was the first major conflict of the Cold War, and unlike the later war in Vietnam, the Communist aggression in Korea was tackled by a multilateral United Nations force. It had begun as a civil war between two rival Korean regimes, each of which was supported by external powers in a fight for control over a Korean Peninsula divided by the United States and Soviet Union in 1948. The North Korean Army had

---

[4] Walker, *A Barren Place*, 34.

moved south on 25 June 1950 to reunite the country, backed principally by China and to a lesser extent by the Soviets. When a United Nations Command force intervened in support of South Korea, it blossomed into a tense Cold War stand-off with the lingering threat of nuclear warfare.

Younger was perhaps better informed about developments in the peninsula than most National Servicemen, for his uncle, the Labour MP Kenneth Younger, was then minister of state at the Foreign Office, where he knew what was going on with regard to British policy towards Korea but did not always agree with it. And while Kenneth tackled the intellectual ramifications of the conflict, his nephew just followed orders. 'I'd no political ideas really at that age,' George said later, 'but we knew very well why we were there, because North Korea had tried to take South Korea. That was good enough for us.'

Until Younger turned 19, however, government policy dictated that he had to see out the remaining months of his 18th year with the 1st Black Watch in West Berlin, still occupied by Allied forces five years after the end of the Second World War. 'It's just for a temporary period until you're old enough,' he was assured. 'I never believed that for a moment. I assumed that it would never happen.'[5]

After some leave, Younger left for West Berlin with Sandy Gilmour[6] who had been in his hut at Fort George. 'It was absolutely fascinating,' he recalled, 'just after the Berlin airlift. One went in through the Iron Curtain in the special train [from Helmstedt], locked up and all that.'[7] George arrived at Charlottenburg Station to be met by Peter Carthew, a friend from Winchester now in the Black Watch. 'However, no-one here was expecting *me* at all and they had heard nothing about me!!' he wrote to his parents. 'They are glad to have me though, as they are rather short of officers at the moment.'[8]

The Black Watch in Berlin was a skeleton unit of only 25 officers, which was also short of fuel and clothes. When George first arrived he was still dressed as an Argyll, although he was able to borrow a Black Watch uniform which he wore when on duty. His parents also posted him further sartorial supplies as well as bed sheets and pillow slips. Younger was based in Montgomery Barracks which was located on the boundary with Communist East Germany. For a future Defence Secretary during the final years of the Cold War, it was a pertinent experience.

'What struck me was that it was still very much the era of reparations

---

[5] Ibid., 35.
[6] Sandy was a half brother of Sir Ian Gilmour, a future Cabinet colleague of Younger's.
[7] Walker, *A Barren Place*, 35.
[8] GY to LLY, 22/9/1950, GYP.

and the Germans were still being pretty roughly treated,' recalled Younger, liberally-inclined even as a teenager. 'I think everybody down to the rank of corporal had a German servant under reparations. We could hire a Volkswagen with a driver anytime we wanted to go out for the night for two and sixpence (12 ½ pence) and he would stay there any length of time, no limits.'[9]

This ease of transport also led to innumerable road accidents. 'To-morrow I am the member of a Court of Inquiry,' George told his parents towards the end of October, 'to enquire into the circumstances of the road accident. . .when six officers going to the Opera ran into a German lorry.'[10] Otherwise, his duties as an orderly officer mainly consisted of chores like the changing of the guard. At night, George would sleep in a special orderly's bedroom. 'I have been twice woken up in the middle of the night by the Military Police', he wrote home in another letter, 'saying that they have caught some of our men walking about the streets at 3.0 a.m. having broken out of barracks.'[11]

> When I answered him [the military policeman] he said he was faced with a very unruly collection of Scottish soldiers and he had locked them in the Guard-room. He said, "You better come and sort them out Sir". So I went into Charlottenburg and found some very drunk "jocks" locked in the Guardroom. I then proceeded to, very diffidently, look into the Guardroom, but as soon as I appeared and they saw that I was wearing my Black Watch uniform, they immediately said, "very nice to see you Sir" and "I don't know how we've got into this mess" and all that sort of thing. I then ordered these soldiers out of the Guardroom and into my truck which they did without a murmur.[12]

To Younger, this incident demonstrated the strength of the regimental system. His Commanding Officer in Berlin was Lieutenant-Colonel Bernard Fergusson, later Lord Ballantrae and governor-general of New Zealand. Despite suffering from heart trouble Fergusson was a lively character who made quite an impression on George. At the end of October Fergusson announced his engagement to Miss Laura Grenfell, a sister-in-law of the actress Joyce Grenfell. 'To say that the news came as a bombshell is to put it mildly', George wrote to his parents (his father knew Fergusson); 'it has caused a complete sensation'.[13]

---

[9] Walker, *A Barren Place*, 35.
[10] GY to LLY, 29/10/1950, GYP.
[11] Ibid., 12/11/1950, GYP.
[12] Autobiographical notes, GYP.
[13] GY to LLY, 22/10/1950, GYP.

The autumn of 1950 was a period of continual disputes with the Soviets over boundaries in the partitioned city. On one strip of mutual territory, a road, Russian soldiers even erected a block. 'Since then we have had sentries facing theirs at opposite sides of the road & armed to the teeth,' George told his parents. 'They put up a banner saying "Korea for the Koreans. Germany for the Germans, go home Tommy" which they obligingly changed to "Go back to Glasgow" when we took over the sentry duty. Their soldiers look very young and *very* dirty, and, according to interpreters who spoke to them had not a clue as to what they were doing!'[14] During a guard duty at the infamous Spandau Prison, George came face to face with Hitler's deputy Rudolf Hess who had famously flown to Scotland in 1941 on a quixotic diplomatic mission.

Younger also had an amusing encounter with John Strachey, Secretary of State for War in the Labour government and the MP for Dundee West. 'He was introduced to the Officers and some of the men,' he wrote to his parents. 'The first thing he asked me was whether I was a relation of Uncle KK [Kenneth], and when I said yes, he proceeded to speak to me as if I was Uncle KK's parent or guardian or something!! He said that they all thought that Uncle KK, if he might say so, was doing most awfully well etc etc!!! He was a most stupid man, I thought.' George clearly was not impressed at having met one of the most prolific and widely read British Marxist-Leninist theorists of the 1930s.[15]

'This week we have had the gayest and most exhausting week I have ever remembered,' George informed his parents in another letter, 'although it was great fun.'[16] Berlin was an ideal posting for Younger. Culturally, even in a city still scarred by severe aerial bombardment, there were two opera houses, one in the East and one in the West, sailing on the Havel, riding, and numerous clubs, favourites being the Officers', the Marlborough and the Blue & White. He even took his platoon to swim and play football at the Olympic Stadium. 'Next time we are going to try going there by Underground', George told his parents, 'we must be careful not to get into one going "Eastbound" instead of "Westbound".'[17]

There were also plenty of parties to attend, at which George would mix with other friends from home like Alasdair Milne and David Montgomery, the latter of whom was in the same company. At one gathering he met the 18-year-old daughter of Commodore Gerald Seymour Tuck, then

[14] Ibid., 25/4/1950, GYP.
[15] Ibid., 1/10/1950, GYP.
[16] Ibid., 8/10/1950, GYP.
[17] Ibid., 5/11/1950, GYP.

deputy commissioner of the Military Security Board in Berlin. She was called Diana, and immediately hit it off with Younger, who was only a year older. 'Diana is the daughter of a Commander [sic] Tuck who is head Naval Attaché in Berlin,' he told his parents. 'She is very nice, but unfortunately, being literally about the only British girl in Berlin, is very difficult to get hold of!!'[18] A shared love of music ensured that George had his fair share of dates with Diana, and together they regularly attended concerts and operas.

In early December Younger received instructions to leave Berlin on the 16th. 'I hope this doesn't depress you overmuch,' he wrote to his parents. 'It doesn't worry me because I reckon by the time I get out there [Korea] either the war will be over or the Argylls will be withdrawn (the 1st of these alternatives looks practically certain). Secondly I get Xmas leave out of it!! Thirdly I see a new part of the world etc. etc.'[19] George's prediction was wrong on both counts.

Younger managed a few days' leave prior to a recreational training course at Aldershot from January to February 1951. He then reported to the Goodge Street Transit Centre, which was actually in Goodge Street Underground station. 'We went in exactly as if you were going to go to the Tube,' he remembered. '[We went] through an extra door and there's an *enormous* warren of tunnels – offices and dining rooms and everything, very strange. Then after a day or two there, we were sent out.'

In the early 1950s, the journey to the Far East took five days. Younger took off from RAF Lyneham in a Hercules aircraft. 'We stopped the first night at Malta, the second night at Habbaniyah in Iraq, the third night in Karachi, the fourth in Negombo, Ceylon, and the fifth night we arrived at Singapore.' From Changi Airport Younger and his fellow officers were transferred straight to the nearest dockyard where they boarded HMS *Unicorn*, an aircraft carrier which was being used as a troopship.

The journey to Sasebo in Japan was more leisurely, and from there he went to Kure and came ashore at the British Commonwealth base. 'We transited there for about a week,' recalled Younger, 'and we were then sent up-country to a battle camp which was called Harimura, not too far from Hiroshima. I had a week's battle camp there, I remember that being very cold – midwinter.' Coldness was becoming a recurring feature of his National Service life, but for an Old Wykehamist barely out of school, and who had never before left the UK, it was also fascinating. From Harimura Younger returned to Kure and was flown to Ilkune in South Korea.

---

[18] Ibid., 15/10/1950, GYP.
[19] Ibid., 10/12/1950, GYP.

The commander of the US Eighth Army in Korea, General Walton Walker, had recently died in a road accident and his successor, General Matthew Ridgway, had just taken over the command. 'It happened that he was on the airstrip', remembered Younger, 'and here was a new draft coming . . . of about company strength (about 120 men), mostly Black Watch, but now being transferred to the Argylls, and he addressed us . . . gave us a pep talk.' The company was then trucked south of Seoul to hook up with the Argylls.

It had become clear that the Allied offensive was failing, a situation General Ridgway was supposed to reverse, and that the front was crumbling under a fresh Chinese offensive. Allied forces were therefore slowly making a rearward movement, digging themselves into a defensive position at each stop as no one was sure when the enemy would appear. The Argylls' eventual withdrawal through Seoul was a nightmare complicated by refugees, appalling weather and traffic jams. After reaching Yodonae they were sent forward again some thirty miles to Changhowon-Ni (alias Frostbite Bridge), south-east of the capital, which was to be their station for the next month.

It was at this stage Younger arrived. 'I was given command of 11 Platoon in "C" Company,' he remembered. 'We had about a week of sitting around on top of a hill waiting for something to happen. Then we started moving and did a whole series of moves without a great deal of action.' The terrain consisted of rice-paddy fields in valleys surrounded by rugged hills. 'C' Company took the top of the hills, 'patrolled forward and when we met the enemy we dealt with them.'

Younger's first brush with the enemy came about three weeks after his arrival. 'A' Company got held up by a determined Chinese machine-gun post and several people were killed, including two friends of Younger's called Mike Hawthorne and John Milner. 'They were both killed in one morning,' he remembered:

> The Chinese (manning the machine gun) were knocked out because I remember seeing them. It's a funny feeling seeing dead bodies for the first time, coming upon the Chinese position and seeing the Chinese chap, two chaps in this case, lying there dead. You don't really want to investigate too closely and you wonder if they are booby-trapped. But I did feel that that was rather a ghoulish performance, but you just have to get on with it. There's nothing much you can do.[20]

---

[20] Walker, *A Barren Place*, 35.

'C' Company then supported the retaliation before steadily advancing north towards the infamous 38th Parallel, eventually reaching a hilltop north of Kapyong.

Younger's platoon were not exclusively Scots although the majority were Argyll National Servicemen with a few Black Watch. Some of the reservists were English, including his platoon sergeant, a Yorkshireman called Dickinson, who was a miner in his home county and used to write to Younger right up until the 1980s. The death of two friends, not to mention the sight of dead enemy troops, had been a shocking introduction to the realities of war, but although still only a teenager, George's acclimatisation to war was stoical. He later reflected:

> It was very upsetting when friends were wounded or killed. But that's part of war. You just have to get on with the job. I was lucky. I didn't have any close shaves apart from being under fire. I just kept my head down. We were always outnumbered. The enemy had hundreds of troops they were quite prepared to sacrifice.[21]

> The first thing I remember very vividly was when it suddenly occurred to me, as I settled down on the top of a hill that first night, was that it's not going to stop. When you're out on an exercise in the army you know it's a day of exercise and you can put your all into it and you know you'll be back to a warm bed or whatever. Then it suddenly occurred to me that here is something that I may be in for weeks and weeks and weeks. If I get wet I shall remain wet. That was a very funny feeling.

Although regular patrols kept Younger occupied, they were also fraught with danger. Mostly, he would be sent out on recce patrols with not more than four men. Younger recalled:

> We were sent out from a hilltop position, so what one was told to do was to go down that ridge, across that bit of valley and find out if there was anybody on the hill [at] the other side. It was quite a long way, and you had to go quite carefully and silently and you were always concerned that you were about to run into something, and occasionally you did. I found it quite nerve-wracking.

Sometimes, he would also be sent out on a fighting patrol, which was supposed to engage proactively with the enemy:

---

[21] *Sunday Post* 25/6/2000.

That would be about seven or eight men. I do remember once going down a long ridge towards the bottom of the valley, and then somebody at the front of the patrol thought he saw something and we all stopped and eventually we did see some enemy. As we were supposed to be bringing back information we decided not to fire on them. On the other hand, they saw us and started firing, but not very effectively. I don't think they knew really quite where we were, but there were bullets whistling round nearby and we quietly withdrew.

Younger would later recount another incident in which his platoon spotted a North Korean soldier on the facing hill. A command came through that the soldier was to be taken out. Younger issued the order to one of his platoon, but the Jock protested that the enemy soldier was not threatening their position. He concurred, and radioed his opinion back to HQ. The order was repeated. Younger passed it again to his rifleman, who aimed and fired. The unarmed North Korean soldier scuttled to safety while the Argyll explained that the wind must have been stronger than he thought. The humanity of this soldier's deliberately bad shot impressed his platoon commander deeply.

Otherwise, in the absence of action, the daily routine revolved around meals. Younger was able to heat his rations over a makeshift fire on the reverse slopes of the hills. The food came in boxes marked 'C rations' parachuted to them by American aircraft. It was not bad: pork, beans and pineapple slices, but the troops soon got fed up with only six culinary variations, and rarely tasted alcohol except for the rum ration. Nights were usually spent patrolling, and if Younger was not doing that then he was on duty. 'I got up about three or four times every night to check the posts and go round everybody,' he recalled. 'You just slept in your sleeping bag with your boots on. You weren't allowed to take them off. You waited for dawn when you stood-to and then, if conditions were good enough, you went down the reverse slope, lit a fire and had some breakfast.'[22]

Trudging up and down a steep mountain to fetch water, rations and blankets soon took its toll, even with the help of a company of 'Gooks',[23] a sort of carrier company led by an Argyll major. Younger was, however, impressed by the sheer organisation of the operation. 'Wherever you were, behind you was always your supporting chaps in the battalion – the

---

[22] Walker, *A Barren Place*, 36–37.

[23] 'The term 'Gook' came from South Koreans saying something that sounded like 'Me Gook' when greeted by troops. Only later did it become a synonym for the enemy, while the friendly South Koreans became known as 'Rak' (Republic of Korea) troops.

quartermaster's people who always seemed to be able to appear out of nowhere with a truck and something hot to eat. They always seemed to have things like blankets and mail from home.'

George's grandmother, Eva McClure, had started sending her grandson a copy of the *Sunday Post* each week. Its couthy blend of gossip, hard news and comic strips helped ease his homesickness. 'It's a very light sort of newspaper but I read it avidly and it was *wonderful*,'[24] he remembered. 'It was her contribution to the war effort. I passed it around the platoon and we all read every last word. I have to admit it was a bit surreal reading The Broons and Oor Wullie there.'

Cultural differences also led to absurd misunderstandings. Younger remembered that black soldiers in a swing band formed by the Scots' US allies were so delighted to hear that the famous Scottish Negro regiment called The Black Watch was on its way that a special jazz performance was mounted in welcome. When they arrived, the colour of their faces and legs caused considerable confusion and disappointment, as did their bagpipes.

'The American heavy mortars liked to be with the Brits because it was dull to be with their own people,' recalled Younger. 'They identified themselves wholly with the Argylls and were great friends. I did in fact meet two of them when I went to the Pentagon later on as Secretary of State [for Defence]. They were still serving soldiers.'[25] The 27th Brigade was a real mixture, comprising the Scots, the 1st Middlesex regiment, American heavy mortars, regulars in the 3rd Royal Australian Regiment, New Zealand gunners, the Indian field ambulance and the Princess Patricia's Canadian Light Infantry. Younger remembered that

the Australians were marvellous, fantastic, very rough and ready but in a problem they were wonderful, always good and always there. They didn't allow anyone other than a regular to go (to Korea); they had a legislative ban. The Canadians were more difficult, a bit clannish and rather over the top in their parties. The New Zealand gunners were marvellous. We had with us one of their officers, who was a Forward Observation Officer, and his signaller. It's unbelievable really but in private life they were reservists called back. The signaller was the owner of a large sheep station in the south island and the officer was his hired hand, so they'd reversed roles. It worked marvellously; they were the greatest of friends.[26]

---

[24] Walker, *A Barren Place*, 38.
[25] *Sunday Post* 25/6/2000.
[26] Walker, *A Barren Place*, 38. George's younger brother Sandy (Alexander James), who later served as a second lieutenant with the 1st Black Watch in Korea, found the Australian regulars less convivial. Unlike George, he was wounded in the leg during his service. He feigned death and had his watch taken by the enemy.

Younger fitted into this cultural melting pot perfectly, and in the long lapses between action he struck up some lasting friendships. 'It helped enormously that all the lads with me were from places like Stirling and Fife,' he recalled. 'We could always talk about home.'[27] When Younger arrived at the battalion he already knew personally more than a quarter of the officers either through his father's association with the Argylls or from his own training at Fort George and Eaton Hall.

At this stage in the conflict there were no mass attacks by the Chinese, as it was largely a 'probing' war. 'The Chinese had followed us down south, but had not yet regrouped themselves,' explained Younger, 'so we were probing northwards to see how far we could get and they were just a screen I think. So every so often they would stop us and get one of our patrols, or at least they would try to.' The patrols would come under attack from small arms, and occasionally rather ineffective mortars.

Younger, of course, had already had one bad experience with a gun when he lost one of his index fingers, and he remembered the heart-stopping feeling of hearing half-sleeping troops cocking their rifles as he patrolled gun posts in the middle of the night. 'I was supposed to be armed with a revolver,' he recalled. 'I thought that was useless and I was offered an Italian carbine which somebody had picked up in the early days of the campaign. It was much lighter than the rifle and quite enough for me to defend myself.' His platoon was armed with Second World War bolt-action rifles and three Bren-guns. They also used two-inch mortars ('which gave a big bang but weren't very effective'),[28] occasionally supported by three-inch models – Vickers .303 machine guns – while the NCOs carried Stens.

Generally, conditions were appalling. 'We lived in Korean cottages which were made of mud and overrun with rats.'[29] But there were also periods of near normality. 'When we got into reserve, which we did at least twice during my period, then funnily enough everything turned pretty quickly [in]to something like a TA camp,' he recalled. 'You got down to the paddy fields at the bottom and after a night of recovery the pipe band appeared and started playing, sports days would be arranged, [and] mobile bath and laundry units would come.'[30]

Although organised football matches were not possible, balls were still kicked around, while 'A' and 'C' Companies organised a shooting match against their old friends in the 5th Regimental Combat Team. Although the targets were tin cans in a paddy field, the Scots won, aided, no doubt,

[27] *Sunday Post* 25/6/2000.
[28] Walker, *A Barren Place*, 39.
[29] *Daily Record* 30/1/1998.
[30] Walker, *A Barren Place*, 40.

by Younger. Idle conversation on 'Frostbite Ridge' also gave rise to rumours, including one that the Scottish Nationalists would return the Stone of Destiny if the Argylls were returned to Stirling.[31]

The troops would get a new uniform every few weeks, retaining only their Glengarry headgear throughout. 'In the winter we had a rudimentary version of what you'd now say is a sort of skiing jacket,' recalled Younger. 'It was made of kapok, quilted things they were, quite good for warming you.' Footwear, however, was less effective. 'We were issued with frost-proof boots – boots FP – which had been made for the Norwegian campaign in 1940 and not used because the campaign stopped.'

> They were very interesting because about 10% of them were absolutely marvellous and were very good and very comfortable. The remaining 90% fell apart as soon as you put them on. They had a leather top and a leather sole, but the trouble was that the stitching had rotted and your sole flapped off. It was no use telling the quartermaster that your boots had broken because it was always your fault, so there were an awful lot of people padding around with boots tied round with the soles half off. It was quite ridiculous.

But then it was so cold that no amount of clothing would have made much of a difference. 'The vehicles had to be started every twenty minutes during the night because the whole thing froze up,' said Younger, 'the anti-freeze and everything. I do remember trying to shave one morning on a hilltop. We poured boiling water into a bowl and by the time I finished shaving it had ice on it, it was that cold.'[32] Even when there was a thaw it caused almost equal misery on account of the mud and treacherous road conditions (there was no tarmac) it would create.

On top of all that, the bitingly cold Manchurian wind covered everything with snow, although it came in handy for washing when clean water ran short. Frostbite was common, but certain operational restrictions were relaxed so that the men could warm themselves by small fires dug into the side of trenches. More importantly, wet socks could be dried out. As a result, Colin Mitchell's 'B' Company had the lowest incidence of frostbite of any front line Allied unit in Korea. But, recalled Mitchell in his memoirs, 'to add to our misery many of us developed tape worm through eating local pigs to supplement the diet of composite rations: it was animal living'.[33]

As January drew to a close, it became clear that some activity was being planned, and sure enough on 25 January the 1st US Cavalry Division

---

[31] The Stone of Scone had recently been taken from Westminster Abbey.
[32] Walker, *A Barren Place*, 40.
[33] Mitchell, *Having Been a Soldier*, 85.

advanced through the battalion area for a 'limited offensive'. Frostbite Ridge no longer constituted the front line and the Argylls were once more in Corps Reserve, ready to move on at two hours' notice. The orders came on 4 February and they transferred to Yoju, a few miles to the north, where, in spite of constant patrolling for a week, they made no contact with the enemy.

Intelligence, however, suggested the enemy was about to attack in strength, so defensive plans were laid and the whole Brigade dug itself in for what seemed inevitable. The attack, however, never came and on 13 February there began a painstaking and mountainous advance which was to last a month. The Allied offensive was finally on the up. Positions were no longer defensive and although there was still heavy snow, a determined effort to shift the enemy – not just Gooks, but also the Chinese – from their mountain positions got under way.

This was a manifestation of the new spirit of the US Eighth Army as imbibed by General Ridgway whose insistence on forward and not rearward movement was by now in place. The Communist forces had dug into well-prepared and camouflaged mountain positions which proved difficult to dislodge. But although important, the role of the Argylls at this point in the campaign was serviceable rather than spectacular. Younger and 'C' Company were seldom in contact with the enemy, and rarely did they encounter opposition or incur casualties. The snow eventually melted, and Korean porters carried supplies several thousand feet up after the Argylls dug into a position.

The month's operations came to an end on 13 March with 'A' Company occupying the record height of about 2,500 ft. There was a rest area in a dry river bed surrounded by paddy fields. It was out of sight and sound of the enemy, and for only the second time in six months the Argylls relaxed and had hot showers. This time, organised football matches were possible and the hopeless looking river bed was transformed into a pitch. The Argylls emerged victorious from the football tournament, and morale gradually revived.

'The combination of loneliness, discomfort, fear and boredom is a pretty harsh cocktail,' Younger told the General Assembly of the Church of Scotland in 2001, 'but there was, then at any rate, a spiritual element to the life of a Scottish battalion fighting for the United Nations in a far off country. Our Padre [J. F.] Macdonald was very active and very popular. He was also very necessary when casualties had to be endured. I will certainly never forget the emotional effect of a drum-head service in a paddy-field while the Argylls were temporarily out of the line for a rest.'[34]

---

[34] Speech as Lord High Commissioner, 20/5/2001, GYP.

It was during one of Macdonald's services that Younger heard the psalm 'The Lord's My Shepherd' being sung by hundreds of men, an almost spiritual experience which he would still speak of decades later. At this point, Brigadier Burke arrived in Korea to guide the battalion through the final phase of their operations.

The next three weeks saw warfare on mountains of up to 4,000 ft in height, near Kapyong, 35 miles to the north-west. On 4 April the Argylls ran into their first, and last, trouble in these mountains. Again, it was not a day of heavy fighting, but the rather routine business of attacking a ridge ahead of the one which had already been secured. 'A' and 'D' Companies did the attacking, and there were several casualties, including two of the platoon commanders. 'B' Company also had some casualties because of an unsuspected minefield the following day, and Younger's 'C' Company, 3,000 ft high up on Daffodil mountain, found themselves established exactly on the 38th Parallel.

By 8 April the Argylls had attacked their last hill and soon after the battalion was withdrawn into the valley at Karim as Brigade reserve. It was during their ten days there that news reached them of their relief by the King's Own Scottish Borderers, albeit with no firm date attached. The 19th ROK [Republic of Korea] began to relieve the Argylls on 18 April and the following day a small advance party left for Hong Kong. There were farewell parties, entertainments and a final Brigade church parade as the troops prepared to leave the peninsula. When news filtered through of a Chinese offensive the previous evening, morale sank as they thought fate might send them back to the front line. Orders to do so actually came through on 24 April, but by then the regiment was already en route to Inchon where it arrived late in the afternoon having passed the KOSB on the way.

Another National Serviceman called Willie Purves was among the regiment relieving the Argylls, at least according to Younger. 'It's a nice story, but actually I brought the rear party up from Hong Kong a few weeks after he had left,'[35] recalled Purves, who as Sir William was chairman of the HSBC when Younger was at the Royal Bank of Scotland. 'He sometimes used to say I saved his life but that was complete nonsense. I can only think that he meant our arrival allowed him and his Regiment to leave.'[36]

There was a dismally uncomfortable last evening ashore in a Korean schoolhouse which contrasted with the comfort they found on board the USS *Montrose* the following morning. As the Argylls steamed out of the harbour that afternoon, the ship's company saluted the battalion with three cheers; the Marine Band played on the quarterdeck and, as it

---

[35] *Scotsman* 7/2/1998.
[36] Sir William Purves to the author, 15/8/2007.

ceased, a solitary piper was seen standing on a gun turret playing the two regimental marches, 'The Campbells are Coming' and 'Hieland Laddie'. Every eye followed the piper's movements as he stopped playing, turned aft and saluted the quarterdeck as he disappeared from view.

The Argylls left behind 31 dead and scores of wounded, many of whom never properly recovered. Nineteen Argylls won decorations for gallantry, including Kenny Muir's posthumous Victoria Cross, and nine had been mentioned in dispatches. Younger counted himself lucky that he was not among the injured, as his brother Sandy later would be. He had been in Korea for just four months, but four months which would provide a context for the rest of his life.

'We arrived in Hongkong last Sunday morning,' George told his parents, 'and there were, needless to say, bands, a speech from General Mansergh to welcome us, a march through streets (with polite handclapping from the crowds as each company passed) followed by free lemonade & buns on the station which were kindly supplied by some keen firm who saw a good advert!'[37] Younger then got the train through the New Territories to Doddwell's Ridge, about three miles from the border which his battalion was to patrol.

'It was difficult to settle down,' George remembered. 'We all returned with horrendous digestive problems. It took a while to recover.'[38] Tapeworm, it seemed, had also travelled from Korea to Hong Kong. Medical checks were quickly carried out, but the lack of air conditioning made the tropical conditions in the city hard to bear. Officers lived in Nissan huts divided into three, although most occupants – including George – had rooms to themselves.

The summer of 1951 was certainly eventful. Younger followed eagerly news of the defection of Burgess and Maclean to the Soviet Union[39] as well as his uncle Kenneth's appointment to the Privy Council in copies of the *Sunday Post* still being dispatched by his grandmother. He also went shopping for cheap tailor-made suits and for swims at Castle Peak. 'On Thursday we had the King's Birthday Parade which was a real feat of endurance!' George wrote to his parents on 10 June. 'It poured the whole day long with the hardest possible torrential rain which soaks you to the skin in 30 secs. Even our kilts were soaked right through and became terribly heavy and uncomfortable.'[40]

---

[37] GY to LLY, 1/5/1951, GYP. General Mansergh later became commander-in-chief, NATO forces (1953–56).

[38] *Sunday Post* 25/6/2000.

[39] Guy Burgess would have been known to Younger's uncle Kenneth, as he worked at the Foreign Office before his defection.

[40] GY to LLY, 10/6/1951, GYP.

In August, the time came to return home. Younger sailed for South-ampton on the ss *Empire Orwell* via Singapore, Colombo, Aden and Port Said along with most of his platoon. Back in England, he served at the Southampton depot for about six weeks as an adjutant under Major John Penman before being released to go up to New College, Oxford. A constant anxiety had been a potential delay in taking up his place, but although the standard period of service was then two years, George had finally secured 'Premature Release' that April. Two years later – a year before he graduated – a ceasefire agreement was signed by North and South Korea on 27 July 1953.

'The Korean War taught me something useful in later life', Younger declared shortly before his death, 'that there is absolutely nothing attractive about fighting a war. As everyone always tells you quite correctly, war is 95 per cent boredom and the rest is horrifying.'[41] But while the experience revised his schoolboy romanticism about war, it also gave him enormous affection for the Army and especially the regimental system.

But above all the Korean War had provided George with a valuable insight into the ways of the world. 'I enjoyed all my service very much. I was lucky. It was varied. It was interesting,' he said later. 'It took me to a part of the world I might never have gone to otherwise . . . It toughened me up a lot because you meet with a lot of very unreasonable people and unfair situations and you realize that life is very unfair, and that's an important lesson.'[42]

Yet for the next fifty years Younger rarely, if ever, talked openly about his experiences in the Far East. There was a family connection. His cousin Susie had settled in Korea and often visited him at Easter Leckie with friends. 'Whereas with an Irish friend George was friendly but not totally tactful,' she remembered, 'with the Koreans he was simply wonderful – and this could have come from his Korean war experience. He was always sad that none of us knew the village where he was stationed the longest.'[43]

It was only as preparations got under way for events to mark the conflict's fiftieth anniversary that he began to reminisce. In early 1998 Younger agreed to be the patron of a trust to plant memorial trees, while in 2000 he wrote, spoke and broadcast extensively on his experience of National Service. On 23 September he attended a reunion of Argyll

---

[41] *Soldier* 2/2002.
[42] Walker, *A Barren Place*, 41.
[43] Susie Younger to the author, 16/7/2007. Susie had converted to Catholicism at Oxford and settled in Korea after working there as a missionary.

veterans at Stirling Castle to mark the fiftieth anniversary of the Battle of Hill 282. But despite all this activity it seemed to Younger as if it had indeed become the 'forgotten war'. 'There is nothing so quickly out of mind as something not in the news,' he said, although he remained proud of his modest contribution to the Cold War. 'We fought to deter the Communists from taking over Korea. The Americans tried to prevent them getting Vietnam and spectacularly failed, Korea succeeded.'[44]

The motto of the 1st Argylls in Korea was *Ne obliviscaris*. Although literally a negative injunction not to forget, it could equally well have been interpreted as a positive command to remember. A month after Younger left Hong Kong, the remaining Argylls paraded to commemorate their dead on the anniversary of the action at Hill 282. The padre, J. F. Macdonald, who had made a lasting impression on one 19-year-old platoon commander with his drum-head services, conducted the brief and poignant service. Some of what he said was particularly appropriate for Younger as he began his adult life. 'Many years ago an old man called John had a vision of the kind of world the United Nations are trying to build,' said Macdonald, 'the ideal for which our comrades fought and died. This vision is something realisable in our day and generation, but it all starts with ourselves. We are the people who count – not the politicians. The first step to the rebuilding of a better world is the rebuilding of our lives.'[45]

---

[44] *Sunday Post* 25/6/2000.
[45] Malcolm, *The Argylls in Korea*, 89.

Chapter 3

'NEW COLLEGE CALLS US WITH HER WYKEHAMISTS'

AFTER THE HORRORS of the Korean War, albeit with a spell of rest and relaxation in the Far East, the cloisters and quad of New College, Oxford must have been a pleasant contrast for Younger when he arrived there in the autumn of 1951. 'New College calls us with her Wykehamists,' wrote John Betjeman in his memoirs *Summoned by Bells*, 'Old home of essays, gowns and lecture lists'.[1] Younger was also summoned by bells, and was joined at New College by two fellow Old Wykehamists, one of whom, Alasdair Milne, was known to him, and the other, Charles B. Guinness, who was not.

It was Guinness who Younger found himself sharing a set of rooms with in the garden quad, as the college authorities thought it would be amusing to see two famous brewing surnames on the same door. Later, he boarded with Mrs Stott on Museum Road, a formidable landlady who requisitioned George's ration book.[2]

Before starting at Oxford, Younger had also reacquainted himself with Diana Tuck whom he had first met in Berlin. He had invited her to the Argyll and Sutherland Highlanders Ball that summer, and collected her from Perth in his Triumph Mayflower sports car, an ostentatious vehicle not entirely in keeping with George's character. After the ball, Diana stayed at South Lodge with the Youngers and on learning that George was heading for New College resolved to press ahead with her own application to study orthoptics at the Radcliffe.

Charles Guinness later recalled that Younger studied modern history dutifully, if not very energetically, and did not show much interest in

---

[1] Betjeman, *Summoned by Bells*, 104.
[2] Mrs Stott's daughter later married the Irish comedian Dave Allen, who, like George, had a missing finger.

university politics, 'although he once took me to hear an eccentric speech by Lady Astor'.[3] He did, however, join the Oxford Union, and also signed up to all the political clubs, mainly to hear good speakers, which ranged from Clement Attlee to Randolph Churchill. But Younger did not last long in the Communist Club. 'It so happened that the first meeting of the Communists that I went to was addressed by a London Councillor and the subject of her talk was "The Atrocities Committed by the Argyll and Sutherland Highlanders in Korea",' Younger remembered. 'I heard then the most incredible load of rubbish that I'd ever heard, so I left them.'[4]

George's uncle Kenneth, then still a Labour MP, used to tell his nephew that if he had attended university from 1929 to 1931, as he had done, then he would have become a socialist too. Younger disagreed, and he subsequently fell out with the Socialist Club too (as distinct from Labour), which split over whether to have sherry at its meetings. He sustained, however, his membership of the Labour Club long enough to encounter a young Shirley Williams, although his allegiance was by then firmly Conservative. Younger's first direct political activity was the unglamorous task of licking envelopes on behalf of various candidates during the 1951 general election campaign.[5]

'I have just had an amusing time in St. Giles' listening to Mr. James Baird M.P. (a Bevanite) addressing an open-air meeting,' George wrote to his parents in the autumn of 1953. 'He seemed rather a nice man and talked a lot of nonsense about British Guiana which his listeners were rather loath to accept. I nearly asked him why he didn't favour freeing other oppressed peoples like the Scots, but as he was Scots and I thought he might think I was a Scottish Nationalist, I desisted from saying anything!'[6] A career as an MP himself, however, was obviously far from Younger's mind. 'Di has been canvassing a housing estate as part of the Arundel bye-election!' he told his parents in another letter. 'She says they were all very friendly, but I must say I should loathe canvassing!'[7] George only joined the Unionist Party in 1954, the year of his graduation.

University is for many students a period of frenetic activity, not all of it related to one's chosen area of study. And so it was for Younger, who indulged in only gentle scrutiny of modern history, a subject which

---

[3] *The Times* 31/1/2003.

[4] Walker, *A Barren Place*, 41.

[5] Charles Guinness also remembered that Younger 'only once got annoyed with me, when I stuck on a stamp upside-down. This was disrespectful to the Sovereign' (*The Times* 31/1/2003).

[6] GY to LLY, 25/10/1953, GYP.

[7] Ibid., 7/3/1954, GYP.

genuinely interested him. The history dons at New College left their mark, however, and years later he could still remember figures like Professor David Ogg, whose Scottish burr fascinated his students, and Raymond Carr. '[He] is really quite good as a tutor,' George told his parents. 'However he is a trifle unrealistic in what he gives us to read; this week we are supposed to read and write an essay on a 4-volume biography of Joseph Chamberlain running to over 2,400 pages!! Charles [Guinness] and I have worked out that it is physically impossible to do it without skipping large amounts!!'[8]

Otherwise, Younger's pocket diary for 1952 gives a taste of his extra-curricular activities: shoots at Leckie, numerous balls, tea with friends, soccer at Winchester, squash, golf (although George was never an addict), Territorial Army (TA), cocktail parties, play readings and, of course, visits from 'Di'. But it was music which turned out to be Younger's main preoccupation during his three years at Oxford, and crops up more than any other subject in his weekly letters home.

George practised his French horn assiduously and sometimes tunefully in his bedroom, and with his fellow-players founded the Oxford University Confederation of Horns. He also participated in the Oxford Orchestral Society (its jubilee concert in 1952 featured Ralph Vaughan Williams conducting his own music); sang tenor in the Bach Choir; and combined the two as part of the Oxford University Opera Society and Orchestra, for which he conducted performances of Gilbert and Sullivan, including *Princess Ida*. 'Once,' remembered his room-mate Guinness, 'dressed reluctantly in tights, he contributed to the music for a production of the Merchant of Venice from the top of New College tower.'[9] Later, Younger would recall fondly the Queenswood Summer Orchestral Course, from which he was never absent.

Together with Diana, Younger also attended several concerts at the then relatively new Edinburgh International Festival from 1951 to 1954. Academically, however, he was not quite as dedicated, and left Oxford with a third. 'Probably my fault', remembered Diana, to whom he had just become engaged. He wrote to her in February 1954 describing trips to the cinema with Charles Guinness and ice skating. 'Otherwise the programme has been work and a little music,'[10] he added. But although Younger had enjoyed his time at Oxford, he later nursed mild regrets. 'The other thing I would have liked is to have had the opportunity to

---

[8] Ibid., 18/10/1953, GYP.
[9] *The Times* 31/1/2003.
[10] GY to DY, 5/2/1954, GYP. Friends remember a framed photograph of Diana being a fixture on Younger's desk at New College.

spend more time at university,' he mused in 1985. 'I was just settling down to it when it finished. If I'd had a chance, I would have liked to do a post-graduate course.'[11]

Soon after Younger sat his finals in the summer of 1954, he and Diana were married at St John the Evangelist's, Bury, Sussex, with the Dean of Rochester officiating. '[W]e were both 22 when we married in 1954,' Younger recalled in 1986. 'Nowadays it isn't so young, but looking back it was amazing. My parents were extremely progressive.'[12] Diana's parents also approved. Her mother had long hoped her daughter would marry a Wykehamist (she considered them clever), while Diana's father, who had once captained HMS *Illustrious*, could talk about ships with his new son-in-law.

George and Diana had been engaged since June the previous year – a newspaper announcement wrongly identifying Younger as a 'boxer' instead of saying he was 'at Oxford' – and they soon began house hunting. A modest inheritance from Younger's grandfather, the 2nd Viscount, allowed the couple to buy a bungalow called 'Carnaughton' in Alva, which enabled George to be near his place of work in Alloa.

Younger remained active in the TA, again with the Argyll and Sutherland Highlanders (this time 7th Battalion), first as a signals officer and then as commander of HQ company. He also devoted the occasional weekend to TA exercises, and never missed the annual TA summer camp, even attending one in the few weeks between graduating and his wedding. Diana used her husband's absences as an opportunity to visit her mother and father at Bury in Sussex where George would join them after his exercises were complete.

Younger adored the TA summer camps which gave him a chance to catch up with locally-based friends like James Stirling and Alick Sheriff while exploring parts of the English countryside and even West Germany during overseas trips. He kept in contact with Diana by telephone and letter throughout. 'This place is really fairly god-forsaken,' he wrote to her in 1959, describing Millom in Cumberland. 'It is *miles* from everywhere, and even the everywhere that it is miles from is not worth much.'[13]

The camps, from Younger's point of view, also provided an opportunity to develop his contacts, including with a young Duke of Kent at the 1957 camp in Yorkshire. 'He is *very* shy and stands on the edge of a group

---

[11] *House Magazine* 7/6/1985.
[12] *Sunday Express* 29/6/1986.
[13] GY to DY, 30/6/1959, GYP. The 1959 summer camp meant Younger missed his daughter Joanna's first steps.

letting others talk if he can get away with it,' he told Diana. 'When the others sheered off however he expanded a lot and was quite easy to talk to on many subjects, although I don't think he was too clued up about tanks!'[14]

Meanwhile, there was also the small matter of starting a family. George and Diana's first son, James Edward George Younger, was born a year after their marriage on 11 November 1955. He was followed four years later by Charles Gerald Alexander on 4 October 1959 and Andrew Seymour Robert on 19 November 1962. All three sons, like Younger, continued the family tradition by attending Winchester. Their only sister, Joanna Rosalind, was born on 16 January 1958, and soon became known as 'Jo-Jo'. That same year there was a family tragedy when George's younger brother Robert, universally known as Bobby, suffered terrible burns to his face and body when a primus stove exploded in his face at Winchester.

The expanding family warranted a move, and in 1959 Younger built a brand new house called 'Easter Leckie'. It was affectionately dubbed the 'Signal Box' (or 'Xob' – 'Box' backwards – by George) and built on George's father's estate at the same time as 'Leckie', a new house in the Georgian style, into which Teddy and Evelyn moved in 1962.[15] It was a close-knit family compound with frequent visitors and regular shoots, but despite the hereditary title, Younger was by no means wealthy. The brewing fortune was long gone, and the couple lived frugally as George embarked upon his first career.

'I was expected to go into the family business,' recalled Younger decades later, 'and I felt a bit of an obligation although I wasn't quite certain I wanted to do that.'[16] The family business was George Younger & Sons, where Younger worked until transferring to its wines and spirits subsidiary, J. G. Thomson & Co., in Leith eight years later. When George started working there in October 1954, it had long since centralised its three breweries at the Candleriggs site in Alloa which had been completely rebuilt since the war, making it one of the most modern in the UK.

The Scottish brewing industry, however, was not in good shape. The war had taken its toll, export trade had declined markedly and increased transport costs also impacted upon local breweries. Nevertheless in 1954

---

[14] GY to DY, 23/6/1957, GYP. The present Duke of Kent was otherwise known as Prince Edward, a grandson of King George V. He had graduated from Sandhurst in 1955 and was a second lieutenant in the Royal Scots Greys.

[15] 'Easter Leckie' was demolished when George and Diana moved to 'Leckie' soon after Teddy's death in 1997.

[16] *VIP* (STV) 17/8/1998.

Scottish Brewers, with its two associated companies, William Younger and William McEwan, accounted for more than half the industry's total capital.

But despite Younger's family connections, there was no rapid rise to the top for the firm's newest recruit. 'I started off working as a labourer in 1954 and did a year at that, malting and so on,' he remembered. 'It was very hard work in those days, shovelling with wooden shovels – no mechanisation. [But] I thought it was terrific.' He added: 'Then I went on the road as a salesman – sold all round Glasgow's 1,000 pubs; fascinating; enjoyed that immensely. The only thing was avoiding having a drink everywhere you went. That side of it was very difficult. But it was wonderful in those days. There were still lots of shipyards. People in Glasgow were absolutely larger than life, and I've had enormous affection for the city ever since.'[17]

George travelled to and from the brewery by bus, and Diana remembers that he alternated daily between the upper and lower decks in order to avoid slipping into a dreaded 'rut'. But he enjoyed the work and within a few years had familiarised himself with the entire production process. Always very domesticated, Younger became renowned on the night shift for taking a frying pan to work so he could have a meal of eggs and bacon in the middle of the night.[18]

In 1958, Younger also played a colourful role in brightening up the design of the firm's canned beers. He and Bob Marshall, a creative young salesman and Scottish regional manager for Metal Box (the can manufacturer), pored over hundreds of photographs of girls who purportedly looked as though they might be somebody's sweetheart. Finally they discovered, in a magazine, the blonde who still adorns cans of Younger of Alloa's Sweetheart Stout – the one-time Hollywood starlet Venetia Stevenson. Younger also worked on the sales and marketing of such brands as Carling lager and Piper export, and became active in the influential Brewers Society. In 1958, four years after joining the family firm, he was appointed to the board of George Younger & Sons.

Musically, Younger also remained active, playing French horn in the occasional orchestra of the Royal Scottish Academy of Music and Drama (RSAMD) – of which he was elected a governor in July 1961 – and in what Diana remembers as the 'amateur' Alloa orchestra. He also became chairman of the Stirling and District Choral Union (SDCU) and arranged for it to take part in the Stirling Festivals of 1963 and 1964. Henry

---

[17] *Scottish Banker* 2/1990.
[18] Younger's pocket diary for 1955 notes night shifts beginning at 10 p.m., week-long backshifts starting at 2 p.m., and dayshifts kicking off at 6 a.m.

Havergal, George's music master at Winchester, was then principal of the RSAMD and was persuaded by his former pupil to conduct the SDCU for one season.[19]

Younger's musical hero had long been the French horn player Dennis Brain, whose unique power and flexibility of tone, as well as an astonishing interpretative sensibility, were a profound influence. Tragically, in the early hours of 1 September 1957, Brain was killed near Barnet as he drove home from a concert at Edinburgh's Usher Hall. He was thought to have fallen asleep at the wheel of his TR2, which skidded, overturned and hit a tree. He was just 37 years old, and his death prompted Younger to put down his thoughts, for the first time, in an occasional diary he would keep until entering the Cabinet in 1979. 'His death is, I feel, a great loss,' he wrote. 'He was a superb technician with his horn and . . . It was always a thrilling experience to listen to him even on the wireless.' He continued:

> He was also a most charming and modest man, who always had time for a chat with an unknown admirer. I first met him in Winchester Guildhall in 1948 after a performance of Schubert's Octet. He had a vintage French Horn with a block painted design inside the bell which he said dated back to the early 19th Century . . . He was to me, and possibly to many others, a symbol of the highest of high standards and a model of perfection in an age when second best has often to be tolerated.

Younger feared that in time 'he will be forgotten by all but a few', although he believed the extent of his fame could 'be gauged by the fact that even ordinary working men seem to have noticed that "the horn player has been killed" '.[20]

In addition to work, musical distractions, the TA and helping to raise a young family, Younger also developed his political interests. Having done nothing more than lick envelopes during the 1951 general election, he began speaking at meetings during the next general election in 1955, mainly Junior Unionist events and 'Any Questions' panels at several local associations. He also campaigned for his cousin, Sir John Gilmour (the former Scottish Secretary's son), and the formidable Alexander Forbes Hendry who, like Younger, was active in the TA with the Argylls and hailed from Stirlingshire. Hendry did not manage to win the Labour-held

---

[19] Rosalind Younger, George's sister, had recently studied music under Havergal at the RSAMD.
[20] Diary entry dated 2/9/1957, GYP. Younger noted the anniversary of Brain's death in his 1958 pocket diary.

seat of North Lanarkshire, and the following year Younger took over the candidacy.[21]

At the age of 28, Younger was hooked on politics, but although it was a welcome first rung on the political ladder, the seat was essentially unwinnable. The 1955 election had seen the electoral high point in Unionist fortunes when the party secured an unprecedented majority of both seats and votes in Scotland. North Lanarkshire had failed to elect a Conservative then, and therefore it seemed unlikely it ever would. The sitting MP was the popular Margaret 'Peggy' Herbison who had made her mark as an under-secretary at the Scottish Office in the early 1950s. Her majority in 1955 had been 5,523 ('it seemed a lot in those days'[22]); in the general election of 1959, Younger was determined to at least dent it.

Despite the likelihood of defeat, Younger tackled the campaign in his typically energetic fashion helped, among others, by Diana's father who came north to act as his driver. He reasoned that the closure of local pits and a historically declining Labour vote could at least make the seat more marginal, while a recent influx of Conservative supporters to the north of the constituency at Bishopbriggs counted in his favour.

Younger, however, told reporters that the biggest issue in the constituency was unemployment. 'What North Lanarkshire really needs more than anything else is light industries,' he said, 'and we believe the coming of the strip mill [Ravenscraig] is going to promote this as soon as it is going to provide strip steel.'[23] The creation of Ravenscraig arose from the politically successful yet economically questionable division of the British steel industry between South Wales and Lanarkshire. Some twenty years later as Scottish Secretary, Younger would frequently find himself defending this particular strip mill, albeit in very different circumstances.

George made no secret of his brewing background during the campaign, telling hard-headed miners that it was an asset in a country heading for increased prosperity through private enterprise. 'As a young business man,' he said at one meeting, 'I am very conscious of the urgent need for North Lanark to be in the forefront of the tremendous industrial developments of the future.' Younger was one of the six youngest candidates in Scotland and his campaign won plaudits. 'That he is dedicated to the Unionist cause', noted one newspaper, 'can be readily seen in his attempt

---

[21] Forbes Hendry represented Aberdeenshire West from 1959 to 1966 and served as president of the Scottish Conservative and Unionist Association when Younger was chairman of the party in Scotland from 1974 to 1975.

[22] *Herald* 4/3/1995.

[23] *Scotsman* 1/10/1959.

to cram every scrap of propaganda, every favourable fact and figure, into his regular 40-minute platform speeches.'[24]

The election campaign was happily disturbed by the birth of Younger's third son, Charles, on 4 October, dubbed a 'campaign baby' by the local press. When he had returned home after a hard day's campaigning to find Diana in the early stages of labour, George was determined to catch some sleep on a camp bed despite the inevitability of his being woken up again just a few hours later. Polling day came on 8 October and Herbison comfortably defeated Younger by 21,152 votes to 14,883. But Herbison did not gloat, instead telling many of her colleagues what an excellent Tory candidate he had been, and that more so than any other Conservative she knew Younger had proved himself at ease with the Scottish working class in general, and mineworkers in particular.

'Back to work again after the Election, having slept it off over the weekend,' noted Younger in his diary. 'All rather disappointed that we did not reduce Herbison's majority, but all W[est]. of Scotland has gone against us, mainly because of unemployment I think.'[25] But George had no regrets. 'Our campaign went v. well and I enjoyed it. Meetings were great fun once they started but I always feel nervous beforehand, perhaps that is a good thing. The speech gets a little tedious after 3 weeks giving the same one but the questions are always fun and even the most hostile audiences took it all in good part.' He continued:

> I expected the result overall to be close, but it was a landslide for us everywhere except W. of Scotland, where there was a small swing to Labour which I had not expected. They got a lot of extra voters out by tremendous use of cars, and unemployment prevented some from swinging to us as elsewhere. All very sorry that Patrick Maitland [former MP for Lanark], Douglas Nairn [Central Ayrshire] and Jack Nixon Browne [Craigton] are out but that's what the swing has done.

But, thought Younger, the overall result was 'wonderful'. Labour, he wrote, had really 'had it' this time, and he believed the opposition would have to make big changes if it were ever to win again. It had to 'drop nationalisation and class-warfare for a start. This may lose them their left wing but their centre and right could then ally with Liberals to make a

---

[24] Undated newspaper clipping, GYP.

[25] Diary entry dated 12/10/1959, GYP. Younger also wrote to John Cranna, secretary of the Scottish Unionist Association, about the campaign. 'I entirely agree with what you say,' replied Cranna. 'The dice was heavily loaded against us from the beginning . . . and the prosperity theme which worked so effectively in England had, as you say, rather a hollow ring in our black spots.' (John Cranna to GY, 13/10/1959, GYP)

good radical reformist government and leave the die-hard Socialists to themselves.' If Hugh Gaitskell, the Labour leader, and like Younger, a product of Winchester and New College, Oxford, 'will only now be honest with himself and lead them this way he can still become Prime Minister before he is too old'. Just four years later, Gaitskell died.

Despite his disappointment, the experience of the 1959 poll had confirmed in Younger's mind that he enjoyed politics and 'would like to take it up in due course'. But he was also conscious of his young family and decided not to get fully involved until they were 'beyond the baby stage so that Diana can join in'. 'If I can get a safe seat after 1964 that would be the ideal,' he wrote, 'but I don't suppose it will happen like that.' The future of George Younger & Sons also presented difficulties, but 'if they get taken over or amalgamated so that I do not see a good future for me, I would be quite prepared to make the break. If they really carry on requiring me, it will be much more difficult, as I couldn't be active in business and an M.P.' However, he concluded philosophically, 'I expect this problem will solve itself one way or the other in due course.'[26]

Alasdair Milne, who later became controller of BBC Scotland and used to see the Youngers occasionally, remembers asking George why he had decided upon politics as a career: 'And he said, because I've something to offer. I said what? And he said, I think I've been very privileged in my background; I'm very comfortable in life; I have a very happy family, but I think I can actually contribute something to make other people's lives better. I said, I think that's a noble aspiration but is that all? And he said, isn't that enough?'[27] Younger's political motivations, like many others of his generation, would remain essentially paternalistic throughout his career in public life.

George remained in place as the Conservative candidate for North Lanarkshire for another four years, and continued to work hard both in the constituency and as a Junior Unionist speaker at events around Scotland. He knew most of the Scottish Tory MPs well, one of whom, the formidable Betty Harvie Anderson, told him forcibly that he 'should never underestimate the importance of Parliament'.[28] He was to find out just what she meant over the next two decades. Younger also braved the podium at the annual Unionist Party conference, most notably during a debate on colonial affairs in 1961. He described as 'naïve' a delegate's suggestion that African nationalism should be allowed to abate itself. 'A thousand times no,' Younger declared. 'This is just the ammunition to

---

[26] Diary entry dated 12/10/1959, GYP.
[27] Interview with Alasdair Milne, 23/1/2007.
[28] GY to Duncan Sutherland, 23/11/2000, GYP.

feed the fires of African nationalism.'[29] The previous year, Harold Macmillan had memorably described the 'wind of change' blowing across the African continent in a speech to the South African Parliament.

Otherwise, it was back to work at the brewery where winds of change were also gathering strength. George Younger & Sons had been at the forefront of plans to merge with some other medium-sized Scottish firms to rationalise industry capacity, but when these came to nothing the breweries became obvious targets for takeover bids. English brewers had always had a substantial interest in the Scottish markets, and they soon cast an eye northwards. 'I'd go to Scottish Council [for Development & Industry] meetings in the 1950s', remembered Younger, 'and watch the big-name companies get picked on one after the other and lose their headquarters.'[30]

But on the other hand, although George 'enjoyed the small business side, particularly its independence', he was irked by the consequential lack of resources: 'you couldn't do anything very much because you were so small.' This period later proved useful as Younger pursued his post-Cabinet career at the Royal Bank of Scotland (RBS). 'Our business was medium-sized but I was continually dealing with individual pubs and their problems,' he recalled, 'putting them in business, taking them out of business and so on.'[31] Even spending £5,000 was an agonising decision. To that extent, he welcomed the mergers 'which brought me into a large company world . . . but I always felt very strongly that there must be a Scottish character and a Scottish headquarters'.[32]

But although George Younger & Sons would itself soon be swallowed up, in late 1959 it had just taken over Blair & Co., the aftermath of which confronted Younger when he returned to work following the 1959 election campaign. 'We seem to have achieved the goodwill of their staff and directors which is vital if we are to keep their free trade,' he wrote in his diary. 'Some of their customers are very touchy about the possibility of being forced to go over to G.Y.'s beer but if we handle it all carefully we may manage to keep most of the trade.' Blair & Co.'s travellers were to continue selling Blair's Beer, while promoting George Younger's only as a sideline. 'We have already started to do their bottling and will shortly consider the brewing of all their beer at Candleriggs. We did not pay too bad a price for Blairs and if we can keep their trade we will not do badly.'[33]

---

[29] *Scotsman* 22/4/1961.
[30] *Business a.m.* 4/4/2001.
[31] *Director* 7/1993.
[32] *Scottish Banker* 2/1990.
[33] Diary entry dated 28/10/1959, GYP.

In April 1960 it was announced that three of the most revered names in Scottish brewing, William Murray & Co. of Edinburgh, John Fowler & Co. of Prestonpans and George Younger & Sons of Alloa, were being taken over by Northern Breweries of Great Britain, a holding company owned by the Canadian Brewing magnate E. P. Taylor. Eventually all Northern Breweries' Scottish interests were combined into a group known as Caledonian Breweries (later United Caledonian Breweries, or UCB) and Viscount Younger – George's father – was co-opted onto the board of the new company. When UCB decided in 1963 to close the Candleriggs Brewery of the now defunct George Younger & Sons, Teddy resigned after much soul-searching because he felt the closure breached promises made by him to his workforce three years earlier. The Youngers of Alloa were no more.

George had begun commuting to Leith in 1962 to work for J. G. Thomson & Co., which was then one of the oldest wine and spirit businesses in Scotland and a subsidiary of George Younger & Sons. His appointment as sales director coincided with some remarkable developments in spirit marketing and distribution which occurred against a backdrop of a social revolution in attitudes towards drink and drinking. Younger was fascinated by a plethora of clever new marketing techniques which he utilised on sales trips to Germany with his colleagues Alick Sheriff (also a TA colleague) and Charles Craig during 1963. The last bottlings, however, were carried out at the Leith vaults in 1964 and ironically, many of J. G. Thomson & Co.'s bonded warehouses later became housing and retail developments under regeneration programmes begun by Bruce Millan – and sustained by Younger – as Scottish Secretary.

In 1963, Younger applied for the job of marketing director at UCB, but although he was interviewed his application was unsuccessful, something he later described as the first great disappointment of his life. Three years later, UCB formally merged with J. & R. Tennent of Glasgow to form Tennent Caledonian Breweries within the giant Bass Charrington Group. Younger remained a director of its subsidiaries George Younger & Sons until 1968, and J. G. Thomson & Co. until 1966, while also adding board positions at Maclachlans (1968-70), John Fowler & Co., and from 1966, Charrington Vintners in London, all of which were happily compatible with his parliamentary duties as an opposition MP.

Just occasionally, Younger's brewing past would bubble up during his political career. In a 1971 Commons debate the Labour MP Willie Hamilton mischievously implied that some MPs would be counting 'the £ s. d. profit' from a government Bill to sell off state pubs in Cromarty, Gretna and Carlisle. He named Sir William McEwan Younger, the new chairman of the Scottish Tory Party, and George, at that time a junior minister at the Scottish Office. 'There is a member of that Guinness family in the Tory Government at the moment', he said, referring to Paul Channon. 'And there is a Younger in the Government who denied he had any more associations with the brewery trade at the moment and we are bound to accept that.'[34] George was defended by Gordon Campbell, the Scottish Secretary, who reminded Hamilton that Younger had severed all his connections with Bass Charrington on being appointed a minister in 1970. Nevertheless, the Shadow Home Secretary James Callaghan said it had 'the makings of a nasty scandal'.[35]

A few years after that skirmish, and once again in opposition, Younger revived his business interests by becoming a director of Tennent Caledonian Breweries from 1977 to 1979 and a diligent attendee at the annual Brewers Society dinner. 'If a bomb dropped on Westminster,' Younger later mused as a Cabinet minister in the 1980s, 'or we were all abolished, I would certainly go back to business.'[36] He did eventually go back to business at RBS, while his youngest son Andrew continued the family tradition by working at Bass after graduating from university. He later became a director of another family's brewery, Hall and Woodhouse, and would happily talk shop with his father, who was content that a ninth-generation Younger was still involved with the brewing industry.

On 15 August 1963, while George was still reeling from the disappointment of being turned down for the post of marketing director at UCB, he was driving home from Leith when he heard on the radio that the Scottish Office minister and MP for Kinross and West Perthshire, William Gilmour Leburn, had collapsed and died while walking on the moors. 'I saw this as an opportunity,' he recalled later. 'I wasn't going to get a better opportunity than that as it was very close to home. It was obviously now or never.'[37]

---

[34] *Scottish Daily Express* 21/4/1971.
[35] *Daily Record* 21/4/1971.
[36] *House Magazine* 7/6/1985.
[37] Autobiographical notes, GYP.

Chapter 4

'YOU'LL DO YOUR DUTY'

YOUNGER WROTE TO THE Kinross and West Perthshire Unionist Association on 1 September 1963 asking to be considered as a candidate in the forthcoming by-election. Ten days later he received a call to say he was on the short-list of four, which also included William Stormont, later (as Lord Mansfield) a minister at the Scottish Office under Younger, and David Anderson, the Solicitor-General for Scotland, who was then on the hunt for a constituency.

As Younger prepared for his interview, he contacted United Caledonian Breweries (UCB) to establish what would happen to his job as sales manager at J. G. Thomson & Co. should he be chosen and go on to win the seat. UCB would 'be prepared to take you back into full time employment if you decided or were forced to decide to pack up within five years of being elected,' his boss replied, 'which I think is a very fair offer. Naturally, however, they could not guarantee that you would be re-instated in your present position.'[1] Thus reassured, Younger then 'had to go through the most exhaustive selection process you can imagine with visits to branches and ladies tea' parties and all sorts of things, to make sure everyone thought I was the right sort of person.' He recalled: 'One lot even asked themselves to tea with us at home, presumably to see if we were respectable and had respectable manners.'[2]

The final stage of the selection took place in Crieff on 18 September and Younger's interview was scheduled for 12.15 p.m. at the Unionist Club. 'At the given time I walked down to meet the executive,' he recalled. 'I answered questions. They said thank you. I walked back to my hotel, and then was summoned back to be told I had been chosen. At the age of 32 I had been offered what amounted to a job for life.'[3]

---

[1] UCB to GY, 12/9/1963, GYP.
[2] Autobiographical notes, GYP.
[3] *Herald* 4/3/1995.

Younger quickly informed the North Lanarkshire Unionist Association that he was resigning as its candidate. This prompted two prophetic letters; one good and the other bad. Susan Hamilton, the efficient organising secretary at Younger's old association, wrote to say she was 'delighted for you & Mrs Younger too . . . I know you will probably be a Secretary of State for Scotland in no time at all.'[4] But a few days later, Marjorie Harvey, who had been Gil Leburn's part-time secretary in the House of Commons, wrote offering her services, 'provided, of course, that nothing unforeseen occurs in the Bye Election!'[5] Marjorie, of course, meant in terms of electoral support. Little did either of them know what was in store.

The Prime Minister, Harold Macmillan, was by then seriously ill. When, in the midst of the annual Conservative Party conference in Blackpool, Lord Home, the Foreign Secretary, read out a letter from Macmillan announcing that he intended to resign the premiership, there was immediate jostling to succeed him. At first, Home's name was not among the contenders, although the recent Peerage Act – prompted by Tony Benn's campaign to disclaim his father's hereditary peerage – provided the constitutional mechanism by which he could leave the House of Lords and stand for the Commons.

As a Scot, the impact of this possibility in Kinross and West Perthshire was palpable, and within days there were rumours that Younger would be forced to stand aside in order to make way for Home if he became prime minister. The local association, however, was distinctly unhappy at the prospect of having an outsider – even a prime minister – foisted upon them. The first indication that something was afoot came on 16 October (the day before Macmillan drafted his final memo of resignation for the Queen) when Younger was canvassing with his agent John G. Robertson.

Calls started coming in from the London press asking Younger if a rumour that he was going to stand aside for Home was true. Naturally concerned, he kept in constant touch with constituency activists at the Blackpool conference, although his formal adoption proceeded as planned at the Salutation Hotel in Perth the following day. 'All speculation linking Lord Home with the candidature in the Kinross and West Perthshire by-election ended in Perth yesterday', reported the *Courier and Advertiser*, 'when the Unionist constituency association unanimously adopted Mr George K. H. Younger . . . as their candidate.'

Major David Maitland Gardner, who had presided over the adoption meeting, was also unequivocal. 'There is no question of Mr George

[4] Susan Hamilton to GY, 25/9/1963, GYP.
[5] Marjorie Harvey to GY, 29/9/1963, GYP.

Younger being asked to stand down in favour of anyone else.'[6] It was also, or so George believed, a huge weight off his mind. 'I feel highly honoured to be here', he told reporters, 'and, after the events of the last few days, somewhat surprised and not a little relieved.'[7] That very day, Lord Home emerged as a candidate for the Conservative leadership and announced his intention to disclaim his peerage and seek election to the Lower House. 'I am so glad that no movement in the stratosphere affected your plans,' wrote one well-wisher to Younger, 'though you must have had some anxious moments.'[8]

Polling day was set for 7 November, and one by one Younger's competing candidates emerged. The Labour hopeful was Andrew Forrester; the Liberal J. A. Duncan Miller; and the Nationalist Arthur Donaldson, a former Scottish National Party (SNP) leader who had stood in the constituency four years earlier. The prospects of victory for Younger were not only good, but virtually guaranteed. Leburn's majority in 1959 had been a whopping 12,248; it would have taken a major political upset to prevent Younger retaining it with a similar lead.

The large rural seat was perfect for Younger, who lived just two miles from the constituency boundary, and the local businessman Lord Rootes loaned him a blue Hillman Imp in order to negotiate its vast size. West Perthshire's small burghs – including Aberfeldy, Callander, Dunblane and Pitlochry – were popular tourist attractions, and although there was little in the way of heavy manufacturing, agricultural industry was predominant. Politically, it was quintessentially Tory territory, and would remain so until another lively by-election in 1995. Younger was to fight his campaign on the government's record, chiefly regional development and industrial policy, both issues instinctively close to his heart.[9]

The campaign began in earnest on Friday 18 October, with three big meetings planned for the following day. But by that point the jostling between Lord Home, Rab Butler and Quintin Hogg had come to a head and Home ultimately 'emerged' as Prime Minister. The Queen invited him to form an administration shortly after 12.30 p.m., but the new Prime Minister was still without a constituency and there were only two vacant seats – the highly marginal Luton in London, for which no one had been selected, and Kinross and West Perthshire, for which someone had. The

---

[6] *Courier and Advertiser* 18/10/1963.

[7] *Perthshire Advertiser* 19/10/1963.

[8] Letter to GY, 18/10/1963, GYP.

[9] Ironically, part of the government's record Younger sought to defend was the opening of the Steel Strip Mill at Ravenscraig, BMC Trucks at Bathgate and Hillman Cars at Linwood, all of which would give him trouble as Scottish Secretary twenty years later.

prospect of the Prime Minister campaigning in Luton was unthinkable, and so Younger's fate was effectively sealed.

That same Friday, Sir John George, chairman of the Unionists in Scotland, summoned Younger to lunch at the Golden Lion in Stirling along with the Kinross and West Perthshire Association chairman, Maitland Gardner. Sir John quickly came to his rather blunt point. 'George,' he declared, 'you'll do your duty for your country and your party.' Younger, however, was understandably reluctant and, at least initially, refused to do so. Ian McIntyre, the head of information and research at party HQ in Edinburgh, was also at the lunch and remembers Younger being of the view that Roxburgh, Selkirk and Peebles (where the incumbent Tory MP had offered to stand down) was a more viable constituency for the Borders-based Home, and that Central Office was being far too cautious in passing this over.[10]

In reality, however, Younger probably realised he was in an impossible position. Sir John assured him his reward would be the next available safe seat in Scotland; besides, there were long-term political advantages in being cast in the role of sacrificial lamb although this was emphatically not part of his calculation. McIntyre then recalls being dispatched to a neighbouring room to draft an appropriately gracious statement with a heart-broken candidate.[11]

The rest of that Friday and the following weekend must have been agonising for Younger, but on Sunday 20 October the following statement was released to the press:

> The appointment of Lord Home as Prime Minister obviously makes it essential that he should have a seat in the House of Commons at the earliest possible moment. It seemed to me in the best interests of the party and the entire nation that I should offer to withdraw my name as a candidate in the forthcoming by-election in the hope that he will allow his name to go forward instead. I have conveyed this offer to the Prime Minister.[12]

The 'invitation' for Home to stand in the constituency was telephoned to the Prime Minister the same day and followed up by an exchange of letters, modest from Younger (written the day before) and grateful from Home:

---

[10] Interview with Ian McIntyre, 19/11/2006.
[11] McIntyre remembers returning to his office with Murray Kemsley after the lunch and receiving a comical cloak-and-dagger telephone call from Maitland Gardner. When Kemsley's phone rang, the caller did not identify himself but said simply: 'Did you have mince scallops for lunch?' Maitland Gardner was thereafter referred to as 'Mince Scallops' (Ian McIntyre to the author, 2/11/2007).
[12] *The Times* 21/10/1963.

Dear Prime Minister,

Your appointment yesterday as Prime Minister seems to me to have made it essential that you should have a seat in the House of Commons as soon as possible.

As you probably know, I have been adopted as Unionist Candidate for the impending Bye-Election in Kinross & West Perthshire, and I now write to say that I would be very glad to withdraw my name as Candidate, if you would allow your name to go forward in my place.

Your appointment has already caused much pleasure throughout Scotland and I can assure you that I and my supporters would give you every help that is within our power.

Yours sincerely,

George K. H. Younger[13]

Home was, of course, aware that Younger had already been adopted as the candidate, but replied that he would be pleased to accept the nomination if the Kinross and West Perthshire election committee decided to invite him. 'It is highly unusual for the . . . Unionist Party,' observed a contemporary account, 'to conduct political business on the Sabbath'. But this was an emergency, and for once rules had to be broken.[14]

John Robertson's wife Una rushed Home's nomination papers to Perth on Monday morning with only minutes to spare (nominations closed at noon) and the election committee met the following day. Many local office holders were distinctly unhappy about having a candidate imposed upon them, even if it were the Prime Minister, preferring the youthful Younger to the elderly Home, but the reality of the situation soon sank in and Home's candidature was unanimously endorsed. John Robertson was released to serve as his agent while 'Mr. Younger's unselfishness and loyal action' was commended.

Maitland Gardner then hastily dispatched a telegram to the Prime Minister: 'At a meeting today the Constituency Election Committee with Mr. George Younger's enthusiastic approval agreed unanimously to invite you to contest the Kinross & West Perthshire Bye-Election as Unionist Candidate. We assure you of our whole-hearted, loyal and vigorous support.'[15] The new Prime Minister had just become a candidate in Britain's third-safest Tory seat.

Lord Home wrote to thank Younger the next day:

[13] GY to ADH, 20/10/1963, GYP.
[14] Howard, *The Making of the Prime Minister*, 96.
[15] *Scotsman* 23/10/1963.

My dear Younger

    I want you to know how much I appreciate your willingness to stand aside in the Kinross By-election. It is no small thing that a young man, happily launched on a political career and with a reasonable certainty of being elected to Parliament, should make this sacrifice. If, as I hope, I am myself successful, I trust that it will not be long before you are able to join me in the Commons.

    Yours ever

    Home.[16]

Shortly after concluding this letter of thanks to Younger with the customary 'Home', the Prime Minister signed an instrument of disclaimer under the Peerage Act. He disclaimed six peerages in all, and styled himself for the first time as Sir Alexander Frederick Douglas-Home.

Despite Younger's relaxed demeanour and gentlemanly language, he was a profoundly disappointed man. He had fought a gruelling contest to secure the nomination for Kinross and West Perthshire, lived just two miles from the boundary where he would have been close to his parents, wife and young family, and above all had been assured of victory in a seat which would have provided a solid basis for him to develop what everyone expected would be a successful political career. Yet within the space of a week, the resignation of one prime minister and the emergence of another – both events which occurred several hundred miles away in London – had seen him go from elation to uncertainty as to when he would enter Parliament, if at all. 'I never doubted for a minute that I had to do it,' Younger reflected thirty years later, 'but it was very hard in the sense that it seemed an absolutely daft thing to do in my own interest.'[17]

Graciously, Younger also agreed to play a full part in Home's campaign, a vital contribution considering how little time the fledgling Prime Minister could actually devote to it himself. 'I became his runner, in effect,' George recalled, and the local party soon rallied round. 'The formidable ladies became tremendously steamed up and were enormously enthusiastic about it all, not least because of the sudden international attention.'[18]

Letters of sympathy also flooded in. Marjorie Harvey, who had offered her secretarial services to Younger a couple of weeks earlier, wrote again on 21 October. 'I was very sorry to learn that you have decided to stand down in favour of Lord Home but quite realise that you hadn't really much alternative!' she said. 'As soon as I heard last week that he was P.M.

[16] ADH to GY, 23/10/1963, GYP.

[17] *Director* 7/1993.

[18] *Herald* 4/3/1995.

I thought it was pretty certain that he would have to contest Kinross & West Perthshire. I only hope all goes well as I gathered originally that the Association wanted a local & not to have someone thrust on them – but perhaps the Prime Minister is different.' She added jauntily: 'I somehow feel the P.M. will not want ¼ of a Secretary!'[19]

Younger's decision had also provoked a political storm. William Marshall, the organising secretary of the Labour Party in Scotland, said he would object formally to Lord Home's nomination, while the Liberal leader Jo Grimond said 'Clearly his [Younger's] arm has been twisted and the candidate has been forced to stand down for the convenience of the Tory party. This is treating the electors of Kinross and West Perthshire with contempt and reducing democracy in this country to farce.'[20]

Such protests, however, quickly blew over, and Sir Alec began his campaign by travelling through the glens to address his future constituents in chalk-dusty schoolrooms and timber halls. 'So, off we went,' recalled Younger later, 'and he did some of the meetings and I did most of the meetings and we generally did it between us. It was certainly quite a circus when you add together my car and other helpers/supporters etc and also, of course, all the press.'[21] Sir Alec generally adhered to the programme of engagements already agreed for Younger, although Diana had a terrible time getting her husband to speaking engagements on time, often finding her car stuck between press vehicles.

Reporters certainly had colourful copy to file during a by-election which almost matched another in Kinross and West Perthshire in terms of national significance. In 1938 the Duchess of Atholl fought a lonely battle against Chamberlain's policy of appeasement; a quarter of a century later, Chamberlain's former Parliamentary Private Secretary (PPS) had wide support in his fight to remain Prime Minister. It left an indelible impression on many local residents and those further afield, including a young Gordon Brown, who later became friendly with Younger at Westminster.[22]

The *Private Eye* satirist Willie Rushton announced his candidacy and campaigned on the basis of 'No Home Rule for Scotland', a deliberate pun on Sir Alec's name. And while that was certainly intentional, the SNP's traditional rallying cry of 'Home Rule for Scotland' was subtly undermined. Meanwhile the Labour candidate, the Glaswegian teacher Andrew Forrester, campaigned with a new bride and his right forearm in

[19] Marjorie Harvey to GY, 21/10/1963, GYP.
[20] *The Times* 22/10/1963.
[21] Autobiographical notes, GYP.
[22] Gordon Brown recalled the by-election in a television profile, *GB: Made in Scotland* (STV) 26/6/2007.

plaster cast following an accident. Two independent candidates also took a stand against what they said was the 'foisting' of Sir Alec upon the constituency. One, Ian Smith, a former wing commander in the RAF, claimed to represent the 'disgruntled rank and file Tories'.[23] Harold Wilson, the Labour leader, depicted the by-election as a contest between vested interests in modern dress and progressive socialist egalitarianism.

Sir Alec and Lady Douglas-Home were still based in Coldstream, although during the by-election they stayed regularly at a friend's house in Comrie. The campaign lasted three weeks, although Sir Alec had only two to travel across the county. It was a lively and non-stop campaign, with packed meetings, 72 speeches from Sir Alec and, above all, top-notch political theatre. As it drew to a close, the Prime Minister cleverly hinted that Edward Heath, the President of the Board of Trade, would soon be collaborating with Michael Noble, the Scottish Secretary, on a white paper to redirect industrial development to Scotland.

As ballots piled up in Perth's Sheriff Court House on 8 November, Younger acted as one of the Prime Minister's counting agents. At 11.45 a.m. the following day, it was announced that Sir Alec had romped home with a majority of 9,328 although George had deliberately lowered expectations by predicting a majority of about half that.[24] Conservative Central Office, and the party generally, breathed a collective sigh of relief. In Luton, where a by-election took place the same day, the party's candidate lost to his Labour opponent. 'Luton was the last page of the old chapter', commented Sir Alec on his party's mixed fortunes, 'and Kinross and West Perthshire is the first page of the new.'[25]

'So at the end of this process,' Younger later recalled, 'I went back to my ordinary job as sales manager and he went back to being Prime Minister of the United Kingdom.'[26] Much later, he became more philosophical: 'For a young man with no political experience, that October was the most extraordinary episode. I gained half a lifetime's experience in a few days.'[27]

Although it was widely expected that Younger would easily top any selection short-list in the months following the Kinross and West Perthshire by-election, his hunt for a seat was far from straightforward. 'There was nothing they [the party] could offer,' he recalled. 'I was told they would do everything they could to help me get selected elsewhere, but you

[23] *The Times* 28/10/1963.
[24] Younger likened the by-election to a football match: 'Home United vs. Wilson Dodgers – A decisive Home Win!' (undated speech notes, GYP).
[25] *Courier and Advertiser* 9/11/1963.
[26] Autobiographical notes, GYP.
[27] Roy, *Conversations in a Small Country*, 179.

can't impose a candidate on a constituency. Probably the best thing they could have done was to keep out.'[28]

The Times speculated that Younger would be offered the candidacy at the forthcoming by-election in Dumfriesshire, where Niall Macpherson, the sitting MP, had been raised to the peerage as Lord Drumalbyn, but instead that safe seat went to David Anderson, the Solicitor-General for Scotland. Then there was Ayr, which by sheer coincidence Younger's great-grandfather, George Younger, had been elected to represent back in 1906. Sir Thomas Moore had been the MP for almost 39 years, but aged 77 (he was then acting for Sir Winston Churchill as Father of the House) he had recently intimated that he would not be fighting the next election, due sometime in 1964.

'I remember we agreed that it would be marvellous to get this young man,' said Bill Taylor, who in 1963 had just become the Ayr Association's agent, 'so he was invited to come down for an interview.'[29] The interview was essentially a formality, and although Younger made a good impression on the selection panel, the office bearers were already thrilled at the prospect of having him as their candidate.

Sir John George, who had been the pivotal figure in Younger's decision to stand aside for Home, had once again intervened, this time in his favour. Sir John, who lived in Ayr, wrote to Younger on 9 November:

> In the great joy of the Prime Minister's magnificent victory, the man who made it possible is apt to be overlooked. No doubt the Prime Minister has already conveyed to you his gratitude, but as Chairman of the Party, I feel I must again acknowledge the tremendous service you rendered to the Party in Scotland and to the nation when you so willingly and at such great sacrifice stood down to make way for the Prime Minister . . .
>
> Your services will never be forgotten, and I hope that the approaches which are being made, or will be made to you from another source will meet with a favourable response from you. If you want to talk over this matter, I shall be glad to meet you. Perhaps it might be as well for you to come down here if you feel disposed to accept. I would take you round the area and let you see the changes which have taken place in recent years – mainly favourable . . .
>
> Once more – my very deep gratitude.[30]

Younger was torn. Although Sir Thomas had always enjoyed healthy majorities of about 6,000, these had fallen to 3,356 at the 1959 poll, and

[28] *Herald* 4/3/1995.
[29] Interview with Bill Taylor, 2/8/2007. Taylor remembers showing Younger minute books recording his great-grandfather's activities as the MP for Ayr.
[30] Sir John George to GY, 9/11/1963, GYP.

with things going badly for the Conservatives nationally, this made it a potentially risky seat. Younger's uncertainty is obvious from a letter he wrote to the Prime Minister on 19 November:

Dear Prime Minister,

You asked me the other day to keep in touch with you in regard to any possible constituency which I might be asked to represent. Things have moved rather more quickly than I expected, and I have now been definitely asked if I would stand for Ayr. As you know, Sir Thomas Moore does not intend to stand at the next General Election, and his majority was approximately 3,300 at the last General Election. I have to make a decision as to whether I will stand for Ayr or not in the fairly near future, and I would much appreciate your own personal advice on this matter. It seems to me that the considerations are as follows:–

1. If I do not take Ayr, there will be no other Scottish constituency vacant, barring accidents, before the General Election. Therefore, If I do not take Ayr, I would presumably not have a constituency at the next General Election.
2. If I do take Ayr, I could not in the meantime take any better constituency that might turn up by accident between now and the General Election.
3. Ayr is obviously highly marginal, and I must accept the fact that I might easily not be elected if I stood there. If that happened, I would then be free to take any better seat that became available after the next General Election.
4. If I did stand in Ayr and win it, it might be by a very small majority and it might, therefore, be a very insecure basis upon which to found a career in Parliament.

Bearing in mind all these factors, I feel that on a balance it would probably be right for me to accept Ayr, although I consider that it is a very difficult decision to make. I would be most grateful for your own advice and if you think fit, I would, of course, be only too pleased to come and see you if you think this is worth while.

I was most grateful for all your kindness to me during the Election, and apologise for troubling you at this time on the question of my next step. If you do wish to get in touch with me, my home telephone number is Gargunnock 274, and my office telephone number is Edinburgh, Leith 2131.

Yours sincerely,

George Younger[31]

Sir Alec's view of Younger's predicament has not survived although perhaps the assassination of President Kennedy on 22 November provided an

[31] GY to ADH, 19/11/1963, GYP.

understandable distraction. Younger's letter, however, overlapped with a
handwritten note from Downing Street expressing yet more gratitude:

> My letter writing has suffered dreadfully from the pressure of events & I am
> ashamed that I did not write long ago to thank you for all the unselfish support
> which you gave me throughout the whole of the campaign in Kinross & West
> Perth. To go through with it all & to see another elected would try a saint but
> you did it all with unfailing goodwill & good humour – I am deeply grateful. I
> do hope that you will soon find a seat which suits you but don't ever be tempted
> to become P.M.! Don't hesitate to come & see me if you want a talk.[32]

It is likely that Younger did speak to Sir Alec about his prospects, probably
by telephone, although he must have overcome any lingering doubts,
for on 2 December Younger accepted the offer and was endorsed as the
prospective Unionist candidate for Ayr.

Almost immediately, Younger's candidacy ran into difficulty. At the
beginning of 1964 Edward Heath, then a reforming President of the Board
of Trade, announced the abolition of Resale Price Maintenance (RPM).
This allowed retailers greater discretion in pricing the goods they sold, but
many Tory back-benchers saw abolition as a charter for supermarket chains
and the beginning of the end for small shopkeepers, a group of voters who
were in those days largely Tory. Younger's initial reaction was along the
lines of 'wait and see', especially when confronted by angry pub landlords in
Ayr. 'Of course the subject of re-sale price maintenance is very dear to me,'
he protested. 'Like the licencees, my own brewery will be affected by it and
at the moment I am studying the implications of the Bill. But I think the
Ayrshire licensees are acting in a very Irish way if they campaign against the
Tories at the General Election. We are the only party that will introduce
safeguards along with the abolition of Re-sale Price Maintenance.'[33]

But more than 600 pub owners in Ayrshire were not appeased and
threatened to field a candidate in opposition to Younger unless the
abolition of RPM was abandoned and Ted Heath resigned. Younger
offered to meet the publicans, a wise move in the circumstances, although
by the time of his first public meeting as a candidate in March 1964, he
bravely faced them head on by declaring his support for abolition. On
11 March, twenty-one Conservatives voted against Heath's Bill on its first
reading and seventeen others abstained, but after much controversy and
further back-bench revolts, the Bill passed its third reading on 13 May and
hardly figured at all in the subsequent election campaign.

Instead, Younger campaigned on the importance of Prestwick Airport

---

[32] ADH to GY, 20/11/1963, GYP.
[33] *Scottish Daily Express* 23/1/1964.

and regional development for Scotland. He also attempted to secure his trump card, a visit from the unexpectedly popular Prime Minister. Sir Alec replied on 21 February:

My dear George

It was good of you to write and ask whether it would be possible for me to visit Ayr and address a meeting at some time, either before or after the Election. Whenever the Election may come I doubt if it would be possible to fit in a visit during the actual campaign. I should, however, like to pay you a visit if it can possibly be fitted in, and if you will give me until early April I will then see whether anything can be arranged.

I am so glad to hear that all is going well and I see no reason why it should not continue to do so.

Yours ever

Alec.[34]

Sir Alec continued to demonstrate his gratitude by regularly inviting George and Diana to functions at Downing Street and Chequers while offering shrewd advice on Younger's campaign to enter Parliament.

There were also less welcome supporters, including Anne, the irrepressible wife of the Scottish Secretary Michael Noble. She spoke in support of Younger at a meeting in Alloway Village Hall, although her contribution was not exactly conventional. The candidate spoke for his allotted time, but Anne quickly became bored and kicked him under the table to indicate her disapproval, behaviour which infuriated Younger's wife Diana, who was also on the platform. She then flashed him a devastating smile and said: 'We want people to know that Unionists are not just political bores like Mr. Younger.' Amid laughter, Anne Noble added: 'People should know Unionists are nice people, that they are fun and amusing, and lead a good life in every sense of the word.'[35] The press latched on to her description of herself as the Tory Party's 'horror comic', while Younger dealt with the fallout among members of his constituency association.[36]

Shortly after Sir Alec asked the Queen to dissolve Parliament, Younger was formally adopted as candidate in Ayr on 24 September 1964 at the Boswell Hall. 'The Socialists, like the Bourbon kings of France, have learned nothing, and forgotten nothing in their thirteen years of exile,' he said, clearly in a colourful frame of mind. ' "Thirteen wasted years" they have called them! How aptly this remark applies to themselves.' The

[34] ADH to GY, 21/2/1964, GYP.

[35] Undated newspaper clipping, GYP.

[36] Bill Taylor, Younger's agent in Ayr, remembers that one member of the association even wanted to send a letter of complaint to Anne's husband, the Scottish Secretary.

speech, and indeed the Conservative campaign in general, represented a government on the defensive. Younger chose to focus on the UK's nuclear deterrent, and carefully exploited internal Labour divisions in doing so. 'They are pledged to give up entirely our own nuclear weapons and rely on the United States to protect us,' he reminded supporters. 'To give up our only ultimate means of defence is a terrifying step and commits us for ever to being unable to face up to any aggressor.'[37]

George's agent Bill Taylor led an enthusiastic band of Young Conservatives on a vigorous campaign in Ayr. As it drew to a close the Prime Minister fulfilled his long-standing commitment by speaking at two meetings on the evening before polling day. It was literally a flying visit. Sir Alec was greeted at the airport by George and Diana, Sir John George, and Sir Thomas Moore, the retiring Member. But while he got a positive reception at the Prestwick event, Sir Alec endured a barrage of heckling at the Station Hotel meeting in Ayr. The Prime Minister joked that someone had said to him on his way to the microphone that he should 'Go home, Home'. 'I have come home to Scotland', he retorted, 'and I am going home to Downing Street tomorrow night and I will stay there for another five years.' At one point his sound system broke down, leading to cries of 'We can't hear you'.[38] Sir Alec paid warm tribute to the candidate, saying he had done most of the spadework for him in the previous year's Perthshire by-election. Responding, Younger thanked him for rearranging his programme in order to visit Ayr, and after lunch at the Station Hotel the Prime Minister flew to Scone for some final campaigning in his own constituency before the polls opened.

It could be that Sir Alec's visit crucially tipped the balance in Ayr, although there were other positive influences. The town had just experienced one of its best ever tourist seasons, and although the local Labour Party had smartened up its organisation since 1959, Younger had worked the seat hard, meeting as many people as possible while stressing local development issues, including the new £2 million passenger terminal at Prestwick and plans for a New Town at Irvine. The Ayr result was announced at just after 1 a.m. on the steps of the courthouse in Ayr; Younger had beaten the Labour candidate, Alex Eadie, by just 1,701 votes in a straight fight. Some of those voting for him even claimed to have voted for his great-grandfather, the other George Younger, half a century earlier.

---

[37] Speech to Ayr Conservatives, 24/9/1964, GYP.
[38] *Ayrshire Post* 16/10/1964. According to Bill Taylor, the wires had been cut in a deliberate act of sabotage. Fortunately, he had a battery-operated hand-held speaker as back-up.

Chapter 5

THE YOUNG TURKS

YOUNGER ARRIVED AT Westminster almost sixty years after his great-grandfather, the other George Younger, had taken up his seat in the House of Commons representing, like his great-grandson, the old burgh constituency of Ayr. Even the constituency office remained the same – 1 Wellington Square – an imposing Georgian square with the county buildings and court at one end and a park in the middle. The House of Commons, to some extent, had always been a family affair. George's uncle, Sir Kenneth Younger, had stood down as a Labour MP in 1959, although his cousin, Sir John Gilmour, had been elected to represent East Fife as a Unionist in a 1961 by-election. Between them, Sir John and George represented the changing face of Scottish Unionism. Gilmour was a baronet, a real knight of the shires who shied away from any overtly political activity while Younger was young, energetic and willing to take on Labour over less than traditional Tory issues.

Although Sir Alec Douglas-Home had narrowly lost the election, the 1964 intake of Conservative MPs, particularly in Scotland, was one of the most impressive in living memory. In all there were twenty-four Unionists returned in Scotland, a net loss of six. Joining Younger was Alick Buchanan-Smith in North Angus and Mearns, like George the son of a Scottish peer; Hector Monro in Dumfries, and Teddy Taylor in Glasgow Cathcart. Teddy was cut from different cloth and fiercely populist in style, but all were fresh faces in marked contrast to more traditional figures like Gilmour and Sir William Anstruther-Gray.

While the old guard took four-figure majorities for granted, Younger and the rest of the young Turks, as they were soon dubbed in the Scottish press, diligently worked their constituencies to consolidate often slim majorities and spread the Scottish Tory gospel. It made for a lively opposition, and Younger had fun gently teasing the formidable Willie Ross, Harold Wilson's new and powerful Scottish Secretary, who just happened to live in Ayr. Some of the old guard, however, gelled with the young Turks. Sir Fitzroy Maclean, the adventurer-turned-MP (who had visited Winchester when Younger was a pupil), supported George throughout his first years as an MP, and even allowed him and Diana use of his Yugoslavian villa in Korčula.

For Younger, it was a relief to be in Parliament at all. After the disappointment in Kinross and West Perthshire, Ayr was a risk, but the gamble had paid off. His majority, however, was predictably slim, and consequently Younger decided not to move to his constituency as he had his parents to support at Leckie, not to mention a wife and children. Juggling constituency life in Ayr with family life in Stirling and political life in London came naturally to Younger, and his base in the capital quickly became the Caledonian Club near Hyde Park. Slightly removed from the rest of London's famous clubland, it nevertheless provided some semblance of a home from home.

Regular boarders at the Caledonian included Younger's friends Alick Buchanan-Smith, Hector Monro and the Edinburgh MP Tony Stodart. 'Another attraction at the Caledonian Club was Mr Godfrey, the Night Porter who was usually there when we got back from the House of Commons', recalled Younger, 'we used to talk round the Night Porter's desk in the front of the Club . . . It was also an attraction that he had a tot of whisky always easily available.'[1] He was a regular guest at the Caledonian Club for the next 15 years.

The perfect opportunity for a maiden speech came during the second reading of the government's Airports Authority Bill on 16 November 1964. Younger supported the Bill, which transferred management of British airports from the government to an independent authority, including Prestwick Airport in his constituency. But he joined forces with the Ayrshire Labour MP Emrys Hughes to condemn the recently-announced development of Abbotsinch (now known as Glasgow Airport) on the basis that it threatened Scotland's existing transatlantic gateway near Troon. 'It seems to me only human nature, and perfectly obvious, that if I were booking a flight from New York I should ask the travel agent where I could go from Prestwick,' said Younger. 'The answer would be, "Nowhere". It is a matter of great importance to the development of the airport and to the development of Scotland as a whole that this situation should not be accepted by anyone.'

Younger called for the urgent development of Prestwick as both a domestic and international flight hub for the west of Scotland, a campaign he was to continue for the rest of his political career. For a mere £750,000, he argued, Prestwick's new terminal could be extended to cater also for domestic services, a view echoed by Hughes. Responding to his maiden

---

[1] Autobiographical notes, GYP.

speech, as was the custom, John Rankin, the Labour MP for Glasgow Govan, praised George and quoted Burns: 'Auld Ayr, wham ne'er a town surpasses / For honest men and bonnie lasses.' He added: 'That is the privilege which the hon. Member has in coming to the House, and I hope that he will live up to it.'[2]

Younger came to enjoy warm relations with several Ayrshire MPs during his twenty-eight years in the Commons, always Labour members such as Hughes, Jim Sillars and later George Foulkes. He in turn was popular with Labour MPs from further afield, including John Smith and the future Scottish Secretary Bruce Millan. During the committee stage of the Education (Scotland) Bill in 1969, which abolished fee paying in local authority schools, Millan complained ruefully that 'the Honourable Member for Ayr can always contrive to make the most unreasonable proposition sound eminently reasonable'.[3]

Later, Younger scored a small yet satisfying victory when Roy Jenkins, the minister for aviation, announced that Scandinavian Airlines would be permitted to operate one extra flight per week from Prestwick, reversing a cut by Jenkins' predecessor Julian Amery. He also lobbied John Stonehouse, the minister for technology, to ensure that Scottish Aviation Ltd (based at Prestwick) was placed on the official list of firms who could tender for government defence contracts. Many, including Younger, feared Prestwick would suffer death by a thousand cuts, something the Member for Ayr was determined to prevent.

George proved to be a natural constituency MP. 'From canvassing he'd quickly pick up all the local issues,' remembered Donald (later Sir Donald) Maclean, who replaced Peter Leggatt as the Ayr Association chairman in 1965, 'but where he came into his own was during questions – I never saw him fazed by a question. That, combined with an incredible memory for faces and names.'[4]

On the morning of Sunday, 24 January 1965, Sir Winston Churchill died aged 90. His send-off greatly impressed Younger who attended the funeral along with every other Member of Parliament. It ended with the impressive sight of Churchill's coffin floating down the Thames, dockland cranes bowed in tribute and accompanied by an RAF fly-past. Together with the fall of the Conservative government just months before, Churchill's death marked the end of a political era. Although Younger had his own link – his great-grandfather would almost certainly have known Winston during his

---

[2] Hansard 702 c95 and c99.
[3] 'A Private Secretary's Tribute' by Kenneth MacKenzie, 2006.
[4] Interview with Sir Donald Maclean, 2/8/2007.

time as an MP – he was typical of the new political era, the crop of which would govern the UK for much of the next quarter century.

Beyond this splendid occasion and Younger's maiden speech, his first parliamentary outing came at the committee stage of the government's Finance (No. 2) Bill which set the Budget for the following year and introduced controversial capital gains and corporation taxes, as well as new taxes on overseas earnings. As Shadow Chancellor, Edward Heath divided the opposition attack on the Bill into three parts, each with its own leader and supporting team of back-benchers. Peter Walker, assisted by Younger, led on capital gains; Tony Barber – a future chancellor – led on the corporation tax; and Edward Boyle led on the overseas financial provisions. They met each morning to plan tactics and launched 'probably the most ruthless amending campaign against a Finance Bill this century'.[5] Younger dealt with two major amendments, one of which concerned stamp duty, during May and July, an experience he found useful, not least because it brought him into closer contact with the next leader of the Conservative Party.

Sir Alec, having stayed on as leader following the 1964 general election, decided to stand down in mid-1965. Before doing so, he devised a new system for Conservative leadership elections, largely to avoid a repeat of the controversy – both internal and external – which had greeted his own 'emergence' as leader when Harold Macmillan resigned through ill health in 1963. As a result, every Conservative MP was to have a vote in a properly conducted ballot for the first time. Three candidates quickly emerged: the former chancellor Reginald Maudling, Enoch Powell and Edward Heath, fresh from his triumph in tackling the Finance Bill. Sir Alec resigned as leader of the opposition on 22 July and, just five days later, Heath became the first Tory leader formally elected by the parliamentary party with 150 votes to Maudling's 133 and Powell's 15.

Younger voted for Heath,[6] with whom he shared a passion for sailing, although many of his Tory colleagues were more attracted by Maudling's relative youth and progressive outlook. His reward came soon after Heath was confirmed as party leader on 2 August, when Younger was the surprise choice to replace Ian MacArthur as Scottish Whip, a position George's great uncle Sir Frederick Thomson – not to mention the 1st Viscount – had also held in the early 1930s.

Although a junior posting within the grand scheme of things, it enabled Younger to get to know every Conservative MP in Scotland, a useful grounding for his future roles as deputy chairman of the party in Scotland and under-secretary at the Scottish Office. He reported to the amiable Willie

---

[5] Walker, *Staying Power*, 41.

[6] Tam Dalyell remembers Younger telling him he had backed Heath.

Whitelaw, the opposition Chief Whip since 1964, and, given their shared Scottish, Army and Winchester roots, quickly became lifelong friends. Whitelaw had not forgotten Younger's sacrifice in Kinross and West Perthshire and for the following two decades – both in and out of government – he would be Younger's first port of call for friendly and shrewd political advice.

The opposition whips' office, located just off Members' Lobby, was known as a pleasant environment in which to work. Willie was assisted by the equally amiable Francis Pym, while Brian Batsford acted as his deputy. Ironically for the new Scottish Whip, Younger had not always obeyed the whip himself. A few months earlier he, Teddy Taylor, Alick Buchanan-Smith and three other Scottish Tory MPs had defied party instructions not to 'overplay' the regional battle for the Ford car plant and signed a motion demanding the government steer its planned new factory to Scotland.

The Labour government's majority of just three also made life in the whips' office interesting. Whitelaw, however, was reluctant to play devious games and impressed upon Younger and his fellow whips that pledges given to one's opponents were sacrosanct. Conservative MPs were not treated quite so honourably. Thirty years later, Whitelaw revealed in a television documentary that he had maintained a 'dirt book' in order to keep Tory MPs in check.[7] No doubt Younger played his own discreet role in maintaining that 'dirt book' while it probably came in handy during a bitter back-bench rebellion over Ian Smith's Unilateral Declaration of Independence (UDI) in Rhodesia towards the end of 1965.

This constitutional break with the British Crown had already dominated the Conservative Party conference, and when it was formally invoked on 11 November, the divisions on the opposition benches deepened. There was still an imperialist faction in the party which favoured not only apartheid but white-majority rule in Rhodesia. The party's liberal wing, on the other hand, favoured stringent sanctions against what was seen as blatant defiance of Crown authority. Whitelaw and Heath cobbled together a compromise, reasoning with potential rebels that as Harold Wilson's government would undoubtedly win a vote to impose sanctions, it was self-indulgent for dissident Conservative MPs to follow their conscience. On the night of the vote, however, 50 pro-UDI Tories and 31 from the pro-sanctions group broke ranks, and the government watched with delight as the opposition split and they won the division by 228 votes. Several years later, on a trip to South Africa, Younger encountered a Rhodesian major whose 'chief complaint was that they don't get Heinz Baked Beans in Rhodesia – so that is the glorious result of Harold's sanctions!'[8]

[7] BBC News Online 1/7/1999.
[8] GY to DY, 27/11/1969, GYP.

Heath's election as party leader was also accompanied by a major reappraisal of party policy, leading to a break with the consensus politics which had dominated the previous two decades. A document, *Putting Britain Right Ahead*, advocated a more regionally-based style of government and was endorsed by the Conservative Party conference at Brighton in October 1965. Heath's leadership also emphasised lower taxation, less public spending, a small state and trade union reform, while priority was given to the aim of EEC membership. This new-look Conservative Party provoked much comment. Stepping off a pavement during the Brighton conference, Younger narrowly avoided being knocked down by a Rolls-Royce. 'Not a Rolls-Royce, Younger,' quipped a horrified colleague. 'Think of the party's new image.'[9]

But Heath had momentum, and it became clear that another general election was imminent. Meanwhile, the Labour government's much-hyped *National Plan* had designated most of Scotland (except Edinburgh) a development area, a scheme – given its consequences in terms of economic aid – which many Tory MPs in Scotland found difficult to oppose, including Younger. Another feature of the government's plan was the creation of a Highlands and Islands Development Board (HIDB) with a huge budget and powers to distribute grants. The Shadow Scottish Secretary, Michael Noble, denounced the initiative as undiluted Marxism, but Younger welcomed the HIDB, although with the caveat that it should have more freedom to act without reference to the Scottish Office and Treasury.

The Bill to establish the HIDB crawled through the Scottish Standing Committee, and after 15 hours of protracted debate, MPs had reached only its third clause by 13 April 1965. George Willis, a Scottish Office minister, moved a motion to extend sittings, but it was defeated by just one vote. Younger was appalled. 'We are an absolute waste of time – a talking shop that cannot do the simplest thing quickly,' he said. 'We need a radical change in the way we conduct our business.' If Scottish MPs had 'really got down to it', he added, the Bill could have been completed in four more sittings.[10] As a newly-elected MP, some must have thought Younger was a young man in a hurry, but within five years he would find himself in control of the HIDB as an under-secretary at the Scottish Office.

The net loss of six Scottish Conservative seats at the 1964 general election kick-started a much needed reorganisation of the party north of the border. The Unionist chairman, Sir John George, who had been so crucial in ensuring Younger entered Parliament, had privately prepared plans for

[9] Undated newspaper clipping, 1965, GYP.
[10] *Scottish Daily Express* 14/4/1965.

reform even before the election, but the result gave him just the impetus he needed to implement sweeping changes. The old East and West Divisional Councils were abolished ('We had the Eastern Divisional Council and the Western Divisional Council,' remembered one party official, 'and never the twain shall meet.'[11]) and replaced with five regional councils (City of Glasgow, Highland, North-Eastern, Central and Southern, South-Western) under the central control of the chairman's office. That office was also expanded and given a general policy committee, while a single treasurer-administered fund was created for the whole of Scotland.

Most radical of all was the name change. The catch-all title of 'Unionist' engineered by Sir George Younger following the merger with Liberal Unionists in 1912 now became the Scottish Conservative and Unionist Association. 'We were looking for everything that could be wrong,' explained his great-grandson. 'One of the things that to many of us was daft was to be calling ourselves Unionists . . .We just thought, well, I'm not a Unionist actually, I'm a Conservative.'[12]

The reforms were announced in January 1965 and approved by the Scottish party conference in April. The old chairman's office soon emerged, rebranded, as the much more formidable Scottish Conservative and Unionist Central Office, with Younger's cousin, Sir John Gilmour, as its new chairman. As a progressively-minded young back-bencher, George fully supported the changes.

But even while the reorganisation was being implemented, the party in Scotland continued to suffer demoralising defeats. Roxburgh, Selkirk and Peebles fell to the 'Boy David' Steel in a March 1965 by-election, and when Harold Wilson called another election at the end of 1966, the Labour Party romped home with an increased majority of 96. The Conservatives ended up with only 20 seats in Scotland, a further loss of four MPs, and Younger's majority in Ayr fell to just 484.[13] The result in 1964 had been bad enough; the outcome two years later was considered by many Conservatives to be disastrous.

Together with much soul-searching at 11 Atholl Crescent, the new Edinburgh home of the consolidated party operation, journalistic eyes turned towards the so-called young Turks of the party. The *Scotsman* even tipped Younger to become the next chairman. 'Surprising as it may seem,' it said, 'he [George] has made a remarkably good impression as an M.P. of clear-headed and firm attitudes. He has lived down his aristocratic

---

[11] Interview with Bob Kernohan, 26/1/2007.
[12] Kemp, *The Hollow Drum*, 110.
[13] Younger's Labour challenger in 1966 was Charles O'Halloran, the first – and popular – Labour provost of Ayr.

connections with the beerage and the suspicion of dynasticism, and established himself as a forceful and thoughtful young man of considerable ability. This is the man on whom Heath's logical eye will probably fasten, and he could well brisken the tempo of party activity considerably.'[14]

The *Glasgow Herald* concurred that 'any restoration of Conservative fortunes in Scotland depends very much on the performance of this group', and according to one young Turk, their aim was to make the Scottish Tories at Westminster 'a force to be reckoned with'. To achieve that, they were quite prepared to borrow a trick or two from the bellicose style of the Scottish Labour opposition prior to 1964.

The new intake of Scottish Tory MPs also felt less obliged than their seniors to defend past actions. 'The new-style Conservative bears no such sense of injustice,' continued the *Glasgow Herald*. 'He tends to rationalise the reasons for the party's decline by saying that the good work done for Scotland in the last five years of Conservative rule simply did not compensate for the inadequate policies of the previous five . . . Most have temporarily put aside private or business interests in favour of political activity in and out of Parliament.'[15] This latter point did not quite apply to Younger. In 1966, perhaps as a consequence of the party's election defeat, he resigned from the board of his old employer J. G. Thomson & Co. and instead joined that of Charrington Vintners in London.

Certain figures at Atholl Crescent also began to look to Younger as a solution, or at least part of a solution, to the party's declining fortunes. Ian McIntyre, a former BBC producer and head of information and research at Scottish Central Office, agreed with the *Scotsman*'s analysis and advocated bringing him in to replace Sir John Gilmour as chairman. McIntyre met with Younger and Alick Buchanan-Smith soon after the 1966 election defeat and found, to his pleasure, that they were in substantial agreement. Michael Noble, with whom McIntyre met separately before that meeting, was also thinking along similar lines, and he followed up on these informal conversations with a 'personal & confidential' letter to Younger on 1 May 1966.

McIntyre divided his articulate and remarkably frank assessment of the party into three parts: the present situation; proposed short-term action; and priorities for the next four years. In short, he thought the present situation was 'much graver even than 20 seats out of 71 would indicate'. If sustained corrective action was not initiated soon, he argued, 'we shall become another Wales', a reference to the 1964 election at which just three Tory MPs were returned in the principality. In essence, McIntyre argued, it

---

[14] *Scotsman* 12/5/1966.
[15] *Glasgow Herald* 23/5/1966.

comes down to a lack of credibility. The Party as a whole just doesn't cut a convincing figure in Scotland any more, in spite of the efforts of 'the class of '59' and the arrival of people like Alick and Teddy [Taylor] and yourself. Perhaps even worse, the Central Office in Edinburgh doesn't convince candidates and others on the voluntary side that we are equipped to lead them out of this wilderness. We therefore stand at the centre of two concentric vicious circles . . .

Hard as it is to face it is still not Michael Noble, or the class of '59 or you and Alick and Teddy and Hector [Monro] who furnish the stock image of the Party in Scotland. It is the [Michael] Clark Hutchinsons, the [John] Brewises, the [Tam] Galbraiths, the [Earl of] Dalkeiths, [and] the Gilmours. They, by their silences, or by what they say when they do occasionally pipe up, destroy half the good you do.

By comparison, said McIntyre, Liberals such as Russell Johnston, David Steel and James Davidson 'appear young and vigorous'. 'If the comparison with youth and vigour were not damaging enough to us,' he added, 'there is our continuing identification in the public mind with landed interests and with agriculture. There is nobody on our side in the House to-day who really speaks convincingly for industrial Scotland, except, in his rather idiosyncratic way, for Teddy.'

McIntyre was equally brutal in his assessment of what action was needed. Sir John Gilmour, he said, was not an 'effective or credible Chairman' – a somewhat unsympathetic remark given Younger's family ties – and nor did he have 'an efficiently led office machine in Edinburgh to sustain him'. Sir John, he said, had failed to act as a proper link between the party in Parliament and the party in Scotland. 'It is not realistic, however, to keep a pussy cat as a watch dog and then complain that he never barks. The only sensible thing to do is replace him with an animal of the appropriate species.'

Then came the crunch:

My proposals for immediate action are:–

   1. That you should replace John Gilmour as Chairman
   2. That John Mitchell [the political secretary] should be removed
   3. That I should be appointed as your deputy, and specifically identified as the executive head of the office.

As I said to you, I think it essential that the Chairman should be an MP, and a politically conscious, 'mainstream' one at that. My initial thought, that we ought to revert to combining the Chairmanship with the Whip's job, may not be on, but so long as someone sensible and in tune with your aims as Chairman were to succeed you (and I presume it would be Alick), this wouldn't much matter.

McIntyre saw the chairman's job as 'a cross between General de Gaulle and the fairy on the Christmas tree – an eloquent figurehead, if you like, sounding off in the country at weekends, performing generalised PR functions at a high level . . . and action as the main energising link between the Party in Scotland and at Westminster.' McIntyre explained:

> There comes a point beyond which it becomes tedious and embarrassing to be associated with failure on the Scottish Tory scale, and I am very close to that point. With you in the chair, I would be prepared to buckle down to four years hard [work], and I think we could achieve something.
>
> You were bothered a little about being in Edinburgh often enough. That would obviously be less of a problem if you stopped being Whip. Even if you didn't, it is not in my view much of a problem. 'Greater things to less must give way', and all that – if you're in London and want to see the deputy chairman urgently, he hops on a plane – as does everyone else at any other level.

McIntyre ended his memo to Younger on a personal note. He had stood in the 1966 general election against David Steel in Roxburgh, Selkirk and Peebles, and although the campaign had gone well he came second, losing by more than 2,000 votes. 'I am simply not interested in remaining associated with the present shambles for more than a few more weeks,' he wrote. 'If I am to go into business or go back to broadcasting, I obviously want to feel free to look at the possibilities as soon as possible.'

'Such are my views,' he concluded. 'Very indelicate to name names, but I think things have gone too far for it to make sense to talk in tactful generalities. All this is primarily for your eyes, but do show it to Willie Whitelaw or anyone else you judge ought to see it.'[16] Such was the backdrop to the next stage in Younger's party political career.

---

[16] Ian McIntyre to GY, 1/5/1966, GYP.

Chapter 6

'ANOTHER NORMAN CONQUEST'

GEORGE YOUNGER BECAME deputy chairman of the Scottish Conservative and Unionist Party on 12 January 1967, reporting to the chairman, Sir Gilmour Menzies Anderson, who was known to everyone at Atholl Crescent as 'Gim'. A dapper moustachioed Glaswegian lawyer who had fought in Burma during the war, Gim had been Sir John Gilmour's deputy since the party reorganisation in 1965.

Although Ian McIntyre had lobbied for Younger to fill the chairman's office, the position was in the gift of Heath. And despite having made a good impression on the party leader during the passage of the Finance Bill in 1965 – and for the last two years as Scottish Whip – Heath instead appointed George deputy chairman. 'You have a tough job before you,' wrote Sir William McEwan Younger shortly after his cousin's appointment, 'but I am sure your thinking is on the right lines.'[1] Aged just 35, George was one of the youngest men ever to hold an office-bearer's position with the Scottish party.

The new role meant Younger had to stand down as Scottish Whip, but there was more than enough to occupy him at the party's HQ in Edinburgh, not least the second major reorganisation of the party since 1965. On 7 June Bob Kernohan was recruited from running the *Glasgow Herald*'s London office to become director-general of Scottish Conservative Central Office; Murray Kemsley reported to him as director of organisation, while Gim delegated responsibility for liaising with MPs and Central Office in London, political education, policy and organising speakers to Younger.

'We have lost ground in Scotland over the last decade and now is the time to take stock and put our house in order,' Gim informed constituency chairmen. 'Our traditional forms of organisation and effort must continue and are of great value but we must at the same time accept change and by greater political activity break out of ourselves into the electorate beyond

[1] Sir William McEwan Younger to GY, 14/2/1967, GYP.

with all its diverse interests . . . We cannot afford to fail.'² A scheme was even mooted to transfer party HQ to Glasgow, but although supported by Younger, Sir William and Gim, the plan came to nothing and was abandoned on grounds of cost.³

The other key players at Scottish Conservative Central Office during this period were Ian McIntyre, who continued to head up information and research, the research officer John Davidson (also Sir Gilmour's son-in-law and later director of the Confederation of British Industry (CBI) in Scotland) and Barry Henderson, who handled the Scottish press and political education as Conservative Political Centre (CPC) officer. The top floor at Atholl Crescent was a happy and stimulating environment, Davidson's desk overflowing with papers, interspersed with packets of biscuits to sustain him during election time. More importantly, all – including George – were younger, more progressively-minded Conservatives who freely embraced new political thinking.

There were soon noticeable improvements to internal organisation and morale as a result of the new regime, which set about assembling an impressive team of candidates, not only for Westminster but to fight increasingly politicised local government elections. Gim was rather unconventional as chairman, but he got things done and gave matters close attention. By contrast, Younger was conventional, focused and cautious, preferring to ensure that everybody was facing in the same direction before committing himself to anything. He and Gim got along well despite being very different characters, and while George typified the 'young Turk' strand within the party, Gim, with his almost Dickensian lawyer's office, represented – at least superficially – the old guard.

Younger enjoyed providing the all-important link between Edinburgh and the Scottish parliamentary contingent in London. He was also hugely energetic, diplomatic and able to draw upon a wide range of business and social contacts at all levels of Scottish society. 'He came to decisions quite quickly and clearly,' remembered Bob Kernohan, 'and they were always reasonable decisions. Unlike a lot of Tory back-benchers then he was a very articulate man; he could put into words in a few minutes what would have taken his parliamentary colleagues fifteen minutes of stumbling speech.'⁴

The new party structure soon had to contend with two by-elections.

---

² CCO 2/7/13, 12/9/1967.
³ Bob Kernohan remembers being recruited to Atholl Crescent on the basis that he, along with everyone else, would eventually move to Glasgow. He even identified suitable premises near Blythswood Square.
⁴ Interview with Bob Kernohan, 26/1/2007.

The first, in March 1967, saw the Conservative candidate Esmond Wright regain Pollok for the party, while the second, in Hamilton seven months later, failed to sustain the Pollok bounce. The Labour candidate, the miner Alex Wilson, was almost a caricature of an old-school trade unionist with no presentational skills, which the SNP candidate, Winnie Ewing, had in abundance. The Conservative candidate also had problems and when the result was declared on 2 November, Ewing had achieved a sensational victory. Psephologists searched in vein for precedents, but in a constituency uncontested just 18 months before there were none.

While Labour lurched from crisis to crisis – the pound was devalued 16 days after Hamilton – Heath's response was swift. He summoned leading Scottish Conservatives, including Younger, to his flat in the Albany at 9.30 a.m. on 16 November. He had inherited a party policy which was strongly opposed to devolution but, he instinctively felt, 'in the light of the evident shift in opinion since that election [1966], it would have been politically suicidal to stick to our guns'.[5] The 1965 document, *Putting Britain Right Ahead*, had advocated a more regionally-based style of government, so Heath was certainly not opportunistic when it came to advocating constitutional reform. Indeed, just weeks before the Hamilton result he told the Labour minister Dick Crossman that 'nationalism is the single biggest factor in our politics today'.[6]

It was decided at the secret meeting to launch a PR offensive against the SNP, while Heath prepared to make a series of visits to Scotland during 1968. In policy terms, it was also agreed that substantive ideas on devolution could only be formulated by Scottish Conservatives and not by the party in London. Younger, like many other Scottish Tories, was open-minded at the prospect of devolution for Scotland, although he believed Hamilton represented more of a protest vote than a genuine desire for Scottish independence.

The Conservatives' Government of Scotland Policy Group met for the first time on 14 December with Younger, as deputy chairman, presiding. He 'confirmed that the terms of reference given to each member of the group were intended to give the widest possible scope. All solutions except actual separation could be considered.'[7] George's cousin, Sir William McEwan Younger, was unanimously elected chairman.

Younger's devolutionary thinking was articulated in a *Scotsman* article which appeared the following day. Largely a point-by-point rejection of

[5] Heath, *The Course of My Life*, 294.

[6] Crossman, *The Diaries of a Cabinet Minister II*, 550–51.

[7] CRD 3/28/7, 14/12/1967. The three MPs on the committee were Norman Wylie, Esmond Wright and Tony Stodart.

Nationalism, George argued that the 'vast majority' of decisions affecting Scotland were already taken by the Scottish Office. 'This is controlled absolutely by Scottish Ministers who are Scottish M.P.s,' he wrote, 'backed by the 71 Scottish Members of Parliament.' This was an over-statement – Scottish Tory MPs did not exactly 'back' Willie Ross as Scottish Secretary – although the point was sincerely made. 'Irrespective of party allegiance,' he continued, 'no government and no Prime Minister could go against the wishes of the united opposition of these Scottish M.P.s.'[8] George would find that political reality was somewhat different when he became Scottish Secretary more than a decade later.

Within a few months, the Government of Scotland Policy Group produced an interim report as a basis for Heath's forthcoming speech to the Scottish Conservative Party conference. The group's intellectual driving force was a Dundee academic called John Berridge.[9] He was convinced that a devolved Scottish Assembly was the only solution and actively converted the chairman, Sir William McEwan Younger, to his thinking.

Bob Kernohan remembers that Younger was also quickly converted. 'He had a wonderful little speech where he would set out the options,' he recalled. 'One was the status quo; one was total opposition to the Nationalists; and the other was something in between. Eventually, he got round to the cliché that the status quo was not an option.'[10] Although Younger had never been an original political thinker, he saw the tactical appeal of seizing the initiative on devolution. '[W]e new Conservative members were a bit radical and reformist in those days,' he recalled. 'And we saw this situation and we felt, well, why not, let's address our minds to whether there's anything wrong with the system.'[11]

Not everyone in the party, however, agreed, and part of George's role as deputy chairman was to keep Heath informed about the obstinacy of some Scottish Tory MPs, like Betty Harvie Anderson, who were not only suspicious of devolution but resented party policy being formulated by non-MPs like Sir William.

Other sections of the party also became increasingly jittery about the party leader's forthcoming speech. 'I feel that Mr. Heath must be both cautious and positive in his presentation of his Perth speech on Scotland,' Kernohan told Younger in a memo, arguing that Heath should present the proposals as 'part of the broad evolution of our existing policy'.[12]

---

[8] *Scotsman* 15/12/1967.
[9] 'I don't think we'll go as far as separation,' Younger told Berridge on recruiting him as the committee's adviser (interview with John Berridge, 7/3/2008).
[10] Interview with Bob Kernohan.
[11] Kemp, *The Hollow Drum*, 110.
[12] CRD 3/28/7, 6/5/1968.

George, however, actively encouraged Heath to be as radical as possible in his conference speech.[13]

In early May, Sir William and Esmond Wright met with Heath in London to unveil the policy group's conclusions – an indirectly-elected Scottish Assembly dealing with some readings of UK legislation. The proposal was considered by a meeting of the Shadow Cabinet on 8 May. 'Though the element of S.N.P. extremism is limited,' observed Heath, 'there is strong feeling that Scotland should have more say in her own affairs.' Sir Gilmour Menzies Anderson, who was also present, added: 'We must get across that we are the Party in favour of change, and what is needed is something positive enough to demonstrate that.' Quintin Hogg also chipped in, humorously observing that 'we are going off very fast . . . on this. Really it is another Norman Conquest!'[14]

The Shadow Cabinet eventually approved Heath's conference speech, fully realising that he had to say something decisive. As delegates arrived in Perth for the Scottish conference, Michael Noble, the Shadow Scottish Secretary, and Younger rounded up Scottish newspaper editors and treated them to lunch at the Central Hotel in Glasgow. As they sipped wine and ate cold trout, Noble sounded them out about a Scottish Assembly while Younger 'helped to explain to the journalists that they [the Conservatives] thought the mini parliament was a jolly good idea'.[15]

Edward Heath publicly unveiled that 'jolly good idea' on the afternoon of Saturday, 18 May. 'I propose that . . . a Constitutional Committee should be set up to examine proposals for the reorganisation of Scottish Government,' he declared.

> We would propose to the Constitutional Committee the creation of an elected Scottish Assembly, to sit in Scotland. What we have in mind is that this Scottish Assembly would be a single chamber, and would take part in legislation in conjunction with Parliament . . . Let there be no doubt about this: the Conservative Party is determined to effect a real improvement in the machinery of government in Scotland. And it is pledged to give the people of Scotland genuine participation in the making of decisions that affect them – all within the historic unity of the United Kingdom.[16]

The response from the Scottish Conservative Party faithful was mixed although Heath won praise from *The Times* for seizing the initiative on

---

[13] When asked in 1992 if he had any regrets, Younger replied: 'I had quite a role in the Sixties in persuading Mr Heath to go for a Scottish Assembly. I do regret that' (Roy, *Conversations in a Small Country*, 182–83).

[14] CRD 3/28/7, 8/5/1968.

[15] *Sunday Mail* 19/5/1968.

[16] Speech to Scottish Conservative conference, 18/5/1968.

devolution. The former prime minister, Sir Alec Douglas-Home, was appointed chairman of the committee, while Younger was given the task of selling the new policy to the party at large. Devolution turned out to be a difficult product to shift. Several Scottish Tory MPs and activists resented what they saw as Heath's *fait accompli*, and complained bitterly to Younger as he gauged views all over Scotland. Others were enthusiastic, but the party was split.

In his haste to modernise the Conservatives, Heath had ridden roughshod over the Scottish Tories with inadequate preparation and little attempt to take the party with him. 'We persuaded Heath it was a good idea,' recalled Younger. 'He was very willing to be persuaded. But we were quite surprised by the strong reaction we got from the Old Guard after the declaration . . . We were surprised by the vehemence of their unhappiness about it.'[17]

At a meeting of the Central Council of the Scottish Conservative and Unionist Association on 17 June 1968, Younger attempted to explain exactly what a Scottish Assembly would mean in practice. It would, he said,

- meet at regular intervals.
- have delegated to it, by certificate of the Speaker, a large part of Scottish legislation.
- discuss, and decide upon, the spending of money within sums allotted by the U.K.
- debate any aspect of Scottish Affairs.

This, explained Younger, would free up Scottish MPs to engage in wider Parliamentary activity. Importantly, he continued, the scheme was

- a Unionist solution.
- not separatist.
- less cumbersome than the Northern Ireland parliamentary system.

'The debate about how it should work has now started,' said Younger, adding that all views would be channelled through the Government of Scotland Policy Group to the Constitutional Committee chaired by Sir Alec and, ultimately, to Heath. One sceptical MP, Patrick Wolrige-Gordon (East Aberdeenshire), asked 'if the Scottish Assembly was a proposal or a commitment'. In a classic Younger-like turn of phrase, he replied that 'there is a commitment to discuss a Scottish Assembly'.[18]

Despite this dissent, Younger remained enthusiastic about the commitment. 'The Conservative Party was, in fact, the Party of Devolution,' he

[17] Kemp, *The Hollow Drum*, 112.
[18] SCUAP Acc 11368, 17/6/1968.

argued. 'Once more, the initiative had been seized by the Party and the eyes of all thinking people were upon us. We must not fail in our duty and it is our task to say how we think the Scottish Assembly should be constituted and what its specific powers should be.'[19] Younger even discussed the proposals with the Queen during an informal luncheon at Buckingham Palace. 'She said she could well understand that Whitehall seemed remote to Scots', he reported to Diana by letter, 'but thinks they feel remote from Edinburgh too.'[20]

Sir Alec Douglas-Home's Scottish Constitutional Committee was far from remote. It travelled all over Scotland collecting evidence from more than 1,000 witnesses while members of the (Scottish) great and the good diligently took notes. Sir David Milne, the former Scottish Office permanent under-secretary, served as the committee's vice-chairman, while Brigadier Sir Bernard Fergusson (who had been Younger's Commanding Officer in Berlin) and the Rev Dr Ronald Selby Wright (whose sermons George had listened to at Winchester) ensured the Army and Kirk were sufficiently represented. The former Australian prime minister, Sir Robert Menzies, also advised the committee on the dynamics of antipodean federalism.

Younger attended just one meeting of the Constitutional Committee at Edinburgh's North British Hotel in late 1969. Sitting alongside officials from Atholl Crescent, he gave his views on how an Assembly might work in practice, while advising the committee on a number of points concerning Parliamentary procedure. Sir Alec's report, *Scotland's Government*, was finally published on 19 March 1970 and contained 34 recommendations. The most important was the creation of a 'Scottish Convention' with approximately 125 members to consider the second reading and committee stages of all exclusively Scottish Bills.

But although Sir Alec's report was comprehensive, it satisfied neither unreconstructed Unionists nor home rulers, although by the late 1960s the Nationalist tide had begun to ebb. The SNP had reached its electoral peak in 1968, performing well in local government elections and opinion polls, but in the absence of another by-election until Jim Sillars won South Ayrshire in 1970, there was no Parliamentary outlet for this buoyant Nationalist sentiment. Interest in Scottish affairs in the Shadow Cabinet had also waned although Sir Alec was by now its most prominent devolution convert. Nevertheless, the Scottish Conservative Party conference in May 1970 endorsed Sir Alec's proposals by three-to-one. The Labour government, meanwhile, had established a Royal Commission on the Constitution and also a Select Committee on Scottish Affairs of which Younger was a member.

George remained an enthusiastic proponent of devolution and even

---

[19] Quoted in a letter from Bob Kernohan to Sir Gilmour Menzies Anderson, 3/9/1968, GYP (copy).
[20] GY to DY, 14/11/1969, GYP.

proved to be progressive on other aspects of constitutional reform, most notably the Labour government's proposals for reforming the House of Lords. This was a somewhat contrived plan concocted by Harold Wilson and Dick Crossman in which two categories of peers would be created: non-voting (largely hereditary) and voting (mainly chosen by party whips). Although these plans did not get very far, the second reading of the blandly-named Parliament (No 2) Bill, which also proposed to truncate the Lords' powers of delay to six months, was debated in February 1969.

'We need a second Chamber,' Younger told the House in his contribution, 'and the question is what it should do and how it should be composed . . . As one personally involved, I agree entirely that the hereditary principle should have no place in a modern constitution in the second Chamber. It has served us well in many ways, but it is no longer appropriate in modern conditions.' This was a remarkably selfless position for the future 4th Viscount Younger of Leckie, although perhaps he had been inspired by the former Earl of Home's sacrifice during the Kinross and West Perthshire by-election back in 1963. 'I hope that the Bill will be carried,'[21] he concluded, but it was not, and 29 years later George took up his place as the 4th Viscount Younger (having served since 1992 as a life peer) in a House of Lords largely unaltered from that of 1969.

There was no mention of Second Chamber reform in the Conservative manifesto for the 1970 general election, although a separate statement of intent for Scotland was produced, albeit with the distinctly unionist title of *Putting Britain First*. Gordon Campbell, who had succeeded Michael Noble as Shadow Scottish Secretary in February 1969 despite speculation that Younger was Heath's preferred replacement,[22] did not much care for manifestos, let alone those with a kilt. He was also lukewarm about devolution – as were many candidates and sitting MPs – despite it having been party policy for almost two years.

'The Conservatives' new-style government will tackle Scotland's problems in Scotland with Scottish advice,' said Younger shortly after his readoption as the Tory candidate for Ayr, 'and not by slavishly imposing the policy of central government as Labour has done. The Conservative Secretary of State will be in the inner councils of the Cabinet as of right, and will thus exercise Scottish influence on all British affairs.'[23] But by 1974, after nearly four years of a Conservative government committed to delivering a Scottish Assembly, Scotland would be no nearer to devolved power.

---

[21] Hansard 777 c131–35.
[22] The *Scottish Daily Express* reported that Heath's canvassers had sounded out Scottish Conservative MPs about 'the trendy figure' of Younger succeeding Noble.
[23] *The Times* 30/5/1970.

Chapter 7

A FOREIGN INTERLUDE

ALTHOUGH YOUNGER HAD spent more than a year in Berlin, Korea and Hong Kong during his National Service, the combined responsibilities of family and work had provided few subsequent opportunities to visit other countries. Life as an MP, even a humble back-bencher, changed all that and during 1968 and 1969 Younger embarked upon two extensive trips, one to the United States and the other to South Africa, two countries which would thereafter fascinate him.

The first was a month-long visit to the United States from 5 November to 7 December, arranged by the Government Affairs Institute in Washington on behalf of the State Department. Primarily, the trip was contrived to educate visiting British MPs in the ways of American politics, but given the dominance of race relations in US public life throughout the 1960s, that issue also figured prominently. On this, Younger was instinctively liberal, and his experience on that journey was to have a profound influence.

Recent events in UK politics also provided a topical backdrop. More than six months before Younger crossed the Atlantic, Enoch Powell had made a controversial speech in Birmingham warning of the consequences of allowing continued immigration from the Commonwealth to Britain. It included an evocative, some might claim provocative, allusion to Virgil. Like the Roman, said Powell, he could see 'the River Tiber foaming with much blood'. To him, the Labour government's legislation to prohibit discrimination on the grounds of race in certain areas of British life, particularly housing, was both offensive and immoral.

The 'Rivers of Blood' speech caused a political storm and Heath swiftly sacked Powell from his Shadow Cabinet. The Conservatives also drafted a reasoned amendment to the Race Relations Bill, fearful that it would result in another revolt like that over Rhodesia two years before. This explained why the party could not support the government even though it deplored 'racial discord'. Nevertheless, forty-four right-wingers, including Powell, voted against the Bill at its third reading. Younger stuck loyally to the contrived party line but was probably appalled by Powell's speech. By the end of that year, he would see for himself the result of racial tensions in another predominantly white, English-speaking nation.

Younger touched down in Washington DC on 5 November and quickly began to absorb the minutiae of the US political system. The State Department had in him the perfect visitor, for George was fascinated by both political and legislative procedure. He was particularly interested in the resolution of disputes between state governors and legislatures, noting in his diary that even when a Bill was completely blocked, a governor could 'go around for months stating that his noble measure was blocked by the other Party and can castigate personally those who voted against'. Imagine, he playfully added in brackets, 'what Willie Ross would have said if a Conservative Scottish Assembly had denied him the Highland Development Bill!' Although Younger realised this tactical political game was 'fraught with difficulties & uncertainties', he approvingly noted that 'it at least gives a more prominent role to backbenchers and gives electors a real chance of influencing policies'.

Younger visited the Gettysburg battlefield on 9 November, something which no doubt appealed to his love of military history, before flying on to Boston, Chicago, Colorado, Denver, San Francisco, the Vandenburg Air Force Base, Santa Barbara and New Orleans. There, he had a long conversation with John Nelson, Jr, a local attorney who had acted in a range of civil rights causes, and for 'negroes' in cases of racial discrimination. 'He is a gentle sort of man, good looking, white-haired, aged about 48-50,' Younger noted later. '[He] has had to suffer personal abuse from whites and has lost some friends and a few clients through what he has done. Generally I would say he is respected beyond the negro community. He is a devout Catholic, [and] very critical of the fence-sitting by the R[oman]C[atholic] hierarchy on the race issue.'

The fact that Nelson had been severely wounded during the Second World War further endeared him to his young interrogator. Younger later wrote up their conversation, paying particular attention to education.

> . . . the hard fact remains that schools in negro areas are predominantly negro, and this, however unpalatable the fact may be, means that *on average* they are poorer and have worse home backgrounds than the whites . . . This is in no respect the fault of the negroes and nothing whatever to do with the colour of their skin. It is to do with the social conditions in which they and their parents live. One finds much the same situation in schools in the poor areas of Glasgow, where no colour enters into the picture. In these areas also there are acute teacher shortages. Naturally the teachers, even when they are not racially prejudiced prefer to teach in the more successful schools.

In spite of these handicaps, the young negro to-day who is industrious and has ability can, and usually will, get to high school and University. His opportunities are vast, and beyond the wildest dreams of his parents. The problem is not the 12–18 year old to-day, nor is it the older negro over 65. The former has vast opportunity, the latter has at least adequate welfare services to support him.

The problem is the vast mass of negroes aged 18–65. They had no educational opportunity *and cannot now get it.* They are the most active generation and they rightly feel frustrated with little means of bettering themselves. They will steadily revolt against society unless something is done, and done quickly.

Although Younger's terminology is clumsy by contemporary standards, Nelson clearly had a profound influence. 'We must force the pace on implementation of the legal rights of negroes,' he added, mixing his own views with those of Nelson. 'Whites must be in the van, forcing implementation all the time. If whites don't, extremists will have a perfect platform for years to come.' Younger conceded:

> All this may seem very impracticable but it is vital that it should be done. The Black–White distrust has gone a long way, and only infinite tact over a long period will have any effect. This must be started now and continued for many many years. Meanwhile white thinks black is incompetent and useless, and black thinks white is overwhelmingly smug and is determined to keep them down by force. Hence the Black Panthers and the Klu Klux Klan; they lead only because no-one else can on either the right or the left. It is to keep these two horrors at bay that we devote ourselves and we must not fail in this task.[1]

Younger then moved on to Miami, Key West, Atlanta for the first few days of December, then North Carolina where he visited friends in Wilson. In the southern states of Georgia and North Carolina, he experienced more directly the problems caused by racial segregation. 'This Senator did not seem to be a great politician,' Younger wrote of a North Carolina state senator who clearly did not make a good impression. 'There is no evidence just now of racial strife but it is potentially there,' he observed. 'Integration certainly exists in the schools as the football teams etc that I saw were mixed, although not in proportion to the population. Black housing is very bad in many towns and ghettos are the order of the day . . . At present the conservative whites rule and are very happy to have as little government as possible.'

The governance of Georgia was even worse. 'One Party State', noted Younger bluntly. 'Southern Democrats have a large and permanent majority.' The then governor, Lester Maddox, was 'despised as an

---

[1] Undated diary entry, c11/1968, GYP.

extremist although he is in theory a Democrat. He is a Baptist and a non-drinker & non smoker.' Traditionally, learned Younger, strong governors had submissive legislators, although a powerful speaker had recently reasserted the power of the legislature, which had promptly removed the governors' reserve fund with which he and his predecessors had been able to 'do whatever they liked'. 'Now Maddox will have a fight with Legislature because he needs money for Teachers' Salaries, Welfare, Mental Health etc and the legislators and the people don't want any more taxes,' recorded Younger. 'Legislature sits for so little time that [there is] no chance of getting much . . . through. Many get no debate, others as little as 10 mins. Public does not like legislature to sit for too long, as their sittings cost money.'[2] Some aspects of political life, as Younger discovered, varied little from nation to nation, and while US politics fascinated him, certain elements of it held little appeal in practical terms.

Younger wrote about his American trip in the *Glasgow Herald* on 11 March 1969, concentrating on the lessons the UK could learn from racial strife in the United States. 'The time to tackle the racial problem is now,' he wrote, 'while it is still manageable in scale. It will be too late if we dither any longer . . . We who live under truly democratic governments are allowing tiny, militant minorities to dictate our policies and mould public opinion, to the detriment of the policies pursued and our own happiness and prosperity.'[3] Those 'tiny, militant minorities' must presumably, in Younger's mind, have included Enoch Powell.

Younger's fact-finding trip to South Africa less than a year later provided a similar, and equally as influential, experience. Although it lacked any official government sponsor, he toured a variety of locations and spoke to academics, journalists, officials and a range of politicians about the former British colony and its future. But in stark contrast to the progressive racial policy in much of the United States, South Africa's controversial policy of apartheid had recently been stepped up.

George began his visit in mid-November 1969, with two days at Kruger National Park where he observed carefully how park authorities combined innovatory tourism with government grants to attract crowds of sightseers. Then, on 17 November, he got down to more serious business, interviewing General R. C. Hiemstra, commandant-general of the South African Defence Force, about the ongoing integration of the country's forces and its National Service scheme. 'He hopes Britain will look again at Simonstown Agreement', recorded Younger in his diary, 'which has

[2] Ibid., c12/1968, GYP.
[3] *Glasgow Herald* 11/3/1969.

been broken in spirit . . . He said R[oyal].N[avy]. had been lukewarm about Simonstown in 1957, but supposed they took a more positive view now. Facilities at Simonstown had been greatly improved since SA took over.' The Simonstown Agreement was the naval co-operation agreed between the UK and South Africa on 30 June 1955. Under the agreement, the Royal Navy gave up its naval base at Simonstown (in South Africa) and transferred command of the South African Navy to the government of South Africa. In return, South Africa promised to allow Royal Navy ships use of the Simonstown base. The stability of this agreement was to occupy Younger intermittently for the next decade.

Another backdrop to the visit was obviously apartheid. Younger had made clear in advance of his trip that he was opposed to the policy, and it featured heavily in his discussions with South African ministers and officials. The secretary of foreign affairs (equivalent to a permanent under-secretary), B. Finnie, told him that he did 'not think the views of UK about apartheid have much effect either way on S.A.' He added:

> They know U.K. and many others do not like it, but it is an S.A. affair and this is their solution. It has many problems but they do not think in the long run it will turn out any worse than the various solutions imposed on the other African States by colonial powers, and probably very much better.[4]

On 19 November Younger visited the 'new, show-piece' Bantu town of Ga-Rankuwa (20 miles north of Pretoria), which, as he noted cynically in his diary, was 'supposed to show the 'good' side of apartheid (=separate development)'. Essentially a planned housing scheme, residents of the town could purchase their prefab housing, buy food in a shopping centre and even purchase Scotch from a well-stocked off-licence. 'It was spotlessly clean', observed Younger, 'and seemed to have quite a large staff. The owner was a smartly dressed Xhosa [a people of Bantu origin] and talked about his business just like any other publican. I have seen many worse off-licences in Glasgow!'

Younger also visited a local nursery school where the 'enchanting' children performed for him a tribal dance. Unemployment was low thanks to nearby factories and the vibrant motor industry while the Bantu had complete control of internal town affairs, aided by 'a few white officials'. 'This sounds all right but when you get down to the power of the Bantu councils things don't look so good,' wrote Younger. 'They don't really have much more power than that of a District Council in Britain for all the major decisions of planning etc are made by the Department of

---

[4] Diary entry dated 17/11/1969, GYP.

Bantu administration; the same goes for education and most other major services, so although they are said to be in local control, they can only act within the framework of measures already pre-determined by the state.' But, he added, it 'must be admitted also that the other African States who have full political rights are mostly a very bad advertisement for giving such rights now'.

The argument of white South Africa, therefore, was that the system may be one of 'white supremacy (which it undoubtedly is) but that it gives the African no less personal rights and freedom that he has elsewhere in Black Africa, and very much more economic well-being'. Younger again wrote at length in his diary:

> I have made great efforts to find out what is the real ultimate goal of apartheid in theory. It appears to be the progressive development of these 'homelands' until they really do have internal self-government. If they then demand full self-government, I am told that they would be given it, but that their economic life would be so bound up with White South Africa that they could hardly afford to break away and pursue a policy hostile to South Africa. However, the eventual granting of full independence (à la Botswana) is a goal that is more respectable than what most people see from apartheid, and if S.A. could be persuaded to accept this officially, it might take some of the heat out of the apartheid issue. I wonder for how long after independence they could continue to practise 'petty apartheid' i.e. in buses and public places. They already are finding that you cannot refuse to give a multi-racial reception for the High Commissioner from Botswana or Malawi and the multiplication of such problems could mean the breaking of the apartheid dawn.

In the meantime, he continued, 'the British conscience will continue to be affronted by the human indignity suffered by these intelligent and civilised blacks and Coloureds who are not considered fit to have normal social relations with their white brethren.' Younger also considered the UK's influence on apartheid:

> Britain must continue to make her voice heard on these issues, for constructive criticism is listened to from Britain far more than anyone would like to admit openly. The flow and effectiveness of this criticism depends on good relations with S.A. and this is where boycotts etc and violent abuse do infinite harm to the cause of keeping Britain's abhorrence of apartheid firmly fixed in the mind of the public of South Africa. Let us not slam doors, but keep them open.

Dr Denis Worrall, a political academic Younger lunched with two days later, was 'impressed at the idea I put to him of encouraging the Nats to specify and work towards an ultimate goal. He agrees that this might make it easier to explain S.A. policies to the outer world.' The governing party until 1948, the 'Nats', or National Party, had recently suffered a split, caused by Dr Albert Hertzog – a fundamentalist advocate of Afrikaner supremacy – who formed a Reconstituted National Party to compete electorally with the Nats. Dr Worrall thought that 'if Hertzog goes far enough the United Party might fold up and join the moderate Nats'. Could they, asked Younger rhetorically, 'then become a moderate coalition to isolate the Afrikaner who is the real believer in total apartheid'?[5]

In Cape Town, Younger was struck by how much like Westminster the South African Parliament was, even down to a debating chamber modelled on the old, pre-1940 House of Commons in London. 'Reading Hansard is interesting', he noted, 'as it shows the extreme difficulty of opposition against such an all-powerful government. The govt does not have to make concessions and so it does not do so, and those who raise injustices etc get a fairly tough time from Ministers.'[6]

Back in the UK, the Springbok (South African rugby team) tour of Britain and Ireland was being greeted with large anti-apartheid demonstrations wherever it went. A young Liberal South African called Peter Hain, later a Cabinet minister under Tony Blair and Gordon Brown, was leading the physical disruption of several matches which had to be played behind barbed wire fences. Although Younger shared their distaste for apartheid, he thought the protestors' tactics were counterproductive. 'They [South Africans] do realise that the vast majority of British people are fed up with demonstrators too and so they take it reasonably calmly,' he wrote to Diana. 'The trouble is that these disorderly demonstrations strengthen the hand of the ultra right wingers here who say that it is no use trying to be friendly to hostile people, and that South Africa should not alter any of its policies and should put up the shutters against the whole world.'[7]

Younger also encountered a lot of hostility to the fact that Britain refused to sell South Africa certain defence hardware, a somewhat empty gesture which simply enabled other European countries like France to scoop up lucrative contracts. Vice Admiral H. H. Biermduh, chief of maritime defence, told Younger it was 'very disappointing to be refused British Frigates' and that he was very 'keen on an extension of NATO to cover S.A., Australia, N.Z., Argentina and Brazil'. Younger was delighted

[5] Ibid., 19/11/1969, GYP. Worrall was later appointed South African ambassador to the United Kingdom in 1984 but resigned three years later to form the liberal anti-apartheid Independent Party back in South Africa.
[6] Ibid., 20/11/1969, GYP.
[7] GY to DY, 20/11/1969, GYP.

to be shown plotting of South African vessels around the Cape. 'Wherever their squadron goes, there is a revolution, or so it seems,' he mused. 'Advance planning for control of shipping in event of war is well advanced and frequent exercises are done. It is quite clear that Simonstown is vital to the free world and we should keep this agreement in letter and spirit.'[8]

On 24 November Younger met M. D. Arendse, leader of the Coloured Labour Party. He had recently won a general election to the Coloured Representative Council after his MPs were removed from the Federal Parliament, although the government had simply 'nominated enough of the defeated candidates of the Federal Party to give them a majority instead!'[9] 'Naturally Arendse is very bitter but maintains he will work within the Law as a responsible opposition,' Younger noted. He also met Tom Swartz, leader of the Coloured Federal Party who had been appointed chairman in place of Arendse. 'Unimpressive man,' he wrote later, 'very apologetic about the humiliating way he has come to office. Why on earth he ever accepted the post is beyond me unless it was old fashioned greed . . . This man is a stooge and according to Sir de V[illiers]. Graaf is also a crook, in that he will do anything if the price is right.'[10]

'I heard the story from both sides as I saw the leader of each party,' Younger wrote to his parents, 'so there is not much I don't know about rigging elections now.' Sir de Villiers Graaf was leader of the United Party in Parliament and a 'very engaging pro-British Afrikaner' who wanted to restore the Coloured Labour Party's representation in the Federal Parliament. 'He is a friend of Michael Noble [the former Scottish Secretary]', Younger noted, 'and has much in common with him I think – a certain relaxed charm, and a good brain. I am not sure if he has any real drive or the cutting edge needed in an opposition leader in his position. He will need to be very cunning to defeat the Nats who have everything rigged their way.'[11]

Younger then spent two 'fascinating' days in Transkei, a large province set aside for Africans with limited self government, providing another useful (along with local government reform) yardstick for him with regard to Scottish devolution. There, he met K. Guyana, leader of the opposition Transkei Democratic Party, who had won a 1963 election but suffered a similar fate to Arendse. 'A very charming and highly educated man,' Younger observed, 'a minister, and obviously fairly well-off. His

---

[8] Diary entry dated 21/11/1969, GYP.

[9] GY to LLY, 25/11/1969, GYP.

[10] Ibid., 24/11/1969, GYP.

[11] Ibid., 25/11/1969, GYP. 'Although he is an Afrikaaner,' Younger added, 'he is ex-Oxford and very British in many ways. His Party (United Party) has been in opposition since 1948, so he has problems!'

knowledge of world affairs is excellent and we had quite a discussion about the Common Market.'

Guyana was firmly anti-apartheid but believed the white man would be essential for a long time to come, particularly in commerce. 'I rather fear he is too nice', observed Younger, 'to tackle the rough fight that would be needed to oust the Govt Party with all its inbuilt patronage and the open support of the S.A. Govt.' And on the rugby tour, Guyana 'expressed strong disapproval of the Demonstrations against the Springboks. "We are sorry to hear they are having a rough time and hope they will do well. It is not for foreigners to interfere with our sport." '[12]

The South African government was actively 'devolving' legislative functions to Transkei, such as justice, albeit with predominantly white magistrates and, more slowly, control of police stations to the local police. 'Transkei is heavily subsidised by S.A. on a "block grant" basis,' noted Younger, again with a Scottish analogy in mind. 'SA gives automatically the same for each dept as was given in 1963 and gives a block sum in addition which is subject to negotiation each year. SA Govt can alter the total amount of the extra grant in any way it likes, but cannot specify in any way how the money shall be used.'[13] 'This is the real aim of apartheid', Younger told Diana from Durban, 'so that as most of S.A. is dominated by the whites, they give other parts over to be dominated by the Blacks.'[14]

Following Transkei, Younger also met with leaders of the Indian community in Durban, who were mostly members of another 'devolved' South African assembly, the Indian Representative Council (IRC). Although Indians had been accepted as South Africans in 1961, for 80 years they had been regarded as 'temporary workers'. 'Political advance is minimal as the Govt appoints who it wants to the I.R.C.,' observed Younger, 'and although it tries to cover different areas and interests, clearly no-one who is an agitator or in disagreement with Govt Policy has much chance of being appointed. Those appointed seem to be mostly successful men with conservative outlook and they behave accordingly.'[15]

As Younger's tour drew to a close, he returned to Cape Town to see Dr Zac de Beer, leader of the Progressive Party and also a businessman in the Anglo-American Corporation chaired by Harry Oppenheimer. His party's aim was progressively to remove all racial discrimination in South Africa. 'The real failure of apartheid is in the economic field,' Younger wrote after meeting de Beer. He went on:

[12] Diary entry dated 25/11/1969, GYP.
[13] Ibid., 26/11/1969, GYP.
[14] GY to DY, 27/11/1969, GYP.
[15] Diary entry dated 28/11/1969, GYP.

In almost every part of the land the job reservation does not work and this will be the real downfall of apartheid. Progressives are quite sure that intemperate criticism and ignorant abuse from Britain does far more harm than good. S.A. must work out its own salvation and all it needs from the outside world is contact as much as possible and friendship and sympathy for problems. Progressives approve of Tory policy of no boycotts and approval of Simonstown Agreement and obviously hope for better relations with Britain in future.

Finally, George saw Rae de Villiers, editor of *The Star* newspaper, who bluntly confirmed most of Younger's suspicions. 'He thinks Apartheid is proving not to work. Job reservation is a sham, the Transkei is a façade and there is little or no industry moving in to it, there is no political future for Bantu in the townships or Indians (who are highly intelligent mostly) and the Coloureds whose only link is with Whites are literally being driven to drink.' De Villiers stressed that 'pressure on S[outh]A[frica] from Britain is disastrous to the Liberal cause in S.A. Britain's role should be as friend and sympathiser and in that role Britain would be listened to.' The anti-Springbok demonstrations, he said, 'have merely brought scorn on Britain and the West for allowing their affairs to be dictated by communists', while de Villiers believed the 'ultimate solution' to South Africa's problems may 'eventually have to be federal – giving full political rights in Provinces with sufficient powers reserved to the (white dominated?) Federal Parliament to reassure the Whites that they would not be destroyed'.[16]

Younger had spent just two weeks in South Africa but the trip, along with his earlier visit to the United States, had provided an invaluable introduction to African politics and the importance of race relations. The South African experience also confirmed Younger's opposition to apartheid, adding an international element to his defence interests and, perhaps most importantly, consolidating his place on the liberal wing of the Conservative Party.

---

[16] Ibid., 1/12/1969, GYP.

Chapter 8

'SAVE THE ARGYLLS'

'HE COMMANDS HQ Co[mpan]y with enthusiasm and efficiency,' commented Lieutenant-Colonel John Fanshawe on Younger's Territorial Army (TA) report of 1962. 'He is most loyal. He is always ready and willing to offer his sound advice. Recommended for command.'[1] George had been active in the TA since finishing his National Service in 1951. In May 1964 he received the award of Territorial Decoration (TD) and, following his election to the House of Commons that October, Younger liked to think of himself as the TA's – and the Argylls' – Parliamentary spokesman.

The TA had continued supplying complete divisions to the regular Army for twelve years after the Second World War, and also furnished much of the UK's anti-aircraft cover during that period. But the end of conscription in 1960 dramatically reduced the Army's size, and in 1961 a number of TA units were amalgamated. During a supply debate on the Army estimates in 1965, Younger lamented that 'the present state of the Territorial Army is anything but a happy one'. 'I can, I think, say so with a certain amount of authority because I am still serving in the Territorial Army.'[2]

The news that the Labour government was preparing a major reorganisation of the TA reached Younger as he was commanding his company at its summer camp in 1965. 'I well remember the occasion when the news came through of what then amounted virtually to the destruction of the entire Territorial Army as we knew it,' he later recalled in a May 1966 debate on the Reserve Forces Bill. 'My instructions were to put the news across to the troops in my command as best I could and to cause as little alarm as possible.'[3]

---

[1] Letter from John Fanshawe, 11/7/1962, GYP.
[2] Hansard 708 c101–02.
[3] Ibid., 728 c317.

Younger was determined to wage a campaign to save what was often referred to as the UK's 'weekend army', and he even resigned his commission (as a major, and second in command of the 7th Battalion) at the beginning of December 1965 in order to lead the fight. His first Parliamentary opportunity came with a debate on the TA on 16 December 1965. 'Of course we want change', Younger protested, 'but, if we want change, we do not want to be destroyed. What sort of an argument is it that says that because this organisation is not perfect it must be destroyed?' The government's white paper called for 'Reorganisation of the Army Reserves', but Younger argued that all that would be left were 'reinforcements', not 'reserves'.

> I want to make the strongest possible protest on behalf of Scotland. The Territorial Army is successful in many parts of the country, but I do not think anyone would disagree with me when I say that nowhere is it more successful than it is in Scotland. Not only has it all the benefits which it has in other parts of the country, but it is in a real sense a part of our national life . . . a part of the life of the community. It is tied up with our history.

Younger also argued that the TA had valuable social aspects. 'The noble Lord, Lord Montgomery, said not long ago in another place – and how true it is – that, when one is planning operations of war, there are at least three alternatives in almost any situation, and the only thing one can be sure of is that the enemy will take the fourth. This is the main fallacy into which right hon. Gentlemen have fallen, thinking that they can absolutely rely upon any future conflict being a nuclear exchange.' So, he reasoned, if the plan in the white paper was adopted there would be an obvious weakness. 'Step by step, therefore, we shall be at the mercy of any enemy because we shall not have anything like sufficient ground forces.' But Younger stressed that he was 'not accusing the Government of doing a Socialist trick. It is not Socialism I am worried about here. My concern is that right hon. Gentlemen have accepted bad military advice, and, in saying that, I should be supported . . . by 90 per cent. of the professionals.'[4]

The Reserved Forces Bill appeared early in 1966 and confirmed Younger's worst fears by proposing a complete reorganisation of the TA, including the adoption of a new title, the Territorial Army and Volunteer Reserve (TAVR). TAVR was to be divided into four units: TAVR I, units available for all purposes; TAVR II, units with a NATO role (TAVR I and II were known collectively as 'volunteers'); TAVR III,

---

[4] Ibid., 722 c1546–51.

home defence units (known as the 'territorials'); and TAVR IV, consisting of bands and the university-based Officer Training Corps (OTC).

Younger was on duty during the second reading of the Bill in May 1966, by which time 18 months of negotiations between the TA and Ministry of Defence (MoD) had produced some degree of consensus. Although he still disagreed with parts of the Bill, Younger conceded that the minister responsible, Hugh Fraser, had 'won the confidence of the people'.[5] The reorganisation and name change took effect on 1 April 1967, but there were immediate problems. In another debate a year later, Younger gave vent to his frustrations. 'Will a future conflict be entirely nuclear, entirely conventional or conventional for a time then nuclear?' he asked, adding that

> whatever happens, the one common factor is the need for reserves. A prolonged conventional war will obviously mean reserves to replace initial losses and the operation of doubling one's reserves quickly to build up forces for such a long conventional war, too, the first thing that would happen would be the disappearance from this country of practically all the Regular forces at present stationed here. How conceivably could any conventional war of any size at all in Europe go on without a major part of our Regular forces here being transferred to Europe very rapidly, and leaving behind in this country absolutely nothing at all?

The government, Younger continued, 'would do a service to the country and to the volunteers who have worked so well if . . . they will reprieve the Territorial Army and let it continue to do the job that it has done so well'.[6]

In 1969 the territorial element of the new force, TAVR III, was disbanded, with its units reduced to eight-man 'cadres'. These became part of a 'sponsoring' TAVR II unit although they continued to wear the badges and propagate the traditions of their forebears. In the longer term the news was a little better. An increase in the size of TAVR in 1971 led to the formation of a number of battalions based on these cadres, while in 1979 the new Conservative government – of which Younger was a member – restored the Territorial Army title and increased its size even further.[7]

Younger's battle to save the Territorial Army paled into comparison to that of another more epic, and ultimately successful, battle, this time to

[5] Ibid., 728 c318.
[6] Ibid., 760 c543–45.
[7] As Scottish Secretary, Younger was honorary colonel of the TA's 154 (Lowland) Transport Regiment, a position officials remember him taking very seriously.

'Save the Argylls'. His affection for his old regiment was undimmed, and George was delighted when his father, then Lord Lieutenant for the county of Stirling, commissioned George to act as one of his deputy lieutenants in July 1968. Younger's 16-year association with the Argylls had temporarily ended in 1965 when he resigned his commission; now he was back in the fold.

The timing was fortuitous. Later that month, the MoD made public its decision to axe the Argyll and Sutherland Highlanders along with a number of other British Army units, arguing that the Argylls had been earmarked as the 'junior' Highland regiment. The context was both economic and international. The Defence Secretary, Denis Healey, had signalled that cuts in defence expenditure were imminent earlier that year and, as Younger's uncle Sir Kenneth observed, there was 'nothing new in the idea that Britain is exchanging an old role in world affairs for a new one'.[8] The Middle East War of June 1967, followed by the devaluation of the pound a few months later, had sealed the Argylls' fate.

A campaign to save the regiment was launched just hours after the announcement. Lt-Col Colin Mitchell, known affectionately as 'Mad Mitch', was about to retire from the Army and provided a powerful symbol of the regiment's past glories. Mitchell had been Younger's company commander in Korea, but as his account of taking on Arab nationalists in the former British colony of Aden was soon to be serialised in a Sunday newspaper, the campaign avoided capitalising on that tale of derring-do in its battle to save the Argylls. Nevertheless, a 'monster petition'[9] was soon initiated by Younger with secretarial support from the Regimental Association.

George articulated the arguments against axing the Argylls to great effect during a debate on the future of the Scottish Regiments in the middle of July. He said the 'Army of the present and of the future' needed regiments of front-line troops with morale, skill and efficiency drawn from a supportive civilian population. That relationship, argued Younger, was particularly strong in Scotland where the Argylls were currently providing at least a third of new recruits.

If abolished, said Younger, 'we threaten about half the recruiting in Highland regiments and about a third in Scottish regiments as a whole'. He continued:

---

[8] Younger, *Britain's Point of No Return*, 1.

[9] Bob Kernohan remembers the petition soon getting out of hand, mainly because regimental enthusiasts thought collecting signatures in what was supposed to be a non-party political campaign should be the first priority of Conservative activists (Bob Kernohan to the author, 12/11/2007).

What conceivable sense is there in that at a time when full-page advertisements are being taken in the newspapers with all kinds of glossy pictures and wonderful wordings by the advertising men to get recruits into the Army? What do the Government do? They select for disbandment the one regiment which is getting the lion's share of the recruits at the moment. It is an absolutely incomprehensible decision. This is what has been found so difficult to put across to the people of Scotland as a whole.

Younger said that in his own experience, the vast majority of those joining Highland regiments requested to join a particular one. 'A figure of 90 per cent. was quoted by General [Freddie] Graham, who should know,' he added. 'He sees personally every recruit to the Argyll and Sutherland Highlanders . . . I beg the Government to think again, to look behind the figures and to see these patterns which occur behind the figures.' Younger continued:

> This is not a game of playing soldiers. The reason for the regimental system is that it works. It enables people to withstand situations that are impossible for human flesh and blood to stand. The fact that the men know that they have to live the rest of their military careers with the same people, and have to go back to their home areas where everyone will know what their conduct has been, is the sort of factor which enables them to withstand more than reason could expect them to do.

The Argylls, argued Younger, had built up an outstanding level of efficiency. 'I do not make the claim that they are the best battalion in the British Army, although there are many who would,' he said. 'I do claim that they are one of the most outstandingly well-trained units that the Government have in the Army. That is one of the main reasons why the people of Scotland are absolutely unable to understand why this regiment has been chosen at this time to be abolished.'

What was more, said Younger, the regiment was a rare success story amid general economic gloom in Scotland. 'When one looks back,' he argued, 'surely one of the things which shines out in the minds of ordinary people as having been successful and having been well done has been the conduct of the Argyll and Sutherland Highlanders, particularly in Aden.'

> People were able to open their newspapers and say, 'Well, somebody is doing a good job. Something is successful in everything all the time.' When there is that sort of feeling people are glad suddenly to find something to cheer them.

Within a few months, however, the Government select the very people who,

through years of work, courage, industry and everything else, were responsible
for producing that one glimmer of sunshine in years of hard graft. That is the
regiment that the Government have decided to disband and abolish. Can they
be surprised that the people of Scotland are raging mad about it?[10]

The Labour government had blundered into a worst-case scenario, both
in terms of policy and, crucially, presentation. Younger exploited it fully.
He also pointed to a more 'sinister' reason behind the decision, a suspicion
shared by Colin Mitchell. 'For years there has been a powerful lobby in
Whitehall against the regimental system,' George alleged. 'They are
motivated purely by jealousy of the glamour and success of our regiments
and their resentment is particularly strong against the Scots. Time and
again they have tried to abolish them, sometimes piecemeal, sometimes
them all, and they have always been thwarted in the end either by a strong
Minister or by a wise Government, or both.' Now, added Younger, 'they
see their chance. The Minister will not stand up to them, and Socialist
Members hate all soldiers, so they have the chance to get their way at
last.'[11]

It was even suggested that disbanding the Argylls was the vengeful act
of military bureaucrats following Mitchell's actions in Aden. And although
the 'Save the Argylls' campaign was avoiding any mention of Aden,
Younger simply could not resist its inclusion in his list of arguments.
Speaking in the same debate, the Labour back-bencher Tam Dalyell (a
childhood friend of George's) argued the case for the Scots Greys, also
under threat of disbandment, while opining the performance of the
Argylls at the Crater.

> I ask my hon. Friend [Younger], is it or is it not true that Colonel Mitchell
> disobeyed administrative and operational orders in Aden given by his Brigade
> Commander, Brigadier Jeffries, and the Army Commander, Major-General
> Tower? . . . If Colonel Mitchell disobeyed orders, why was he not relieved of
> his command? For example, is it or is it not true that during the Aden operation
> an order was given that grenades were to be kept at regimental headquarters,
> and is it or is it not true that when an inspection was made by senior officers,
> grenades were found to be distributed among the platoons of the Argyll and
> Sutherland Highlanders?

Then came the crunch. 'I had better be very blunt about it,' declared
Dalyell. 'Is it not true that the Argylls in Aden, far from being the superbly

[10] Hansard 768 c1073–76.
[11] Undated speech notes, GYP.

disciplined force which they were claimed to be by the British Press, in fact suffered from a lack of discipline? Is not that the actual truth of what happened?'[12]

'Younger', recalled Dalyell much later, 'interrupted me in genuine anger saying that I had made a scandalous allegation.'[13] The Scottish press had a field day, providing a noisy and unashamedly patriotic backdrop to the speeches of Tory MPs while fuelling the row about what 'Mad Mitch' did, or did not do, at the Crater in Aden. 'Mr. Younger is no lightweight or backwoodsman,' Dalyell wrote to *The Times* two days after the debate. 'He is one of Mr. Heath's most energetic and trusted lieutenants . . . If Mr. Younger and his colleagues choose to make the claim that the Argylls should be retained, partly on account of "their outstanding success in Aden", then you cannot be surprised if some Government supporter feels bound to scrutinize this episode under a microscope.'[14] But the row, as Dalyell later conceded, 'hugely enhanced Younger's reputation with the public in general and his own party in particular'.[15]

Meanwhile, the Save the Argylls campaign had been phenomenally successful. By August 1968 letters were flooding in at a rate of 10,000 a day to the home of General Sir Gordon Macmillan, who had set a target of a million signatures, while mail was also arriving at the home of the Duke of Argyll. Once the million-signature target was reached, the plan was for Younger to deliver the petition to the House of Commons.

Younger also found himself tackling the long-term position of the Conservative Party in terms of defence policy. He wrote to Major-General Freddie C. C. Graham, whom Younger had first met at a TA camp in 1959,[16] to assure him that he was working on the Conservative Defence Committee (a party policy group) 'to find out what sort of commitments we may get from them'. He cautioned, however, that a likely outcome was that a new Conservative government could only reprieve the Argylls if it still existed. If the axe had already fallen, added Younger, then 'they could not be committed to reactivate the 1st Battalion but would, I think, try very hard to find a way of doing so'.[17] Graham replied in early November, saying that Younger's idea of amalgamating two regiments with the 'clear understanding that they will be reactivated separately at the first

---

[12] Hansard 768 c1087.
[13] *Independent* 27/1/2003.
[14] *The Times* 18/7/1968.
[15] *Independent* 27/1/2003.
[16] GY to DY, 7/7/1959, GYP. 'I was very impressed with him,' Younger reported to his wife. 'It is the first time that I have met him on duty and he seems to me to be an excellent chap.'
[17] GY to FCCG, 25/10/1968, GYP.

opportunity' had some merit. He had finished his letter by scrawling triumphantly: '750,000 today!'[18]

Major-General Graham meant signatures, and by the middle of December there were 1,086,590 of them, easily surpassing the target of a million. 'To the sound of skirling pipes,' reported *The Times* on 13 December, 'with a strong whiff of blazing heather . . . one of the largest petitions ever presented to Parliament steamed into Euston station last night.' The reception party included the colourful Margaret, Duchess of Argyll, resplendent in a red feather hat and furs and, of course, Mad Mitch.

The campaign organiser, Brigadier Ian Stewart, presented 22 Scotch whisky cartons containing the signatures to Younger, who replied: 'This petition is not an attempt to resist change, but an earnest plea that some role shall be found that is of use to our country for regiments whose skill and loyalty are irreplaceable.' The boxes were then loaded into a bullion van for safe keeping until Younger could present it to the Prime Minister, 'in case', quipped one campaigner, 'the Minister of Defence tries to steal it.'[19]

Younger presented the petition to Parliament on 17 December. Amid cheers from crowded opposition benches, the whisky boxes were carried into the Chamber by attendants and placed in front of the clerks' table. Afterwards, Younger said: 'I am very optimistic that the sheer weight of support for this petition will convince the Ministry of Defence that it would be in the interests of the Army to think again.'[20]

It did not, and the government simply ignored pleas to 'Save the Argylls'. 'Having produced this petition with over 1 million signatures,' Younger said during a defence debate in March 1969, 'it is beyond belief that the Government have made no effort to meet the wishes expressed in it. Even if they thought the whole thing to be a nonsense, they could have recognised that this was a manifestation of ordinary people, unconnected with me, or anyone, expressing a strong opinion and that something should have been done to meet the feelings expressed.'[21]

The campaign fizzled out soon after delivery of the petition, and the Argylls remained in limbo. The government refused to budge, while tension grew between the regiment and the Conservative Party. Major-General Graham wrote to Younger again in June 1969 implying that the Conservatives were softening their position on reinstating the Argylls once

[18] FCCG to GY, 5/11/1968, GYP.
[19] *The Times* 13/12/1968.
[20] Ibid., 18/12/1968.
[21] Hansard 779 c1438.

it regained power. 'I know only too well that politicians are kittle cattle', he wrote, 'but don't tell me that our side is already swithering on their decision given to me?'[22]

Younger wrote to reassure him on 26 June:

> Gordon Campbell [the Shadow Scottish Secretary] is pretty sound on these matters, having been a leading supporter of mine during the campaign, and I am confident that he can deal with the Shadow Cabinet effectively. We must still keep in mind the question as to when the moment will arrive for a further push to keep the issue in the public eye. My own view is that it is probably still best to hold off until the Autumn, but this could well change if there is a reappraisal of defence strategy before then.[23]

The suspicion, however, lingered, and a meeting of the Save the Argylls campaign committee in September noted 'that it had been some time since a statement had been made by the Conservative Party about their promise to "Save the Argylls"'. Younger promised to discuss it with his colleagues, while the meeting also resolved that in 'view of the troubles in Ireland and the general shortage of troops, it was agreed that Mr. Younger and his colleagues should press the Government for a post-ponement of the amalgamation and disbandment of the various units due to take place in the next two years'.[24]

The trouble brewing in the Province, ironically, proved to be the clinching factor in securing the future of the Argylls. 'I had a talk with her [the Queen] about the Argylls about which she was quite friendly', Younger reported to his wife following lunch at the Palace, 'and still obviously hoping that something will turn up to save the day.'[25] Something did, but sectarian violence on the streets of Northern Ireland was perhaps not what Younger and the regiment had in mind. The Argylls were saved, although reduced to company strength, and in 1971 the Conservative Defence Secretary, Lord Carrington, announced that it would be restored to battalion status. A year later, the Argylls did a tour of duty in Northern Ireland and subsequently played an important role in the peace process during the 1990s, as well as in Iraq where it helped recruit, train and deploy units of the new Iraqi Civil Defence Corps. But in March 2006, and despite a valiant effort to revive the old 'Save the Argylls' rallying cry, the regiment was subsumed within the new Royal Regiment of Scotland.

---

[22] FCCG to GY, 11/6/1969, GYP.
[23] GY to FCCG, 26/6/1969, GYP.
[24] Minute dated 29/9/1969, GYP.
[25] GY to DY, 14/11/1969, GYP.

In conjunction with the campaign to Save the Argylls, Younger had also been campaigning more subtly to secure Colin Mitchell as a Conservative candidate for the next general election. He dismissed this as 'just a rumour' in July 1968, a few months before Mad Mitch was due to leave the Army. 'When Colonel Mitchell comes out of the Army his first priority will be to get himself a job,' said Younger, 'but should he show any desire to become a Conservative candidate – and he probably will – he will go through the selection committee and be interviewed in the normal way.'[26] This was a slightly disingenuous position, as both the SNP and Liberals were equally as keen for Mitchell to be 'interviewed in the normal way'. Younger's persuasive charm, however, did not fail and Mitchell was duly selected as the prospective Conservative candidate in the Liberal-held constituency of West Aberdeenshire.

Defence policy played a small but important role in the 1970 general election campaign. Labour claimed that Conservative defence policy amounted to the reintroduction of conscription, a spurious charge swiftly rebutted by Younger. And as polling day approached, he revealed that an incoming Conservative government would create a reserve force of around 25,000 men along the lines of the old Territorial Army. Having helped save the Argylls, Younger was determined to restore the TA to its former glory. Luckily for him, he would soon be in a position of some influence as a member of the new Conservative government.

---

[26] *The Times* 22/7/1968. Younger's pocket diaries for 1968 and 1969 record at least three private meetings with Mitchell.

Chapter 9

IN AND OUT OF OFFICE

THE CONSERVATIVE PARTY fought the June 1970 general election holding just 21 seats in Scotland, and although this increased slightly after the poll, Edward Heath was reportedly displeased that the party's revival north of the border had not been stronger. Colin Mitchell, however, won West Aberdeenshire, while in Ayr, Younger again secured a good majority. The result was:

G. K. H. Younger (Conservative)	22,220
J. M. Craigen (Labour)	17,770
L. Anderson (SNP)	2,186

Younger's majority had increased ten-fold since 1966 and, for the time being, it looked as if Ayr might finally become a safe seat. He had long been spoken of as a 'coming man' in Conservative circles; now the Scottish Office provided a destination.

In 1970 the department was divided into four Departments – Agriculture and Fisheries, Home and Health, Education, and a Scottish Development Department (SDD) covering infrastructure, environment, planning and local government – all of which reported to the new Secretary of State for Scotland, Gordon Campbell. Several free-standing Divisions also reported direct to the permanent under-secretary, a short-tempered but effective man called Sir Douglas Haddow, the most important of which was the Regional Development Division (RDD) headed up by James McGuinness – the doyen of Whitehall regional development specialists – which kept a watching brief across all economic issues of interest to the Scottish Secretary. Younger occupied what was generally known as the 'development' brief, giving him responsibility for both the SDD and RDD.

Younger was the natural choice. He had long supported the pioneering regional policies implemented by Michael Noble as Scottish Secretary in the early 1960s, something which had also impressed the new Prime Minister, Edward Heath, enough to make Noble a somewhat short-lived President of the Board of Trade in his new administration. Younger's strong relationship with Heath was also an important factor in his appointment to the Scottish Office as was his continuing friendship with Sir Alec Douglas-Home, who once again became Foreign Secretary. All were present at the usual dinner for the new government hosted by Heath at 10 Downing Street on 1 July, the eve of the new Parliamentary session.

Joining Younger at the Scottish Office were Alick Buchanan-Smith (home, agriculture and fish), the folksy Teddy Taylor (health, education and social work), and the rather remote minister of state, Lady Tweedsmuir (deputy to the Scottish Secretary with special responsibility for local government reorganisation). Previous governments had designated junior Scottish Office ministers anonymously, and not very informatively, as 'Joint Parliamentary Under-Secretary of State'. Campbell agreed that his ministers' letterheads should for the first time reveal their responsibilities, so Younger's read 'JPUS for Development'.

Younger already knew Teddy well, and Alick was a close friend from their shared digs at the Caledonian Club. Relations with Gordon Campbell however soon became strained. Although Teddy regarded him as helpful, George and Alick felt the Scottish Secretary was aloof and infuriatingly non-political in style. Instead, Sir Douglas Haddow emerged as the most influential figure in the Scottish Secretary's immediate circle although his tendency to advise against Younger's policy initiatives added to the development minister's frustration. Haddow treated all the junior ministers as if they had just left school but got on well with Campbell who, as a former diplomat and civil servant himself, felt more comfortable taking his lead from senior officials rather than the fickle political mood of the day.

Younger's first appearance at the dispatch box came during a debate called by the Labour MP for Caithness and Sutherland, Robert Maclennan, on the future development of the Highlands and Islands. The government had pledged itself to a 'vigorous' regional policy in the recent Queen's Speech and Younger, following in the footsteps of Lord Home, found himself in charge of Highland development, or more specifically the recently-created Highlands and Islands Development Board (HIDB).[1] He had already met, briefly, the HIDB chairman, and had arranged to visit Inverness at the end of July in order to meet other board members. 'I have no doubt that in these [past] five years the Board has been able to catch

[1] As minister of state at the Scottish Office from 1951, Home had responsibility for an old consultative body called the Highland Panel.

the imagination of the Highlands and Islands and that it is now well-established as an effective organisation for Highland development,' Younger told the House. 'The new Board must retain and develop this image.'[2]

SQUARING THE CIRCLE

A Scottish Office brief presented to Younger on becoming a minister in June 1970 gives some idea of the myriad of development issues which were to occupy him for the next three-and-a-half years. Not only was a major review of regional policy under way, but a decision on the future of iron and steel in Scotland was imminent. The coal industry was also facing problems, as was shipbuilding, predominantly the Upper Clyde Shipbuilders (UCS), and both were at risk from large redundancies. In the case of UCS, Heath would later U-turn disastrously on his pledge not to bail out 'lame-duck industries' with public money.

At least, following six years of a Labour government obsessed with 'planning', there was a plethora of bodies to assist Younger in tackling these problems. The Scottish Economic Planning Council (set up by Willie Ross; Campbell dropped the word 'planning'), of which Younger became deputy chairman, coexisted with four local Economic Planning Consultative Groups for the Borders, Tayside, the North East and the South West. There was also the Scottish Economic Planning Board, consisting of officials from all the government departments concerned with economic development in Scotland, although responsibility for regional policy and industrial grants was still the preserve of the Board of Trade in London together with its Scottish office in Glasgow.

In September 1970, a young economist (and leading authority on regional policy) called Dr Gavin McCrone took up his post as head of a new economic and statistical unit which would make information directly available to the Scottish Economic Planning Board and Council. This proved to be a key appointment under the influential James McGuinness, and Dr McCrone was to work closely with Younger right up until the mid-1980s when George was Scottish Secretary.[3]

Even before the 1970 election Labour had probably been intending to alter the machinery of industrial regeneration in Scotland, and now the Scottish Office under Gordon Campbell had to mastermind yet another 'new deal'. Over the past ten years public investment had increased from

---

[2] Hansard 803 c633.
[3] When James McGuinness retired in 1972, McCrone succeeded him as under-secretary and head of the RDD, while retaining the role of chief economic adviser.

£120m to about £400m, but this massive figure soon disappeared as part of the new government's general economy drive. The existing regional employment premium, worth about £40m to Scottish industry, was due to be scrapped by 1974 with no obvious replacement in sight. The government claimed its 100 per cent tax allowances, building grants and enhanced cash aid under the Local Employment Acts meant there was no overall decrease in funding. 'The Government have decided that the balance of advantage for Scotland lies in the new system,' Younger told MPs during a debate on Scottish affairs in February 1971. 'It is a system not only of investment allowances but of better grants . . . and more generous criteria under the Local Employment Acts as to the number of jobs per pound of loan given.'[4] He said it had become clear that the old system of industrial incentives was simply not working.

But even its replacement did not last long. In August 1971 Campbell, George, Scottish Office officials and a Tory businessman, Hugh Stenhouse,[5] prepared proposals on an even more extensive reform of regional aid which were fed into a Cabinet Office review. This led to the 1972 Industry Act (covering the whole of the UK) and the creation of Regional Development Grants – which were automatic for qualifying industries – and Section 7 Selective Financial Assistance – for which a firm had to apply.

The Department of Trade and Industry (DTI) also replaced the old Board of Trade and Ministry of Technology. Although Stenhouse and James McGuinness proposed the creation of a non-governmental body to be called the Scottish Development Agency (SDA), the idea was rejected by the Cabinet. Instead, the DTI established an office for Scotland in Glasgow (the Scottish Industrial Development Office) with its own staff under the direction of an industrial adviser called Denis Kirby. Willie Ross, the former and future Labour Scottish Secretary, would eventually get Cabinet approval for an SDA, but in the meantime joked that Mr Kirby should get a grip.

'I think we shall see that the Industry Act and the new system will prove to be a major watershed in changing the continual trend of adverse economic forces in Scotland', said Younger, 'to one which will get us into a much more prosperous phase, with expansion coming not only to Britain as a whole but in particular to Scotland, something for which many of us have fought for a long time.'[6] Godfrey Robson, who became

---

[4] Hansard 810 c1800–01.

[5] Hugh Stenhouse had resigned as treasurer of the Scottish Conservative Party to become chairman of Upper Clyde Shipbuilders. He died in a car accident in November 1971.

[6] Hansard 847 c1628.

Younger's private secretary shortly after the Industry Act became law, says his minister's personal view on the merits of using taxpayers' money to support industry was never clear. But 'he understood Scotland, and that mattered to him even in the face of conflicting views within the government'. Robson said Younger's strength came in 'squaring the circle, defending Scottish interests and speaking very effectively to a brief'.[7]

By the summer of 1973 there were signs of economic recovery. Unemployment in Scotland was falling, although it was still roughly twice the UK average, while the new Industry Act had produced 4,000 applications for regional incentives at a total value of £89.7m. There were also other, admittedly minor, achievements in terms of infrastructure. Gordon Campbell always regarded his greatest achievement as fast-tracking the reconstruction of the A9 from the Central Belt to the Moray Firth, using the needs of the emerging onshore North Sea oil industry as a bargaining chip with the Treasury. Younger also officially opened the M73 motorway early in 1972, by which point he was tipped for promotion to the new position of Minister for Industrial Development at the DTI. Instead it went to the former champion athlete and broadcaster Christopher Chataway, although both Younger and Alick Buchanan-Smith continued to be spoken of as Campbell's natural successors as Secretary of State.

'MR YOUNGER, SPECIAL AGENT!'

Younger's self-discipline, commitment to Scotland and leadership skills made him almost a textbook minister. Although George, like Heath, was no ideologue, his cousin Sam Younger remembers viewing him as a rather boring establishment figure. 'I had a sort of in-built prejudice because I regarded myself as radical,' he recalled. 'We would sometimes go up to Easter Leckie and one particular memory I have is being all ready to find George as this lily-livered member of the establishment who would be strung up at the time of the revolution.'

> But I remember in 1970 or 1971, when George was an under-secretary, having a drink on a Saturday evening and the phone going. It was for George so he went off and didn't come back for about half an hour. Diana said something like 'it's ridiculous letting your number be known and having all these people ringing you up.' I remember George saying, 'Diana, these people elected me; I must be available to them.' I remember being quite impressed by that, as until then I'd seen him as the mill owner who would grind his workers into dust; that was my first experience of his essential decency.

[7] Godfrey Robson to the author, 6/11/2007.

Sir Kenneth Younger, Sam's father, also used to visit his brother and nephew at this time and noted rather patronisingly in his diary that although Younger seemed 'to be doing a creditable job as under-secretary of state', he did not have 'an interesting mind'.[8] Part of this was intellectual snobbery from a former Foreign Office minister, but it accurately captured his nephew's self-assurance. In order to be considered 'interesting' by his uncle, George would constantly have had to question himself and his position within society. Self-analysis, however, was not really George's thing.

Nor was original thinking, although Younger recognised a good idea when he saw it. The notion of a 'Scotland West' tag for industrial promotion purposes was not new when he arrived at the Scottish Office in June 1970, but it was George's enthusiasm which made it a reality. In October he set up the Scotland West industrial promotion group to complement existing self-help activities in the area as well as successful work by the independent and bipartisan Scottish Council (Development and Industry) (SCDI).

Much industrial investment in Scotland was from overseas. There were 110 American firms alone, many of which were located in or around the New Towns of Glenrothes, East Kilbride and, later, Livingston. As *The Times* reported in May 1971, Younger 'had been courageously stomping the country with talk of Scotland emerging soon as "the industrial pace-maker in Britain" '. The Budget, George had said in April, created the conditions for success and before very long the Jeremiahs who were talking of nothing but woe would look very foolish and irrelevant. 'George Younger is no Jeremiah himself,' continued the report. 'As well as preaching hope, he has attempted to set Scots' eyes on European opportunities.'[9]

These European opportunities were given added impetus by the UK's imminent membership of the Common Market, and in September 1970 Younger visited its Commission HQ in Brussels before attending a conference of European regional planning ministers in Bonn ('Mr Younger, Special Agent!' proclaimed a *Daily Record* headline). On his return, George announced a Scottish Office drive to attract German investment in order to strengthen Scotland's economy and utilise its surplus labour, particularly in petrochemicals and ancillary industries. 'German industry not merely wishes to expand abroad,' said Younger, 'but it has to do so.'[10]

---

[8] Interview with Sam Younger, 6/7/2007.
[9] *The Times* 14/5/1971.
[10] Ibid., 12/9/1970.

He set about co-ordinating a plethora of regional, county and burgh promotional efforts into a single all-Scotland campaign with the Scottish Office acting as a conduit. 'As the Minister for Development I see my job as that of acting as a catalyst – to bring people and ideas together and to sell Scotland,' Younger explained. 'To this end I am prepared to go anywhere within reason so long as I get results for Scotland.'[11] The SCDI provided match funding for £20,000 a year from the Scottish Office, half of which was to be spent on promotion and the remainder on establishing a permanent representative in Germany.

'I hope that no one will sneer at the necessary efforts to co-ordinate and bring together the efforts of the many agencies in Scotland which are going out to England and abroad to encourage new investment and industry to come to Scotland,' Younger told MPs. 'If we sit back and just complain about our difficulties and troubles we shall not get the new jobs and the new investment which we need.'[12] George was a natural salesman, his decade at George Younger & Sons having equipped him with some useful transferable skills. In 1963 he had visited Germany to sell Scottish wines and spirits; in 1971 he flew there to sell Scottish industry.

Younger charged Lord Taylor of Gryfe,[13] chairman of the Forestry Commission and a director of British Railways, with ensuring that Scotland's industrial community did more than just 'sit back and complain'. In May 1971 a 'Europe in Scotland' committee was formed, while the general onslaught was formally launched by George on 1 October. The *Glasgow Herald* applauded Younger as 'the most impressive member of Gordon Campbell's team, though he has had the unenviable task of trying to attract industry to Scotland at a time when the economic circumstances militated against it'.[14]

Younger had always been instinctively European in outlook, and loyally supported Heath in his determination to join the Common Market in early 1971, a zeal which led to significant dissent among both government ministers and back-benchers. Although Alick Buchanan-Smith, George's friend and colleague at the Scottish Office, had been one of the three-man ministerial team who negotiated entry to the EEC, the other young Turk at St Andrew's House, the vehemently anti-European Teddy Taylor, resigned in protest.[15] 'George Younger beat me in a debate in front of an audience of miners and their families,' recalled Jim Sillars of the debates

[11] *Glasgow Herald* 12/9/1970.
[12] Hansard 810 c1805.
[13] Lord Taylor was a Labour life peer and former chairman of the Scottish Co-op.
[14] *Glasgow Herald* 4/4/1972.
[15] Taylor's place was taken by the Dumfries MP Hector Monro, another friend of Younger's and fellow Caledonian Club resident.

surrounding EEC membership. 'He was "yes" and I was "no". He told
them that to vote "no" would bring disaster on the country, with massive
job losses. They believed him.'[16]

THE PROPERTY-OWNING DEMOCRACY

Younger's development brief also extended to more home-grown areas,
chiefly Scotland's historically problematic housing stock. There was an
imbalance between owner-occupiers and council tenants in Scotland,
mainly due to the relatively low level of local authority rents compared
with rising house prices. In his capacity as chairman of the Scottish
Housing Advisory Committee, Younger worked hard at formulating a
comprehensive housing policy. He was determined not to concentrate on
any one mechanism, although he recognised that a property-owning
democracy was economically desirable.

A Housing (Scotland) Bill appeared halfway through 1971 which
changed the whole structure of housing subsidies while standardising
the existing, rather spasmodic, system of rent rebates. There was also a
rates revaluation that year, something which was to have more serious
consequences for Younger more than a decade later. His solution was a
system of rent rebates for council house tenants on lower incomes. 'The
schemes are the same for all tenants in all parts of Scotland,' explained
Younger, 'they effectively reduce rents taking full account of family
circumstances to levels that eliminate hardship, and the cost is borne
mainly by the Government, not by the local councils and the ratepayers.'[17]
This, he said, not only meant rent reductions but more money for
landlords to keep housing in good repair. 'In that period all the rhetoric
was about how people valued their housing', recalled Sir Muir Russell, a
housing official at the time, 'and George's constant experience as a
politician was that it was the centre of his constituents' lives. Ensuring
they paid a decent level of rents was all part of George's philosophy.'[18]

This was especially true of Glasgow where the housing stock had been
crumbling for decades. The previous Labour government had committed
to building an additional 50,000 houses in Scotland, many of them in
Glasgow, but had failed to meet its own target. 'The present Government
are not going to base the housing programme on a set of targets plucked
out of the air which we would have no chance of fulfilling,' Younger
warned MPs early in the new Parliament. 'The question is whether we can

---

[16] *Sun* 12/9/2000.
[17] *Shelter Magazine* 1/1974.
[18] Interview with Sir Muir Russell, 21/5/2007.

build houses when and where they are needed and at the right cost. That is what we are addressing ourselves to at the moment.'[19]

Nevertheless, George plucked out a target of his own in aiming to improve 1,000 houses a year over the next decade. His private secretary during that time, Godfrey Robson, remembered the problem of tackling Glasgow's serial housing failure as a huge undercurrent of Younger's time as development under-secretary. A valuable ally was Sir William Gray, who was both the city's Labour lord provost (1972–75) and chairman of the Scottish Special Housing Association (1966–72).

There was also a total of £5m to improve Glasgow's environment while Heath also announced the creation of a sixth New Town in the Stonehouse area of Lanarkshire. Although this was eventually shelved by a Labour Scottish Secretary in the late 1970s, it demonstrated Younger's commitment to interventionist policy. He also reduced day-to-day interference in the internal affairs of Scotland's New Town development corporations, and remained committed to the likes of Livingston, Irvine, Glenrothes and Cumbernauld on becoming Scottish Secretary in 1979.

CREATING A MONSTER

Beyond Younger's remit of development, he also assisted on a broader range of Scottish Office issues, some less welcome than others. One was local government. Lord Wheatley's Royal Commission on Local Government in Scotland had reported in 1969 and by February 1971 the Scottish Secretary was ready to unveil his proposals for a legislative response with the subsidiary aim of quelling demands – and fulfilling a Tory pledge – to establish a Scottish Assembly.

Gordon Campbell's scheme broadly followed the Royal Commission's recommendations, albeit with some concessions to local considerations. He agreed with Wheatley's proposal for a massive West of Scotland regional authority (embracing 2.5 million people), and another covering the whole Highland area, as 2 of 7 large regions. Campbell also broadly concurred with the recommended second layer of 37 district councils, including the 4 cities, which would take up more local functions. But his white paper departed from Wheatley in several important respects. Orkney, Shetland and the Western Isles were given separate status as 'island authorities'; the Scottish Borders and Fife became regions in their own right as a result of intensive lobbying; while some Conservative-voting areas on the fringes of Glasgow (such as Bearsden and East Renfrewshire) were kept out of the city's district authority.

---

[19] Hansard 808 c1732.

Wheatley's seven regions therefore became nine, and his 37 districts swelled to 53. On the face of it, the Scottish Secretary had thoughtfully reshaped local government according to local desires, but grassroots Conservatives – and some Scottish Tory MPs – were furious. The main bugbear was the new West of Scotland region (later renamed Strathclyde) – smaller than that planned by Wheatley but still guaranteed to consolidate socialist control in the west of Scotland. Campbell was unrepentant, believing it was necessary in order to avoid inter-council conflict over planning issues, a view not shared by some of his ministerial colleagues, including Younger. George was unhappy with the scheme in general and resented Campbell for being unwilling to listen to his junior ministers. Ordinary party members were also dismayed and took to bypassing Campbell (who hated party functions) in order to air their grievances with either George or Alick Buchanan-Smith. Officials remember that the pair – rather than Campbell – often acted as the friendly face of the Scottish Office.

Although Younger had to handle several crucial stages of the Local Government (Scotland) Bill in the House, he often felt as if was being kept out of the loop by an increasingly aloof Gordon Campbell. He discussed the Bill with Michael Noble, who had just left the government ('He is very relieved to be out of office and will take a few months' rest'), while dining at a London club, Boodle's, in November 1972. 'Discussed L.G. Bill & he is *for* the West Region,' Younger recorded in his diary, 'but he thinks we will be defeated on several other points (incl Cowal to go in with Argyll District). He is going to ask Douglas Haddow to dinner & try to convince him that defeat will come, and he had better prepare alternative courses.'[20]

But even this high-level intrigue was ultimately to no avail. On 4 December Younger had the unenviable task of winding up for the government on the Bill's second reading. 'In the course of my life I have had to split up Scotland six times for the purposes of my commercial activities,' he said, alluding to his career in brewing. 'Each time I have finished with a different result, and I have been struck with the great difficulty of splitting it up, because it is so unbalanced in terms of population.'

> Let us not forget that this is the end of 10 years of consideration and discussion during which every conceivable effort has been made by three successive Governments to consult as many organs of opinion as possible. We cannot please everyone in making a major change of this sort, but the time has come for the Government to make their views known to Parliament and for Parliament to pronounce its judgement on those views.[21]

---

[20] Diary entry dated 13/11/1972, GYP.
[21] Hansard 847 c1041.

The increasingly unpopular Bill then moved on to its committee stage and transferred to the House of Lords the following year. The resident Scottish Office minister in the Upper House, Lord Polwarth, was less than enthusiastic. He wrote to Younger on 18 October 1973 to moan about the legislation, quoting what he had just written in a separate letter to Gordon Campbell. 'We have been taken [so much] for a ride by D. Haddow & [Sir] A[lan]. Hume [secretary of the SDD] – that we have now lulled ourselves into believing Strathclyde is the right solution,' he scrawled. 'I believe we are creating a "monster" which will one day greatly embarrass us in central government and which, under the pretext of efficiency, etc, will create an inflated bureaucracy which will be remote from the *people* – for whom *local* government should exist.' He added triumphantly: 'I know George Younger broadly agrees with me.'

Instead, Polwarth urged two regions instead of just one (Strathclyde) as a compromise although he probably realised it was too late to make such a major change. 'I'm sorry you're landed with such a vile task on Monday,' he told Younger sympathetically. 'I can but wish you the best of luck in whatever you have to cope with!'[22]

The Bill did pass, just as a miners' strike and the three-day week brought chaos and the suspension of normal government, eventually leading to the February 1974 general election. The first elections to the new two-tier councils were held in May 1974, several months after Younger and Gordon Campbell had left the Scottish Office. The results deepened Conservative dismay as it became clear the reorganisation had done little for the party's electoral appeal in local government. By the end of the decade Younger openly admitted that the reform had not been a success and promised that the next Conservative government would undertake yet another review.[23] Ironically, however, the regions in general and the mighty Strathclyde Regional Council in particular proved to be responsible and did not cause the embarrassment predicted by Polwarth. Although Younger had many running battles with Labour-run local authorities as Scottish Secretary the following decade, that particular 'monster' region gave him very little trouble.

Gordon Campbell had said repeatedly that local government reform would take precedence over proposals for a devolved Scottish Assembly, a Conservative commitment since Heath's 1968 Declaration of Perth. Even so, it seemed to many that the Prime Minister had simply lost interest in constitutional reform although Heath protested that he could not

[22] Lord Polwarth to GY, 18/10/1973, GYP.
[23] Younger was true to his word. On becoming Scottish Secretary in 1979, he appointed his friend Lord Stodart to conduct a review.

pre-empt the deliberations of the Royal Commission on the Constitution, which finally reported at the end of October 1973. It recommended a directly-elected Scottish Assembly as well as major changes in Wales and Northern Ireland, but as its publication clashed with striking miners, the report received relatively little media attention.

Younger, although he had also failed to make much of it during the last three years, remained supportive of Scottish devolution but probably realised that other factors took priority. Elements of the Conservative grassroots, however, remained stubbornly unreconstructed. At the 1973 Scottish conference in Perth, a proposal calling on the government to reaffirm its commitment to a Scottish Assembly was heavily defeated by a show of hands, while an alliance of Young Conservative delegates and the South Aberdeen MP Iain Sproat (also Campbell's PPS) led an attempt to kill off completely any commitment to devolution. Campbell's subsequent conference speech was rambling and interrupted by hecklers. When Heath spoke the following Saturday, he did not even mention the word 'devolution'.

'IT'S SCOTLAND'S OIL'

Despite both internal and external tensions, Younger ably equipped himself as a minister. He never lost his temper, managed to make even the unreasonable sound eminently reasonable, and enjoyed gently teasing often angry Scottish Labour MPs while lucidly outlining what the government had done, intended to do and more importantly why. Everything was couched in consensual tones and a congenial spirit. 'I have the chance of putting the headmaster – the right hon. Member for Kilmarnock [Willie Ross] – right on a point of grammar,' he joked during one exchange. 'It seldom comes to a humble member of the lower fourth to do that.'[24]

George could also turn away wrath with silky earnestness. When Ross brusquely told him to wash out his ears, Younger thanked him for his helpful suggestion. Even James Callaghan, not a man given to needless compliments, once compared Younger with his uncle Kenneth, a former Labour MP and minister, in that they could both reduce ministerial speeches to around four minutes. These skills were of particular value when cries of 'It's Scotland's Oil' – perhaps the SNP's most enduring slogan – began to ring loudly in Unionist ears in the early 1970s.

As development under-secretary, Younger was one of the first government ministers to visit an oil rig in the North Sea – the Forties Field in 1971 – where he found considerable excitement over new geological

---

[24] Hansard 847 c1032. Younger meant Ross's ignorance of the word 'mered', as frequently used by the Ordnance Survey.

readings. North Sea oil development therefore occupied much of Younger's time from 1970 to 1972, and he was never in any doubt as to its value to the Scottish (and UK) economy, particularly in the long term.[25] He championed it relentlessly, not least because the recent war in the Middle East had demonstrated that the UK could not rely upon 'shaky regimes' for its energy supplies.[26]

Oil development (specifically licensing policy) was, of course, initially a DTI responsibility and later fell under the Department for Energy, although the Scottish Office was responsible for ensuring the associated infrastructure – roads, housing, airports and ports – was in place. Despite this, Whitehall rarely consulted St Andrew's House on oil matters, although a 'standing conference' (which later became the Oil Development Council) was convened, chaired jointly by Sir Peter Emery from the DTI and Younger from the Scottish Office.

Its inaugural meeting was held in the impressive surroundings of Inverness Castle's council chamber, but while Younger's flight was delayed by fog, Sir Peter breezed in on time. 'He therefore started the meeting,' recalled its secretary, Kenneth MacKenzie, 'reading from a very cautious Whitehall brief which confirmed that very little of the action on the North Sea discoveries would come to Scotland apart from a few token gestures to the inescapable fact that we provided the nearest landfall.'

> The assembled tweedy suited 'coonty cooncillors', chairmen of harbour authorities and would-be industrial suppliers were getting increasingly restive at all this and, come coffee time, it was no easy task for the secretariat to keep the party sweet. Into this ominous atmosphere, however, strode our gallant champion [Younger] with a brave and sunny smile and the glad tidings that the government was going to rebuild the entire A9 and restore double track on the railway to Inverness in recognition of the importance of North Sea oil developments. It was not quite Mafeking night but the whisky flowed freely at lunchtime and the Standing Conference on North Sea oil was off to a brilliant start.[27]

In terms of government 'high politics', however, Younger was largely a spectator. Gordon Campbell's rigid sense of formal departmental bound-

---

[25] A Fife businessman called David Anderson, however, wrote to Younger in November 1972 to express his concern about the speed at which North Sea exploration appeared to be developing. 'I remember you mentioning that you thought that oil would not be very important after 20 to 30 years,' he wrote, 'because by that time we would almost entirely be producing power from nuclear sources' (*Press & Journal* 2/1/2004).

[26] Speech dated 8/12/1973, GYP.

[27] 'A Private Secretary's Tribute' by Kenneth MacKenzie, 2006.

aries meant he deferred unequivocally to the DTI over the development of oil exploration even though it predominantly took place in Scotland. The situation was worsened by a developing Whitehall view that the Scottish Office was needlessly stalling exploration projects through its overly-bureaucratic planning processes. This was unfair, particularly as many had already been approved without recourse to a public inquiry.

Lord Polwarth – who later complained so bitterly to Younger about local government reform – had joined the Scottish Office in 1972 specifically to deal with North Sea oil development. Previously a respected chairman of General Accident and a Bank of Scotland governor, Polwarth was a surprisingly effective speaker in the Lords as minister of state, but not exactly a success as a politician. His appointment was also frustrating for Younger. Having covered North Sea oil for two years, it was widely expected that he would be upgraded along with the increasingly-important brief; instead his responsibility for Regional Development was transferred to Polwarth. This was, as Godfrey Robson recalled, 'a bolt out of the blue, and a real setback for George . . . it was very frustrating for him to become a virtual onlooker at all this [North Sea oil development]'.[28]

In 1973 a fifth Scottish Office department, the Scottish Economic Planning Department (SEPD), was created to oversee economic development in general, and North Sea oil in particular.[29] Polwarth was dubbed 'Lord of the Oil' in his capacity as chairman of the new Oil Development Council while Younger, typically, showed no sign of being unhappy at being passed over. Polwarth, however, was not a success. Frustrated by his lack of familiarity with London-based ministers, the Lord of the Oil did not exactly complement a Scottish Secretary with an already weak political hand to play.

The government's handling of the North Sea oil industry had become increasingly Byzantine. Heath had one final, and largely successful, attempt at consolidating it when he created a new Department of Energy under Lord Carrington in January 1974. Carrington's move from the Ministry of Defence (MoD) also led to Younger's first ministerial promotion. 'While meeting CBI in St. A[ndrew's]. House about the 3-day week [which had started on New Year's Day] in Industry etc. called out by Godfrey Robson to speak to P.M. on telephone,' recorded Younger in his diary on 8 January. 'He asked me to go as Min. of State Defence to replace Ian Gilmour who is to be S[ecretary]. of S[tate].'

---

[28] Godfrey Robson to the author, 6/11/2007.
[29] Sir Nicholas Morrison had by this point succeeded Sir Douglas Haddow as permanent under-secretary at the Scottish Office.

He said I had done 3½ years at Scottish Office and should go South of the Border for a while. I gladly agreed. It is a good move in every way – a subject I like and non-Scottish experience is very necessary if I am ever to be right for SofS Scotland. Teddy Taylor is to succeed me to his astonishment! Hector [Monro] very sad not to get a change but Alick happy to stay with his present jobs.

The changes generally are to put Carrington, [Patrick] Jenkin, [David] Howell & [Peter] Emery to new energy ministry. This is v. welcome but would have been better if a Scot were included. Polwarth's role is a mystery, but we are told it continues meantime until Carrington thinks about it.[30]

It was the perfect promotion for Younger after more than three years at the Scottish Office and, as he observed in his diary, defence was a subject which had fascinated him since childhood. Letters of congratulation poured into Younger's Stirlingshire home, including a creative note of approval from Invergordon Distillers:

> From Fort George back in '51
> A soldier somewhat Younger
> Left Scotland for Korean shores
> To fight for Britain's honour.
>
> You've soldiered since in statesman's ways
> Now – thanks to Ted's good sense
> We're proud and pleased to welcome you
> As Minister for Defence.[31]

Younger's move to the Ministry of Defence also neatly overlapped with a developing interest of his in relation to regional development. A report by Sir Henry Hardman, a former permanent under-secretary at the MoD, had been published in 1973 recommending the 'dispersal' – or relocation – of certain MoD jobs to stimulate regional economies. One proposed location was Glasgow, and when Younger got wind of the fact that the Defence Secretary (then still Lord Carrington) had effectively vetoed the city in some internal correspondence, he had asked Gordon Campbell to intervene. Campbell, however, refused to do anything because he had not been officially privy to the communications.

Undeterred, Younger persuaded Carrington's minister of state, Ian Gilmour, to come to Glasgow and inspect several potential sites. The visit

---

[30] Diary entry dated 8/1/1974, GYP.
[31] Letter to GY, 10/1/1974, GYP.

had a comical conclusion when the government convoy was stopped by the police on its way back to Glasgow for having unwittingly neglected to pay its toll on crossing the Erskine Bridge. As Godfrey Robson reasoned with the local constabulary, Younger and Ian Gilmour doubled up with laughter in the back seat of a limo. The previously hostile line began to soften. Kenneth Baker, minister for the Civil Service Department (CSD), said the government supported dispersal where 'technically possible', and that Glasgow's claim would be considered alongside parts of England and Wales. 'You know our difficulties,' Gilmour wrote to George, 'but if I may say so I thought you and Glasgow put up a very good case. But then so did Cardiff!'[32]

Now as minister of state in succession to Ian Gilmour, Younger had a real chance to ensure the policy became a reality. He had his first day's briefing at the MoD two days after his appointment. 'Security is very tight,' observed Younger in his diary. 'I am to concentrate on procurement & speak for RAF in Commons. Saw briefly Sir James Dunnett [PUS], Sir Michael Carver [chief of defence staff] & Sir Herman Bondi [chief scientific adviser] but briefing will take a week or two. Not much Parlt. Work – what a contrast to Scottish Office! Big issues will be Nugent Report [which reviewed MoD land use] particularly Lulworth & Tain and dispersal.'

However, added Younger, 'Sir. J. Dunnett [has] already made it clear they are strongly against moving to Glasgow but might consider Cardiff. Tony Buck [minister for the Royal Navy] also said he was anti dispersal. This is going to be difficult for me, but Kenneth Baker (C.S.D.) says he is coming to see us as he disagrees with MoD view. At least he will be an ally!'[33]

Unfortunately for Younger, not to mention the Conservative government as a whole, the whole issue quickly became academic. He enjoyed just a few short weeks in his new role, answering some questions in the House but taking part in no debates, before Heath asked the Queen to dissolve Parliament in order to go to the polls on 28 February. The *Scottish Daily Express* tipped Younger to succeed Campbell as Scottish Secretary should Heath be returned for a second term.

'The Conservative government has only done 3½ years of the five years' mandate it was given in 1970,' Younger told a capacity audience prior to his adoption in Ayr. 'It has faced up with tremendous courage to all the long-standing problems which have held Britain's prosperity back ever since the war.'[34] The choice, he said, was between continued stability

---

[32] Ian Gilmour to George Younger, 26/11/1973, GYP.

[33] Diary entry dated 10/1/1974, GYP.

[34] Undated newspaper clipping, GYP.

under Heath or a Labour government which would capitulate to the trade unions.

Younger's four years as a minister had unwittingly anticipated his future Cabinet career. A successful stint at the Scottish Office had given way to a shorter spell at the Ministry of Defence. Only later would he be the senior, as opposed to the junior, minister in each department. Until then, however, five years of opposition would see Younger preoccupied not only with the same two areas – Scotland and defence – but with the fluctuating fortunes of the Scottish Conservative Party.

Chapter 10

'THE LONG FIGHT BACK'

IN THE GENERAL ELECTION of February 1974, Younger managed to increase his majority in Ayr to just over 5,000 votes. The result was:

G. K. H. Younger (Conservative)	21,626
J. A. McFadden (Labour)	16,528
C. D. Calman (SNP)	4,706

It was one of the best results for the Conservative Party in Scotland, but nationally it was a different story. A resurgent Liberal Party fatally damaged the Tories and helped Labour to scrape a narrow majority – 301 seats to 297 – despite winning fewer votes than the Conservatives. Edward Heath clung on for a few days, hoping to negotiate a coalition with Jeremy Thorpe's Liberals, but it was not to be.

Having spent a few weeks at the Ministry of Defence (MoD) as minister of state until the February election, Younger served as the Conservatives' deputy defence spokesman in the political limbo which spanned March–September. With another electoral contest imminent (it was thought at one point, although not by Younger, that another election could follow in June), he was also invited to become chairman of the Scottish Conservative Party in the belief that he would help steady the ship.[1] Although the party had lost just two seats overall, the rise of the SNP (which gained six seats, four at Tory expense) and the humiliating defeat in Moray of Gordon Campbell, the outgoing Scottish Secretary, had dealt a severe blow to party morale.

Steady it he did, and together with Alick Buchanan-Smith – who worked hard at presenting Scottish Tory MPs in the Commons as sharp and positive – Younger patiently tried to whip a demoralised party back

---

[1] Younger succeeded his cousin, Sir William McEwan Younger, as chairman. His appointment also marked a return to the tradition of having an MP as chairman.

into shape. 'We are going to have the hardest working four months that the Scottish Tory Party has seen for many years,' Younger told the *Scotsman* in June. 'My impression is that we are all ready for whatever comes, and I think we will give a good account of ourselves.'[2]

But no amount of organisation – or reorganisation – could avert further woe. At the autumn poll the SNP made even more headway, adding another four MPs to constitute its famous 'football team' of 11 representatives. The Scottish Conservatives were reduced to just 16 members, its lowest headcount since the beginning of the century. Even more worryingly, the SNP secured more votes than the Tories and came second in some 36 Labour-held constituencies, a political shift which focused both Labour and Conservative minds in terms of devolution policy (see Chapter 11). As the gloomy news poured into party HQ at Atholl Crescent, Younger admitted the party had 'taken a mauling'[3] and blamed tactical voting by Tory supporters who backed the SNP in order to topple Labour members. Standing once more in Ayr, George hung on with a majority of 3,219, a decrease of almost 2,000 votes since February.[4]

Inevitably, newspapers began to run political obituaries of the once mighty Unionist Party. Younger said publicly that activists and MPs had to 'build a new party structure with an organisation in every street', but beyond this fighting talk there was even more gloom among party activists. 'For the Party in Scotland . . . the coming year will not be an easy one,' Younger warned constituency chairmen in December. 'The lessons of the 1974 Elections are now being learned: over the next twelve months they must be applied. This will require effort and understanding from every section of the Party . . . We have always fought for Scotland. And, in the storms that lie ahead, we must ensure that Scotland does not bear an unfair share of the country's burden.'[5]

Effort and understanding, however, were not forthcoming. Younger was instead bombarded with memos and letters from activists across Scotland, many of them quite hostile. Russell Sanderson, who soon became a firm friend of the Youngers, also kept the chairman in touch with numerous other complaints. 'The main point which comes across', he wrote on 14 November 1974, 'was that the loss of the October election was due almost

---

[2] *Scotsman* c6/1974.

[3] *The Times* 12/10/1974. Younger was assisted throughout the election by the young candidate Ian Lang, a future Scottish Secretary.

[4] Younger's Liberal opponent in October 1974 was a trainee teacher called Murray Tosh, who dramatically endorsed Younger on the eve of poll and defected to the Conservatives. He later became an Ayr councillor and chairman of the Ayr constituency association, as well as a Tory MSP.

[5] Letter to constituency chairmen, 30/12/1974, GYP.

entirely to the record of the Government 1970–74. This may be unfair in your eyes, [George], but it comes across again, and again, and again, and I must pass it on.'[6]

Younger also rejected allegations that Atholl Crescent was out of touch with party members. In fact, he said, 'the grass roots of the Party had such a variety of views on . . . policy that some people tended to the belief that Central Office was out of touch if their own particular point of view was not accepted as official policy'.[7] At a meeting of the party's Central Council in November, Younger asked if 'it was not perhaps our own fault' that the party had failed to attract new people. And oddly, considering his mild disposition, he suggested that 'the Party in Scotland must become more militant and aggressive'.

A committee to 'consider all aspects of the Party in Scotland with particular reference to the lessons to be learned from the last two General Elections'[8] was established and Younger threw himself into yet another shake-up of the Scottish Conservative organisation. Younger was, as in his few years as deputy in the late 1960s, a natural chairman and adept at handling the more difficult elements within the party, particularly over the divisive issue of devolution.

Resources at Atholl Crescent were tight following two election campaigns, and there was talk of redundancies and a sale of party assets as part of a general economy drive. In an effort to ensure all this was co-ordinated professionally, Graham Macmillan, a talented Tory organiser in Yorkshire, was persuaded by Younger to return to his native land in the new post of director of Central Office. 'This is the moment when Scottish Conservatives must begin the long fight back after the defeats of 1974,' declared Younger at the May 1975 Scottish conference. 'So, out of defeat is arising like a phoenix, a new Scottish Conservative Party. It is younger, more vigorous and more broadly based than in the past but it retains a firm belief in the basic principles of the Party.'[9]

The 1975 Scottish conference, however, was not a success, and Younger's defiant rhetoric masked serious problems with the ongoing reorganisation. 'It is not that this is at all complicated in substance', the Scottish party treasurer Charles Bell reported to Mrs Thatcher – the new Conservative leader – on 5 August, 'but it certainly is bedevilled [sic] by personalities and by long standing differences between the East and West of Scotland.' He continued:

---

[6] Russell Sanderson to GY, 14/11/1974, GYP.
[7] Minute dated 1/11/1974, GYP.
[8] Minute dated 1/11/1974, GYP.
[9] Speech to Scottish Conservative conference, 15/5/1975, GYP.

We are at the final somewhat critical stage. I think both George and I would have some confidence that we might be able to secure acceptance of all parties by early Autumn. This would be difficult for a new Chairman who will be unaware of – and indeed positively surprised by – the personal pettiness which accompanies talks of this kind. George is both aware and immune. I know you are anxious to have this decision taken. May I suggest one or other of two alternatives. Either, and preferably, that the announcement be delayed until October or, if that is not possible, that George be asked whether he would continue to associate himself during the Recess specifically with this subject to the point of final decision. I rather fear the advent of a new Chairman might give rise to a concerted attempt to take us back to square one. That would really try the patience.[10]

Younger was in his element as chairman, and was even tipped to replace Alick Buchanan-Smith as Shadow Scottish Secretary. 'George Younger has a lot going for him – hard-working, intelligent, popular, and a good speaker,' gushed one newspaper. 'In ten years at Westminster, he's never embarrassed colleagues. Certainly the safer choice. So should Mrs T. play safe or gamble?'[11] He also won the approval of long-serving Scottish party grandees although at grassroots level there was grumbling about him not being available more often in Scotland because of his defence commitments.

Younger stood down as chairman in September 1975, having told Mrs Thatcher in February that he would find it difficult to combine the two jobs as well as look after his constituency. He attended his last meeting to discuss the reorganisation in August after which Russell Fairgrieve (the MP for West Aberdeenshire) continued negotiations with the UK party chairman, Lord Thorneycroft, to forge a closer relationship between the Scottish and UK parties.

'May I thank you, George, for the pleasant experience of the past fifteen months or so?' wrote a senior party official in October 1975. 'You have got us over a very trying period.' He continued:

After the October defeat much of what happened was, I suppose, inevitable. People were bound to flail about, and the Chairman's Office was an all too obvious target. I marvelled at your unfailing courtesy under what at times must have been extreme provocation. It was magnificently done and undoubtedly quietened things down to the point where we could, with relatively little

[10] Charles Bell to MT, 5/8/1975, GYP (copy).
[11] Undated newspaper clipping in GYP. The 'gamble' was Teddy Taylor.

trouble, give the Forbes Hendry Report[12] a decent burial at Perth a week or so ago. The Germans have a word for it – *viel larm um nichts* [much ado about nothing]. Whether they are or not one cannot say, but the Party ought to be grateful to you for all you did – and that at great personal inconvenience. I certainly am.'[13]

'A SOUND DEFENCE POLICY'

Younger's other major preoccupation throughout 1974 and 1975 was defence, a policy area of long-standing interest to the former Argyll and Korean veteran. From March 1974 he assisted Ian Gilmour, who had been Defence Secretary during his short stint at the MoD before the election. 'A sound defence policy,' George told the Commons in late 1974, 'whoever is in charge of it, in any country at any time, must always provide some margin to allow for the unexpected.'[14] Harold Wilson's minority government was already moving towards major cuts in defence expenditure, and Younger warned that rumoured cuts of about a third would severely reduce the effectiveness of the Armed Forces and undermine the UK's NATO commitment. 'The Labour left, much of it openly sympathetic to Communism,' he said rather melodramatically, 'is trying to do from within Britain what 25 years of Russian effort from without has failed to do.'[15] Such sentiments were to become recurring themes of Younger's defence career – both as a front-bencher in 1975–76, and as Defence Secretary in the late 1980s.

The election result of October 1974 had effectively sealed Edward Heath's fate, and when Mrs Thatcher challenged him for the Conservative leadership in early 1975, Younger probably voted for Heath out of loyalty. Astutely, however, he wrote to the new leader offering to advise her on Scottish issues. 'Thank you for your kind letter,' she replied on 16 February. 'I shall need a lot of advice about Scotland but am ready and willing to take it. I believe that the problem is the same as further south – people lost *faith* in us and our job is to restore it.'[16]

Younger received a call from Thatcher just three days later. 'I am delighted that Mrs. Thatcher has appointed me as Shadow Secretary of State for Defence in her new Shadow Cabinet,' he said in a statement. 'It will be my main task to fight all moves by the Government to weaken our

---

[12] The Forbes Hendry Report proposed that party conferences should be enlarged to about 1,500 members and extended to three days. The chairman, Colonel Forbes Hendry, was a former MP for West Aberdeenshire.
[13] Letter to GY, 14/10/1975, GYP. The author of this letter is unidentified beyond his first name, 'Thomas'.
[14] Hansard 883 c1279-80.
[15] Speech to Scottish Conservative conference, 17/5/1974, GYP.
[16] MT to GY, 16/2/1975, GYP.

defences, and to see that Scotland gets a better share of defence expenditure and jobs.'[17] Mrs Thatcher had purged the Tory front bench of Heathites, sacking six while promoting six new faces to the Shadow Cabinet, one of which was Younger.

Although essentially a Heathite himself, Younger was rated by Thatcher who had received positive reports of his performance as deputy defence spokesman over the previous few months. He accompanied her on her first, oddly tumultuous, visit to Scotland the week after his appointment. 'Mrs Supercool!' screamed the *Daily Record* headline on 22 February, referring to her whistle-stop tour of Edinburgh and Glasgow. Her visit boosted morale among Scottish Tories for the first time in years although she was vague on policy.

She did a walkabout at Edinburgh's St James Centre with Younger and Alick Buchanan-Smith in tow. The enthusiastic crowd of 3,000 was so large that police had to clear a path for her leading to the relative serenity of a jewellery shop. Mrs Thatcher was given an equally rapturous welcome at a party rally in Glasgow, where she reiterated her party's commitment to a directly-elected Scottish Assembly. That pledge, and the new Conservative leader's popularity north of the border, did not last for long.

Although Younger did not play a prominent part in Shadow Cabinet discussions, he quickly proved himself an able proponent of what he called 'a new military approach' in both the Commons and in the media. The recent context was stark. In a statement the previous December, Labour's Defence Secretary Roy Mason had announced a reduction in defence expenditure as a proportion of Gross National Product (GNP) from 5.5 to 4.5 per cent over the next ten years. This, argued Younger in an article for *The Times*, was an 'arbitrary and politically motivated cut' which meant the government was essentially following a policy of unilateral disarmament.

By contrast, he wrote, the Soviets and non-Soviet Warsaw Pact countries continued to improve their defences far beyond strictly defensive needs. 'There is no reason, therefore,' argued Younger, 'to believe that the Soviet intention for the long-term – the total dominance and ab[s]orption of Western Europe – has changed in any way, and it seems that, while on the political level the Soviet Union pursues a policy of détente, there is no sign that the word détente has any real meaning for the military part of the Warsaw Pact.' Defence policy, he said, needed 'stability as a safeguard against the vicissitudes of alternating political whims imposed on a fluctuating and unpredictable GNP'.[18]

---

[17] Statement dated 19/2/1975, GYP. Younger's deputy was initially Peter Walker, a future Cabinet colleague, and subsequently the eccentric former MI6 agent Cranley Onslow.
[18] *The Times* 19/3/1975.

Younger's new approach on defence, however, had to be slotted into the continuing party policy review headed up by Sir Keith Joseph. At a Shadow Cabinet meeting on 11 April 1975, Younger emphasised that the 'power resides in T.[ransport] H.[ouse] not Parliament; we must try to increase the chance of a split'. This meeting also marked a decisive break with Heath and the beginning of a more strident direction for the Conservative Party. Although this offended Heathites like Ian Gilmour and Francis Pym, there is nothing to suggest that George disapproved. Instead, he concentrated on tactics as opposed to the party's philosophical direction. 'The great majority of Scots do *not* wish to break up Britain,' he observed. 'Conservative defectors in Scotland had a more attractive haven to go to than in England.'[19] That haven was the SNP.

A debate on the government's defence white paper was fixed for 6–7 May in the House of Commons, and the Shadow Cabinet met again on 28 April to discuss tactics. Younger proposed to base his attack on three main points: exposure of the white paper's contradictions; criticism of an additional £110 million cut announced in the Budget; and the ramifications for industry. 'He stressed the need to alert the public to the dangers ahead and to embark on a long-term exercise to rekindle public interest in defence matters,' recorded a minute. 'He warned of the need to be clear about what cuts in other public spending programmes we would have made and the need to qualify and cost our alternatives.'[20]

'George Younger, as well as putting the Scottish Party's point of view [as party chairman],' said Mrs Thatcher at the Scottish conference in May, 'is the next minute arguing the case on defence for Britain as a whole. It is said that national defence is a Government's first duty – and with George Younger we have little chance of forgetting it.'[21] In all, there were four opposition debates on the defence white paper, covering the Army, Air Force and the Royal Navy. Cuts to the latter, argued Younger, were the worst of all the proposed reductions. The Russian Navy, he said, was expanding, while the government proposed reducing the UK's fleet by almost half. 'Unless NATO and its member nations wake up to the threat that is now so glaringly obvious,' Younger told MPs, 'we may lose our ability to defend our nation from a slow death by the strangulation of the nation's trade.'[22]

The Labour government argued that its reduction of defence expenditure as a proportion of GNP would bring UK spending into line with

---

[19] Lord Hailsham's diary, 11/4/1975, MTF
[20] Minute dated 28/4/1975, GYP.
[21] Speech at Caird Hall, Dundee, 17/5/1975, MTF.
[22] Hansard 895 c540.

that of France and Germany. Younger made much of this in debates, pointing out that as both countries had larger GNPs than the UK, it was hardly surprising that they spent proportionately less on military hardware. The bitter debate over the defence white paper was also played out against the backdrop of the government's referendum on whether or not the UK should remain within the European Common Market. Younger was firmly in the pro-Europe camp, where he would remain throughout his political career, but believed the poll was more a cynical ploy to manipulate the Labour Party than gauge the mood of the British people.

Younger used the 1975 summer recess to visit Northern Ireland, meeting the Royal Anglians and familiarising himself with MoD commitments in the Province. In September, he also accompanied Mrs Thatcher on a visit to the BP exploration rig, *Sea Quest*, in the North Sea. While she pledged to denationalise the oil industry, Younger warned of threats to oil installations from terrorism and pollution. Another favourite theme was the need to standardise equipment across NATO which Younger claimed could save as much as 30 per cent on the cost of defence hardware.

The Conservative Party conference in October marked Younger's first – and only – set-piece outing as Shadow Defence Secretary in front of party delegates. 'We must not forget that the decisions we take now are determining what we shall be able to do (or not to do) for our defence not to-day, but in 1985 and beyond,' he said in summing up the defence debate, little knowing that he would in fact be Defence Secretary beyond 1985. 'We must assume the historic mantle of the prophet crying in the wilderness, and we must warn, warn, and warn again of the dangers of neglecting our defences. The Free World is sailing into great danger and the crew must be woken up before it is too late.'

Again, he attacked the government's white paper:

And so we have had a 'Jekyll and Hyde' White Paper or rather a 'Mason and Benn' White Paper. Dr [Roy] Mason warns us in horrifying terms of the threat we face while a few pages on, Mr [Tony] Benn assures us that we can therefore slash our defences . . . Every one of our NATO allies has stated clearly and publicly that our cuts are dangerous to the alliance. Even a Labour Government cannot ignore such a unanimous view.

Younger welcomed *détente* between East and West, but warned:

What we face to-day is not an open military assault, but a much more dangerous two pronged attack. The preaching of detente to weaken our resolve to maintain our defences, and systematic subversion of every free institution throughout the free world. There is no sign that the Soviet Union has altered its policy in any way . . . but every sign that this subversion is everywhere being most successful. We are losing this battle now because Britain is asleep and our free institutions are themselves being subverted while we sleep.

Somewhat melodramatically, but in language not untypical for the period, Younger also warned about the 'enemy within'; militants in the trade unions and, more pertinently, the IRA. He ended with a quote from Somerset Maugham ('someone with plenty of wisdom but no pretence to strategic military expertise'): 'When a nation values anything more than freedom it will lose its freedom – and the irony of it is that if it is comfort or money that it values more, it will lose that too.' 'And so let this message go out from this Conference to the whole nation,' concluded Younger in bombastic style. 'The Conservative Party's determination to maintain our defences is as strong as ever. Our allies may fear the socialists but they need have no fear of us – for we will see to it, that Britain will not let them down.'[23]

The mid-1970s was an interesting period in international defence. In South Africa, the Simonstown Agreement (witnessed by Younger on his trip to South Africa in 1969) once again came under scrutiny; Northern Ireland remained in limbo following the collapse of the Sunningdale Agreement; the so-called 'Cod Wars' with Iceland captured the domestic imagination; and the United States' new defense secretary (Donald Rumsfeld) pursued *détente* through the SALT (strategic arms limitation) and MBFR (mutual and balanced force reduction) talks with the Soviet Union. Nevertheless, as 1975 drew to a close there were rumours that the Labour government was planning to cut defence spending for the second time in a year.

The Armed Forces Bill was debated in December, and Bill Rodgers, minister of state at the MoD, said he would resign rather than agree to cuts that undermined the collective security of the West. In a powerful condemnation of the proposals, Younger demanded consultation with NATO allies before any cuts were implemented. Ominously, he added, if these undertakings failed, the opposition would be forced to conclude that ministers were being increasingly influenced 'by those in their midst who seek to overthrow our Western way of life'.[24] The government, Younger concluded, had a responsibility not to the left-wing Tribune group, or even to the Labour conference, but to the nation as a whole.

Politics is full of ironies, and in the slow-moving realm of defence procurement, one future irony passed across Younger's desk at the end of

---

[23] Speech to Conservative conference, 9/10/1975, GYP.
[24] Hansard 902 c487.

1975. The UK's fleet of Nimrod surveillance aircraft were by then old and tired, and the choice for a replacement lay between US-manufactured Boeing AWACs (or E3As) or a cheaper home-grown alternative. Although the 1970 Conservative government had cancelled Marconi's contract to build that domestic alternative, the company was pitching a UK refit of the existing Nimrod AEW (Airborne Early Warning) planes as an alternative to the US purchase. Kenneth Warren, a fellow Conservative MP, wrote to Younger on 26 November to tell him of private discussions he had held with the MoD minister Bill Rodgers, who was keen to avoid paying £200m for eight Boeings when there was a chance of a British alternative costing only £70m. Warren hinted that the pulse-doppler radar used by the Boeings could be jammed, and said Marconi Radar Ltd had estimated a cost of £40m to convert the Nimrods by 1980. 'To embark on such a venture sounds wonderful', wrote Warren, 'but the U.S. Government is saying that we have got to buy [Boeing] AWACs if they are to approve the building of three hundred Harriers by McDonnell-Douglas [US defence contractor]. They need the Harrier more than we need Boeing's E3A. I would be prepared to call their bluff.'[25] Younger's reaction to this is not known, but eleven years later one of his first acts as Defence Secretary was to cancel the whole Nimrod AEW programme following years of rising costs, practical difficulties and political posturing.

In January 1976, after little under a year shadowing defence, Younger was sacked from the Shadow Cabinet. This was probably nothing personal and was thought to stem from Mrs Thatcher's belief that as defence became a bigger political issue, it needed more of a heavyweight (in terms of experience) to tackle it. That heavyweight was Ian Gilmour, who was for a few weeks Younger's chief as Defence Secretary in the dying days of Heath's government.

For Younger it was bitterly disappointing, and an almost unbroken line of advancement within the party since he became Scottish Whip in 1965 was seemingly at an end. Yet shortly before being dropped, he played a small part in earning his party leader an enduring nickname. Almost from the moment Thatcher became leader of the opposition she had attached great importance to East–West relations and believed that a more strident position in relation to the Soviet Union was desirable. Younger shared this view and pressed her to articulate it in a now famous speech at Kensington Town Hall in January 1976. In it, Mrs Thatcher accused the Soviets of being 'bent on world dominance'.[26] Her speech attracted attention in Moscow, and the Soviet Ambassador in London even

---

[25] Kenneth Warren to GY, 26/11/1975, GYP.
[26] *The Times* 29/1/1976.

protested to the Foreign Office, while *Red Star*, the Soviet Army news-paper, denounced her as 'The Iron Lady'. Ironically, what had been intended as an insult became a badge of pride that Thatcher was happy to wear for the rest of her political career.

Younger heard the news of his dismissal while visiting St Andrews where his children James and Joanna were studying, and despite the bad news went ahead with a meeting at the university.[27] Thatcher's decision was greeted with incredulity. Norman Fowler (who was also removed from the Shadow Cabinet) later wrote that Younger 'for no sensible reason was moved out of his position as Defence spokesman',[28] while Julian Critchley wrote to say 'I am very sorry – and surprised.'[29] Tam Galbraith, the Glasgow Hillhead MP, also wrote to Younger on 18 January. 'I had no idea when I was "wading into" you about yr very persuasive Central Council speech that your shadow responsibility had been removed from you,' he said. 'It's a most unpleasant experience but I am sure with that silver tongue of yours it will only be a temporary eclipse. However in the meantime I suppose the anti-Assemblyists will have to work even harder!'[30]

Another Conservative MP dropped Younger a line the same day: 'It is beastly hard to make an impact with such a subject in a short time. In my view you *were* coming across well in the House and outside; certainly the % of GNP approach will never be more dented! Sure, only a temporary check – but one your friends regret.'[31] Younger's friend David Mitchell, then an official in the Scottish Conservative Party, also wrote in philo-sophical terms:

> You will be fully aware of those 'twin imposters Success and failure' and have the character to cope with both so very well. It must be somewhat hard for you having battled all last year with the job of Scottish Chairman and Defence Spokesman to find yourself suddenly as a reward with nothing at all – but then there is no thanks in the political game and the swings and changes of personal fortune combined with those of a party make it a very difficult corner.[32]

The press reaction to Younger's removal was also largely sympathetic, although some commentators thought that perhaps he had not been aggressive enough in attacking the government. One editorial warmly

[27] Younger stayed with his second cousin, John Purvis, the night after the event. 'This was the first occasion I witnessed his great resilience and his amazing ability to rise above any setbacks,' recalled Purvis (John Purvis to the author, 5/4/2007).

[28] Fowler, *Ministers Decide*, 83–84.

[29] Julian Critchley to GY, 16/1/1976, GYP.

[30] Tam Galbraith to GY, 18/1/1976, GYP.

[31] Letter to GY, 18/1/1976, GYP.

[32] David Mitchell to GY, 17/1/1976, GYP.

welcomed Gilmour's appointment but added: 'This is not to say that Mr Younger failed. Far from it. It is to say that the Tory party needs a Defence spokesman of the weight and experience in this field at this time.'[33] George told reporters he was disappointed but would continue his defence work from the backbenches. 'I appreciate that Mrs. Thatcher has to make changes from time to time,' he told the *Scottish Daily Express*. 'This will enable me to play a stronger part in Scottish affairs. With the current dispute over devolution, we need every Scotsman we can to put across the great dangers of slipping towards separation, which no one wants. I will continue to be a loyal lieutenant to Mrs. Thatcher and will give her every ounce of support.'[34]

Younger's friend, Alick Buchanan-Smith – who continued as Shadow Scottish Secretary following the reshuffle – wrote to Diana Younger two weeks later with more words of support:

> My dear Di,
>
> I thought I should let you know how shaken many of us are by the Shadow Cabinet changes. What happened to George is quite unexpected and totally undeserved. Particularly to those of us who knew just how much George was doing with the services, it was a surprise.
>
> Really, one begins to wonder if there is any justice in politics! What I feel is very rough, is that George, against his own better judgement and to the knowledge of the Leadership, did two major jobs for six months of last year – and both well. It is galling that only eleven months were allowed for the single job. I wonder what thanks there are!
>
> Considering all this, George has reacted marvellously – as we would expect! What I value, is the tremendous support he has pledged for me.
>
> Yours
> Alick[35]

There turned out to be justice in the long term. Almost exactly ten years after he was sacked from the Shadow Cabinet, Younger was appointed Secretary of State for Defence.

SOUTH AFRICA REVISITED

Although Younger was now a humble backbencher, he was determined to continue speaking on defence even if he could not do it from the platform of the Shadow Cabinet. Before his sacking, he had arranged two foreign

---

33 *The Times* 16/1/1976.
34 *Scottish Daily Express* 16/1/1976.
35 ABS to DY, 28/1/1976, GYP.

visits, one to Brunei and a return visit to South Africa. This time, Diana accompanied him on both. The former trip involved hasty reorganisation, and the sultan was no doubt bemused to be presented with Mrs Thatcher's 'senior' colleague as opposed to her Shadow Defence Secretary. The long flight, however, gave George time to come to terms with the shock of his removal from the Shadow Cabinet.

The latter trip was enlivened by a bright young official called J. Stauch, who was determined to make the South African tour as much fun as possible for George and Diana. Younger revisited many of the places he had seen seven years earlier but the context to this trip was bleaker even than in 1969. The neighbouring state of Angola had recently become independent and a civil war was raging, a conflict exacerbated by foreign intervention along Cold War lines.

Younger found the Angolan situation highly engaging and it permeated most of his discussions with South African government ministers and officials. He flew to Johannesburg on 26 February where he and Diana lunched with J. van Dalsen, the senior deputy secretary for foreign affairs, before embarking on a scenic drive of Pretoria, a visit to the Klapperkop Military Museum and a performance of *Joseph and his Amazing Technicolour Dreamcoat* at a local theatre. After more than a year of chairing the Scottish Conservative Party and shadowing defence, a break – albeit a working break – was for George much needed.

The most bizarre appointment of Younger's itinerary was a meeting with Marquhand de Villiers, a local director of Lonrho (the London and Rhodesian Mining Company, described by Edward Heath as the 'unpleasant and unacceptable face of capitalism' in 1973) and a friend of the UK-based businessman 'Tiny' Rowland. De Villiers was an infamous political 'fixer' in South Africa and proved surprisingly frank over lunch, telling Younger that Lonrho had been trying to topple the Rhodesian prime minister, Ian Smith, for more than a year, at one point under the guise of a constitutional conference comprising Smith and the black Rhodesian political leaders Joshua Nkomo and Ndabaningi Sithole. Sithole was also busy trying to topple the Zambian president Kenneth Kuanda and had been arrested under Smith's orders on a 'trumped up' charge. Younger recorded the related intrigue in his diary notes:

> Lonrho discovered via Kaunda and London that Kaunda and Nyerere [president of Tanzania] were to meet on Sat 21 Feb 1976 and publicly withdraw support from Nkomo, Sithole and Muzorewa [Zimbabwean nationalist politician and bishop] thus leaving no-one for Smith to talk to on opening the way for a 'guerrilla' solution. De Villiers [therefore] asked to see Smith on Thursday 19 Feb. Smith sent an emissary called Fletcher.

De Villiers told Fletcher about the Kaunda–Nyerere plan and pressurised him to get Smith to pre-empt this by an immediate announcement of an intention to treat with Nkomo & bring him in to Govt with clear objective of a complete handover of power within 3 years and African participation now.

Result was Smith's announcement next day of the offer to London coupled with attack on Lonrho. This bought time but risked Nkomo being ditched – which risk gets greater each day.

De Villiers wants it passed to London that there is only one hope of avoiding invasion of Rhodesia by guerrillas followed by a Marxist regime. This hope rests on Smith resigning now (as Nkomo can't negotiate any more) handing over to Nkomo as caretaker plus offer by Britain (or someone else?) of full compensation for property to any Whites who wish to leave (possible cost £100m). If this happened, within 3 years Zimbabwe would have majority rule and be part of a pro-Western bloc consisting of Zambia, Malawi, Zimbabwe, South Africa, Lesotho, Bostwana and ? Zaire.[36]

Younger was an unlikely Cold War emissary but although De Villiers' fear of a guerrilla invasion was mistaken, his timescale was not. Just over three years later Bishop Muzorewa was elected as head of a black majority government under a new constitution negotiated with Ian Smith, and by the end of 1979 the Conservative government – of which George had become a member – negotiated the Lancaster House agreement which granted Rhodesia independence and created the new state of Zimbabwe.

On Thursday 4 March Younger met with the then minister of defence – and future prime minister – P. W. Botha, whose wife entertained George and Diana over lunch. A trip to the all-important Simonstown followed, where he saw Admiral Johnstone, chief of the South African Navy. The following day Younger met D. Venter, the assistant director of the South African Institute of International Affairs ('A red-bearded leftie-looking man & rather shy & retiring'), who told him he considered South Africa to have 'made a big mistake in identifying itself as fighting for the West against Communist incursion into Africa. SA ought to be identifying itself as an African Power fighting to keep Africa for the Africans.'

Later that day Younger lunched with Harry Oppenheimer and four colleagues from the Anglo-American Corporation. 'All v. worried about Rhodesia & think [Ian] Smith is already past the eleventh hour,' he noted in his diary. 'Maximum pressure on him to settle with Nkomo. Consider the S.A. incursion into Angola was very ill-advised . . . All have good impression of Margaret Thatcher.'[37] One can only assume that Younger

[36] Undated diary entry c2/1976, GYP.
[37] Diary entry dated 5/3/1976, GYP.

communicated the existence of a South African fan club direct to his party leader on returning to the UK.

Although social issues had dominated Younger's earlier visit to South Africa, this time it was a subordinate consideration. Instead, he visited Mr Richter, who ran the Bantu Investment Corporation, and Dr Jacobs from the South African Reserve Bank, who was 'shattered to hear that UK had 60% of GDP in public expenditure'.[38] Finally, on 5 March, Younger visited two officials at the Industrial Development Corporation of South Africa. 'I was struck by the similarity of what they do to the role of the National Enterprise Board and the Scottish Development Corporation!' mused Younger in his diary, no doubt with memories of his time in charge of development at the Scottish Office. 'They have been going for 30 years in a *very* non socialist state! However they do *invest* in undertaking & pull out when they can sell advantageously. They aim to make a profit & operate like a normal business.'[39]

On returning to the UK, Younger made full use of his accumulated intelligence. He used the *Ayrshire Post* to call for diplomatic and economic sanctions against the Soviet Union until 'she has withdrawn every Cuban soldier from Angola. We should suspend all talks for further arms agreements which Russia very much wants to achieve; we should stop cultural exchanges and cut off her access to our superior technology until Russia demonstrates that she will allow freedom to other nations without imposing military might on free peoples.'[40]

A week later, in a speech to what must have been a bemused gathering of the Dunoon Ladies' Lunch Club, Younger attacked the government for proposing 'to send literally millions of our money to an obscure revolutionary regime in Mozambique'.[41] He also contributed to a Commons debate on the strategic implications of Angola on 30 March, while in 1978 Younger produced a paper with the Edinburgh West MP James Douglas-Hamilton on 'Soviet Foreign Policy in Africa'.

Younger continued to speak on defence issues throughout 1976, often styling himself as a former 'minister of state for defence'. He joined a NATO tour in June at the invitation of Raymond Seitz, then first secretary at the US embassy (and later US ambassador to the Court of St James), whom George and Diana had met during a US visit in April. Younger obviously believed that by maintaining a high profile on defence issues he might return to the MoD as a minister when – and if – the Conservatives won the next election.

---

[38] Undated diary entry c3/1976, GYP.
[39] Diary entry dated 5/3/1976, GYP.
[40] *Ayrshire Post* 5/3/1976.
[41] Speech to Dunoon Ladies' Lunch Club, 12/3/1976, GYP.

THE RIGHT APPROACH?

Back in the UK, the remainder of the 1974 Parliament was dominated by devolution and the development of the party's Scottish policies in the run-up to the next general election. In 1976 Younger sketched out what he considered to be the essentials of 'Cons[ervative] Policy' on the back of an old press release:

Economy – live within our means – Taxes – cut? Profits?

Housing – Encourage home-buying. Sell Council Houses.

Health – More money and more choice.

Education – Uniformity and lower standards or higher standards & more choice.

Defence – Maintain or cut.

Foreign Affairs – Strike attitudes or stand up for Britain.

EEC – Co-operate or not?

Social Security – Indiscriminate or concentrate?

U.K. – Together or not?[42]

This was, essentially, the manifesto on which the Conservatives would fight the 1979 general election. It sprang, in part, from *The Right Approach*, a seminal statement of Conservative aims and values produced by Sir Keith Joseph in the autumn of 1976. But although Younger was interested in the development of policy, particularly on housing and development, he was by no means a policy wonk.

One housing policy, the so-called 'Right to Buy', was first floated by various Conservatives in May 1976, and Younger was a frequent evangelist for the cause. 'It is now time for Conservatives in Scotland to rescue council tenants from the monopoly landlord that the Labour Party has imposed upon them,'[43] he said at a Conservative Women's Conference in early 1977. At meeting of the Scottish Policy Group, Younger also urged that 'houses must be sold', although 'care must be taken not to set extravagant targets for house sales'.[44] He also suggested that 'Councils should be made to submit schemes to the Scottish Office for the sale of council houses, much like they had to on comprehensive education.'[45]

Speaking at the 1978 Scottish Conservative conference, Younger

---

[42] Undated notes, GYP.

[43] Speech dated 12/2/1976, GYP.

[44] CRD 4/15/9, 22/4/1977.

[45] Minute dated 24/2/1978, GYP.

articulated the policy in more detail. 'We know that over 60% of Scots would like to own their own homes,' he proclaimed, 'yet [the] Labour Government is now deliberately preventing them from doing so, by refusing permission to local councils to sell houses even when they and their electors wish this to be done.' Why, Younger asked, 'should they be forced by Labour to pay rent at ever increasing amounts for the rest of their lives? They will have paid out huge sums and will have nothing to show for it at the end of the day.' Although the council house system had been a good one, he continued, 'for the most part it no longer meets the needs and aspirations of ordinary people'.[46]

Another area of interest to Younger was the rates. Although his mentor Sir Alec Douglas-Home had famously cautioned against tampering with local government finance in the early 1960s, Younger was in complete agreement with Mrs Thatcher when it came to the increasingly unpopular rating system. 'I have never been a great friend of the rating system,' he said during a Commons debate in late 1976. 'I have always thought – and still think – that the rating system has reached a stage where it is unrealistic and difficult for ordinary people to understand and that it is time it was brushed aside.'[47]

Younger returned to the Conservative front bench in November 1976 as a junior spokesman on Scottish affairs.[48] He was soon attacking Bruce Millan, the Scottish Secretary, for 'passing the buck' of huge expenditure rises to Scottish ratepayers through a 4 per cent cut in the rate support grant. 'Mr. Millan seems to wash his hands of these problems although they are the results of his Government's failure,' he chided. 'His lack of concern makes Pontius Pilate seem by comparison to have been a most conscientious and concerned citizen.'[49] Younger said rate rises should instead be capped by the government.

There was also wide dissatisfaction, not least among Scottish Conservatives, with the Tory-instigated 1975 local government reorganisation which had created the massive, Labour-dominated, Strathclyde Region. 'In some parts of Scotland it [the reorganisation] *has* been a success, but in too many areas it has not,' Younger said in a party political broadcast. 'For that reason we are urgently studying how best it can be changed. But it is irresponsible to pretend that it can be done overnight.'[50] He also addressed the May 1977 Scottish Conservative Party conference on the

---

[46] Speech to Scottish Conservative conference, 12/5/1978, GYP.
[47] Hansard 918 c115–16.
[48] The vacancy had been created by Teddy Taylor's promotion to become shadow trade spokesman.
[49] Speech to Glasgow University, 2/12/1976, GYP.
[50] PPB script dated 25/4/1976, GYP.

subject. Revealingly, Younger scribbled on his speech notes: 'Dare I add Overspending by the local authorities?'[51]

Of course, abolishing the rates was all well and good, but the question of an alternative was as yet unformulated in Tory minds. At another Scottish Policy Group meeting on 24 February 1978 Younger declared: 'There must be a commitment to abolish the rates because they are seen as unfair. However, we must have a clear alternative in mind. If local income tax is the only option, then a way must be found to make it work.'[52] Although a local income tax was ruled out by the next Conservative government, most other aspects of Younger's thinking came to fruition when he became Scottish Secretary: rates increases were capped; a review of the local government reorganisation was set up (chaired by Younger's friend Lord Stodart); and he did dare to mention overspending by local authorities.

On other policy areas, Younger was more cautious. Greater parental choice in schools was often mooted but he 'questioned the practicality of this as many parents would wish to send their child to the school with the good reputation, thereby creating a system in which the poorer schools became poorer'. The contrary argument was that it would 'make the poorer schools improve and lead to a choice in types of schools'.[53] When Younger took over at the Scottish Office in 1979, parental choice was legislated for, although in a milder form which fell neatly between these two viewpoints.

On regional development too, Younger was moderate and certainly not Thatcherite in his thinking. He believed strongly in government intervention, a view strengthened by his time in charge of development at the Scottish Office, and he broadly supported the powerful new Scottish Development Agency (SDA) established by the Labour Scottish Secretary Willie Ross. 'I want to make it quite clear that the new Conservative government has no intention of abolishing the SDA or reducing its effectiveness,' Younger said in a speech to the Central Council of the Scottish Conservative Party, referring to calls from colleagues for it to be wound up. 'We shall encourage it in every way we can, while giving it new guidelines.'[54]

On this detail, Younger and Mrs Thatcher broadly agreed, but on dispersal, the policy of relocating London-based civil servants to the regions, there was no such unanimity. George had supported dispersal

---

[51] Speech to Scottish Conservative conference, 14/5/1977, GYP.
[52] Minute dated 24/2/1978, GYP.
[53] CRD 4/15/9, 22/4/1977.
[54] Speech in Motherwell, 4/11/1978, GYP.

while a minister at the Scottish Office and MoD, but it was by no means the standard Conservative line. In particular, Younger lobbied for defence jobs to be transferred to Glasgow – as recommended by the Heath-commissioned Hardman Report – but frequently encountered hostility from his Tory colleagues.

In July 1977 Lord Peart announced that more than 5,000 MoD jobs would go to Glasgow by the mid to late 1980s, while 1,000 Ministry of Overseas Development jobs would also be transferred to East Kilbride. While this was popular, for obvious reasons, with Scottish MPs of all political hues, a sizeable number of English MPs representing commuter belt areas were bitterly resentful. The issue came up at a Shadow Cabinet meeting on 4 December 1978 which Younger attended in place of Teddy Taylor. He knew he had a fight on his hands, and recorded its blows in his diary:

> I had to battle hard to avoid them abandoning dispersal altogether. They were in a great panic about how many English marginals were 'in danger' (e.g. Bath, Gloucestershire and in London) because Defence workers from there did not want to go to Glasgow or Cardiff. A very anti-Scottish attitude was shown and no-one showed any sign of being sympathetic at first. I pointed out that work was well advanced at East Kilbride with the O[verseas].D[evelopment]. M[inistry]. offices, and that St. Enoch site was also under preparation for the 4000-odd to go to Glasgow. This cooled them a bit and they eventually agreed not to abandon the principle but to say we would review the actual detail of which departments would go. Mrs. T. said that if Scotland rejects the Assembly we would have to try to be as helpful as possible. But if Scotland chose an Assembly they would get nothing. That just shows the attitude of hostility we now have to counter.
>
> Once more I doubt Mrs. T's coolness. She rattles on, arguing everything & is a bad chairman. She gives me the impression of being very much under strain and is no doubt feeling that everything is going wrong for her just now.[55]

Younger also served, from the end of 1975 until 1977, on the Authority of Government Group chaired by Lord Carrington, which had been set up by Mrs Thatcher to consider how a future Conservative government would deal with widespread industrial action. Trade unions had brought down Ted Heath; Thatcher was determined the same would not happen to her.

Other members included Ian Gilmour, William Waldegrave and the

---

[55] Diary entry dated 4/12/1978, GYP.

former leader of the House of Lords, Earl Jellicoe. Younger played an active role in discussions and advocated the creation of a permanent government body 'to prepare and administer contingency plans for the event of a challenge to the authority of government'.[56]

The Carrington Committee produced recommendations in 1978, but by then Mrs Thatcher seemed to have lost interest. 'I feel very strongly that we ought, without any publicity, to devise a permanent strategy for planning ahead, with the aim of being ready to meet industrial action with effective counter measures,' George wrote to Mrs Thatcher on 14 February 1979. 'As the Carrington Report suggested, there is a lot that can be done in preparing and designing government undertakings so that they have alternative methods of supply etc., adequate stocks to withstand siege, and some basic preparation for the use of volunteers where appropriate.'[57]

Mrs Thatcher did not share Younger's sense of urgency. She replied on 22 February saying that some thinking was already being done on the basis of Carrington's report, 'but you will remember from its content that the main action can only be taken in Government. There is obviously a limit to what we can do outside, and I think it would be a mistake to reconvene that particular committee now.' She added in her own hand, with a hint of paranoia, 'You will remember that it contains "outside" people.'[58]

Continuing industrial action after Mrs Thatcher arrived at Downing Street, and particularly the miners' strike of the mid-1980s, vindicated both Lord Carrington and Younger. Trade unions were legislatively neutered, and by the end of the decade the 'Authority of Government' vis-à-vis organised labour was unquestioned.

CONSTITUENCY MATTERS

Although Younger's majority at the second general election of 1974 had been a healthy 5,098, he was careful not to take his eye off the constituency ball during the 1974–79 Parliament. As ever, the fate of Prestwick International Airport occupied his thoughts, particularly in light of the Labour government's extensive programme of nationalisation. At first it seemed as if Scottish Aviation Ltd (SAL) would be excluded due to its low financial turnover, but by April 1975 it emerged that it would in fact come under state control. 'I greatly fear for the future of jobs at SAL

---

[56] PG/40/75/11, 6/7/1976, GYP.
[57] GY to MT, 14/2/1979, GYP.
[58] MT to GY, 22/2/1979, GYP.

under nationalization,' Younger said at the AGM of the Ayr Conservative Association. 'There is a great danger that the management will be filtered off to some vast headquarters just like the other nationalized industries, and that Prestwick would at best become a branch factory producing small parts for other nationalised factories.'[59]

Tony Benn, the minister responsible, maintained that it would be for the newly nationalised British Aerospace to decide Prestwick's future, so Younger joined forces with the Labour MPs David Lambie and Jim Sillars to lobby Lord Beswick, the minister of state for industry. The trio put forward a proposal – backed by Prestwick's management – that the government should support a civil version of the 'Jetstream' project (a small twin-turbo airliner), enabling the RAF to immediately release ten aircraft. In the event, SAL became a division of British Aerospace on 1 January 1978.

And as the debate on the Scotland Bill continued in the Commons, Younger argued against devolving responsibility for air traffic control to a Scottish Assembly on the basis of his Prestwick experience, saying that the UK-wide British Airports Authority (BAA) and Civil Aviation Authority were best equipped to handle it. 'I can see no advantage in breaking up this system', said Younger, 'and in devolving it to a new and inexperienced legislature the main concern of which is the internal running of part of the United Kingdom.'[60]

Younger was also engaged in battles to save the Seafield Sick Children's Hospital in Ayr during 1978, and more controversially the Craigie College of Education, which was threatened with the axe along with several other further education colleges. Although George accepted that the number of trainee teachers in Scotland had to be reduced, he did not believe closing teacher training colleges was necessarily the way to do it. Bruce Millan, the Scottish Secretary, had lost a division in the Scottish Grand Committee in early 1977 over the plan, and in November Younger led a delegation of Ayrshire and Dumfriesshire MPs to lobby him against closure. 'We repeated the overwhelmingly strong case for retention & he indicated he would be announcing his decision very soon,' Younger recorded in his diary. 'W[illie]. Ross & I agreed afterwards that our impression is that Craigie will be saved, as will Craiglockhart, but Callander Park is more doubtful. Press speculation that Harry Ewing [a Scottish Office under-secretary] would resign if this happened, but I doubt it.'[61] Millan did reprieve Craigie, although without making a firm

---

[59] Speech to Ayr Conservative Association, 3/4/1975, GYP.
[60] Hansard 954 c347.
[61] Diary entry dated 24/11/1977, GYP.

commitment as to its long-term future. It eventually closed in 1993, becoming part of the newly-constituted University of Paisley.

Away from the twin parliamentary preoccupations of defence and devolution, Younger also remained busy in the House of Commons itself. In 1976 his name came near the top of the ballot to introduce a private member's Bill, enabling him to present the Control of Food Premises (Scotland) Bill on 22 December 1976. Its aim was to prohibit the sale of food in circumstances where there was likely to be danger to health and it received cross-party support from Robin Cook, Hector Monro and Russell Johnston. As it was an uncontroversial measure which essentially closed a legal loophole, it won government backing and cleared the House of Lords in July 1977.

ONWARD TO VICTORY

In September 1977 the Shadow Scottish Secretary, Teddy Taylor, proposed 'a major effort to put across the Scottish "Shadow" Team *as a team*'. Besides Taylor, the trio comprised Younger and the Edinburgh MP Alex Fletcher.[62] Taylor said they should go 'on safari' throughout Scotland and organised a joint press conference on 4 September to announce their plan 'to take over St. Andrew's House'. It was a bold move intended to present the trio as a Scottish Office ministerial team-in-waiting, and from 5 September until 1 October they energetically toured the nation.

Younger met representatives of the Highlands and Islands Development Board, the Scottish Special Housing Association, Scotland's New Towns and its power stations, while also embarking upon a 'token' agricultural visit. On Monday 3 October there was another joint press conference, this time in Edinburgh, describing the highlights of the tour. 'We now have a good picture of Scotland's main problems,' Taylor said. 'Everywhere, we were spoken to as the next government of the Scottish Office. We will now follow up these matters in Parliament and are ready to take over as soon as possible.'[63]

With Callaghan's government now lacking the legislative luxury of a majority, all eyes were on a possible snap general election. Younger remained busy with the Scottish Policy Group, which met on 24 February 1978 'to identify any gaps in pledges made to date, with a view to a manifesto and a statement of aims and themes being produced by Teddy Taylor for Perth in May'.[64] This statement of 'aims and themes' caused

---

[62] Fletcher was that rare creature, a comprehensively-educated Tory, while Taylor was a product of the selective High School of Glasgow. Younger, of course, topped them both with Winchester.

[63] TT to GY, c9/1977, GYP.

[64] CRD 4/15/15, 24/2/1978.

problems of its own, particularly for Younger. As he noted in his diary on 15 March:

> T[eddy]T[aylor]'s 'policy document' for the Conference is somewhere in Mrs. T's office. I asked Adam Butler [the son of Rab, who worked in Thatcher's private office] to find out what procedure it is going through as it will be very unacceptable in its present form. T.T. says it is coming before an all-day 'shadow' after Easter. It is a good effort but is full of pledges the Shadow have never heard of and is written in T.T. 'journalese'. T.T. says to collect all my amendments & put them in late en bloc.[65]

Younger's amendments turned out to be pretty scathing. 'No reasons are given for adopting particular policies', he complained in a memo, 'and these policies are not placed in the context of any general approach or principles, either overall or within in subject.' In that sense, he added, 'it does not come anywhere near the level of "The Right Approach" . . . Rather, it reads like a shopping list of policies, some very vague indeed.'[66]

Taylor's document, in the end, was knocked into shape and appeared as a little blue pamphlet in May 1978. *Onward to Victory: A Statement of the Conservative Approach for Scotland* was a sort of tartan *The Right Approach* and sought to draw together recent statements by the party's Scottish spokesmen. 'It is not a manifesto or a complete synopsis of all our policies and pledges,' they explained in the preamble. 'But it shows the *manner* in which a Conservative Government would approach the problems facing Scotland.'

Onward to Victory advocated a second industrial revolution in Scotland, a central theme of Conservative policy being to 'assist and encourage the transition from the old declining industries of the past to those which can make the profits on which well-paid and secure jobs will be based in the future'. The Scottish Conservatives would encourage small businesses, pursue 'a fair and balanced regional policy', and use North Sea oil revenue 'sensibly'. In addition, it stressed the importance of the individual, pledged to reduce taxation and introduce the 'Right to Buy'. Similarly, parents would have the 'Right to Choose' in terms of their children's schooling, while intriguingly it also stressed 'Community' alongside the more traditional Tory commitments to uphold law and order.[67]

Meanwhile, British politics was in flux. The so-called Lib/Lab pact (in which David Steel's Liberals propped up Callaghan's government) was hanging on a thread, an arrangement Younger had always believed was,

[65] Diary entry dated 15/3/1978, GYP.
[66] Undated note, GYP.
[67] *Onward to Victory*, 16.

if nothing else, unconstitutional. As Labour no longer had a working majority, every by-election during the 1974–79 Parliament had the potential to inflict even more damage on a beleaguered administration. Many did. Although the Scottish Conservatives failed to recapture Berwick and East Lothian following the death of the Labour MP and constitutional academic John P. Mackintosh, the opposition received a welcome boost from the Bournemouth East poll in late November 1977. 'Good result in Bournemouth East bye election (9% swing to Cons),' Younger recorded in his diary. 'Liberals disastrously down to 3rd place and only just saving deposit. Another nail in Lib–Lab pact. How long can Steel keep with it?'[68]

A few days earlier, Younger had been among front-bench spokesmen who discussed tactics with Mrs Thatcher. 'Her view is that Callaghan can hang on for a long time as he has everything to lose by going early,' Younger noted. 'We must deflate his "all is well" image about the economy, and fight on general philosophical grounds of a left take-over when election comes.' There was also discussion of internal party affairs. 'It was generally agreed that we produce plenty of good propaganda, but no-one reads it. (Winston [Churchill] had clearly not even read "The Right Approach".)'[69]

Younger also found time to keep up his contacts in the Scottish media and business community, social occasions he enjoyed both for their conviviality and networking opportunities. He lunched at the Garrick in November 1977 with a *Scottish Daily Express* executive called Jimmy Macmillan, whom Younger knew from Stirling circles. 'We agreed wholly on the disasters which have befallen the *Scottish Daily Express,* and the reasons for them,' he wrote in his diary. 'He [Macmillan] confirmed that they are now disengaging from Nationalism as fast as they can without appearing too obvious about it. I suggested a campaign to regenerate Glasgow & West Scotland by massive sales of houses to create home ownership. He is enthusiastic about this . . . The *Express* will be strongly for the Union & Scotland within it.'

Younger was interested in the business aspects of the media industry, noting that the *Express* had 'to find their place again on the right of the popular dailies'. Meetings like this also provided him with useful political feedback. 'He [Macmillan] obviously knows all about the strengths & weaknesses of T.T.! He thinks I am more for the national scene & was better than Ian Gilmour at Defence!'[70]

[68] Diary entry dated 25/11/1977, GYP.
[69] Ibid., 22/11/1977, GYP. Winston was a grandson of the wartime prime minister.
[70] Ibid., 23/11/1977. By 1977 the *Scottish Daily Express* was suffering from declining circulation.

He also found time for more relaxed encounters. 'Lunch with Jeffrey Archer in a superb 7th floor flat on Albert Embankment overlooking the Thames,' recorded Younger in late 1977. 'Jeffrey is a millionaire again thanks to Jackie Onassis resigning from board of her publishers because of J's book "Shall we tell the President?" Actually it was not the book but an article about it in *Boston Globe & Mail* which offended her. J in great demand for TV interviews all over U.S. as a result. He wants the name of a good hotel in Scotland where he can revise his next book.'[71] Younger suggested the Turnberry Hotel in Ayrshire, and for six weeks in early 1978 Archer revised what was to become one of his biggest sellers, *Kane and Abel*.[72] George and Diana were also regular attendees at Archer's famous champagne and shepherd's pie parties.

The 1974–79 Parliament was also very lively, providing plenty of the political theatrics that both fascinated and entertained Younger. In December 1977 there was a late-night debate on the sacking of Peter Thompson, a senior sheriff who had enraged the government by campaigning for a referendum on devolution. The Scottish Secretary tabled a motion for him to be removed, but it required a majority of both Houses of Parliament in order to pass. 'Robin Maxwell Hyslop & the hard-line Tories [were] determined to support the sheriff in order to spite [Michael] Foot who has handled it very badly,' recorded Younger in his diary. 'He should never have arrogated to himself the decision as to whether to hear Thomson[*sic*]. I, and most Scots Tories supported the Govt as Bruce Millan has carried out the law (1971 Act) with complete correctness. We won, but the Press tend to support Thomson, in absolutely blissful ignorance of the facts.'[73]

Younger also attended a meeting to discuss inaugural elections to the European Parliament due in 1979. 'Govt now wants (next week) to finish clause 1 & then move to Cl. 3 so as to deal with the voting method,' wrote Younger. 'I can't make out if our anti Europe lot are going to filibuster or not. After much argument, we decided to have a 3 line whip to be there but we can actually vote either way.' Younger had always been sympathetic to arguments for more representative voting systems, particularly for the proposed Scottish Assembly. He added: 'Many Tories hate PR & anyway they think embarrassing the govt is more important than believing in Europe. I think that sort of trick usually bounces back! Mrs. T just back from yet another tour – NATO, Brussels, & Yugoslavia. She seems in good form.'[74]

[71] Diary entry dated 22/11/1977, GYP.
[72] A 2008 Jeffrey Archer novel, *A Prisoner of Birth*, included a character called Munro. 'He is a little like the late George Younger,' explained Archer. 'People who have achieved the most amazing things, and hide it' (*Financial Times* 8/3/2008).
[73] Diary entry dated 5/12/1977, GYP.
[74] Ibid., 7/12/1977, GYP.

Although the Labour government was wracked with internal divisions and external pressures, the Conservative opposition was far from harmonious. This led to political rows which both amused and frustrated Younger, who always placed party loyalty above self interest. One such row blew up in March 1978 between Humphrey Atkins, the Conservative Chief Whip, and Teddy Taylor over a vote on the Local Government (Scotland) Bill. Younger recalled that

> T.T. wanted to vote because we had won in ctte but Russell [Fairgrieve] told H[umphrey] that the Party in Scotland did not want this amdt. (putting local elections on to Tuesday). TT again thinks R[ussell] is working against him but he is wrong. Russell Fairgreave merely answered questions (correctly). Truth is that H does not want to keep Party to vote on anything Scottish, because they get bolshie. It makes me mad when remembering how the English block all devolution & then won't bother to work the present system. T.T. again v emotional in the lobby & H had heated argument with him. Eventually he simmered down & we won't vote![75]

Nor was this sort of spat confined to the party in Scotland. Later that year Younger attended a stormy meeting of the 1922 Committee which took place shortly after Winston Churchill and John Biggs-Davison were sacked from the front bench for voting to end sanctions in Rhodesia instead of abstaining as per the Shadow Cabinet line. Even a decade after Ian Smith's Unilateral Declaration of Independence, events in the former British colony could still split the Conservative Party. Julian Amery, son of Leo, and Maurice Macmillan, son of Harold, led the onslaught. Younger recorded:

> Humphrey Atkins was present and took much criticism although mostly veiled. He replied at the end rather feebly saying he would report all views to the Leader. He has handled it badly, as a free vote would have been adequate, and avoided this mess. On the other hand it was a Shadow Cabinet decision so perhaps not his fault. It is basically the same nonsense as took place in 1976 over the Scotland & Wales Bill second reading. That too would have avoided much bloodshed if a free vote had been allowed.
>
> Fortunately (for the Leadership) Amery & Co so overdid it that most uncommitted opinion in the Party was against him even among many who themselves voted to end sanctions. The Macmillan, Amery, Churchill clique has had far too much influence with Leadership on a 'family pressure' basis for

---

[75] Diary entry dated 14/3/1978, GYP.

too long. It is to be hoped that this episode will lessen their influence at least for a time.

Winston behaves very badly. He is big-headed, uses his grandfather's name in rather an odious way and always suits himself rather than the Party. He has a lot to learn.[76]

In November 1978 the government announced formal sanctions against the car manufacturer Ford for breaking a five per cent pay limit and instead awarding its workers a 17.5 per cent increase. 'We are, as usual, in difficulty as to whether we have an all-out attack on Govt for this next week or not,' recorded Younger in his diary. 'The media (exc[luding the] *Mirror*) very critical of arbitrary nature of sanctions, but some Tories think the public likes to see Jim standing up to the Unions even if they do it by clobbering management!'[77] In the end, the opposition opted for a supply day debate not about Ford but concerning the use of sanctions. On 7 December Younger recorded:

At lunch in H of C, Mrs. T was expressing determination to defeat Govt over Ford sanctions and to vote against the Xmas adjournment to expose them for clearly trying to get rid of Parl[iamen]t for as long as possible. In the event the left staged a revolt on the formal estimates motions (defence spending was a prominent feature) & talked until closure at 1745. They then voted on all 5 resolutions. Thereafter there were more points of order, [and] the House was nearly out of control. The Govt had completely lost control of its own supporters & Mrs. T and Norman St John Stevas laid into them so effectively that they abandoned the Ford Sanctions debate at about 2030. On the whole a win on points for us. They avoided the sanctions vote which they would have lost, but will now have to face it again by some means next week. It has exposed the left-wing to public view again & this must help us.

The 1922 Cttte was in a very stupid mood, and objected to the idea of voting against the Xmas adjournment on the grounds that this would be an incursion into a backbenchers realm by the front bench. I should have intervened (but didn't) to defend the idea. Peculiar situations often need peculiar remedies, and Mrs. T's idea was worth while.[78]

Relations between Younger and Mrs Thatcher by this point were warm, with the events of late 1976 now a distant memory. He even defended her

---

[76] Ibid., 10/11/1978, GYP.
[77] Ibid., 29/11/1978, GYP.
[78] Ibid., 7/12/1978, GYP.

honour in complaining to Lady Birk, the environment minister responsible for an exhibition in Westminster Hall to mark the fiftieth anniversary of the equal voting rights for women. A portrait of Thatcher was given a more prominent place after Younger objected that it was 'tucked away as though she was nobody'.[79]

An issue which many MPs – both Labour and Conservative – probably wished could have been tucked away was devolution for Scotland. Younger had supported the creation of a Scottish Assembly since Edward Heath's Declaration of Perth in 1968, and the Labour government's ill-fated legislation to establish such an assembly dominated the 1974–79 Parliament.

---

[79] *The Times* 19/7/1978. Younger sent Thatcher Lady Birk's response. 'I can only say "Well done!"', Mrs Thatcher replied. '*Very* well done!' (MT to GY, 21/7/1978, GYP).

Chapter 11

'A PERPETUAL BED OF NAILS'

THE SUCCESS OF THE SNP at the February 1974 general election once again brought the devolution issue to the fore. It had bubbled below the surface of Heath's troubled administration, but the sudden political reality of seven SNP MPs on the opposition benches, rising to eleven in a second poll eight months later, caused panic in the ranks – both Conservative and Labour. Consequently, the Parliaments of 1974–79 were more concerned with constitutional issues than any other since the war.[1]

The Conservative manifesto at the uncertain first election had more or less fudged the issue, claiming that the findings of the recent Kilbrandon Report would merely be studied. 'Devolution – the delegation of authority away from the centre within our country – is the opposite of independence,' it read. 'Much administrative devolution has already been carried out. Our aim is to achieve the most effective and acceptable form of further devolution.'[2] The fact that a Conservative government had had nearly four years to achieve an 'effective and acceptable' form of further devolution was simply ignored.

Alick Buchanan-Smith, who was soon to emerge as the standard bearer for the pro-devolutionists within the party, was appointed Shadow Scottish Secretary soon after the first election defeat. 'I have always felt it was a neck and neck between Alick and yourself,' Tony Stodart wrote to Younger, expressing hope that he was not too disappointed, 'two who *fully* measured up to the job – or for that matter to any other. Perhaps one thing to reflect on is that S[ecretary]. of S[tate for Scotland]. lies over a perpetual bed of nails!'[3] As both Buchanan-Smith and Younger would soon discover, that perpetual bed of nails was very uncomfortable indeed.

---

[1] This constitutional scrutiny applied not only to Scotland but also Wales, Northern Ireland (where the Troubles continued) and membership of the European Union (subject to a referendum in 1975).

[2] Conservative manifesto, 2/1974.

[3] Tony Stodart to GY, 12/3/1974, GYP.

Tory minds quickly turned to the Unionist response. Buchanan-Smith established a 'Devolution Group' to examine the Conservative reaction, and invited Younger to join as well as Ian MacArthur, Alex Fletcher, Iain Sproat, Michael Ancram and Malcolm Rifkind, a bright young lawyer who had recently been elected to represent Edinburgh Pentlands. Two memos were circulated at the group's first meeting on 10 April, a populist set of proposals from Teddy Taylor, and a more cautious list of options from Younger. Focusing more on the financial aspects of devolution, George said it was 'probably true that Scotland . . . gets more money by this method [the block grant] than it would by any other'. But, he added, 'this method is invisible and cuts no ice with the public. Perhaps we should in future allocate a global sum, voted after debate at Westminster and leave Scotland (either Scottish Office or Assembly) to have complete freedom in its allocation within Scotland.' Furthermore, a 'clearly defined proportion of all oil and gas revenues (not only Scottish) could be included. In this way Treasury would keep control over the total sums (which they are well equipped to doing) but not the breakdown within Scotland (which they are ill equipped to do).'[4] With SNP cries of 'It's Scotland's Oil' still ringing out, Younger clearly intended this as a means of silencing them.

Despite the 1973 Scottish Conservative conference having rejected Heath's devolution policy, by mid-1974 many leading Scottish Conservatives still supported the creation of a Scottish Assembly, although they differed as to how much power it should have. When Buchanan-Smith's 'Devolution Group' reported just before the Scottish party conference in May 1974, it again fudged the issue. 'All indications are that the support of the S.N.P. is likely to increase,' it accurately predicted, as October's election would show. 'There is a need, stronger than ever before, that the Conservative Party should have an identifiable and definite policy on devolution which it can put to the Scottish people.' The group (of which Younger was still a member) recommended basing the oil exploration and production divisions of the Department of Energy in Scotland and the creation of a minister of oil production with a seat in the Cabinet. Crucially, the report continued, 'The Committee believe it would be desirable to establish some form of Scottish Assembly.' Its powers, however, were to be limited. First and second readings would continue at Westminster, while membership would – at least initially – be indirectly elected from the new regional and district councils. This, the group believed, would reconcile the demands of the Scottish electorate with 'objections that have been raised within the Scottish Conservative Party membership'.[5]

---

[4] Minute dated 10/4/1974, GYP.
[5] Report dated 9/5/1974, GYP.

There was no direct mention of Home's 1970 proposals, but this new scheme was heavily derivative, albeit with an additional oil dimension based on Younger's own proposals. The report fed directly into Heath's *Charter for a New Scotland* which was unveiled and endorsed by the May Scottish Conservative conference, and subsequently included in the October 1974 manifesto. 'The policy changes since the election are nothing short of dramatic,' boasted Younger to the *Scotsman*. 'If they [Labour] produce a plan [for a Scottish Assembly] we shall look at it and if we agree with it we shall say so . . . [but] it will clearly be seen that we took this seriously long before they did.'[6]

In September, Harold Wilson's minority Labour government had begun to take the government of Scotland seriously with a white paper, *Democracy and Devolution*, which pledged to implement the Kilbrandon proposals of 1973. For the first time, all three major UK parties – as well as the SNP in Scotland – were committed to some form of devolution.

The general election of October 1974 gave the Nationalists an additional four seats, which convinced Younger and other leading Scottish Conservatives that a coherent devolutionary scheme was necessary. Six days after the election, Alick Buchanan-Smith and George announced at a press conference that Tory MPs would support the Labour government's scheme for a directly-elected Assembly. Edward Heath, still party leader despite two consecutive defeats, also remained committed to a Scottish Assembly. His successor, however, had other ideas.

'The Scottish party itself was deeply split,' remembered Thatcher in her memoirs, 'with the critics of devolution representing much grassroots opinion pitted against the left-leaning Scottish party leadership of people like Alick Buchanan-Smith, Malcolm Rifkind and George Younger.'[7] Yet in her first, tumultuous, visit to Scotland as leader on 21 February 1975 (accompanied by Younger as Scottish chairman and Buchanan-Smith as Shadow Scottish Secretary), she reiterated her party's support for a Scottish Assembly, even boasting that it had 'led the field' in supporting the 'distribution of decision making and administration'.[8]

Meanwhile, the party's two devolution groups continued to meet, with Younger playing an active role. Despite the recent electoral success of the SNP, he believed that 'most people still feel that they are really

[6] *Scotsman*, c6/1974. 'In any case,' Younger added, 'people are not going to vote for or against the Labour Party on the grounds of devolution but on the grounds of the socialisation or nationalisation of our whole lives.'
[7] Thatcher, *The Path to Power*, 322.
[8] Speech in Candleriggs, 21/2/1975, MTF.

Conservative or Labour, even if they vote for the Nationalists'.[9] The real task, thought Younger, was educational rather than constitutional: if only Scots could appreciate the existing machinery of government, he argued, demand for independence would subside. But more broadly, George still thought the Home proposals of 1970 were the best option, and 'as near as we would ever get to uniting the English Party and the Scottish Party'. If asked what the Conservatives would implement in government, he said, 'we should say "of course, Douglas-Home".'[10]

Buchanan-Smith, Younger and Malcolm Rifkind sounded out colleagues during the spring of 1975 and concluded that although most MPs thought the starting point should remain the Home proposals, 'it ought to be possible to put much more attractive clothes on the skeleton of the proposals we had at the last election'.[11] Some Scottish MPs and Shadow Cabinet members, however, feared that even such a modest compromise was too close to full separation. On 11 April the Shadow Cabinet agreed that 'the Party should not be motivated simply by electoral considerations in its formulation of its devolution policy: mistakes would involve drastic consequences for the whole United Kingdom.'[12]

'Alick Buchanan-Smith is working flat out to make sure we have policies that Scotland needs,' Mrs Thatcher told Scottish Conservative Party delegates on 17 May 1975. 'I would simply underline today all that he said in Thursday's debate on the Government of Scotland. We are committed to a directly elected Assembly.'[13] Buchanan-Smith was certainly working flat out and personally favoured PR (proportional representation) elections, as did Younger, who believed it would 'balance out to some extent the concentration of the population in the South West'. A joint Tory/Labour policy on this was touted, but Younger was conscious, as ever, of the political consequences. It 'would allow the Scottish Nationalists to pose as the only gallant defenders of Scotland's interests; and if what was produced was universally condemned by the Scottish Press, we would be in the position of looking like English lackeys, following the English line.'[14]

By the time the Study Group met next on 1 October 1975, Younger and Buchanan-Smith were pushing for Conservative proposals to go much further than Douglas-Home's in anticipation of a government scheme expected to give extensive legislative and executive devolution

[9] CRD 4/15/8, 16/1/1975.

[10] Ibid., 18/3/1975.

[11] ABS to WW, 1/4/1975, GYP (copy).

[12] CRD 4/15/8, 11/4/1975.

[13] Speech dated 17/5/1975, MTF.

[14] CRD 4/15/8, 2/7/1975. Younger later agreed to become a vice-chairman of the Scottish Campaign for a Representative Assembly.

to Scotland. At another meeting on 21 October, the Shadow Scottish Secretary warned that the Conservatives 'were in the position of having to react to Government proposals, which would probably go further than our own'. 'If', he added, 'we were to hold back and cling rigidly to the Douglas-Home proposals we should make ourselves isolated and irrelevant to the devolution debate.'[15]

That same month – October 1975 – Younger also stood down as chairman of the party in Scotland, having served his pre-agreed year-long term. John Davidson, a senior Scottish party official who had also recently stood aside, wrote to Younger on 27 October:

> Like you I am depressed by the state of the Party where friends in Scotland are serving us ill. Of even greater concern is the attitude of your colleagues in the South who may present the SNP with a huge and undeserved bonus by adopting a stance [that] could make the English Tories seem ignorant, insensitive and colonial in their attitude to Scotland. I fully share your views on devolution and it is up to you to stop our English MPs from fraternal assassination![16]

The 'friends in Scotland' to whom Davidson referred were a noisy and articulate band of Scottish Conservative MPs led by the colourful Member for Glasgow Cathcart, Teddy Taylor, and including the formidable Betty Harvie Anderson. All were resolutely unreconstructed on the devolution issue and built opposition among Tory MPs throughout 1975.

Still senior Conservatives laboured over the devolution issue. The Shadow Cabinet on 12 November somewhat vaguely resolved to support only a scheme which 'retained the UK'. The following week's meeting elaborated a little further, asserting that it was 'fully committed to a Scottish Assembly, together with a share for Scotland in the revenues from North Sea oil', but that the 'grant of powers to any Scottish Assembly should recognise the ultimate legislative and executive authority of Westminster'.[17]

Malcolm Rifkind – then a federalist – was invited to prepare yet another paper for circulation before the 26 November Shadow Cabinet. This document, which was circulated to Shadow ministers on 23 November, included a crucial shift in Conservative thinking on Scottish devolution. Although the proposed Scottish Assembly would be directly elected, it would not have an executive of its own and instead be an

---

[15] Minute dated 21/10/1975, GYP.
[16] John Davidson to GY, 27/10/1975, GYP.
[17] CRD 4/15/8, 19/11/1975.

'integrated' chamber of the UK Parliament. Although contrived, Rifkind was clearly trying to appease Teddy Taylor *et al*. Agreeing, Mrs Thatcher clearly intended Heath's devolution policy to suffer death by a thousand cuts.

The Devolution Policy Group, as it was now called, next met on 26 November 1975 with Willie Whitelaw in the chair and Younger, Nick Edwards, Rifkind, Graham Wynn (from Conservative Central Office (CCO)) and an increasingly uncomfortable Alick Buchanan-Smith in attendance. At Shadow Cabinet the same day, Rifkind's paper was approved although it was agreed that Conservatives should 'try to avoid making a number of firm, long term, detailed commitments on the subject [of devolution], as it was thought that the Government proposals were unlikely in their present form to survive a prolonged period of debate, during which public opinion might change considerably.'[18] The retreat was well under way.

Younger, however, remained enthusiastic, and when the government's white paper, *Our Changing Democracy: Devolution to Scotland and Wales*,[19] finally appeared a few days later, he enthused to the Pentland Autumn Fair that

At last we have a White paper on Devolution as a basis for action, and Scottish Conservatives who have pursued this aim since 1968 must welcome this historic step. Of course there are many respects in which the details of the Government's proposals are wrong but that is no reason for condemning the whole thing as the SNP have done . . . Our task is to improve the Government's proposals which are in many ways ill thought out and disappointing.[20]

Mrs Thatcher also remained on message but increasingly hedged it with reservations and conditions while some Shadow Cabinet members began considering a simple motion condemning the white paper outright. 'Unless it is qualified by some form of commitment to devolution or to the Assembly,' Buchanan-Smith protested in a letter to Whitelaw, 'it will be interpreted in Scotland as the first step in the Conservative withdrawal from devolution. . .to talk always in terms of generalities does not encourage confidence!'[21]

Once again, the perpetual bed of nails had exposed deep divisions in the Conservative Party. A directly-elected Assembly was simply unacceptable

[18] Minute dated 26/11/1975, GYP.
[19] This committed the government to devolutionary assemblies for Wales and Scotland, the latter with 142 members, but excluded the Scottish Development Agency from the new executive's remit.
[20] Speech to Pentland Autumn Fair, 29/11/1975, GYP.
[21] ABS to WW, 30/12/1975, GYP (copy). In a Freudian slip, Buchanan-Smith had originally written 'withdrawal from Scotland'.

to the majority of MPs. In a memo circulated by Buchanan-Smith, the Shadow Scottish Secretary attempted to make senior figures see sense. Voting against the Bill and it nevertheless going on to a second reading, he argued, would enable Labour to exploit the Conservatives as scapegoats. If the party did not make up its mind soon, he warned, 'There is danger of the Party splitting still further in different directions.'[22]

The year 1976 was a stressful one for the Scottish Conservative Party, and also for George Younger and Alick Buchanan-Smith personally. In January Younger was sacked, without any warning, as Shadow Defence Secretary (see pp. 123–127), while in December Buchanan-Smith would resign as Shadow Scottish Secretary.

Mrs Thatcher's scepticism about devolution had hardened by January and she continued tacitly to encourage anti-Assembly elements within the party. The Commons debate on the government white paper was set for mid-January, and on 6 January the Shadow Cabinet again discussed its ever-changing position. It agreed to support an Assembly but oppose a separate executive (as proposed by the white paper), which was curiously judged likely to 'lead to further demands for separatism'.[23] A referendum on Scottish independence was also out of the question, as was Younger's favoured electoral system for the new Assembly. Mrs Thatcher was to speak first in the four-day debate.

By now, it seemed as if outright opposition to the white paper was just another cut away. Ominously, Graham Wynn, who covered constitutional issues for the Conservative Research Department, warned Whitelaw that if the party came out firmly against an Assembly then the Scottish Party 'would be split down the middle both in Parliament and in the country'.[24] Eleven Scottish Tory MPs were judged to be firmly pro-Assembly, including Younger, while only five were thought to be deeply opposed.

Beyond the Parliamentary Party, (broadly speaking) most prospective candidates were devolutionists; most constituency chairmen had become reluctant Assemblyites; while both the Federation of Conservative Students in Scotland and the Scottish Young Conservatives were also keen supporters of devolution. Only when it came to constituency activists was there a recognisable majority against. Younger later reported the views of Scottish businessmen to Mrs Thatcher. They were, he said, evenly split between pro and anti-Assembly, but 'even those who were against the idea . . . agreed (with one exception) that a commitment by the

---

[22] Undated memo, GYP.
[23] Minute dated 6/1/1976, GYP.
[24] CRD 4/15/10, 31/3/1976.

Conservative Party to make no change whatsoever in the present situation was unrealistic politically.'[25]

George spoke in favour of 'maximum devolution' at a special meeting of the Central Council of the Scottish Conservative Party in Edinburgh on 11 January 1976. Delegates voted by 103 to 60 in favour of a Rifkind-drafted resolution which reaffirmed the Council's 'commitment to a directly elected Scottish Assembly' but condemned the government's white paper as 'unworkable'.[26] The official opposition amendment to the government motion, however, affirmed the need for a Scottish Assembly but omitted the words 'directly elected'.

Although both Younger and Buchanan-Smith had reluctantly accepted the 'third chamber' compromise, they were far from happy. Meanwhile, the diehards grew in confidence, forming a patriotic 'Keep Britain United' group – which included Teddy Taylor and Iain Sproat – just a week before the 1976 Scottish Conservative Party conference. Uncharacteristically, Younger hit out at the group during a speech in Wick. Describing it as a 'front' for all those opposed to devolution, 'its aim is to stampede the Conservatives into abandoning their long-standing belief in decentralisation and devolution on the basis of a short, sharp, scare campaign.' This, argued Younger, had to be resisted, because 'the place to which they are leading us is the political wilderness. By various counts between 60% and 80% of Scots want some form of Devolution, and over half want some sort of Assembly. Scottish Conservatives were first in the field eight years ago with a proposal for an Assembly and to go back on it now would quite simply be political suicide.'[27]

At the Perth conference the following week, Mrs Thatcher once again reiterated Conservative support for devolution, although she was careful not to go into too much detail. Thereafter the issue languished as MPs awaited publication of a Bill based on the white paper, although in September Lord Home and Edward Heath called for any devolutionary scheme for Scotland (and Wales) to be subject to a referendum, a proposal which Younger supported. *The Right Approach*, an influential statement of Conservative aims and policies, also appeared that autumn, and included a typically vague Assembly commitment.

Finally, in November 1976, the government's Scotland and Wales Bill was unveiled. Unlike the white paper, this retained the posts of Welsh and Scottish Secretaries and therefore proposed two rival executives: one to be controlled by the Assembly's first secretary, and the other by the secretary

---

[25] GY to MT, 5/5/1976, GYP.
[26] *Scotsman* 12/1/1976.
[27] Speech dated 7/5/1976, GYP.

of state. Whitelaw established a steering committee to guide future work on the Bill, but the time had come for Mrs Thatcher to inflict the unkindest cut of all.

All hell broke loose after a marathon Shadow Cabinet meeting the following month, which ended in the early hours of Thursday 2 December after the decision was taken to oppose completely the Scotland and Wales Bill on a three-line whip. Whitelaw's support for the U-turn had been crucial. 'I had no illusion that this could be done without some resignations,' recalled Thatcher in her memoirs. 'I wanted to minimize them, but not at the expense of failing to lance the devolution boil.'

The morning after the Shadow Cabinet meeting Malcolm Rifkind, George Younger, John Corrie (the Scottish Whip), Hector Monro, Hamish Gray and Russell Fairgrieve (the Scottish Party chairman) all went to see Mrs Thatcher, arguing that Alick Buchanan-Smith should be given special dispensation to abstain in the vote or else all six of them would resign their front-bench posts. 'I could not agree to this,'[28] remembered Thatcher, so five days later Buchanan-Smith and his deputy Malcolm Rifkind resigned from the Conservative front bench.[29]

'Whatever the niceties of parliamentary procedure,' the Shadow Scottish Secretary told reporters, 'in reality to vote against the second reading of the Bill would be a vote against the principle of devolution.'[30] Mrs Thatcher recalled: 'Four other front benchers wanted to go, but I refused their resignations and even allowed one of them to speak against our line in the debate and vote with the Government. No Party leader could have done more. To replace Alick Buchanan-Smith I moved Teddy Taylor, whose robust patriotism and soundness had long impressed me, from Trade to become Shadow Scottish Secretary.'[31]

Mrs Thatcher's first choice, however, had been Betty Harvie Anderson, a staunch anti-devolutionist and friend and neighbour of Younger's parents in Stirlingshire, but when she refused,[32] the mantle fell on Taylor. George had only returned to the front bench in November as a junior spokesman on Scottish affairs (specifically local government),[33] and his pragmatism dictated that it made more sense to acquiesce (albeit under

---

[28]   Thatcher, *The Path to Power*, 325–26.

[29]   'It was a big decision for him as he felt very divided loyalties – to the country or to the party,' Janet Buchanan-Smith recalled. 'Incidentally when he died, he was against the plans for devolution. Too much water had flowed under too many bridges!' (Janet Buchanan-Smith to the author, 6/2/2007).

[30]   *The Times* 9/12/1976.

[31]   Thatcher, *The Path to Power*,325.

[32]   Betty Harvie Anderson to MT, 8/12/1976. Harvie Anderson could not stomach the continuing commitment to a 'directly elected' Assembly.

[33]   Sir Malcolm Rifkind remembers Mrs Thatcher initially being reluctant to reappoint Younger to the front bench, but changed her mind following representations from colleagues.

protest) rather than quit over the issue. Instead, he and others argued that allowing the party a free vote would be a sensible compromise in the circumstances, although *The Times* reported that only three other members of the Shadow Cabinet backed Buchanan-Smith's stance, including Lord Hailsham, who would also have resigned had it not been for an intervention from Lord Carrington.[34]

On 8 December – the day of Buchanan-Smith's resignation – the Shadow Cabinet issued a statement explaining its decision to vote against the Bill following its regular Wednesday meeting. 'We do so because we oppose the *method* of devolution proposed in it,' it read. 'Our belief in the *principle* of devolution and the need for a directly elected Assembly for Scotland, as expressed in our second pledge, remains unaltered.'[35]

The Shadow Cabinet's decision caused dismay among constituency associations in Scotland, and the backlash was politically messy. John Bowis, a CCO official, visited Scotland on 13 December and found that the 'majority felt the commitment to devolution had been betrayed'. 'I regret to say I met not one single person who understood the Shadow Cabinet's decision and approved it.' Bowis also spoke to a number of people who 'regretted that George Younger or Alex Fletcher has not been appointed. On balance however, Teddy Taylor's appointment was not disapproved of, because it was felt that, whatever his views, at least they will be vociferous in Scotland.'[36]

Many were impressed that Younger agreed to stay on as one of Taylor's deputies. Having been in the Shadow Cabinet until the beginning of that year, he was technically senior to Taylor in the party's hierarchy. Younger had also yet to make up his mind as to how he planned to vote on the second reading of the Scotland and Wales Bill on 13 December. 'I do not intend to vote against the Bill,' he told *The Times*. 'In all probability I shall be abstaining. I think it is a bad Bill, and it needs major improvements, but I am firmly of the belief that the House of Commons ought to debate this thoroughly.'[37]

At the final division, 42 Conservatives including Edward Heath, Russell Fairgrieve and Younger either abstained or were paired under the 'conscience clause' sanctioned by Thatcher. There were five – including Buchanan-Smith, Hamish Gray and Malcolm Rifkind – who voted with

---

[34] A similar situation arose over sanctions against Rhodesia in 1978, when several MPs defied the Tory whip. 'It is basically the same nonsense as took place in 1976 over the Scotland & Wales Bill second reading,' Younger wrote in his diary. 'That too would have avoided much bloodshed if a free vote had been allowed' (diary entry dated 10/11/1978, GYP).

[35] CRD 4/15/8, 8/12/1976.

[36] CCO 20/11/82, 13/12/1976.

[37] *The Times* 11/12/1976.

the government. Labour was just as divided, with 29 of its MPs abstaining and ten even voting with the Conservatives. Overall there was a 45-vote majority for the Bill, but an awful lot more unhappiness – on both sides.

Meanwhile, Mrs Thatcher trod a delicate line between her own opposition and those who still supported devolution by denouncing the government scheme as 'a thoroughly bad Bill'. But although she was superficially effective in criticising the government's plans, it became increasingly obvious that Mrs Thatcher could offer no constructive alternative to this 'bad Bill'. 'Our proposals lack credibility because . . . they have not been sold,' assessed a CRD briefing. 'In addition, there is a widespread belief that not even the leadership of the Party really believes in them.'[38]

By the beginning of 1977 the Conservative Party was preparing to jettison the last remaining elements of its devolution policy. By then, Francis Pym had replaced Willie Whitelaw as the Shadow Cabinet's main devolution spokesman, and while Pym wanted to make the government's Bill 'work-able', the new Shadow Scottish Secretary, Teddy Taylor, wanted to bury it. '[I]t was & is very hard to see all the things he [Buchanan-Smith] has worked so hard for falling about his ears,' wrote Janet Buchanan-Smith to Younger soon after the disruption. 'However, I am sure things will look up soon. You really must be having quite a tough time yourself, knowing in which direction that wee man from Cathcart is going off in next!'[39]

The direction soon emerged although Younger was determined to handle amendments to the Bill in a constructive manner. Labour back-benchers were not quite as reasonable. On 10 February the government was forced to accept an amendment from the Welsh Labour MP Leo Abse, signed by 80 Labour MPs, to hold consultative referendums in Scotland and Wales. Even worse was to come. On 22 February Michael Foot,[40] who was nominally in charge of devolution policy for the government, tabled a guillotine motion in order to ensure the Bill's survival. This, however, was defeated by a majority of 29, including 22 Labour MPs who voted with the opposition. Devolution, for the time being, was dead, and the nine-year-old Conservative pledge to set up a Scottish Assembly effectively died with it.

Even before the demise of the Bill, the Shadow Cabinet had begun

---

[38] CRD 4/15/11, 20/12/1976.

[39] Janet Buchanan-Smith to GY, 28/1/1977, GYP.

[40] One of Michael Foot's officials dealing with devolution at the Cabinet Office was Michael Quinlan, who would later be one of Younger's permanent under-secretaries at the Ministry of Defence.

toying with the idea of a constitutional conference as a way out. Francis Pym saw it as something which would unite both pro- and anti-devolutionists, but Teddy Taylor did not agree, arguing that it 'would restrict the party's freedom to slide away from the devolution commitment'.[41] Nevertheless, the Shadow Cabinet agreed that an all-party convention should be proposed, with the caveat that it would not be committed to implementing its conclusions if the Conservatives were returned to power.

Younger unveiled the new initiative when he took over as chairman of the Scottish Policy Group at a meeting two days later. But although outwardly loyal, he was in fact continuing to agitate behind the scenes to avert any further watering down of the Assembly commitment. George even put his name to a letter sent by Buchanan-Smith to Mrs Thatcher at the end of March 1977:

> At present it is not possible to envisage the political situation in Scotland that will face the next Conservative Government. Whatever the wishes of some sections of the Party, it may be necessary for the next Conservative Government to introduce legislation providing for a substantial devolution of powers to a directly-elected Scottish Assembly. By maintaining our existing commitment to such an Assembly the freedom of action of the next Conservative Government to take such steps as may be necessary will be greatly strengthened.[42]

Thatcher replied on 5 April saying she had not retracted the Assembly pledge and did 'not intend to do so'.

> Exactly what we say in an election campaign must depend upon the circumstances at the time of that election; the progress of the all party talks; and the proposals, if any, the Government has advanced in the meantime. For the moment, I agree with you that we should keep our options open. There are dangers in suggesting a detailed policy prematurely. We are committed now to an all-party convention, without preconditions, to see whether or not it is possible to reach any degree of accord on the issues raised by the call for devolution. I am sure that would be the best way forward.[43]

Despite her private, and strongly held, beliefs regarding devolution, Thatcher was clearly trying to be conciliatory. However, on 27 April the Shadow Cabinet agreed that the line for the forthcoming Scottish Conservative Party conference should be that an all-party approach was

[41] CCO 20/11/82.
[42] A draft of the letter was sent by ABS to GY, 17/3/1977, GYP.
[43] MT to ABS, 5/4/1977, GYP (copy).

the best way forward. With a minimum of fuss and opposition, Mrs Thatcher was able to jettison quietly her party's devolution pledge during her speech in Perth just two weeks later.

By July 1977 the government had resurrected its legislative proposals, this time as two separate Bills covering Scottish and Welsh devolution. The Scotland Bill fast became a millstone around the government's neck. Although it did pass its second reading on 14 November, 16 of Labour's February dissidents again withheld their support. Instead there were several wrecking amendments, the most destructive of which was tabled by the London-Scottish MP George Cunningham. It stipulated that 40 per cent of the total Scottish electorate had to back an Assembly for the Scotland Act to take effect. It was carried as a result of Conservative abstentions on, appropriately enough, Burns Night in 1978, and did more than anything else to scupper devolution for Scotland.

Younger's position had now hardened, and his was one of six names – along with Mrs Thatcher – on a reasoned amendment calling on the government to set up a constitutional conference to report no later than July 1978. On 16 November 1977 the government guillotined the Scotland Bill in order to ensure its survival, something George said it did 'without a shred of any normal justification'.[44] This time, however, the Bill survived with a majority of 26. The remainder of the debate on the Bill was long and tedious, a flavour of which is provided by Younger's occasional diary from the period:

24 November 1977
Long talk with John Smith [the devolution minister and future Labour leader] after Division. He does not care about details of Scotland Bill – they will now get it one way or another. He is confident that referendum vote will be 'Yes'. Thinks Alick has been courageous. He is against 'umbrella' organisations for referendum as Labour will not work with SNP. I stressed that we don't want to fight it as a Party as this will embarrass pro-devolutionists in Tory Party & anti's in Labour Party. He agreed & thinks campaign should be fairly low key anyway . . .

5 December 1977
1615 steering ctte for Scotland Bill. Francis Pym in charge. I arrived a little late to find I am to do clauses 24–32. Only a minimum of instructions as I just make my own rules.

---

[44] *The Times* 17/11/1977.

7 December 1977

Two very boring days on Scotland Bill. Poor attendance and no meaning-ful dialogue with govt. who need give way on nothing now they have a time-table . . .

8 December 1977

Govt has been defeated twice this week – once on Cl. 40 of Scotland Bill & once in Lords over defence. But this doesn't matter any more, they soldier on![45]

Nevertheless, throughout January 1978, Younger took an active part in debates, dealing with amendments on the rate support grant for local authorities, while urging that general economic powers (including regional development) should not be devolved. 'I have felt that strongly all through,' he reasoned, 'in spite of other views I may have held on devolution.' Younger argued that Scottish industry functioned within a UK context, whether the SNP liked it or not. 'My final point is to make a plea for the Assembly itself,' he added. 'If the Bill becomes law and the Assembly is set up, it will have a massive task. The Assembly will have a tremendous number of difficult decisions to make . . . Let us not overload it with many extra matters at this stage.'[46]

In early May 1978 the Scotland Bill was carried, and received Royal Assent on 31 July. In his memoirs, Norman Tebbit praised Whitelaw's role in the steady watering down of the party's devolution commitment. 'At the time he took on responsibility as our spokesman the Party had favoured devolution,' he observed. 'By 1978 we opposed it but no one could quite remember how or when the U-turn had been made. It was the stuff of genius.'[47] Even so, and despite the Cunningham amendment, Younger fully expected a Scottish Assembly soon to become a reality.

Meanwhile, Younger's reference to 'umbrella' organisations in his 24 November 1977 diary entry precipitated yet another internal row. Charles Bell, a senior figure in the Scottish Conservative Party's volunteer wing, wrote to Mrs Thatcher on 19 December proposing a cross-party 'no' campaign in the planned devolution referendum. This was to include figures like the Labour peer Lord Taylor, who was also a friend of Bell's. He offered to explore, consult and then report back. 'At that stage, however, it would be necessary to bring in Teddy,' he wrote ominously.

---

[45] Diary entries dated 24/11/1977, 5, 7 and 8/12/1977, GYP.
[46] Hansard 942 c397–99.
[47] Tebbit, *Upwardly Mobile*, 160.

'We are all agreed that it would be very desirable for you to tell him rather than that it should come from anyone else.'[48]

Younger recorded subsequent events in his diary:

> 11am. A blazing row in the smoke room between Teddy & Russell Fairgreave because of letter by Charles Bell to M[argaret].T[hatcher]. re a possible join-up with 'Scotland is British' for the referendum. T[eddy].T[aylor]. feels very threatened because C.B. has been cooking this up since Nov. and has told R[ussell] & M.T. but not T.T. It is quite understandable that T.T. was not told as in the past he is thought to have told the Press everything too often.[49]

That evening Taylor bashed out a furious letter to Mrs Thatcher, protesting that he had met with Younger, Fletcher and Fairgreave to consider the most 'helpful' way of co-ordinating preparations for the referendum and that they all knew nothing of Charles Bell's parallel plans. The four of them, added Taylor, had agreed that the Shadow Cabinet should consider forming an umbrella organisation 'with which we would be associated'.[50]

'The row', continued Younger in his diary, 'rumbled on all day & eventually TT insisted that he & I & Alex Fletcher went to see M.T. at 1030p.m.'

> T.T. very emotional saying his authority being undermined etc. M.T. v. conciliatory & more or less admitted he should have been told (without actually saying so). But still T.T. went on. Eventually after ½ hr or so M.T. told him he must learn to accept knocks & be more resilient. 'We all have knocks. I have had many especially over Scotland etc.' Finally he was forced out of the room & Alex & I took him for a coffee. He will never stand the strain of [the] S[ecretary] of S[tate for Scotland] job if he flaps as badly as this. I can't imagine what M.T. thought of it – she had had a busy day & looked exhausted.[51]

James Callaghan's minority government was by now struggling daily, and with an election rumoured for October 1978, thoughts soon turned to the Conservatives' Scottish manifesto. In late March Taylor sent Fairgreave, Fletcher and Younger a 'shot' at a draft of the Scottish manifesto bashed out on his own typewriter. George annotated his copy with large question

---

[48] Charles Bell to MT, 19/12/1977, GYP (copy).

[49] Diary entry dated 7/2/1978, GYP.

[50] TT to MT, 7/2/1978, GYP (copy).

[51] Diary entry dated 7/2/1978, GYP.

marks, particularly the section dealing with the 'Government of Scotland'. It included the usual anodyne pledges to bring government closer to the people: 'To this end we will initiate urgent discussions between all parties committed to the maintenance of the Union with a view to arriving at a reform of the structure of Government [here Younger added hopefully in his own hand, 'and the setting up of an Assembly'] which will take account of Scotland's needs and desires and which does not involve the additional cost, bureacracy [*sic*] and conflict inherent in the Labour Party's Scotland and Wales Bill'.[52]

But despite Younger's attempts at redrafting the manifesto, it effectively sounded the death knell for any Conservative-backed Scottish Assembly. There also remained the tricky question of how Scottish Conservatives were to vote in the referendum on 1 March 1979. A meeting of the Scottish Conservative and Unionist Association's Central Council in Motherwell on 4 November decided they should vote 'no' although there was a conciliatory caveat. In his speech Teddy Taylor urged 'understanding and respect' for any Conservatives who felt compelled to campaign for a 'yes' vote. But a communication from the SCUA president Russell Sanderson – a good friend of Younger's – to constituency association chairmen a month later was subtly different. 'Let me make it quite clear that in campaigning for "No",' he explained, 'the Party will not be campaigning against Devolution for Scotland but only against the type of devolution contained in the Act.'[53]

Younger dined with Sanderson, Francis Pym and the SCUA vice-president Alistair Smith at the Caledonian Club on 16 November.

> We talked round and round the problem of how to express a 'No' as 'no – but' to avoid being too negative. It is very difficult as there is only agreement between the various strands in the Party to be not too negative. There is no agreement at all about what alternative we could devise to the govt's Scotland Act. T[eddy].T[aylor]. is being amenable as he is very depressed at our failure in Berwick & E Lothian [Labour had held the seat in a by-election] & the polls this week show us 23% Lab 51% & SNP 21%.
>
> Francis is still to make speeches on devolution and will try to keep a positive lead. We all expect a clear 'Yes' vote and only hope we may have a respectable 'No'. Only TT still thinks we might get the noes off the ground and win. I think the present scheme is very bad and dangerous, but we must have an end to this business and a 'Yes' is probably the best way.[54]

[52] TT to GY, 21/3/1978, GYP.
[53] Russell Sanderson to constituency association chairmen, 11/12/1978, CCO 20/11/86.
[54] Diary entry dated 16/11/1978, GYP.

This belief, of course, was never publicly articulated by Younger, but his tactical unease was clear during a speech he made to the Heriot-Watt Conservative Association on 17 November. 'Amongst the No campaigners', he said, 'there will of course be some who want no change at all, but there will also be many, like myself, who want to achieve substantial constitutional change, but who regard the present plans as defective, dangerous and bad for Scotland.'[55]

In his diary on 20 November Younger recorded:

A very depressing meeting with M.T. about the Scottish situation after Berwick & E. Lothian, and before the referendum. Francis Pym, Leon Brittan, Peter Thorneycroft, Alex Fletcher & Russell Fairgreave were present. Mrs T. seemed v. edgy and is clearly feeling the strain of adverse polls (particularly re herself), divisions in the Party (Ted [Heath] on incomes policy plus the revolt on Rhodesia sanctions etc). She is not a good chairman & there was no structure to the meeting. Everyone just kept on saying their piece. Alex Fletcher talked much nonsense – Russell Fairgreave very thick & T.T. his usual self with many trivial headline-grabbing suggestions to make. Peter Thorneycroft is the best as he does actually carry out what he says he will do, and the details of referendum literature etc. are in hand. He will see that they actually happen.

No Scots had any worthwhile solutions to our poor showing [in the Berwick and East Lothian by-election] but I (and Russell) emphasised that our negative attitudes to devolution & other Scottish issues undoubtedly have their effect. The referendum is to be fought constructively & Mrs. T. will take part. She wants Alec D[ouglas]-H[ome] and Harold Macmillan to appear with her as those Scots ex-PM's cannot be matched by Labour.

M.T. jumped at detailed points & did not seem to be able to look objectively at the situation. She sees it all in personal terms, possibly because of the conflicting advice which the Scots always give.[56]

Like many in the party, Younger was concerned that the referendum would simply reopen the Conservatives' devolutionary wounds. Various umbrella and party campaigns got under way towards the end of November 1978, and Younger's diary recorded continuing presentational difficulties with the Conservative stance:

We held a lobby conference yesterday (T.T., AF & me) to explain why & how Tories would campaign for a 'no'. A very dim response & not much in the Press to-day exc the *Scotsman* saying *we* are trying to get M.T. to come up in the campaign!

[55] Speech to Heriot-Watt Conservative Association, 17/11/1978, GYP.
[56] Diary entry dated 20/11/1978, GYP.

What *actually* happened was that Press referred to a (wrong) report that M.T. was *not* going to campaign. TT said this was not true – no decision had been taken. Press then said 'do you want her' & we couldn't say any other than yes!

A dreadfully stupid Scottish Members Meeting where Fletcher [Iain] Sproat & others tried to blame Atholl Cres[cent] for being lukewarm for the 'no' vote. I defended them as such accusations are quite untrue.[57]

Number 11 Atholl Crescent housed the Scottish Conservative Party's central office and, by the end of 1978, years of devolution 'fun and games' had damaged grassroots morale. At Westminster, the Shadow Scottish Team struggled to deal with a demanding media, while Francis Pym desperately tried to demonstrate that some intellectual rigour under-pinned Conservative thinking on devolution by publishing a series of pamphlets.[58] Even consistent anti-devolutionists within the party were unhappy at how the referendum was being handled. 'The unsophisticated and apolitical average person understands a "Yes" or "No" attitude,' wrote Betty Harvie Anderson to Lord Thorneycroft, the UK party chairman. '"No-but" makes little sense and the reaction is to wonder what on earth the Tory party is seeking to do.'[59]

Younger was dispatched, along with Taylor and Fletcher, to constitu-encies across Scotland to 'encourage and advise them' as to the party's position. Mrs Thatcher's visit to Scotland was set for 19 January, while it was 'agreed that a recommendation to vote No on the part of Lord Home would carry great weight in Scotland'.[60] Home did so in a speech at Edinburgh University, urging Scots to vote 'No for a better bill', and many believe his intervention fatally eroded support for the 'yes' cam-paign.[61] Jim Sillars would later remark caustically that having begun his career by helping to betray Czechoslovakia, Lord Home had ended it by betraying his homeland.[62]

Younger spoke widely during the referendum campaign and appeared to have shed any remaining qualms he had about devolution:

The Government is clearly determined to ignore Parliament's 40% rule and to push this measure through, however small the 'Yes' vote may be [he told the

---

[57] Ibid., 29/11/1978, GYP.

[58] *The Conservative Party and Devolution: Four Viable Options* appeared in December 1978, as did a short guide to the Scotland Act of 1978.

[59] Betty Harvie Anderson to Peter Thorneycroft, 13/12/1978, CCO 20/11/85.

[60] CCO 20/11/86.

[61] Thorpe, *Alec Douglas-Home*, 456. Sir Alec later defended his move. 'The Act as drafted was divisive,' he told *The Times* in 1995. 'I'm sure it was right to vote against it' (*The Times* 10/10/1995).

[62] As Neville Chamberlain's PPS, Lord Home had supported appeasement and the Munich agreement which granted Hitler large chunks of Czech territory.

Stirling University Federation of Conservative Students]. It is therefore vital that everyone who wishes to vote 'No' should do so. The Scotland Act is now being exposed to the public at last and its dangers are clear for all to see. It has no money of its own. Its powers are ill-defined and confusing and it will fatally weaken Scotland's influence in government where it is needed as never before.

'The plot has been rumbled just in time,' Younger continued. 'They are trying to palm off Scotland with a second-best scheme which will leave us as second-class citizens of the U.K. Surely we can do better than this, and heed Lord Home's advice to take a little more time to devise a better scheme more worthy of Scotland's vital role in the U.K.'[63]

When the referendum vote finally took place on 1 March (St David's Day), a bare majority of those voting said 'yes', but it was well below the required 40 per cent of the total electorate. 'For the moment,' said Thatcher, 'devolution was dead: I did not mourn it.'[64] Parliamentary horse-trading soon began, although the Scotland Act required the government to repeal the legislation following the referendum vote. 'Jim [Callaghan] was strongly in favour of delaying [repeal] and forcing the Tories to table a motion of no confidence,' recorded Tony Benn in his diary for 14 March. 'If we went ahead with the repeal he thought the Party would split, but if we resisted the Tories in a vote of confidence the Party would stick together.'[65]

This turned out to be wishful thinking on the Prime Minister's part. When the SNP put down a censure motion on the government's failure to implement devolution, the Conservatives augmented it with a motion of no confidence. This was debated on 28 March, and after an eloquent debate Callaghan's beleaguered administration fell by just one vote. The subsequent Conservative manifesto merely promised further 'discussions about the future government of Scotland'. Younger, who probably voted 'no' in the referendum, had mixed feelings as he prepared for the 1979 general election. Nevertheless, the failure of the referendum had given the Conservatives a useful boost as the long-awaited campaign got under way. 'At last the end of this Parliament', Younger wrote with relief in his diary on 5 April, 'and all have gone home.' He continued:

We stayed for a 1922 meeting in Central Hall Westminster for Mrs. T to address us plus candidates. A very successful occasion except that Peter Thorneycroft spoke for too long . . . [he] told us of his strategy for the Campaign. He will let

[63] Speech to Stirling University, 15/2/1979, GYP.
[64] Thatcher, *The Path to Power*, 430.
[65] Benn, *Conflicts of Interest: Diaries 1977–80*, 471–72.

Labour start on Monday 9th & we will start in earnest later in the week. He believes Labour will do anything to keep off their record & will keep [Tony] Benn & Co wraps. Uncle Jim Callaghan is their best hope with this mornings [*sic*] MORI Poll still giving us a lead of 13%.

Mrs. T. was without notes and therefore at her best. There will be no 'bribes' except the main pledge to reduce direct taxation. The theme is to restore the balance in (a) taxation (b) Rights and duties of Trade Unionists (c) Law and Order (more police & better pay) (d) Incentives (e) Defence.

We will be attacked over cuts in public spending, but what is the alternative? It is to make private citizens cut their standards [therefore] less to spend on the family etc.

The big issue is our *free* society as against the Socialist one. You cannot have *personal* freedom without *economic* freedom. She was v. warmly received and I think we all hope she can sustain her line when the bullets start flying.

'It will be interesting to look back on this day,' reflected Younger. 'The general opinion of all is that we shall win this election although some think by a fairly small margin. As of now I agree. There has been a fundamental shift of attitude over the past three years, and I believe the people want a change. The left, with an appalling record are on the defensive and no Labour MP to whom I have spoken genuinely expects to win.' And, he observed, 'As many friends have said to me, if we can't win in these conditions, can we ever? One thing is certain; if we lose, Britain will become a basically Socialist state, and one wonders if one would want to live in it.'[66]

---

[66] Diary entry dated 5/4/1979, GYP.

Chapter 12

GENTLEMAN GEORGE

'YOU KNOW THERE are times, perhaps once every thirty years, when there is a sea-change in politics,' James Callaghan told his adviser Bernard Donoughue shortly before polling day. 'There is a shift in what the public wants and what it approves of. I suspect there is now such a sea-change – and it is for Mrs Thatcher.'[1] He was right, and as a result of that sea-change Margaret Thatcher became the first female prime minister of the United Kingdom.

In Scotland, Tory fortunes were revived following the October 1974 debacle. The party's share of the vote increased from 24.7 to 31.4 per cent, bringing a net gain of six seats despite a relatively low Labour-to-Conservative swing. The result appeared to vindicate Tory opposition to a Scottish Assembly. Furthermore, the failure of the March referendum had convinced Mrs Thatcher that most Scots did not seriously want devolution.

In Ayr, Younger's majority remained steady at 2,768, while the SNP, which had returned an impressive eleven MPs in the second election of 1974, was reduced to a rump of just two. Mrs Thatcher was thrilled by the results in Scotland but disappointed at the defeat in Cathcart of Teddy Taylor, who had been Shadow Scottish Secretary for the past three years. This created a vacancy at the Scottish Office. Alick Buchanan-Smith, who had quit the Tory front bench in 1976, was out of the question due to his pro-devolution sympathies, while Alex Fletcher, although able, was not seen as experienced enough.

The mantle, therefore, fell to Younger, who at the age of 49 became Secretary of State for Scotland and a member of Mrs Thatcher's first Cabinet. Having assumed that Teddy would get the job, George had expected to return instead to the Ministry of Defence, perhaps as minister of state. But becoming Scottish Secretary, as he later said, was 'the pinnacle of ambition for any Scottish MP'. 'I remember remarking to my wife Diana that henceforth I could never feel in any way unfulfilled as a politician. I had arrived.'[2] A year later, he reflected: 'I'[d] been preparing

---

[1] Donoughue, *Prime Minister*, 191.
[2] *Scotland on Sunday* 10/10/1993.

for this, I suppose, for 15 years in Parliament.'[3] Nevertheless, when the call came from Downing Street, George was more than a little shell-shocked.

Younger's pocket diary entry for Saturday 5 May reads simply: 'To London. Mrs T. 1100.' 'Many Congratulations,' wrote his old friend Jeffrey Archer. 'I was delighted [as] it will give me another excuse to hate Scotland.'[4] Jack Maclay, who had been Scottish Secretary from 1957 to 1962, also wrote with some advice. 'I admit that there were moments when one had to remind oneself that it was "great fun",' he said, 'but . . . Otherwise, James Stuart's [Scottish Secretary from 1951 to 1957] only comment when I took over from him was "If you've any friends in Scotland prepare to lose them now" I found my friends *remarkably* tolerant! You certainly will.'[5]

'I was not by nature a tremendous admirer of the Scottish Office', Younger admitted in a radio interview a few years later, 'and indeed, like most of the rest of the Scots, I didn't know much about it when I got into Parliament.' The 94-year-old department was, he thought, a very 'typically British compromise' that had by and large worked very well.[6] At Dover House in London and St Andrew's House in Edinburgh, Younger inherited his predecessor Bruce Millan's private secretary, Kenneth MacKenzie, and also his permanent under-secretary, Sir William Kerr Fraser. Although still reeling from the demise of a Scottish Assembly he had meticulously planned for, Kerr Fraser got along well with his new political chief. Both were thoroughly Scottish and viewed the Scottish Office as a counterweight against the centralising tide which flowed into Whitehall.

The ministerial team was also strong. Alex Fletcher (education and industry), Russell Fairgrieve (health and social work) and Malcolm Rifkind (home affairs and environment) were appointed under-secretaries, while Lord Mansfield (who had lost out to Younger in the selection for Kinross and West Perthshire in 1963) was made minister of state with special responsibility for the Highlands and Islands. Another key appointment proved to be that of James Mackay as Lord Advocate.

Younger's first Cabinet meeting took place the following week. 'We were in high spirits and were looking forward to seeing how Britain's first woman prime minister would tackle the job,' he remembered. 'We were not kept waiting. Dead on time, Mrs Thatcher came down the stairs and with a welcoming smile swept into the Cabinet Room.'

---

[3] *Open to Question* (STV) c.1980.
[4] Jeffrey Archer to GY, 7/5/1979, GYP.
[5] Jack Maclay to GY, 7/5/1979, GYP.
[6] *Playing the Scottish Card* I (BBC Radio Scotland) 9/9/1985.

As soon as we were seated, it was clear who was in charge. I will never forget Margaret's first words: 'Some of you may be thinking of writing your memoirs. No one can do so without my permission. I will not be giving permission. So don't bother.'

We were all rather bemused. Nobody actually said anything. People turned to each other with raised eyebrows but after a slight pause for digestion we got down to considering the contents of the Queen's Speech which would open parliament in just over three weeks.

Instead of congratulating everyone on the election victory Mrs Thatcher had chosen to dictate autobiographical terms. Another taste of the new Prime Minister's style came a few days later. '[W]e had started business when in came Jim Prior, two or three minutes late,' remembered Younger. 'Margaret stopped, looked him in the eye and said: "You're late. Don't let it happen again." Jim looked cross and pretty put out but he had no option but to sit down and say nothing. I must say it was pretty effective. It was like getting a ticking-off from a headmistress . . . I made a mental note not to be late after that!'[7]

Mrs Thatcher's first public speech as Prime Minister happened to be at the annual Scottish Conservative Party conference in Perth on 12 May. She described Teddy Taylor's defeat in Cathcart as a 'bitter blow'. 'We lost our standard bearer at the hour of victory,' she added. 'It is a tribute indeed to his inspiration and his leadership that the army can march forward when its Captain has fallen.'[8] Considering that the army's new chief, George Younger, was sitting alongside Thatcher as she spoke, a few observers were shocked at her insensitivity.

It is likely that relations between the Prime Minister and her first Scottish Secretary were initially unsure. Although Younger had toed the fluctuating party line on devolution, he had offered to resign in support of Buchanan-Smith back in 1976, just months after he had been sacked as Shadow Defence Secretary. But George had been loyal throughout, and Mrs Thatcher valued almost nothing more than loyalty. His first few weeks in the job were dominated by preparations for the first direct elections to the European Parliament. For Younger, it was a useful context for forthcoming talks in Brussels on Scotland's farmers and fishermen, while there was also a family consideration. Of the five Scottish

---

[7] *Scotland on Sunday* 10/10/1993.

[8] Speech to Scottish Conservative conference, 12/5/1979, MTF. The late Conservative councillor, Brian Meek, remembered Younger's quip to him as they listened to Teddy Taylor railing against Europe: 'Do you know he eats Rolos and smokes cigarettes at the same time? Quite remarkable' (*Herald* 28/1/2003).

Tory MEPs returned at the election, one was John Purvis, Younger's second cousin on the Gilmour side of his family. Soon after, he arranged for all the Scottish MPs, MEPs and their spouses to meet the Prime Minister over lunch at Chequers.

Mrs Thatcher announced soon after taking office that she intended personally to visit selected government departments. The Scottish Office was second on her list (the Department of Energy had been first) and she travelled north on 11 July with a large entourage including her PPS Ian Gow. She stayed at Bute House, the Secretary of State's residence in Edinburgh's elegant New Town, where the Prime Minister seemed relaxed, kicking off her shoes with a whisky in hand. Diana got to grips with Mrs Thatcher's daily schedule, which involved an early rise and a boiled egg for breakfast, while the Prime Minister charmed her Scottish Secretary's frequently resident children. Joanna remembers watching as Mrs Thatcher failed to flinch when Ian Gow, clad only in a towel and clutching a wash bag, marched past her open door.

The Prime Minister held talks with senior Scottish Office officials, giving Younger an important opportunity to explain Scotland's needs. Although Sir Keith Joseph, the Industry Secretary, had recently scrapped regional development grants, job-related selective financial assistance survived, and Younger ensured other downgradings took place in stages.[9] He probably also raised the long-standing issue of dispersing civil service jobs to Scotland, on which he had fought an often lonely battle during the previous five years.

A statement was finally made to Parliament on 26 July, detailing a truncated plan under which 1,400 MoD jobs would be transferred from London to Glasgow, together with 650 Overseas Development posts to East Kilbride. That evening, Younger reflected on the last few months in what was to be his final diary entry:

> End of session and we look back on three months of hard running by the new Government. Mrs. T. very dominant and leading all the way. She is not a very good chairman of Cabinet as she talks too much herself, and never lets an argument develop without her steering it all the time. But she doesn't bear grudges and after hammering at you for an hour in a very aggressive way, she can see your point of view and even change her own.
>
> An example is Dispersal, just announced to-day. Four weeks ago she heard me talking about it to Christopher Soames [leader of the House of Lords], and

---

[9] First to be cut back was the scope of assisted areas, including many in Conservative constituencies. Gavin McCrone remembers Younger asking 'do they look like people about to be downgraded?' as several Tory MPs from the north-east of Scotland filed past at an airport.

snapped 'You're not going to get it, none at all'. However we have got it, the key was a deputation of Scots Tory MP's led by Iain Sproat who came to see her 2 weeks ago. She was so impressed that in Cabinet she backed me all the way. So did Willie [Whitelaw], [Michael] Heseltine and (just) [Jim] Prior, also poor Nick Edwards. They wouldn't listen to him over Wales & he will have a tough time.

Looking back over three months Scotland has done well in very bad circumstances. I beat Keith Joseph over Regional Policy by [getting] a reasonable deal for Scotland – also on shipbuilding, by 2 years cash plus I hope some 'orders' for Govan [shipyards]. Presentation of the Scottish Office has been v. successful so far in the Press & TV etc, and the family have been a great help. Now for a 2 week holiday & back to the mêlée![10]

This diary entry highlighted several important themes which typified Younger's seven years at the Scottish Office: his realistic yet robust relationship with the Prime Minister; a willingness to fight his corner with support from Cabinet colleagues like Willie Whitelaw; his determination to get the best 'deal' for Scotland; and the formidable 'presentation' skills which would prove so important to his approach as a Scottish Secretary in a nation which regularly returned a majority of Labour MPs.

Younger remembered well taunts that Gordon Campbell, his boss at the Scottish Office from 1970 to 1974, had no mandate to govern, and similar charges were levelled at George. They sounded hollow from two lonely SNP MPs, but reverberated from Labour's 44 members, and grew louder following the 1983 election. As the *Scotsman* assessed near the end of 1979, Younger had 'had to tread the thin line between conceding in private and yet refusing to acknowledge in public the lameness of his own party's political mandate north of the Border'.[11]

UNFINISHED BUSINESS

'I ask the House to repeal the Scotland Act today,' said Younger a month after the election. 'In doing that I know that the Scotland Act has very few friends.'[12] Bruce Millan and the future Scottish Secretary Donald Dewar taunted him about his previous support for an Assembly, conveniently ignoring the fact that it was Labour legislation which required him to repeal the Act. Younger, meanwhile, did his best to sound consensual and reminded his opponents of the new government's pledge to hold all-party talks on the future of Scottish governance.

---

[10] Diary entry dated 26/7/1979, GYP.
[11] *Scotsman* 30/11/1979.
[12] Hansard 968 c1338.

Even had that commitment been genuine, circumstances made it impossible. Reeling from the loss of all but two seats in the election, the SNP resolved to ditch devolution and press for full independence, while the Labour Party – with the majority of Scottish seats – resented the government's zealousness in repealing the Scotland Act so swiftly. Younger's position had also hardened. 'The Parliamentary debates on the Scotland Act were devastating,' he later explained, 'and although 99 per cent of the time I don't agree with Tam Dalyell, he certainly did have a devastating point in pointing out that you cannot have one brand of MP representing Scotland and another in England and Wales.'

The West Lothian Question had, in other words, convinced Younger that there were only two options: a federal system ('I personally don't think I favour that but it would work.') or the status quo, which he had once insisted was 'not an option'. Anything else, he believed, was 'constitutionally illiterate'.[13] What was more, the March referendum had shown that 'that particular scheme did not set the Scottish people on fire'. Two-thirds of the electorate had either voted no or had not voted at all, he argued, and to initiate constitutional change you needed a resounding 'yes'. Interestingly, Younger maintained that a directly-elected Assembly remained government policy, but would not happen until 'we have a scheme which ties in with devolution as a whole for the UK'.[14]

The SNP refused to take part in the Inter-Party Group on the Government of Scotland, which concluded its talks in June 1981. The outcome was a typical Unionist compromise. The Scottish Grand Committee (SGC) was beefed up while the Select Committee on Scottish Affairs, which had last met in the late 1960s, was revived with seven Tory and six Labour MPs, one of whom, Donald Dewar, became chairman.[15]

On 15 February 1982 the Scottish Grand Committee (in its new guise) also met for the first time in Edinburgh. Younger used it to announce a package of measures to tackle youth unemployment, while the SNP's Donald Stewart derided the gathering (in the old Royal High School, which had been refurbished for use as the Scottish Assembly) as nothing more than a talking shop. Younger agreed. 'It is by its very nature a talking shop,' he conceded in 1983. 'It would obviously be wrong for the Scottish Grand Committee to have any powers that would override the power of Parliament.'[16] For MPs, the novelty of meeting in Edinburgh on

---

[13] *Playing the Scottish Card* III (BBC Radio Scotland) 23/9/1985. Younger told Arnold Kemp that the West Lothian Question was 'an absolute show-stopper' (Kemp, *The Hollow Drum*, 123).

[14] *Why I am a Conservative* (BBC Scotland) c10/1980.

[15] Both Younger and Dewar had been members of the original Select Committee on Scottish Affairs.

[16] *Scottish Portrait Magazine* 8/1983.

Monday mornings soon wore off, while officials pondered the political consequences of a planeload of Scottish MPs crashing en route to London on a Monday afternoon.

Younger, however, remained conscious of nationalistic sentiment in Scotland, and tried to compensate for the lack of institutional reforms by stepping up his pseudo-nationalist rhetoric. 'We have our own style of government in Scotland, which we use and we develop to suit our own needs,' he said at the 1984 Scottish Tory conference. 'Scotland, while fully part of the United Kingdom, *is* governed from Edinburgh, and as long as I am there that's the way it's going to be.'[17] By and large this approach worked. Younger had moved into New St Andrew's House with the ripples of the devolutionary argument lapping against him, but by the end of 1982 he could confidently, and not inaccurately, proclaim that most people in Scotland were no longer interested in 'a Scottish Assembly as a practical proposition'.[18]

LEGISLATIVE BEGINNINGS

In retrospect, the early 1980s was a difficult time to be Conservative Scottish Secretary. Strikes still gripped the country, unemployment reached 236,000 in 1980, and Margaret Thatcher was – by all accounts – set to lose the next election. Younger, on the other hand, was riding high, and his first two Bills (on housing and criminal justice) could even be described as radical – and specifically Scottish – reforms. Presentation was also a key consideration. 'I had a very strong and clear perception of how I wanted the Scottish Office to work,' he told an interviewer in 1985. 'It was a well-tried and effective instrument but I still felt that by 1979 it was not personal enough. It hadn't a high enough profile.'[19]

Younger recognised that the Scottish Office had to rectify this to fill the vacuum left by the rejected Assembly, and set about clarifying his junior ministers' titles and duties. Soon they no longer had to introduce themselves as 'Joint Parliamentary Under-Secretary of State for Scotland' with responsibility for education, but instead as the Scottish minister for education, health, etc. This clarity of language extended to Younger's first major piece of legislation, the Tenants' Rights etc (Scotland) Bill, an overtly political title Malcolm Rifkind insisted upon in spite of civil service demands for the more prosaic 'Housing (Scotland) Bill'.

George presented the Bill to Parliament on 14 January 1980. It

[17] Speech to SCUA conference, 9/5/1984, GYP.
[18] Scotland's Record Acc 7330/79, 29/10/1982.
[19] *Scotsman Magazine* 7/1985.

proposed a tenants' charter and, having concluded that the private housing shortage in many areas of Scotland could not be rectified by building alone, the so-called 'Right to Buy'. Younger claimed the government had already received 30,000 inquiries, while the former Scottish Office minister Hugh Brown dubbed it the 'bribe of the century'. But such a massive transfer of wealth was difficult for even the opposition to oppose and Rifkind cleverly threw the argument back at uncomfortable Scottish Labour members, saying the measure would make the single greatest contribution to the creation of a property-owning democracy in the last century. It proved hugely popular, but also depleted public sector housing stock, which some councils later tackled by suspending the policy in property 'hotspots'.

Beyond its initial presentation, the Bill was guided through Parliament by Rifkind, a good example of Younger's willingness to delegate. He was determined not to repeat the mistakes of Gordon Campbell in failing to spread his workload, which then left him free to concentrate on being Scotland's voice in the Cabinet. It also enabled George to keep going in an often arduous job; officials remember him never showing the strain, unlike his predecessors Willie Ross and Bruce Millan. He even asked the Lord Advocate if he could shoulder responsibility for planning issues. 'I said it wouldn't do as it was an executive decision,' recalled James Mackay, later Lord Mackay of Clashfern, 'all I could do was advise on and defend his decision in court if it was challenged.'[20]

Rifkind, therefore, also dealt largely with Younger's next piece of reforming legislation, the controversial Criminal Justice (Scotland) Bill. Its wider stop-and-search powers for the police provoked fury from the civil liberties lobby, which Younger dismissed as 'hysterical'. The Bill also provided the Labour MP Robin Cook with an opportunity to amend Scotland's homosexuality laws and bring them into line with England and Wales. 'It is unreasonable oppression', argued Cook, 'and this House should lift it from them.'[21] Although personally liberal on such matters, Younger asked MPs whether it was right to make such a change when people had had little chance to air their views. Nevertheless, in a free vote MPs backed Cook's amendment by 203 to 80. On social issues, George's record was mixed. He had backed liberalisation of Scottish divorce laws in 1970, but voted to restore hanging for terrorism in 1975, and for killing police or prison officers in 1983.

Even after only six months in office Younger had made his mark. The *Scotsman* noted that he had quickly escaped Teddy Taylor's populist

---

[20] Interview with Lord Mackay of Clashfern, 25/1/2007.
[21] *The Times* 23/7/1980.

shadow and 'quietly established his own firm command of the Scottish Office in a way which has impressed the civil servants, even though it has yet to impress the voters'. Also, 'as a member of an explicitly Right-wing Government, he has like all the others, been handed the public sector hatchet. Yet he has managed to wield it with remarkably little injury to his own basic instincts as a middle-ground, consensus politician.'

So far, assessed the *Scotsman*, Younger had 'made striking progress in working with rather than against so much of Scotland's institutional Establishment – in local government and the trade unions – which is controlled by Labour.' 'We might disagree,' the Scottish Secretary would tell opponents in the umpteenth protest delegation to New St Andrew's House, 'but we all know that Scotland is just the right size for us to do this together by co-operation rather than conflict.' 'It sounds trite,' said the *Scotsman*. 'Yet there is something in the man's personality and disarming candour which gives it the force and conviction of a manifesto that can be believed.'[22]

Donald Dewar, chairman of the Scottish Affairs Select Committee and, from 1983, Labour's Shadow Scottish Secretary, agreed. 'If you attack him, he just smiles back and nods his head in agreement,' he complained. 'The more you attack, the more he nods.'[23] Younger also nodded at hostile delegations from the Labour-dominated Convention of Scottish Local Authorities (COSLA). 'These are concessions which may mean a good deal to Labour both locally and nationally,' judged the *Scotsman*. 'And the political style of the Laird of Leckie is to accumulate some political credit for the harder times that undoubtedly lie ahead.'[24]

Younger needed political credit when, in December 1979, he published statistics showing that a 20 per cent cut in Scottish Office staff would save £9.8 million and cost 1,400 jobs. Again this was carefully contrived. If the Scottish Secretary was to demand cuts from local authorities in Scotland, he had to demonstrate that he practised what he preached.

'EXCESSIVE AND UNREASONABLE BEHAVIOUR'

Tales of Younger's handling of hostile delegations from COSLA were legendary. He would smile broadly, determined to look for an area of common agreement – however small – which he could then present to the media as a breakthrough in negotiations. 'Gentlemen,' he would say after a barrage of complaints, 'if I was sitting where you are sitting I would have

---

[22] *Scotsman* 30/11/1979.
[23] *Scottish Daily Express* 30/1/2003.
[24] *Scotsman* 30/11/1979.

said exactly the same thing. But let me share with you my problems.' Dick Stewart, the formidable leader of Strathclyde Regional Council, tried to pick fights but usually failed, complaining that 'It's just like punching a balloon.' On another occasion, Stewart told Younger that he was the worst ever Secretary of State for Scotland. 'Just a minute, Dick,' he responded, 'have the chocolate biscuits reached you yet?'[25]

The Scottish Secretary, however, was not always consistent. At first he assured COSLA he would not seek legislative powers to restrict rate increases, instead using an old 1930s statute that empowered him to withhold grants from authorities which incurred 'excessive and unreasonable expenditure', a phrase which came to loom large in contemporary political rhetoric. But when the innocuous-sounding Local Government (Miscellaneous Provisions) (Scotland) Bill was presented to Parliament, Younger's amiable relations with COSLA were to be sorely tested.

Younger had come under pressure at the 1980 Scottish Conservative conference to protect ratepayers from the 'blatant disregard' of some local authorities in the face of appeals to reduce public spending.[26] The most contentious clause of the Bill therefore strengthened the Secretary of State's hand in controlling 'excessive and unreasonable expenditure'. Younger issued local authorities with an ultimatum to bring their spending under control, but by April 1981 only six councils had produced satisfactory budgets. Twenty-nine authorities still exceeded Scottish Office guidelines by more than 20 per cent, most notably Lothian Regional Council, which intended to spend £62m more than the government deemed prudent. A 50 per cent increase in Lothian's rates, the highest in Scotland, had been the last straw for Younger and a prolonged fight became inevitable.

It reached its bloodiest in July 1981 when Younger himself was accused of 'excessive and unreasonable behaviour' in moving an order to cut the rate support grant payable to Lothian Regional Council by £47m. The council refused to comply and within weeks the Scottish Office was clawing back millions from Lothian's budget. George exuded reasonableness, pointing to staffing cuts implemented by him at New St Andrew's House. 'The vast majority of Scottish local authorities of all parties are doing their best to save money,' he had reasoned the previous year. 'A few aren't and I think the writing is on the wall for them.'[27]

At Westminster the legislation was dubbed the 'Lothian Regional

---

[25] *Herald* 28/1/2003.
[26] *The Times* 8/5/1980. Younger's predecessor, Labour's Bruce Millan, had also tried to reign in high council spending.
[27] *Scotsman* 21/5/1980.

Council (Abolition) Bill', and an apocryphal tale described the Scottish Secretary carrying his son's shotgun to a south Edinburgh gunsmith for repair. A pedestrian recognised him, noted the gun and pointed up the hill. 'Lothian Region's that way, George.'[28] Ultimately, however, Younger won the battle, albeit with a smile on his face. Not only did Lothian have to back down, but the Conservatives (led by the pro-devolutionist Brian Meek) overturned Labour's tiny majority at the 1982 regional elections and won control of the authority.

Cabinet colleagues were impressed by the Scottish Secretary's hands-on approach. Mrs Thatcher was also delighted, asking Scottish conference delegates in 1984, 'do the ratepayers of Lothian look on George as some ruthless tyrant because he has cut their rates by 25 per cent? On the contrary, they reckon he's a jolly good fellow, and so say all of us.'[29]

It struck some observers as odd that Strathclyde Regional Council, long a Scottish Tory bogeyman, did not suffer the same fate as Lothian. 'Just after the election in 1979,' recalled Kenneth MacKenzie, 'George invited Dick Stewart from Strathclyde Council to Bute House for a quiet word – I don't know what he said – and from then on they played ball in terms of the settlement from the Scottish Office.'[30] In distributing the grant Younger always ensured that Strathclyde Region did relatively well. It was effectively a policy of divide and rule: Dick Stewart hated hard-left Labour councillors in Lothian and could be relied upon not to give them full backing through COSLA. It was also rumoured that Mrs Thatcher gave her Scottish Secretary the option of abolishing Strathclyde as she geared up to scrap the Greater London Council, but George would have known instinctively that it was not a realistic option.

But while rate-capping won right-wing plaudits, Younger recognised the practical difficulties in trying to interfere with the local authority decision-making process. Nevertheless, the Local Government (Miscellaneous Provisions) (Scotland) Act was just the beginning of a dramatic change in relations between central and local government, particularly financially. In this sphere, George and a centralising Scottish Office led the way within the UK. It began with greater control of total local authority expenditure; continued with changes to how councils could spend money in general; moved up a gear with power for the Scottish Office to dictate how individual authorities could spend money; and culminated – in 1985–86 – with the abolition of the rates and their replacement with the Community Charge.

[28] *The Times* 12/9/1981.
[29] Speech to Scottish Conservative conference, 11/5/1984, MTF.
[30] Interview with Kenneth MacKenzie, c2005.

LEFT. Sir William Orpen's portrait of the 1st Viscount Younger of Leckie. A cabin boy, as Lord Birkenhead quipped, who aspired to run the ship, his career anticipated his great-grandson's in several important respects.

BELOW LEFT. Teddy and Evelyn Younger, George's parents. The 3rd Viscount Younger eschewed politics for farming and forestry while his wife devoted herself to the WVS and Girl Guides. George's love of music and sense of humour came from both parents.

BELOW RIGHT. George with friend. His was a contented childhood 'happily' interrupted by the Second World War.

RIGHT. Younger playing his French horn at school. Dennis Brain was his main influence. 'He was to me, and possibly to many others', he wrote in his diary when Brain died in a car accident, 'a symbol of the highest of high standards.'

BELOW. George (far right) with friends in Korea. 'It was on a Korean hillside on a dark, dank, cold night in 1951 that I really came of age,' he later wrote. The conditions were harsh but the experience with the Argylls life-changing.

BOTTOM. With brothers Bobby (left) and Sandy (middle) in Territorial Army gear. The TA enabled George to maintain links with the Army as a civilian, first as a signals officer and then as commander of HQ company in the 7th Argylls.

ABOVE. George and Diana's wedding day. 'We were both 22 when we married in 1954,' Younger recalled in 1986. 'Nowadays it isn't so young, but looking back it was amazing. My parents were extremely progressive.'

LEFT. Younger promising to bring peace and prosperity to North Lanark during his first general election campaign in 1959. The experience convinced him that politics would be his chosen career rather than brewing or business.

RIGHT. 'Up with the Tories.' Diana and George campaigning in Ayr with a rather distracted young Conservative.

BELOW. George and Conservative leader Edward Heath surprise a constituent during a visit to Ayr. Heath liked the forward-looking Younger and appointed him deputy chairman of the Scottish Conservative Party and later a minister at the Scottish Office and Ministry of Defence.

A foreign interlude. Six months after Enoch Powell warned of rivers foaming with blood, Younger got to grips with race relations in 1960s America . . .

. . . and later in South Africa, where he worked hard to understand the ultimate aim of apartheid.

BELOW. At a Parliamentary Press Gallery function with the Scottish Secretary Gordon Campbell (second right) and the minister of state Lady Tweedsmuir (middle). Younger found Campbell's apolitical approach to the Scottish Office frustrating and was determined not to repeat his mistakes on becoming Secretary of State himself in 1979.

Younger sets off for Bonn on his quest to attract inward investment to Scotland. George was a natural salesman: in 1963 he had visited Germany to sell Scottish wines and spirits; in 1971 he flew there to sell Scottish industry.

The Young Turks (l–r), Ian MacArthur, Teddy Taylor, Hector Monro, Alick Buchanan-Smith and George. Teddy looks as if he is about to detach himself from the group, as he did over thorny political issues like Europe and devolution.

ABOVE. George with sons Andrew and Charlie at the Winchester/Eton match, an annual family fixture. In 1997 Younger was appointed Warden, the highest accolade for an Old Wykehamist.

LEFT. Andrew helps out his father in Ayr during the 1979 general election campaign. Younger's appointment as Scottish Secretary following the Tory victory changed his family's life for more than a decade.

At the Secretary of State's official residence in Edinburgh. Bute House became a working home from home for (l–r) Diana, George, Andrew (picture), Charlie, Joanna and James.

And at work in London, Younger in his usual place next to Willie Whitelaw at the Cabinet table as Mrs Thatcher seeks clarification on a point. Like Willie, George did not slot easily into the 'wet' and 'dry' categorisations favoured by contemporary commentators.

Diana and George chatting to Willie Whitelaw outside St Paul's Cathedral en route to the Royal Wedding of Prince Charles and Lady Diana Spencer in 1981. Behind Whitelaw is Alec Home.

Seeing off Gorbachev at Edinburgh Airport. Initially, the future Soviet leader had no intention of telling waiting journalists that Marshall Ustinov had died. George, who advised him that he had no choice, later joked that he had given Gorbachev his first lesson in democracy.
Picture: The Scotsman Publications

ABOVE. Lord Mansfield looks on as Alex Pollock presents George with a silver bed of nails to mark his becoming the longest continually-serving Secretary of State for Scotland in 1985. Events that year – not least the rates revaluation and a lengthy teachers' strike – demonstrated how sharp those nails could be.

RIGHT. A favourite family photograph of George as Defence Secretary, wearing his personalised jacket and specially-commissioned Defence Council cap badge.

The Anglophile 'Cap' Weinberger listens intently to Younger at a Washington function. They forged a lasting friendship as their respective nations' defence secretaries during the twilight of the Cold War.

Margaret Thatcher unveils Younger's portrait at the Scottish Office in 1988. In her speech the Prime Minister recalled looking around the Cabinet table as ministers discussed a thorny issue. 'What do normal people think?' she wondered out loud. 'George, you tell us. You're normal.'

Visiting the 1st Battalion Argyll and Sutherland Highlanders on the Falkland Islands as Defence Secretary. Many of those serving were sons of Argylls George knew from home.

George also encountered some of the Falkland Islands' more naturalised inhabitants. Foreign trips were full of lighter moments.

Younger's introduction to the House of Lords as Lord Younger of Prestwick in 1992, sponsored by friends Humphrey Atkins (Lord Colnbrook) and Lord Sanderson of Bowden. George and his father Teddy (as the 3rd Viscount Younger of Leckie) sat in the Upper House together until the latter's death in 1997.

With the Queen and Prince Charles (back to camera) at 'The Great Event' to celebrate the monarch's 40th year as head of state. Behind Her Majesty is Robin Gill, who founded the Royal Anniversary Trust of which George became chairman.

Younger in his Knight of the Thistle regalia at the Thistle Chapel in Edinburgh's St Giles' Cathedral. The highest honour for a Scot and one he shared with friends Lord Home and Viscount Whitelaw. *Picture: Julian Calder.*

LEFT. George outside Holyroodhouse as Lord High Commissioner to the General Assembly of the Church of Scotland in 2001 (Sir Robin Blair was Purse Bearer). He held the position again the following year, by which time he was already seriously ill. *Picture: Mark Cator*

BELOW LEFT. With sons Charlie (left) and James (right) dressed as members of the Royal Company of Archers. George once joked that the ceremonial bow and arrow were the 'ultimate deterrent'.

BELOW RIGHT. Andrew – who was admitted to the Archers after his father's death – holding the picture featured bottom left while wearing George's old uniform, which fitted him with few alterations.

George presiding over the Royal Bank of Scotland board in 1998. Together they successfully acquired NatWest, the biggest takeover in British banking history. (Back, l–r: Emilio Botin, Juan Inciarte, Miller McLean, Norman McLuskie, Iain Robertson, Sir Robin Duthie, Lawrence Fish, Ian Grant, Fred Goodwin. Front, l–r: Dr George Mathewson, Bob Speirs, Eileen Mackay, Murray Stuart, Bill Wilson, Sir Iain Vallance, Sir Angus Grossart, Viscount Younger of Leckie)

George and his daughter Joanna before her marriage service at the House of Commons crypt. George and Diana enjoyed a close relationship with all their children.

George on his 17-foot Norfolk Oyster *Karmelia* with family and friends. 'One thing I look forward enormously to when I retire is going sailing when I want to,' he said in 1998. Sadly, George's retirement was truncated by illness and his desire went unfulfilled.

'BATHGATE NO MORE'

Within three days of taking over as Scottish Secretary Younger was faced with the closure of Singer in Clydebank, Prestcold in Glasgow and Monsanto Chemicals in Ayrshire. More industries disappeared over the next two years: Lawsons of Dyce, Massey-Ferguson, the Wiggins Teape[31] pulp mill at Fort William, Talbot at Linwood, the aluminium smelter at Invergordon[32] and, eventually, the entire truck factory of BMC at Bathgate.

'When I took office,' Younger recalled in 1980, 'sitting on my desk were a whole series of major redundancies which had been sat on or delayed or held over until after the General Election. Most of them were too far gone, but I and Alex Fletcher have made a major effort on every one of them to see if we could save anything from the wreck – and we've had some success in this.'[33] Others accused Younger of abandoning Scotland's historic industries. 'Bathgate no more,' sang the Proclaimers in a song which likened the closures to the Highland clearances, 'Linwood no more'.[34]

Although closures of this sort were statutorily outside Younger's brief as Scottish Secretary, he inevitably had to deal with the resulting job losses. In terms of presentation, he was also determined to strike a moderate tone. 'We wanted to take people with us', Younger explained,

> rather than to be seen kicking them in the teeth. Keith Joseph, while a most humane man, appeared unsympathetic, and perhaps too quick to explain [that] it was impossible to bail out a factory faced with closure. I knew this but felt there was a necessary healing process that had to take place first. I therefore spent much time discussing with representatives of the firm and its workforce whether there was any way we could save the threatened factory. I explained this to Mrs Thatcher more than once and she said I should handle it in my own way, provided I understood there would be no more money from central government.[35]

There were, of course, uncomfortable echoes of two Heathite phrases: 'lame-duck industries' and the 'unacceptable face of capitalism' in all of this. Younger skilfully steered a middle way between the two. 'While we

---

[31] Younger's daughter Joanna worked for Wiggins Teape after leaving university.
[32] Despite the government offering £100m to another buyer, by mid-1982 Younger was forced to concede that one could not be found.
[33] *Scotttish Daily Express* 8/5/1980.
[34] 'Letter from America' was a number-three chart hit for the Proclaimers in December 1987.
[35] *Scotland on Sunday* 17/10/1993.

see no benefit in pouring vast sums of taxpayers' money into firms or industries which have no future,' Mrs Thatcher told the Scottish Conservative conference in May 1979, 'we will certainly not turn a blind eye to industries which need assistance to overcome the problems of transition.'[36]

The Talbot car factory at Linwood was one such industry. Rumours surfaced in early 1981 that its French parent company, Peugeot-Citroen, wanted to close Linwood and instead concentrate its car manufacturing in France. Younger offered them £40m in government grants to remain in Scotland, but on 11 February the closure of Linwood with a loss of 4,800 jobs was confirmed, provoking widespread fury. George had to be in Brussels for fisheries talks and wanted Alex Fletcher to make the Commons statement, instead of the industry under-secretary Norman Tebbit, whom he considered unsympathetic. Private office ingenuity ensured that Fletcher did make the statement, in which he described the closure as disastrous news for the West of Scotland. Tebbit was apoplectic and later burst into Younger's office demanding that he sack his private secretary. When the official asked the Scottish Secretary what he had said in response, George replied, 'Absolutely'.[37]

Younger also turned on the charm when he faced an angry meeting of Strathclyde councillors soon after the announcement. He pointed out that government grants were available to any budding industrialist who wished to set up shop on the redundant site. 'It doesn't matter what they do,' said Younger, perhaps a little lightheartedly, 'if they want to make rubber ducks, we will do what we can to help.'[38] He did everything in his powers to save Linwood, but in reality, he explained, 'how could we ever compel a private company making huge losses to stay here? That simply isn't the real world.'[39]

The Scottish Secretary almost relished persuading the Prime Minister to save another factory from closure. 'She liked arguments and I liked arguing with her,' he later recalled. 'When I pleaded for special measures in such cases as the pulp [mill] closure at Fort William, she always started by insisting that nothing could be done and realities had to be recognised. But in the end I was never turned down on anything I wanted for Scotland.'[40]

But 'Madam Tango', as Younger jokingly referred to the woman

[36] Speech to Scottish Conservative conference, 12/5/1979, MTF.
[37] Interview with Godfrey Robson, c2005.
[38] *Guardian* 13/2/2003.
[39] *Current Account* (BBC Scotland) 12/3/1981.
[40] *Director* 7/1993.

known generally as 'Mrs T', could dig in her heels, even when presented with a compelling case. After talks at the Govan shipyard ('I learnt a lot of new words!' he told an official after one meeting[41]), he asked Thatcher for temporary financial support to secure a foreign order for three bulk carrier ships. 'Margaret disliked this idea intensely and based her opposition on the way these ships were being financed,' Younger recalled. 'She exploded with scorn that they were to be financed by one source, leased by another and operated by yet another. This sounded awful, but it was in fact the way that many, perhaps most ships throughout the world are financed and operated.'

> I stuck to my arguments and when she saw that I was swinging the meeting my way, she turned on me and said: 'All right. If you think this is such a good idea, you can have it if you pay it from Scottish Office funds.' This was outrageous, as it was not within Scottish Office responsibility but under the Department of Trade and Industry. However, I took up her suggestion as I was fairly confident that the ships would be successfully built and sold so no money would be needed. After three anxious years, the Scottish Office was relieved to find we were in the clear and no money was needed.[42]

Not all of Younger's fellow MPs, however, were impressed by these tactics. '[E]ach SoS, instead of considering the National Interest – still less Government policy in the strategic sense – has to "fight his corner",' complained Alan Clark to his diary. 'So the three heavies (Jim Prior, Michael Heseltine and Peter Walker) get the support of ponces like Younger and Edwards (Nicholas, SoS for Wales) who need funds for their wanky little principalities.'[43]

The Scottish Secretary's principality certainly needed funds, and like most of his predecessors, Younger was prepared to fight for them. Another right-wing MP thought Younger was lazy ('he used to leave the Scottish Office at five every night'), complacent ('he was happy to manage the decline of the Scottish Tory Party') and certainly not-Thatcherite ('all he was interested in gaining was the approval of Labour council leaders in Scotland'), although this animosity was probably more personal than political.[44]

On a visit to Scotland in 1989, Edwina Currie reckoned that the 'problem in part is that George Younger . . . poured money into Scotland

---

[41] Gavin McCrone to the author, 13/1/2008.
[42] *Scotland on Sunday* 10/10/1993.
[43] Clark, *Diaries: Into Politics*, 352.
[44] Private information. The MP in question had lost his seat at the 1983 general election.

and let the Labour councils, especially in Glasgow, take the credit.'[45] While in 1984 an unnamed Cabinet colleague told the *Daily Telegraph* that Younger would present Scotland 'as an industrial graveyard down to its last national assets, and then intimidate us with the bogey of separatism'.[46]

Whatever the case, Younger's presentational skills were formidable, so much so that Labour often found itself unable to dent the credibility of what could easily have been a lame duck ministry. His private secretary, Kenneth MacKenzie, remembers witnessing him 'purveying sweet reason' one afternoon in Glasgow, where George was meeting the Scottish Trades Union Congress (STUC) to discuss yet another major industrial closure.

> George was able to convey his total sympathy and understanding [said MacKenzie] of all that was being depicted, by saying something to the effect that of course it was all really just the result of the government's policies, as if the government was some entirely separate entity on another planet or an extraneous factor like the weather which just had to be accepted. The STUC succumbed to his charm and the delegation gratefully withdrew.[47]

Curiously, Mrs Thatcher appeared to tolerate Younger's approach while simultaneously attacking 'subsidy junkies' in other parts of the UK. The Scottish Conservative conference of 1981, however, was not good for the Scottish Secretary. Many delegates were alarmed at the effects of public spending cuts and the recession on Scottish industry; unemployment stood at 287,000, while the party in Scotland was polling just 15 per cent. In their speeches, Younger and Thatcher tried to placate them with news of companies which were expanding, but the conference noticed instead the much longer list of closures. One delegate, Arthur Bell, said he was running his business with little left over for himself or his workers. 'It was the cry of a Conservative whose patience was running out,' observed *The Times*.[48]

RAVENSCRAIG

'After all these industrial troubles,' reflected Younger in 1993, 'it was not surprising that I felt I had to dig my heels in over Ravenscraig. A lot of industry had gone by then and I decided it was a bridge too far.' Like so

---

[45] Currie, *Diaries 1987–1992*, 134.
[46] *Daily Telegraph* 21/3/1984. The article was entitled 'Lame ducks in a grouse moor sanctuary'.
[47] 'A Private Secretary's Tribute' by Kenneth MacKenzie, 2006.
[48] *The Times* 11/5/1981.

many other major industrial employers, Ravenscraig had come to Scotland under the interventionist eye of the former Scottish Secretary Jack Maclay, who argued that locating a steel strip mill in Lanarkshire was vital to broaden Scotland's industrial base and rebalance steel production across the UK.

Essentially, however, it was a rather woolly political compromise. Geographically, Ravenscraig – unlike its counterparts in South Wales – was hundreds of miles from its main markets, but faced with the issue in 1979, Younger thought it was simply a matter of political reality. 'It was such an important factor in the Scottish economy,' he argued. 'It was the biggest customer of Scottish Electricity and Scottish Rail as well as employing 4,000 people directly. I could not allow it to go without a fight. I let it be known that I would strongly oppose any closure and that message got through to Margaret.'[49]

The Scottish Secretary, therefore, was prepared to stake his political reputation on the survival of the plant. The Cabinet was to decide Ravenscraig's fate in December 1982, although most ministers accepted that its closure would be politically and economically unacceptable. Mrs Thatcher's thinking was crucial, although she was inclined to back Younger and Patrick Jenkin, the Industry Secretary, both of whom wanted it kept open. George also had no qualms about pre-empting a Cabinet decision in public. On 5 December he told a meeting of Scottish Young Conservatives at Peebles that it was 'our duty to see that our steel industry survives in a condition ready to take advantage of the economic recovery', although he conceded that 'trimming and reorganization' would be necessary.[50] Although there was much talk at the time of Younger resigning if the Cabinet decided to close Ravenscraig, this was never likely. 'Mr Younger can be relied upon to do the decent thing,' judged *The Times*, 'and resigning over Ravenscraig would not be at all decent.'[51]

Once again the Scottish Secretary galvanised the Scottish lobby, which extended well beyond St Andrew's House. He enjoyed good relations with Gavin Laird, general secretary of the Amalgamated Engineering Union, and more importantly Tom Brennan of the steel union. As the Cabinet worked towards a decision on Ravenscraig, it did so against a backdrop of reshuffle speculation. John Nott had asked to stand down as Defence Secretary, and Younger had been tipped as his successor. 'He knows that

---

[49] *Scotland on Sunday* 17/10/1993.
[50] *The Times* 6/12/1982.
[51] Ibid., 10/12/1982. When Arnold Kemp asked Younger if it was a resignation issue, he replied obliquely: 'Yes. I don't recall actually ever saying that to Mrs Thatcher's face but it was pretty clear to everybody. Everybody knew.' (Kemp, *The Hollow Drum*, 59).

reshuffle thinking has persuaded Downing Street that he is indispensable – or irreplaceable,' observed *The Times*. 'And so, without having laid his resignation on the line – despite that carefully cultivated lobby impression – he stands to win the hand. Ravenscraig will be saved, although slimmed down, he will get much Scottish credit for his Pyrrhic victory.'[52]

Ravenscraig was saved with a three-year reprieve, but the MoD job instead went to the charismatic Michael Heseltine. 'Well done!' scrawled Russell Sanderson. 'Just a line now that the world knows you have won the day – and by all accounts the economic argument on Ravenscraig! It is good to know that your plans worked out, as there was no way that the P.M. could let you go to the wilderness whatever anyone says!!'[53] Politics more often than not beat economics north of the border, and indeed Scotland had played a major part in forcing Edward Heath to U-turn on his economic policies in 1973. George, recalled the BBC journalist John Cole, believed Thatcherite economics were also being modified by politics, 'and he had been known to murmur, with a glance back at a famous decision of the Heath era: Upper Clyde Shipbuilders is alive and well, and living at Downing Street'.[54]

By 1985 production was up at Ravenscraig, removing one argument for its closure in 1982, while the steel it produced was of such high quality that some customers specifically requested it. Workers at the plant had also refused to go along with demands during the miners' strike to decrease production, earning the gratitude of Mrs Thatcher. This was an important factor when Norman Tebbit, the Trade and Industry Secretary, suggested closing the privately-owned Alpha works in South Wales, followed by Ravenscraig three years later. Although this gave Ravenscraig another stay of execution, its finishing mill at Gartcosh was to be closed as part of the so-called Phoenix II industry restructuring.

Finally, on 7 August 1985, the government delivered both good and bad news: Ravenscraig was to be reprieved for another three years, but Gartcosh would close with the loss of 700 jobs. Iain Lawson, a Conservative Parliamentary candidate, resigned in protest, while several Scottish Tory MPs with neighbouring constituencies also put their heads above the parapet, including Younger's friend, the Dumfries MP Sir Hector Monro. Sir Hector's reward was to be ousted as chairman of the Scottish Conservative back-bench committee by Bill Walker, the stridently right-wing MP for Tayside North, with support from English colleagues.[55] Younger

[52] Ibid., 10/12/1982.
[53] Sir Russell Sanderson to GY, 20/12/1982, GYP.
[54] Cole, *As It Seemed To Me*, 264.
[55] The election was swiftly re-run with only Scottish Conservative MPs voting. Sir Hector won.

was appalled by the party infighting but remained aloof, and initially tried to resist the Gartcosh closure. Iain Lawson remembers speaking to Younger at a Conservative Party event soon after: 'He said to me at the end of the evening, "Keep kicking the doors".'[56]

But by October 1985 Younger found himself increasingly isolated in Cabinet on Gartcosh, not that such an impression did him any harm in Scotland. On 19 December he finally ruled out a reprieve, saying he had been persuaded by BSC that the future of Ravenscraig would not be prejudiced by the closure of Gartcosh. In fact, he argued, the closure of the finishing mill might even be to Ravenscraig's long-term advantage.

ONE OF US?

During 1980 and 1981 the government's popularity plummeted as unemployment rocketed and a prolonged recession was felt throughout the country. Mrs Thatcher insisted that however bad things were, her monetarist economic policy was necessary for the UK's long-term recovery. Younger agreed that short-term pain was necessary for the long-term health of the economy and, crucially, revenue from North Sea oil made that short-term pain slightly more bearable.

But although in agreement on the central thrust of the government's economic policies, the Prime Minister and her Scottish Secretary parted company on ideological grounds. While Mrs Thatcher enthusiastically imbibed the wisdom of Hayek and Friedman, Younger was essentially pragmatic. 'I'm not a devotee of Mr Friedman,' he once protested, 'but the facts of life are terribly important [and] we've overspent more than the economy's been earning for a very long time.'

Younger often echoed Thatcher's good housekeeping analogy to explain government policy. 'We're like somebody who keeps going back to the bank manager, every week or every month,' he said, 'and we simply can't go on like that.'[57] These televised explanations of commonsense economics were valued by Downing Street, and although not a member of the Cabinet's main economic committee, George frequently attended when Scottish interests were under discussion and, from 1981 to 1984, was also one of the 'three wise men' of the 'Star Chamber', the committee on public expenditure priorities chaired by Lord Whitelaw. This met only when disputes emerged between a spending department and the Treasury; as Scottish Office spending was governed by a block grant, George was deemed neutral enough to help arbitrate those disputes.

---

[56] Interview with Iain Lawson, 2/4/2007. Lawson joined the SNP the day Gartcosh closed.
[57] *Why I am a Conservative* (BBC Scotland) c10/1980.

Scottish Office spending was, however, subject to Mrs Thatcher's desire to ensure that government money was well spent. In 1984 Downing Street issued a decree that every departmental minister, accompanied by his permanent under-secretary, had to justify expenditure personally to the Prime Minister and her efficiency adviser. Having heard that Norman Tebbit (DTI) and Leon Brittan (Home Office) had endured bruising encounters, Younger rehearsed his script with Sir William Kerr Fraser and took a calculated risk by asking if the Scottish Office graphics unit could make a slide from a postcard he had picked up on a sailing holiday in Oban. This depicted a kilted Scotsman climbing a hill with the caption 'Looking for lost coins among the heather'. Later the next day, Younger concluded a successful but testing session by revealing the slide. As Kerr Fraser switched the light back on, everyone watched with relief as Mrs Thatcher's face cracked into a smile and the Scottish Secretary departed with his spending plans intact.

Not every secretary of state was quite as fortunate, and Cabinet discussions often became heated. Younger quickly learned how to handle these, as 'any minister who lost the argument would either have to accept this or bring the matter back in some other way'. More often than not Willie Whitelaw would liaise with the relevant minister's department and arrange a new paper which reflected Thatcher's point of view. 'She was quite happy to be got round in this way because she had extracted her price,' recalled Younger. 'Of course, Willie was absolutely supreme and always treated her with the utmost respect.'[58] Whitelaw sat next to the Prime Minister as her deputy, and sometimes Younger would sit to his left. Officials got used to hearing him declare: 'I must go and have a word with Willie.' Having a word with Willie often ensured not having to have a word with Mrs T.

Although regularly categorised as being on the left of the party, Younger was bemused by the 'wet' and 'dry' tags favoured by the media. 'I don't accept any of these funny labels which are going around,' he said when asked to align himself. 'I have never understood who is thought to be wet and who is thought to be not wet.' Personally, he had no taste for divisions of right and left within the Conservative Party. 'I find I do not wholly agree with either wing, and disagree with both wings on some issues,' he explained. 'As far as I am concerned, I am a Conservative and not a socialist, and that is quite sufficient ideological difference for me.'[59]

Nevertheless, Younger recognised that Mrs Thatcher's first Cabinet included several members who were certainly not on her wing of the

[58] *Scotland on Sunday* 10/10/1993.
[59] *Why I am a Conservative* (BBC Scotland) c10/1980.

party. 'Jim Prior, Christopher Soames, Peter Walker, Ian Gilmour and Francis Pym all had great reservations about her economic policy,' he recalled.

> In fact, these 'wets' as they were known, sealed themselves off by never challenging her. It used to entertain me enormously to read in the newspapers about this threat from the dissidents in cabinet. They quite revelled in it and were happy to be characterised in this way. But with the exception of Jim Prior they never opened their mouths. We all knew that they wanted to, but they did not combine and challenge policy. Margaret was pleased about that.[60]

One of Thatcher's biographers placed Younger firmly in the middle section of the Cabinet, what he called 'the ballast of steady loyalists who took their cue from Willie Whitelaw'.[61] Peter Walker was another Cabinet minister Younger admired for quietly working on his brief while occasionally making carefully coded speeches to indicate areas of concern. It was a subtle balancing act which clearly worked for both Younger and Walker, and was appreciated by the Prime Minister. 'There was once a long discussion in cabinet on the inner cities and we could not reach a conclusion,' he recalled. 'Eventually Mrs Thatcher decided it had gone on long enough and said: "Well, we've got to get somewhere. Now what about George? You're a normal person, what do you think?"'[62]

But even humour could not prevent left–right tensions within the Cabinet coming to a head over the anti-inflationary 1981 Budget. Sir Ian Gilmour, Peter Walker and Jim Prior thought its defiance of Keynesian logic was 'astonishingly perverse', but opted not to resign, while Younger and Mark Carlisle, although supportive, 'expressed their reservations in a more minor key'.[63] The reshuffle which followed saw Peter Walker survive, Carlisle and Gilmour sacked and Prior exiled to Northern Ireland.

Nevertheless, even the reconstituted Cabinet could be stimulating and occasionally fun. 'A fascinating by-product of cabinet meetings is notes,' recalled Younger. 'Christopher Soames used to sit next to me and I cannot recall a cabinet meeting when he did not send at least six notes to somebody.' Mrs Thatcher, he said, 'pretended not to notice'.[64] The Chancellor, Sir Geoffrey Howe, was also an occasional note scribbler.

---

[60] *Scotland on Sunday* 10/10/1993.
[61] Campbell, *The Iron Lady*, 441.
[62] *Scotland on Sunday* 10/10/1993.
[63] *The Times* 13/3/1981.
[64] *Scotland on Sunday* 10/10/1993.

One in Latin, passed to Younger in the summer of 1982, read: *Ex Hibernia Semper Aliquid Novum*. Translated, it means: 'Out of Ireland always something new.'[65]

Sir Geoffrey, like George, was an Old Wykehamist, as was Willie Whitelaw. Curiously, despite Mrs Thatcher's distrust of party grandees she adored all three, although relations with Howe would later turn disastrously sour. But in the early 1980s the trio were steadfastly loyal, sound on policy and good on delivery. Younger, in turn, regarded the Iron Lady with bemused affection, aware of her faults but respectful of her energy, focus and command of detail.

Their personal styles, however, were completely different. Mrs Thatcher distrusted some civil servants she suspected to be Labour-inclined; Younger always assumed his officials were politically impartial, even when they urged caution. And while the Prime Minister consumed paperwork, the Scottish Secretary preferred officials to brief him while he signed documents in the back of his ministerial car. 'George's priority was always people rather than paper', remembered one private secretary, 'and I think he made a pretty shrewd judgment that there is more mileage for a secretary of state in taking salutes than in signing Statutory Instruments, so he wisely got the latter task delegated to the junior ministers.'[66]

While Michael Heseltine modernised management structures at the Department of Environment, Younger believed it was not for him to interfere with internal Scottish Office affairs. 'Once you start trying to run the mechanics of the office for the civil service you're lost,' he explained, 'you're lost because you lose their [civil servants'] confidence and you're lost because you haven't the time to do it.'[67] And unlike the eloquent Willie Ross, Younger would happily rely on speeches prepared by officials, although he would add a little personal embellishment.

Although committed to public service, Younger believed that politics was a job almost like any other, and was determined to make time for his family and wife Diana, always an important consideration in both his public and private life. He lunched regularly with friends like Jeffrey Archer and family members such as 'Bill' McEwan Younger; attended 'Old Gang' luncheons at the Dorchester; indulged his love of opera at Covent Garden; and took time out one afternoon to play French horn in honour of his old music master. A senior official was even astonished to encounter Younger queuing to cast his vote when the chancellorship of his *alma mater* fell vacant.

[65] Sir Geoffrey Howe to GY, c1982, GYP. Sir Geoffrey was paraphrasing, inaccurately, the Roman historian Pliny the Elder, who had written *Ex Africa semper aliquid novi*.
[66] 'A Private Secretary's Tribute' by Kenneth MacKenzie, 2006.
[67] *Playing the Scottish Card* II (BBC Radio Scotland) 16/9/1985.

The Scottish Secretary also took civil servants into his confidence, relying on them for advice and inviting some to family weddings. Consequently, they enjoyed working for him, despite being conscious that some issues were off-limits in terms of small talk. On a cold night in December 1981, Younger and his wife even got dressed up to watch Kenneth MacKenzie and his fellow thespians tread the boards in the Edinburgh Civil Service Dramatic Society's Golden Jubilee production of *Sabrina Fair*.

Younger also had a knack of quickly reducing complicated issues down to a single, often pithily amusing point. John Graham, his private secretary from 1983 to 1985, remembers a rather serious group of people briefing him on cable television. 'He sat politely and listened to technical stuff which wasn't his bag,' recalled Graham, 'then he said: "so you're telling me that in principle there could be a channel which showed nothing but *Tom and Jerry*?" They looked baffled but eventually one said, "well yes, it's all about special interests". 'I'll go for that,' replied George.'[68]

His was an intuitive intelligence which did not seem to need hard graft. Good at mastering a brief and reaching quick decisions, Younger also relished the traditional trappings of his office. An ardent Royalist, he enjoyed the plethora of Holyrood garden parties, dinners and duties as minister in attendance to the Queen in his capacity as keeper of the Great Seal of Scotland. For a former Argylls man, the splendid views of Horseguards from Dover House were an added bonus, and Younger would sit happily in his office with the windows open so he could hear bands practising for the annual Trooping the Colour.

George's broad remit at the Scottish Office also allowed him to indulge his love of the arts. In Glasgow, he helped find the Burrell Collection a permanent home, backed a garden festival as part of its ongoing regeneration, and authorised a new building for the Royal Scottish Academy of Music and Drama, of which he had once been a governor. And in Edinburgh, a refurbished school on Belford Road became the Scottish National Gallery of Modern Art, then the only public gallery in the UK with a permanent collection devoted to modern art and the largest single collection outside the Tate in London.

Unstuffy and relaxed in dealings with his private office, when planes were delayed or a car failed to turn up, recalled Kenneth MacKenzie, Younger 'took it with wry but philosophical equanimity and did not harry the hapless private secretary to conjure up alternative transport out of thin

---

[68] Interview with John Graham, 6/6/2007.

air or magic the fog away. And even when it clearly was our fault or we
landed him in an embarrassing mix up, he kept his sense of humour and
we plodded on.'[69] His staff grew accustomed to his preference for a holdall
packed like a kitbag rather than a suitcase, and the need to ransack his
briefcase from time to time in search of a free pardon or Royal Warrant
which had gone astray.

And although Younger was an effective media performer, particularly
on television, he never attempted to 'manage' media coverage in the
modern sense. That was left to Alex Pagett, the Scottish Office's chief
press officer, who could never quite understand his boss's lack of interest
in the newspapers he laid out for him each morning. 'He would go straight
to the back of *The Times*,' remembered John Graham, 'which was running
a fantasy portfolio competition. George would check to see how he was
getting on, then he'd look at the front page of the *Herald* and *Scotsman* for
a minute or two, and then get on with his inbox.'[70] At the end of a long
meeting, Younger would often look at his watch and tell officials that
he would like to go and watch the popular BBC satire, *Yes, Minister*, on
television.

Diana provided George with invaluable support. Despite bouts of ill
health[71] she threw herself into the duties of a Cabinet minister's wife,
endearing herself to the press corps while organising social events for
Cabinet ministers' wives with Lady Howe. She also ensured that visitors to
Bute House (parts of which she energetically refurbished) felt like members of the unusually close Younger family. 'This sprang naturally from
their own close family life', recalled MacKenzie, 'but they took particular
trouble to make sure that we saw as much as was possible of our wives or
husbands and that they could share in any suitable occasion.'[72]

The weekly routine of a Scottish MP was pretty arduous; that of a
Scottish minister even more so. 'I am in London Monday, Tuesday,
Wednesday and Thursday,' George told an interviewer in 1983, 'the rest
up north: mostly in Edinburgh, but I spend at least one day in Ayr every
few weeks.' He continued:

> I try also to get to my own home in Stirlingshire so that the grass can be tamed.
> I do lots of gardening, play some tennis. In the winter I shoot, and in the

---

[69] 'A Private Secretary's Tribute' by Kenneth MacKenzie, 2006. One such mix up occurred in
November 1985 when a private office oversight prematurely revealed approval for a £100m
brewery takeover in a letter to a constituent. Younger had to make a statement of apology to the
House.

[70] Interview with John Graham.

[71] Diana suffered from celiac disease, a common symptom of which was fatigue.

[72] 'A Private Secretary's Tribute' by Kenneth MacKenzie, 2006.

summer try to fit in some sailing. I was educated half in Scotland and half
in England. So I am a bit of a half breed, I suppose. I have always lived in
Scotland, the contrast is delightful, because every week-end when I go home to
Scotland you feel it's different: more relaxed. But I enjoy representing Scotland
in London.[73]

On weekends at Easter Leckie Younger would work in his study – also the
drawing room – with opera or organ music playing at top volume. The
irony was not lost on George's children that it was them, rather than their
father, demanding that the stereo be turned down.

Younger's relationship with his four children – James, Joanna, Charlie
and Andrew – was close and diligently democratic. No matter how busy
his week, George would burst into their bedrooms at around 7 a.m., open
all the curtains and suggest a menu of breakfast options. He would then
cook the majority choice, although the scrambled egg would usually get
burnt. George was always very domesticated – perhaps as a result of
his National Service – and always ensured chores were divided equally
between his offspring. The same principle applied to their education and,
in his final years, to the family estate.

The younger Youngers also provided a useful foil for George's rather
offbeat sense of humour. He loved watching high-quality slapstick comedy
like *Morecambe & Wise* and *The Two Ronnies* on television, and applied some
of what he saw to otherwise monotonous duties such as washing dishes.
One of his favourite jokes was to place each item he had dried back in the
wash pile, while faking a war-wound and talking like an old-Etonian
colonel.

Like his father, Younger also enjoyed using pet names for food and
people. Steak and kidney became 'Kate and Sidney'; mackerel was
'McKerrel' (spoken in a Morningside accent); and a Crunchie was a
'Charles Runcie' (Archbishop Robert Runcie's fictitious brother). Even
Cabinet colleagues did not escape odd nomenclatures. Geoffrey Howe
was referred to as 'Hoffrey Jew'; Maitland McGill Crichton was known as
'Monday-Tuesday-Wednesday' (an Argylls nickname which also applied
to his habit of phoning George during week-day meal times); his father
was dubbed 'Dangrad'; and Hill & Robb, the family solicitors in Stirling,
were known affectionately as 'steal and rob'.[74]

George regularly played his French horn at home, with his children
joining in on piano, flute, violin or oboe. And from the moment they were
old enough, Younger also encouraged his children to take messages from

---

[73] *Scottish Portrait* 8/1983.
[74] Charlie Younger to the author, 15/2/2008.

often inebriated constituents who called to debate the finer points of everything from local policing to the relative merits of the caller's wife. Often amusing, it wore thin at times, although the Member for Ayr always insisted that his home number should be 'in the book'.

Weekend chores were largely dictated by Diana, but George actually enjoyed otherwise mundane tasks like mowing the grass and weeding as it allowed him to switch off completely from political concerns. He loved bonfires and would chop logs (shades of Gladstone at Hawarden) wearing a favourite duffel coat which his children remember being worn for more than 40 years. In that sense George was completely lacking in any materialistic sense, and it was Diana who supervised his sartorial considerations, although he always took care to wear his regimental tie on appropriate occasions. An avid collector of Green Shield Stamps, Charlie Younger remembers his father being thrilled when he had accumulated enough to buy a Black & Decker drill, even though DIY was never his forte.

Occasionally youthful high spirits interfered with the security at Easter Leckie, chiefly lights and panic buttons which had been installed by beds and certain doors in 1979. When George's eldest son James had some university friends to stay on a particularly cold night, one decided to test out a panic button just as they were preparing for bed. Within seconds police cars roared up the drive and several officers knocked on the door. Younger was mortified when he found out and apologised profusely to the police. 'Aye, dinnae worry sir,' replied one policeman. 'We kept yer son talking on the doorstep in his pyjamas for quite some time.'[75]

Security for even middle-ranking Cabinet ministers was, however, a serious matter. It emerged in 1982 that Younger's name was among those on an apparent IRA hit-list found in the flat of the suspected terrorist Gerard Tuite, while several letter bombs were delivered to his constituency and departmental offices. Then there was the October 1984 Conservative Party conference in Brighton. The Youngers were asleep in Room 710 when an explosion shook the Grand Hotel in the early hours of 12 October. George knew immediately that it was a bomb, although Diana managed to remain relatively calm while he tried to attract attention by sticking a metal coat hanger out of the window. Their bedroom door was wedged shut, but firemen managed to gain access and ushered the Youngers down an external fire escape, instructing them not to 'look right' as they did so.

To their right was a yawning chasm where several floors of the hotel had once been. Luckily, George and Diana's room was in a tower structure adjoining the main building. Independently secure, it had escaped any

---

[75] Interview with James Younger, 9/11/2007.

major damage from the blast. They reached ground level wearing pyjamas, although George had managed to put on a suit over his. Police told them to keep moving up a side street, and eventually they stumbled across a guest house run by a gay couple (with whom they later kept in touch). Diana phoned their children to tell them what had happened, but getting back to sleep was impossible. Famously, Marks & Spencer opened early so those who had lost their clothes in the bombing could get new ones. According to Diana, the sight of several Cabinet ministers – including Sir Keith Joseph clad in a silk dressing gown – filing along the street was quite a spectacle for early-morning bus queues.

Although the bombers missed their main target in the Prime Minister, the whip Sir Anthony Berry was killed, as was John Wakeham's first wife Roberta, while Norman Tebbit and his wife were seriously injured. For Younger, the tragedy also struck close to home. Donald Maclean, his constituency chairman in Ayr, and his wife, Muriel, were in the room in which the bomb exploded. Although Muriel was not killed in the explosion, she later died of smoke inhalation while Donald recovered in the Royal Sussex County Hospital. 'At Brighton I had nothing,' recalled Sir Donald (he was later knighted), 'it was all gone in the blast. My sister was holding the fort for me here [in Ayr] and I phoned her up to get some stuff put together. Without any fuss George picked it up, brought it down and took it to me at the hospital. He was quite content to go through security and made no effort to throw his weight around as a minister, something that made quite an impression on the Brighton Police.'[76]

Despite the trauma of Brighton, Younger was always relaxed about his personal security and during the summer recess made time for sailing on the west coast of Scotland, often joining Sir David Montgomery on his yacht *Colymbus*. These family holidays were not without dangers. Once, when George ran the yacht ashore off Arisaig, he hastily pulled down his yellow sou'wester and headed below deck to avoid a ferry boat loaded with tourists that was chugging alongside to offer help. Younger managed to get *Colymbus* towed off while Joanna and his sons expressed thanks without putting his head above the hatch. Newspaper headlines referring to the Scottish Secretary 'running aground' or 'losing his way' were just too much for him to risk.

On another occasion, when *Colymbus* was completing a race into Oban Bay under spinnaker, the halyard was found to be jammed at the top of the mast. George owned up to having hoisted it and was sent aloft in the bosun's chair. All was calm until it became apparent that a Caledonian

[76] Interview with Sir Donald Maclean, 2/8/2007.

MacBrayne (CalMac) ferry was steaming at a rate of knots into the harbour from Mull, full of locals and tourists, and creating a large wake which caused *Colymbus* to roll heavily from side to side. Younger could only hold on for dear life, gripping the mast and shutting his eyes. On arriving back on deck, his views on CalMac were strictly off the record. Otherwise, sport generally passed George by. He enjoyed going to the rugby, fishing (with Russell Sanderson) and playing an occasional round of golf, but Andrew Younger's main memory is of his father routinely binning the sport section of the family's Sunday newspapers.

George would self-deprecatingly recount yachting mishaps to his constituency staff on his regular days in Ayr. After morning surgeries at his constituency office on Wellington Square (also used by his great-grandfather when MP for Ayr) he would break for a fish-and-chip lunch at the County Hotel, before a round of constituency engagements organised by his agent Bill Taylor. He continued to patronise the Tennent's Trophy at Ayr racecourse, and from 1982 to 1986 both encouraged and approved the financing of rolling stock on newly-electrified railways in Ayrshire. During election campaigns, George and Diana stayed with the Mac-Andrews – Joe and Eileen – at their house on Racecourse Road.

He also continued to defend Prestwick against repeated threats to its status as Scotland's transatlantic gateway. Younger dispatched several sales missions to North America to attract custom, lobbied to lift restrictions on cargo flights, approved a £28m upgrade of the airport's road link to Glasgow and backed British Caledonian routes claims against British Airways in Cabinet in July 1984. But Prestwick's operating losses continued to rise while passenger figures continued to fall. Although Younger fought, and won, a vigorous Cabinet battle with the Transport Secretary, Nicholas Ridley, who argued that it should close, the resulting reprieve in April 1985 gave Prestwick just four years to improve its economic performance.

Inconveniently, there were no flights from Prestwick to London, so Younger often faced a mad rush to get from Ayr to Glasgow Airport, which was near Paisley. Another private secretary, Godfrey Robson, remembered being in the shuttle lounge at Heathrow and watching his chief react to a friendly wave from an unfamiliar – but distinctly elderly – fellow passenger. Suddenly, Younger asked, 'how's your mother these days?' 'Good of you to remember,' replied the other passenger. Robson assumed he had remembered who he was after all and on being told that Younger remained none the wiser said, 'but you asked about his mother'. 'Oh well,' said the Scottish Secretary, 'you have to take risks now and again.'[77]

[77] Sir Malcolm Rifkind's memorial service speech, 26/4/2003, GYP.

Otherwise, on Sunday evening he and Diana would get the sleeper to London, where they rented a one-bedroom flat on Cundy Street in Pimlico, often shared with their daughter Joanna and son Charlie, who were then working in the London area. Every Wednesday morning during the parliamentary session the Scottish Office ministerial team would meet at Dover House to discuss issues and plan strategy. Younger's instinct for the core of any issue allowed him to rattle through the morning's business efficiently, while detecting early on if someone had concerns and ensuring they got to articulate why. His subtle sense of humour also made these 'prayer' meetings as much fun as they could possibly be.

En route to his office in Dover House (where Diana oversaw the installation of a kitchen), Younger regularly passed a splendid full-length portrait of his great-uncle Sir John Gilmour, who was Scottish Secretary from 1924 to 1929. Although Younger was only a boy when Sir John died in 1940, there were some interesting parallels in their Scottish Office careers (both reformed the rates and took on local government). While Gilmour had been the first post-1745 Secretary of State for Scotland,[78] his great nephew was to become its longest continually-serving.

As Scottish Secretary, Younger was also acutely aware of the family debt he owed to his great-grandfather, the 1st Viscount Younger. When the Scottish Conservative & Unionist Association (SCUA) celebrated its centenary in 1982, the future 4th Viscount paid tribute to the 'great guiding hands of the middle years such as Sir George Younger, my great grandfather, who first insisted on the paramount importance of organisation'. Nothing changes, mused Younger, 'tariff reform, the Irish Question, deceased wife's sister'.[79]

The SCUA president, Lord Home, who had encountered the 1st Viscount as a young candidate in Lanark, remained a hugely respected figure within the Scottish Conservative hierarchy. George was often in touch with him for advice, and in 1983 he and Diana were two of only fourteen guests at a Chequers luncheon hosted by Mrs Thatcher to mark Home's eightieth birthday. Younger also urged the former prime minister to serve as Lord High Commissioner to the General Assembly of the Church of Scotland, a Royal appointment on advice from the Scottish Secretary. 'We have given the possibility the closest thought but with great regret have decided that the hazard is too high,' replied Home. 'I can do

[78] The post had been known as Secretary for Scotland until 1926, when Stanley Baldwin elevated it to full Cabinet rank.

[79] Speech to SCUA, 26/11/1982, GYP. This was a reference to the Deceased Wife's Sister's Marriage Act 1907, which allowed a man to marry the sister of his deceased wife. Sir John Gilmour (Younger's great-uncle) had, in fact, married his deceased wife's sister.

almost anything but stand & that would be inevitable for longish periods
while Elizabeth's asthma takes charge when she gets tired & is crippling
when it does so. What crocks we are!'[80]

FALKLANDS AND THE KHAKI ELECTION

'Margaret was extremely fortunate in her choice of enemies,' mused
Younger in 1993, 'starting with General Galtieri when he seized the
Falklands in 1982. Before that happened, there were real fears that we
may not win the next election. After we retook the Falklands, there was
never any doubt that we would.'

The invasion of the Falklands was a potentially major debacle for the
Prime Minister. 'She had made her name since 1975 as the Iron Lady,' said
Younger. 'Strong defences, particularly against the USSR, were her constant
theme. What was the worth of all her rhetoric if she was beaten by a bankrupt
South American dictator? It could well have been the end of her.' Thatcher
was always clear in her own mind that any peace deal or compromise would
be regarded by the country as a fudge, although diplomats continued to seek a
solution while the task-force sailed towards the South Atlantic.

Younger was unable to make the emergency Cabinet meeting convened on Friday 2 April, but thereafter listened intently as novel solutions
were canvassed. 'Those took many forms,' he recalled, 'perhaps we could
acknowledge Argentine sovereignty and then lease back the islands? Some
in the Cabinet were attracted to these ideas and they were not foolish to
feel this way because the risks of the operation were very obvious.'[81]
Younger, as a former Argyll, and Willie Whitelaw, a former Guardsman,
were acutely aware of what British soldiers would face when they engaged
the enemy on barren Falklands terrain.

The invasion also had political consequences, claiming the scalps of the
Foreign Secretary Lord Carrington, often a Cabinet ally of the Scottish
Secretary, and the Lord Privy Seal (and Commons Foreign Office spokesman) Humphrey Atkins, who was also a family friend. 'We all know that we
are in a very high-risk business and that there is always the chance that the
cards will fall in a manner which one would not wish,' replied Atkins to a
note from Younger. 'This, of course, doesn't help much when they do, but
the understanding and good wishes of one's friends are an enormous help.
All the very best to you – I hope your new neighbour at the Cabinet table is
agreeable!'[82]

---

[80] ADH to GY, c1985, GYP.
[81] *Scotland on Sunday* 17/10/1993.
[82] Humphrey Atkins to GY, 14/4/1982, GYP.

Although Younger had qualms about the human cost of engagement in the Falklands, he was fully behind Mrs Thatcher's chosen course of action. 'Margaret's real strength as a leader was never more apparent or more necessary,' said Younger admiringly.

> She saw with greater clarity than anyone that what was needed was not a face saving formula but a reversal of the military humiliation that Britain had suffered. It was not just a lucky break. She earned every bit of it by taking the most difficult decisions of her life. Most male politicians would have gone for a diplomatic solution, even if it was a bad one. She didn't and she was proved absolutely correct.

He was also appalled by accusations that the Prime Minister revelled in the fighting. 'I was with her in her room in the House of Commons when the news of the sinking of HMS *Sheffield* came in,' Younger remembered. 'I have never seen her more distressed or upset. To suggest she ordered the *Belgrano* to be sunk to scupper any hope of peace is simply ridiculous. Its sinking probably saved many British lives.'[83]

Younger's friend on the opposition benches, Tam Dalyell, vehemently disagreed. 'To me, it was plain as a pikestaff,' George later explained. 'If you have a huge and very vulnerable fleet in the area, there's only one option: eliminate the danger. The direction the ship was steaming at the moment it was hit may be of some rhetorical interest, but it is of no fundamental interest at all . . . In my view, he [Dalyell] simply couldn't resist the wonderful role of hammer of the *Belgrano*.'[84]

Even the Scottish Secretary, however, grew uncomfortable at the Prime Minister's jingoistic desire to exploit the conflict. In May Mrs Thatcher delivered a rousing speech to the Scottish Conservative conference in Perth following the recapture of South Georgia. 'It reminded me of the Nuremberg Rally,'[85] he told a friend after witnessing the delegates' enthusiastic response. Nevertheless, Younger was in no doubt 'that her courage and success over the Falklands transformed her political position both at home and abroad'.[86]

As a result of events in a faraway island of which most Britons knew nothing, Mrs Thatcher had been transformed into a strong leader. There were also domestic factors in her – and her party's – improved fortunes. By the beginning of 1983 the government's seemingly harsh economic

---

[83] *Scotland on Sunday* 17/10/1993.
[84] Galbraith, *Inside Outside*, 185–86.
[85] Young, *One of Us*, 273.
[86] *Scotland on Sunday* 17/10/1993.

policies finally seemed to be working, while the opposition was split between a self-destructing Labour Party and the breakaway SDP. A 'khaki' election to capitalise on the post-Falklands mood was inevitable.

In Scotland, Younger's balance sheet was pretty positive. He had helped firms like Weir's, Collins, British Aerospace and Ferranti through the recession, although by his own admission there had also been some failures. Talbot had gone at Linwood; Invergordon had won only a temporary reprieve; while a replacement was still being sought for the pulp mill at Corpach. Younger cheerfully brushed aside accusations of not having a mandate, claiming his party was in a majority outside Strath-clyde. 'I love politics and I want to continue in politics for as long as possible,' he told the *Glasgow Herald* just before the election. 'I have to earn a living. I can't retire and I don't want to.'[87]

'Whatever the more blinkered critics say, Thatcherism has not had a free run in Scotland,' assessed Allan Massie in the *Spectator*. 'In each of the critical decisions, George Younger and the Scottish Office have been found articulating the need to protect the Scottish interest against the free play of market forces.'[88] Younger would have had no quibble with that analysis, telling one interviewer that he 'would like it to be remembered that I steered Scotland through the recession with as little damage as possible and enabled it to come out from it, relative to the rest of Britain, much stronger'.[89]

In the event, the general election of 1983 was a triumph for Mrs Thatcher and a relief for Younger. The Conservatives won a landslide and, despite boundary changes and a reduced share of the vote, retained 21 MPs in Scotland. In Ayr, the boundary revision had replaced Labour-voting mining communities with Tory-inclined areas such as Troon, giving Younger his largest ever majority of 7,987. Labour, however, delivered its worst UK performance since the Second World War. On election night George Foulkes (the Labour MP for the neighbouring seat of South Ayrshire) vowed to make life for Younger 'untenable'.

It had been widely assumed that Younger would receive Cabinet promotion in return for services to Thatcherism in Scotland, but it was not to be. He was disappointed, but loyally told reporters he was perfectly content to stay at St Andrew's House. Joining him there were a new team of ministers comprising Michael Ancram, the impressive John MacKay (formerly a maths teacher in Oban) and the mutton-chopped Allan Stewart. Hamish Gray, meanwhile, had lost his Highland seat to a

---

[87] *Glasgow Herald* 2/6/1983.
[88] *Spectator* 5/3/1983.
[89] *Scottish Portrait Magazine* 8/1983.

young Charles Kennedy and was therefore elevated to the Upper House as Lord Gray of Contin in order to become minister of state.

Although the election represented a remarkable turnaround for the government, the economy remained fragile, and the Chancellor, Nigel Lawson, was able to give the Cabinet a reasonably upbeat assessment of future prospects on 21 July. 'Recovery patchy but quickening,' noted Younger during the meeting. 'Unemployment levelling off. Inflation 5½% 1983 and 1984. *BUT* world growth slower than expected. Public Exp[enditure] & Gov[ernmen]t borrowing running ahead.'

The Scottish Secretary then gave Cabinet his assessment, not just of the economic picture in Scotland, but across the UK. He felt that the next '6 months [were] critical' and 'Recovery the vital factor'. But, he added, 'Int[erest] rates [were too] high', as were imports and earnings. More cuts were inevitable, for which, said George, 'realism [was] needed' while 'PR [was] essential'.[90] Younger had always been adept at managing the public relations of government decisions in a Scottish context, a skill he would need more than ever in the two years which followed the general election.

Two days after this Cabinet meeting George's mother Evelyn died on holiday in the north of Scotland, having been involved in a traffic accident several weeks before. Always close to his parents, Younger was at least able to visit them regularly as his ministerial duties meant he was often in Scotland. He and Diana continued to live in their modest stone-and-timber house on the estate, while the 3rd Viscount lived close by in a mock Georgian house, from which he ran 1,000 acres of farmland. One of George's two younger brothers, Bobby, had restored a sixteenth-century castle on the estate ('Old Leckie'), while the other, Sandy, lived in a cottage called 'Wester Leckie' and worked in printing. His sister, Rosalind, had long settled in Australia with her husband Tom Cropper, who farmed a property at Willow Tree in New South Wales.

Soon after the election, Younger requested that his wife Diana be more fully involved in the planning of individual engagements. This included a visit in early September 1983 from the Prime Minister, who was recovering from a minor operation. '[H]ow marvellously you have managed to combine style and tradition with basic comforts in that dauntingly large building!' Mrs Thatcher wrote to Diana afterwards. 'Our break at Bute House proved to be an oasis of calm and rest in an otherwise very hectic programme.'[91]

There was a sartorial crisis when Denis, the Prime Minister's devoted husband, discovered he had forgotten to bring cufflinks for a formal

[90] Cabinet notes dated 21/7/1983, GYP.
[91] MT to DY, 5/9/1983, GYP.

dinner. George came to the rescue by lending him a pair, which Denis later returned along with cufflinks of his own as a thank-you present. '[T]he air of Scotland must have been what she needed to complete her recovery from her operation,' wrote the Prime Minister's private secretary (and future Cabinet secretary) Robin Butler, 'because she has been full of energy and right back in top gear.'[92]

But despite the success of the visit, when another chance for Cabinet promotion arose the following month, Younger was again passed over. The Trade and Industry Secretary, Cecil Parkinson, resigned after a personal scandal, and the Scottish Secretary had been tipped to replace him. Speaking to reporters outside his home George conceded it was 'inevitable' that the Parkinson affair would damage the government. When asked if it was not more accurate to say that it would not be forgotten until the next scandal broke, he replied: 'The next scandal won't be in the Scottish Office anyway.' Standing next to him was Diana, who quipped wryly: 'It had better not be.'[93]

MINERS' STRIKE AND SCARGILL

Despite his desire to leave the Scottish Office, Younger was determined to make the most of the situation. Muir Russell, his private secretary since 1981, remembers sitting in the Secretary of State's office in Dover House and George saying 'well, the time to be really radical and have new ideas is when you've just won an election with a good majority'.[94] This good majority, arguably, led to complacency in the ranks. The 1983–86 period could be described as the wasted years of Thatcherism, and for Younger too the opportunity provided by the landslide majority was inexplicably squandered.

Instead, the Scottish Secretary increasingly became the victim of events and generated little by way of original policy. Younger simply responded to events, chiefly two bitter strikes – miners' and teachers' – while he pushed for just one specifically Scottish initiative, abolition of rates and the introduction of what became known as the Poll Tax.

'If [Mrs Thatcher] was fortunate in facing General Galtieri in the Falklands,' mused Younger in 1993, 'she was even more fortunate in facing another incompetent general in her next battle, Arthur Scargill, president of the NUM. He was both the problem and the solution.' He continued:

---

[92] Robin Butler to DY, 10/9/1983, GYP.

[93] *Glasgow Herald* 17/10/1983. George told some journalists he would 'even' go to the Northern Ireland Office if it meant escaping St Andrew's House.

[94] Interview with Sir Muir Russell, 21/5/2007.

In this battle, she had to display powers of planning, cunning and adaptability that some might have thought she did not possess. The miners had brought down the Heath government in 1974 and we knew very well that this threat would come again once Scargill was elected union president in 1981. He was driven by political aims, not industrial ones. Nothing we could ever pay his members would satisfy him. He had to be beaten in open battle.

The Prime Minister had played a long and careful game. In the face of a threatened miners' strike in 1981, Mrs Thatcher had ordered an uncharacteristic climb-down over pit closures. 'But it was a tactical retreat,' said Younger. 'We knew Scargill would be back spoiling for a fight one day.'

A group of ministers led by Nigel Lawson, then Energy Secretary, secretly began planning for Scargill's next move. It included Younger because of his responsibility for Scotland's electricity supplies. He recalled:

> At meetings throughout 1982 and 1983, we planned our strategy. Maximum coal production was ordered and the Treasury allocated extra money to pay for it. Nuclear and oil-fired power stations were made ready . . . I was particularly glad to get Inverkip oil-fired station ready on the Clyde because I made the decision in 1972 to make it an oil-fired station. But to my embarrassment, the subsequent rise in oil prices meant it had hardly been used. It would be soon.
>
> As well as stocks, we had two other advantages working for us. First, the trade union law on secondary picketing which was to prove crucial for controlling the strike from spreading to other industries; and secondly the break up of the rival Union of Democratic Mineworkers in the Nottinghamshire coalfield [it actually broke *away* from the NUM].
>
> Thus it was when Arthur Scargill, unbelievably, started the strike in March 1984, he played into our hands. All our preparations were enhanced by the fact that he struck at a time when the warmer summer months meant low usage of coal.

There followed a year of bitter strife on the picket lines. 'We frequently had to support the police, the Home Secretary, Peter Walker, by now energy secretary, and Ian MacGregor, chairman of the coal board,' remembered Younger, 'in dealing with the violence organised by Scargill, often against the wives and families of its own members.'[95]

As Scottish Secretary, Younger was also responsible for policing north of the border, and he no doubt drew on his experience of the Carrington Committee in opposition, which had devised strategies for dealing with

---

[95] *Scotland on Sunday* 17/10/1993.

supply problems caused by industrial action.[96] And unlike the battle with
General Galtieri, this time he had no qualms. The strike, he told a
Parliamentary Press Gallery lunch, was 'an assault on many of the things
Britain stands for'.[97] Although he had previously been prepared to fight
for Scottish pits, strike action, he said, had taken the matter out of his
hands.

'The outcome was another victory for Margaret Thatcher,' recalled
Younger, 'the far-sighted planner who sacrificed the short term for the
long-term good of the country.'[98] It was a victory which had required
'necessary ruthlessness to see the matter through',[99] and the fact that the
Prime Minister did so left a profound impression on her Scottish
Secretary. So much so, that he recalled the dispute in correspondence
with Baroness Thatcher shortly before his death.[100]

By the middle of 1984 Younger had became a favourite party spokesman in a crisis. At the height of the miners' strike he was wheeled out to
dampen rumours of a planned coup against the Prime Minister, assuring
reporters there was 'no sign of widespread and deep unrest'.[101] George
was also valued by Downing Street as a polished television performer,
even on subjects beyond his departmental remit. When a row blew up
over the government prohibiting GCHQ (Government Communications
HQ) staff from joining a trade union, Younger was put up to be grilled by
the Labour MP-turned-interviewer Brian Walden on ITV's *Weekend
World*.

Forestry policy was another example of Younger's remit extending
beyond purely Scottish issues. Although the Forestry Commission (FC)
was based in Edinburgh, it was a Great Britain body which just happened
to have a Scottish chairman[102] and a Scottish director-general. The
Scottish Office had no formal responsibility for forestry policy although
the FC was answerable to what was known as the 'triumvirate' – the
Secretaries of State for Wales (Nick Edwards) and Scotland, and the
Minister of Agriculture (Peter Walker and Michael Jopling).

The triumvirate met regularly and Younger soon emerged as its 'lead'
minister. Practically, it made sense. FC HQ was in Scotland, as was most
new forestry planting, but politically, the dynamic within the triumvirate

---

[96] See pp. 134–135.
[97] *The Times* 12/7/1984.
[98] *Scotland on Sunday* 17/10/1993.
[99] Ibid., 10/10/1993.
[100] See pp. 293–294.
[101] *The Times* 13/7/1984.
[102] Initially the FC chairman was the former Labour minister Lord Mackie. He was succeeded in 1979
by Sir David Montgomery, who had been in Berlin with George while on National Service.

was rather strange – two supported the government orthodoxy which dictated that FC assets (i.e. land) should be sold off or privatised, while only one (Younger) urged caution and stability. 'A lot was sold but not as much as there could have been,' recalled the FC director-general at the time, George Holmes. 'George recognised that you needed some continuity.'[103]

SCOTTISH DEVELOPMENT AGENCY

The Scottish Development Agency (SDA) – established in 1975 by a Labour government – also provided institutional continuity. Modelled on the Highlands and Islands Development Board, which had operated since 1965, its wide-ranging remit included urban renewal, factory building and the promotion of industry and technology. There were many in the Conservative Party who wanted the SDA scrapped following the 1979 general election, but Younger soon realised that it was a useful arms-length tool for countering both the recession and accusations of government indifference.

In January 1980, George issued the SDA with fresh guidelines to reduce its employment-protection role and enable it to facilitate – rather than provide – investment. He also appointed Robin Duthie as chairman and, in 1981, recruited George Mathewson as chief executive, forging the basis of a close working relationship which endured well beyond Younger's time at the Scottish Office.

During 1982 the SDA put more than £11m – double the previous year's figure – of equity and loans into Scottish companies. Most came in small amounts, the SDA acting as a facilitator in securing private investment of three or four times as much as its own grant. Despite the recession, the agency was busier than ever. Its small business advice team was growing constantly; in Dundee it was preparing to build a technology park inside a new enterprise zone; and in the East End of Glasgow private housing was being built for the first time in nearly a century. A shopping centre had also replaced the city's old St Enoch railway station, while work was under way on a £36m Scottish Exhibition and Conference Centre on the banks of the Clyde.

But while the SDA was undeniably successful, its interventionist bent was not exactly Thatcherite. 'Margaret was suspicious of the SDA', recalled Younger, 'but I persuaded her to accept it by turning it into a strongly private enterprise-orientated body.'[104] Unequivocally, he told the *Scotsman*: 'Together with my Department it is a really vital part of our long-term strategy.'[105]

---

[103] Interview with George Holmes, 17/9/2007.
[104] *Scotland on Sunday* 17/10/1993.
[105] *Scotsman* 21/5/1980.

In addition to the SDA's £100m budget (the separate Highlands and Islands Development Board got around £30m), £287m in Regional Development Grants was also spent in Scotland during 1982–83, as well as £20m of Section 7 Selective Financial Assistance under the 1972 Industry Act. Shortly after the 1983 election, Regional Development Grants were phased out despite a strong fight by Younger and his chief economic adviser Gavin McCrone, and although Section 7 Assistance survived, its job creation criteria were considerably tightened.

Most of this regional aid went to oil (and related) industries, which was understandable given the crucial nature of the North Sea oil market (although some officials argued that it should be excluded), estimated to be worth about £3 billion in 1983. Most operating needs were supplied locally and sustained some 100,000 jobs, mostly in Aberdeen and the north-east of Scotland. Younger buoyantly spoke of surveys suggesting there was even more oil than previously thought, while his government privatised the British National Oil Corporation and eroded its monopoly by allowing private enterprise to transport gas ashore from oil terminals. The SNP struggled to sustain its resonant attacks of the 1970s but with only two MPs left, cries of 'It's Scotland's Oil' now sounded a little hollow. Scotland's oil, however, became Mrs Thatcher's saviour in cushioning the effects of a recession and her government's economic policy.

Regional aid was also crucial to the success of the so-called Silicon Glen – the 70-mile-wide area between Ayr and Dundee – which employed 40,000 people in microelectronics and was perhaps the real economic success story of Scotland in the 1980s. By 1983, few American firms did not have offshoots in Scotland. The SDA had an investment office in New York City, although ironically the attraction for US companies lay as much in state intervention as it did in free enterprise. Younger lobbied for Section 7 grants to be awarded to three major inward investors – Hewlett Packard in South Queensferry, National Semiconductor at Greenock (which invented and manufactured the Dolby C noise-reduction chip) and Shin Etsu Handotai of Japan at Livingston. Prestwick Airport in George's constituency also received £12.3m of investment to increase its Jetstream production rate.

But although Silicon Glen was a short-term success, it proved to be a long-term mirage. The electronics sector was weak when it came to software, and although companies like NEC would happily manufacture advanced technology (in its case, computer chips) in Scotland, it would research and develop that technology elsewhere. In a country which needed permanent jobs, this was far from ideal, but Younger's aim was to reach a sustainable balance whereby the number of jobs created in electronics outstripped those being lost in traditional industries. Although in 1996 Silicon Glen produced 35 per cent of Europe's PCs, by the beginning of the twenty-first century more than 10,000 workers had been made redundant.

Younger also tackled the age-old complaint that potential overseas investors had to knock on half a dozen doors to settle in Scotland, instead of just one in the Republic of Ireland. Jointly, therefore, the SDA and Industry Department for Scotland (IDS, formerly the Scottish Economic Planning Department until it was renamed in 1980) began to operate 'Locate in Scotland', which from 1981 to 1985 secured £1,300m of inward investment and 30,000 jobs for Scotland despite hostility from Whitehall. Based in Glasgow, Locate in Scotland had a Cockspur Street office near Whitehall which also acted as a 'Scottish Centre' for the Scottish Council (Development and Industry), the Scottish Tourist Board and representatives from Scotland's five New Towns (Livingston, Glenrothes, Cumbernauld, Irvine and East Kilbride).

All of those New Towns were thriving, particularly Livingston. Still expanding in terms of population, Livingston was also home to NEC's new semi-conductor plant, as well as Mitsubishi's video-recorder assembling facility.[106] And while by the end of 1984 English New Town Corporations had mostly been wound up, in Scotland Younger promised that none of Scotland's five would disappear before 1990, and then only once they had reached their projected populations.

Meanwhile in Edinburgh, the financial services sector was booming without any help from the SDA. The summer of 1983 saw the creation of Adam & Company, a would-be Coutts named after Adam Smith, while a UK-wide restructuring of Trustee Savings Banks (TSB) had seen the four Scottish TSBs grouped together to form, following intensive lobbying, Scotland's own TSB. The two Georges – Younger and Mathewson – also lobbied (separately) against attempts either to merge with (Hongkong and Shanghai Banking Corporation, or HSBC) or take over (Standard Chartered) the Edinburgh-based Royal Bank of Scotland (RBS). Although some at the Scottish Office believed the HSBC proposal (it had offered to make Edinburgh its European HQ) to be beneficial, the chairman of RBS favoured the Standard Chartered offer.

In the event, the Scottish Office lobbied against both. The Foreign Office argued that as HSBC was headquartered in the British colony of Hong Kong it could not be excluded, while the governor of the Bank of England was opposed to HSBC on the grounds that he could not control it. 'This

---

[106] The president of Mitsubishi, N. Katayama, thanked Younger for attending the opening ceremony of its Livingston factory in 1984. 'Scotland is pretty and pleasant,' he wrote. 'I will encourage to enlarge our business' (N. Katayama to GY, 25/5/1984, GYP).

gave us a chance to come through the middle', recalled Gavin McCrone, who presented the Scottish Office case to the Monopolies and Mergers Commission (MMC), 'but I do not think Norman Tebbit ever forgave us.'[107]

As Trade and Industry Secretary, Tebbit asked the Prime Minister if she wished to reconsider the MMC's decision to deny both offers. He believed the MMC's reasoning to be weak and Mrs Thatcher was known to be sympathetic to consolidation in the banking sector. Timing, however, was everything. Her son, Mark Thatcher, had recently gone missing in the Sahara Desert. Understandably distracted, she ignored Tebbit's request and the commission's ruling was upheld. Almost two decades later George Younger was chairman, and George Mathewson chief executive, of what had become the world's fourth-largest bank by market capitalisation, still headquartered in Edinburgh and still a major employer.

Attracting 'inward investment' to Scotland required constant entertaining and foreign visits. George and Diana were excellent hosts and effortlessly charmed delegations from Canada, China and even the Socialist Federal Republic of Yugoslavia (talks on constitutional similarities between Scotland and Croatia took place at Bute House). In September 1980 – and again in November 1985 – Younger visited Japan, taking with him Diana, bonhomie and specially-commissioned bilingual Scottish Office business cards. The Foreign Office, meanwhile, regularly sent visiting dignitaries to Scotland for a day or two.

'All that is part of stressing that Scotland has its own government', explained Younger, '[which is] expected to do the honours to international people as well as just operate ourselves.'[108] During one visit by Mikhail Gorbachev in December 1984 the Scottish Secretary unwittingly became one of the first people outside the Politburo to learn of Marshall Ustinov's (the Soviet defence minister) death. As a result, Gorbachev had to leave Scotland early and could not attend a banquet at Edinburgh Castle being held in his honour. George asked him what he would tell journalists at Edinburgh Airport, something that had not occurred to him. Initially, Gorbachev intended to tell them nothing, but when Younger explained that that was not possible, he declared: 'I shall tell the truth. I shall tell them that Ustinov has died.'[109] This important fact, of course, had not yet been revealed in the USSR so it was a risky decision for Gorbachev. George later entertained officials with the tale of how he had given the future Soviet leader his first lesson in democracy.[110]

---

[107] Gavin McCrone to the author, 13/1/2008.
[108] *Scotsman Magazine* 7/1985.
[109] Interview with John Howe, 11/12/2006.
[110] Gorbachev succeeded Chernenko as leader three months after his visit to Edinburgh.

Just hours after Gorbachev's departure, someone hit upon the idea of inviting the occupants of nearby old people's homes to the Edinburgh Castle banquet. 'In the event we had these old people rolling into the Great Hall on their zimmers,' remembered Alex Pagett. 'George came in and he and his wife treated these people with the same reverence and respect he would have accorded to Mr and Mrs Gorbachev. He exploited the opportunity for a beneficial cause, and we got some good media out of it.'[111] In just over a year's time, Younger would find himself dealing with the Soviet Union in a very different capacity at the Ministry of Defence.

EDUCATION AND HEALTH

Although Younger could look back on a strong record in terms of industrial development and tackling local government, he adopted a much more hands-off approach to two policy areas now considered to be the bread and butter of domestic politics – health and education. During his six-and-a-half years at the Scottish Office, there was no legislation to reform the NHS in Scotland, despite the state-run health service being fully under Younger's remit,[112] while beyond the reasonably radical Education (Scotland) Act of 1980, Scotland's historically distinct education system barely passed through the in-tray at Dover House. Indeed, the Scottish (formerly 'Scotch') Education Department (SED) was older than the Scottish Office itself and constantly produced huge submissions for Younger's attention. One day, he was lunching with staff as roadworks rumbled on outside St Andrew's House. 'Another SED submission in preparation I think,' he quipped.[113]

This was partly a symptom of the contemporary media agenda. Throughout the 1980s the news headlines were dominated by industrial matters (and therefore employment) and local government finance, which in turn dictated the Scottish Secretary's political agenda. To be fair, Younger did focus on further and higher education, but then largely because it was important to the booming microelectronics sector. Many of Scotland's universities (then under Whitehall control) offered electronics-related courses, while a national Educational Development Centre specialising in microelectronics was established at the Paisley College of Technology.

The Education (Scotland) Bill contained the only major change to

---

[111] Interview with Alex Pagett, 13/7/2007.
[112] Scottish health boards were, however, compelled to follow the example of the NHS in England and introduce General Managers.
[113] John Miller's memorial service speech, 26/4/2003, GYP.

schooling north of the border of Younger's incumbency. It proposed giving parents greater choice between local authority schools, while amending the assisted-places scheme to include an income-linked subsidy. As with most other Bills introduced during Mrs Thatcher's first government, it was stridently opposed by the Labour Party in Scotland, although there was broad support when Younger ordered all Scottish schools to phase out use of the belt by July 1984.

Another reason for Younger's relative neglect of education policy was probably his own background. A product of the private sector in both Scotland (Cargilfield) and England (Winchester), the Scottish Secretary's direct experience of state schooling was, through no fault of his own, limited to constituency visits. The rolling strikes that hit Scottish schools throughout the winter of 1984 and most of 1985, however, could not be ignored.

Although Scottish teachers had accepted a 4.5 per cent pay increase in April 1984, almost half the Educational Institute of Scotland's (EIS) members had voted to reject it, so they were determined to get more in 1984–85. The EIS and other unions asked for an external salary review, but when Younger failed to respond, staff boycotted new curriculum development – which delayed the introduction of microcomputers into Scottish classrooms – and unions called a one-day strike to take place in December 1984.

Eventually, Younger announced that a salary review could only be considered by the Scottish Joint Negotiating Committee, an internal body composed of teachers and employers. If, he said, it agreed a package on pay and conditions then he would endeavour to implement it using resources from the Scottish block grant.

But by March 1985 the dispute rumbled on. The EIS had deliberately singled out schools in Scottish ministers' constituencies for indefinite strikes, including Ayr, where it also planned to stage a rally of 18,000 teachers. Yet still Younger insisted there would be no independent review, while he urged local authorities to open their schools during holidays and recruit private tutors in order to combat the strike's crippling effects.

For once, Younger's tried-and-tested technique of charming trade unionists while seeking common ground had failed him. He still, however, attempted to sound conciliatory. '[A]lthough Government doesn't have vast sums of money to throw around,' he protested in July 1985, 'I am broadly sympathetic to their concerns.'

> I accept that they feel underpaid, overworked, and not appreciated. But the trouble over the past five months has been the rigid attitude of one union only, the EIS, which has prevented the normal, sensible discussion between the two

parties. They hooked themselves to the idea of having an independent review body when they should have seen perfectly clearly there was no way this Government could ever agree to that without wrecking its entire anti-inflation policy. If we had granted one, everyone else would have wanted it too. It was a classic error of trade union negotiators fixing on to something which the bosses cannot give.

Younger said the EIS had until October to accept his outstanding offer in relation to an internal pay review. 'They missed the bus last year, through not taking up my offer,' he said bluntly, 'I am anxious that they should not miss next year's bus as well.'[114]

By early September 1985 local authority employers and teachers' unions were at least meeting for talks, but there was little optimism that a deal could be reached. Teachers had already rejected Younger's offer of a ten per cent salary increase over four years and John Graham, his private secretary, remembers feeling that the Scottish Secretary was not entirely engaged with the circumstances behind the strike. 'The thing that I remember of those meetings was that he was outraged by the standard of turnout, saying these people were scruffy,' he recalled. 'I suppose they were fairly scruffy by today's standards, and quite unwittingly they were doing themselves damage by not dressing smartly.'[115]

As September wore on, teachers in England voted for all-out strikes and work-to-rule, while in Scotland they were warned that time was running out. In December, by which point the dispute affected the whole country, Mrs Thatcher asked a group of Cabinet ministers led by Willie Whitelaw (and including Younger) to report directly to her.

THE PEASANTS' REVOLT

Fortunately for Younger, he avoided having to handle the final months of the teachers' strike through an unexpected move to the Ministry of Defence in January 1986. His promotion to a UK ministry also neatly sidestepped another hornets' nest, the abolition of the rates and its replacement with what was formally called the 'Community Charge', but became more widely known by the nomenclature 'Poll Tax'.

As a keen student of history at Winchester and Oxford, Younger should have been aware that the historical precedents were not good. In an old school notebook he had noted 'The Causes of the Peasants' Revolt'.

---

[114] *Glasgow Herald* 2/7/1985.
[115] Interview with John Graham.

These included a failure 'to remedy economic troubles arising out of the Black Death', and a 'vague socialism', although the 'immediate cause' was the 'Pole Tax'.[116] There were also historical warnings in the Scottish Office archives. In 1894 one of Younger's predecessors as Scottish Secretary, Sir George Otto Trevelyan, referred to his fiefdom as a country 'where people have always been so much alive to the question of rating'.[117]

Sir William Kerr Fraser remembers George being alive to the question when he met him for the first time after the May 1979 general election. 'He [Younger] said I don't want to get into policies at the moment but we really must do something about the Rates,' remembered the then permanent under-secretary. 'I said well, whatever you're going to do, be absolutely sure about whatever you put in its place.'[118]

Younger had long been critical of the rates, and had lobbied for a party commitment to abolish them prior to the 1979 general election. 'I have never been a great friend of the rating system,' he said during a Commons debate in late 1976. 'I have always thought – and still think – that the rating system has reached a stage where it is unrealistic and difficult for ordinary people to understand and that it is time it was brushed aside.'[119] Initially, however, the issue was kicked into the long grass when a 1981 green paper suggested various alternatives – including a local income tax option backed by Younger – but nothing conclusive.

At the back of Younger's mind was an imminent rates revaluation in Scotland. While Michael Heseltine simply deferred it in England and Wales, there was little room for manoeuvre north of the border, where revaluation was mandatory every five years unless Parliament voted specifically to defer it. The last had been in 1978, and with another due in 1983 – election year – Younger asked Parliament to do just that. But, as he later observed, 'after the one postponement, we were simply running out of excuses and had to go ahead in 1984'.[120]

The long-delayed revaluation triggered an almighty row. Although fiscally neutral overall, it threw a heavier burden on domestic and small-business ratepayers, particularly in large urban areas which tended to be administered by Labour councils. In Edinburgh, where Younger had earlier focused his attack on local government spending, ratepayers faced increases of 40 per cent. And on the Capital's Princes Street, shops like Jenners found themselves paying twice as much as a similar store on London's Oxford Street.

[116] Old schoolbook marked 'G.S.L. 1946', GYP.
[117] Campbell-Bannerman Papers Add 41231 f8.
[118] Interview with Sir William Kerr Fraser, c2003.
[119] Hansard 918 c115–16.
[120] Butler, *Failure in British Government*, 62.

Although the Scottish Office had expected big rises as a result of the postponement, it was caught off guard by the reaction. Younger vainly pointed out that the average domestic rates bill had only risen by 17 per cent, only a third of which was a result of the revaluation, the other two thirds being the consequence of increased spending by local authorities.

Nevertheless, the Scottish Secretary was widely blamed, not least by Thatcher, although he had attempted to forestall the impact by ending industrial derating. Late publication of revised valuations just prior to the issue of rates notices also hampered Younger. By then, it was simply too late to implement a generous scheme of transitional relief.

Local Conservative associations, never known for political perspective, reacted furiously. Even Sir James Goold, the Scottish party chairman and a golfing buddy of Denis Thatcher, angrily waved his own revaluation form at a journalist. Younger patiently explained that he had confused his new rateable value with the relatively modest increase he would actually have to pay once the rate poundage had been set (a common confusion fuelling the protest). Goold was publicly contrite, but the damage had already been done.

Even the mild-mannered and popular Willie Whitelaw suffered from the backlash. He visited the affluent Glasgow suburb of Bearsden during the furore and was repeatedly heckled during a speech to a largely Tory audience. 'Following Willie's visit there was a right royal rumpus,' recalled Younger years later. 'Mrs Thatcher was keenly aware of what would happen if her old ladies in Finchley suddenly found themselves facing a ten-times increase in their rates bills.'[121] To make matters worse, a hitherto safe Tory regional council seat (North Kyle) comprising a quarter of Younger's Ayr constituency fell to Labour in a by-election shortly after. Younger and Whitelaw now united to demand a replacement for the rates, and quickly.

Nearly half the Cabinet attended a Chequers meeting on Sunday, 31 March 1985, at which, as Mrs Thatcher recalled, 'the community charge was born'.[122] When Kenneth Baker (a friend of the Scottish Secretary's since the early 1970s) and William Waldegrave finished their presentation, Younger and his *de facto* deputy Michael Ancram – who had arrived late due to a delayed flight – re-emphasised the importance of the reform for Scotland. In his memoirs, Baker claims Younger declared: 'all my political life I have been waiting for this'.[123] Although it was not a very George-like utterance, he was certainly pleased with what he had heard.

[121] *Sunday Times* 1/4/1990.
[122] Thatcher, *The Downing Street Years*, 648.
[123] Baker, *The Turbulent Years*, 122.

Pressure from Younger, Whitelaw and ministers at the Department of Environment for an alternative to the rates had proved decisive. There were several strands of thinking in the Scottish Secretary's mind. Following his long-running battle with high-spending Labour councils over rate-capping, the Community Charge appeared to him an ideal means by which to control local authority expenditure and therefore alter the whole culture of local government in Scotland. What George called the 'ratepayers of Troon' were also an influence. 'In a place like Troon,' he explained, 'which had very high rateable values, they had to pay lots of money, well over £1,000 a year in rates, so I wanted to do something about that.'[124]

As a diligent constituency MP, Younger understood their grievance and, indeed, the Community Charge did more for the ratepayers of Troon than any other option previously canvassed. 'I myself have always felt that the main difficulty with the present system is that it's based on property,' he told Brian Walden in 1985.[125] While George's home-owning constituents felt they were shouldering the burden of high-spending councils, their council house neighbours (often multiple earners) paid relatively little along with their rent – although many did not even realise it. So by making everyone pay something towards the cost of local services, the rates burden would be spread wider and, in theory if not in practice, bills would come to a level which everyone could afford. Younger also believed a typical ratepayer had to 'feel something in his pocket' in order to correlate higher council spending with pressures on an average household budget.

In the summer of 1985, Younger appeared to confirm that a Community Charge was the government's favoured option during a television interview. He had also given strong hints at May's Scottish Conservative conference in Perth, the run-up to which had seen heated exchanges between Younger and the Chancellor Nigel Lawson about the amount of Treasury relief available to cushion the revaluation. Whitelaw and Lord Home backed the Scottish Secretary, and the relief fund was subsequently increased from £36m to £50m, generosity Lawson emphasised with obvious irritation as 'exceptional'.[126]

'The fact is, that for too many people, this year's rate demand has come as a thunderbolt,' Mrs Thatcher had told delegates in Perth. 'And I know how commercial ratepayers feel – I spent my early years living above the shop.'[127] Younger had been determined to tell conference that an autumn

---

[124] Autobiographical notes, GYP.
[125] *Weekend World* (ITV) 12/5/1985.
[126] *Guardian* 8/5/1985.
[127] Speech to Scottish Conservative conference, 10/5/1985, MTF.

Bill would abolish the rates, but soon realised such a timescale was unrealistic. Instead, in a crucial passage of his conference speech cleared by Number 10 just minutes before he rose to speak, George proclaimed that 'the status quo is not an option',[128] the same phrase he had used twenty years earlier about Scotland's constitutional position. This came as news to Scottish Office officials watching the speech on television, but simply riding out a stormy conference was, like the status quo, not an option for an increasingly embattled Scottish Secretary.

Although protocol prevented civil servants being present at a party conference, Younger's officials would certainly have tried to dissuade him from using his 'status quo' line at any ministerial meeting. In general terms, they did not share their political master's zeal for the Community Charge and flagged up a number of obvious difficulties. As a flat-rate tax it would be regressive in practice and was bound to be seen as unfair; a universal obligation to pay would bring into the system a large number of people who had not been previously involved; those who relied on benefits for income would need them increased to survive financially; awkward issues would arise in relation to those – for example, students – who were not based throughout the year in a single local authority area; and finally, it would require completely new, complex and costly administrative machinery.

But officials were telling Younger what he did not want to hear. He accepted that the scheme was not perfect but, on balance, he believed the inequities of the 'status quo' to be even greater, although he was prepared to concede the possible need for an extended transitional period to act as a palliative. Very quickly, however, his determination for it to be introduced ahead of the next general election took precedence. Sir William Kerr Fraser was especially cautious, and he warned Younger about the intractable practical problems of the proposed tax. 'You don't have to face the music on the doorstep in Scotland,' was Younger's usual response, 'so you can't understand why we need this so badly.'[129]

Drafting a specifically Scottish Bill began soon after the launch of the *Paying for Local Government* green paper, and continued in earnest after Younger moved to the MoD in January 1986. Contrary to popular myth, Scotland was never intended as a poll tax 'guinea-pig'. In fact, the reform was always intended to apply to Great Britain as whole, and only appeared in Scotland first under pressure from Younger. As the MP

---

[128] *Scotsman* 10/5/1985. 'I accept on behalf of the Government that we are expected to take action on our thoroughly unsatisfactory system of local government finance,' *The Times* reported Younger as saying. 'The present system as it stands is not an option' (*The Times* 10/5/1985).

[129] Butler, 101.

Steve Norris put it, 'our Scottish colleagues are trail-blazers rather than guinea-pigs'.[130]

Some observers believed that those of Younger's colleagues in White-hall who had reservations about the whole project were playing a Machiavellian game. Knowing that they were unlikely to win in any debate round the Cabinet table, they thought that if they let the Scots go first they were giving them enough rope to hang themselves. If the Scottish attempt at legislation foundered, the tax would never be introduced in England and Wales. Separate legislation north of the border also suited Younger's mantra that Scotland was governed from Edinburgh, not London. Local government in Scotland had long been controlled by the Scottish Office while many UK reforms, such as Right to Buy in the early 1980s, had been legislated for in Scotland before England.

But despite George's insistence that the Community Charge was vital for the Scottish Conservatives' electoral prospects, the 1987 general election was disastrous for the party in Scotland. It lost more than half its MPs and Younger only narrowly held on in Ayr, a result overshadowed by another Tory landslide in England. But despite his close shave, Younger's view, shared even by some Scottish Tories who lost their seats, was that the Community Charge had played only a minor role in the swing against them.[131]

Curiously, in the interminable blame-game which followed, Younger's name rarely featured. He continued to defend it as Defence Secretary – even when Labour opponents taunted him about his own greatly reduced bill under the new tax – and believed it had more or less settled down in Scotland. 'It didn't really get a bad name from a political point of view', he said, 'until it was introduced in England.'[132] Nevertheless, George had shown uncharacteristically poor political judgement in handling its in-troduction. When asked in 1993 if he thought it had been a misjudgement by Mrs Thatcher, Younger replied: 'Well, I do think it was a misjudge-ment by us all really.'[133]

As with all political gaffes, accounts of the Poll Tax saga often conflict. While one of Thatcher's biographers believed Younger overreacted to the revaluation of 1985, Ian Lang saw him as 'cautious about climbing aboard this emotional bandwagon'.[134] On balance, it appears that George simply allowed his determination to abolish the rates to take precedence over

[130] Ibid.
[131] One Tory MP who lost his seat, Younger's PPS Alex Pollock, disagreed.
[132] Autobiographical notes, GYP.
[133] Kemp, *The Hollow Drum*, 183.
[134] Lang, *Blue Remembered Years*, 82.

finding a replacement which was both politically and fiscally practical. Another lapse was having devoted too little attention to the Scottish Conservative Party. Younger's private office regularly received pleas for him to spend more time meeting activists, to which he responded without enthusiasm. Had relations been better, then perhaps the overreaction of figures like James Goold might have been pre-empted, and the quixotic expectations of the 'ratepayers of Troon' brought back down to earth.

Whatever the case, it fell to George's successor at the Scottish Office to present the snappily-titled Abolition of Domestic Rates Etc. (Scotland) Bill to the Commons in late 1986. Then, Malcolm Rifkind hailed it as a 'radical and reforming measure which will abolish a discredited and unpopular local tax'.[135]

CENTENARY CELEBRATIONS

On 6 January 1985 George Younger became the longest-continually serving Secretary of State for Scotland. His ministerial colleagues, aided and abetted by his private office, chose to mark the occasion several months later by means of a well-orchestrated plot. Believing he was due to attend a routine black-tie dinner at Admiralty House one evening in July, Younger went home to change for dinner. The engagement had been noted in his diary as 'inessential', and when on the day it seemed he might duck out to have dinner with Diana, she feigned a headache to sustain the plot. When George arrived alone at Admiralty House he found not only his wife, but 19 of the 20 ministers who had worked with him at the Scottish Office since 1979 (the exception, the former Lord Advocate James Mackay, was busy with court duties in Edinburgh).

Alex Pollock, Younger's PPS, made the main speech which concluded with the presentation of a miniature bed of nails made from silver by the jewellers Mike and Trish Hurst in John MacKay's Argyll constituency. It was Ray Gunter, a former Labour minister for labour, who had first likened his own job to a bed of nails, and for a Scottish Secretary mid-way through a turbulent year, it was an appropriate symbol.

July 1985 also saw several events to mark the centenary of the Scottish Office. The Queen opened an exhibition at Edinburgh's Inverleith House organised by the retired St Andrew's House official John S. Gibson, who had written an accompanying book called *The Thistle and the Crown*. There was also a large reception at Edinburgh Castle and a dinner at the Palace of Holyroodhouse, to which every surviving Scottish Secretary (and their wives or widows) had been invited.

---

[135] Hansard 107 c200.

As an essentially pragmatic politician, Younger could justifiably draw
inspiration from them all. The Scottish Office had a habit of compelling
its incumbent ministers to 'go native', fighting to get the best deal for
Scotland regardless of ideology or political reality. Younger was no
different, and in interviews to mark the centenary he cited easing
Scotland's reliance on heavy industry while championing a reprieve
for Ravenscraig as his proudest achievements.

But to Ronald Faux of *The Times*, Younger was in 1985 the 'minister too
good to get ahead'. Noting that he had once again been passed over for
promotion (to Energy Secretary) that autumn, Faux said that 'a more
politically ambitious man might have felt justified in thinking he was destined
to be ever the best man and never the groom'. With things going badly in
Scotland, the argument went, an experienced hand was needed on the tiller.
'But even under moderate siege,' continued Faux, 'Younger remains a calm
and astute politician . . . but until Mrs Thatcher redeems her pledge he is
likely to remain at the Scottish Office, a calm figure in a stormy landscape.'[136]

THE WESTLAND AFFAIR

'Margaret Thatcher made a terrific effort to understand Scotland',
reflected Younger in 1993, 'and she did go that extra mile to win the
hearts of the Scottish people. But she remained puzzled as to why it was
she appeared to raise so many hackles in Scotland.' He went on:

> The truth is her character as a powerful English woman made her an easy
> target for her political enemies in Scotland whatever she did. This ungenerous
> and chauvinistic attitude does not cast great credit on us Scots but it is typical of
> our somewhat inward-looking attitude. Scots, even socialists, expect women to
> keep their place. Everyone who ever canvassed during her time experienced
> the coarse and uncivilised abuse about 'that bloody woman'. No doubt this was
> largely due to the fact that so many of them were traditional Labour supporters.
> For many of them, the Archangel Gabriel would have been rejected if he was
> thought to be a Tory.

'Margaret', concluded Younger, 'was not blameless herself in her actions
in Scotland, but she did far more good than harm'.[137] By the end of 1985,
however, even the staunch loyalist Younger had his doubts about the
Prime Minister's staying power.[138]

---

[136] *The Times* 23/9/1985.
[137] *Scotland on Sunday* 17/10/1993.
[138] Robert Gordon, Younger's last private secretary at the Scottish Office, remembers lunching with
him in a Whitehall pub early in 1986 and being left in no doubt as to his views in this respect.

And while he had no ambitions to occupy Number 10 himself, Michael Heseltine, the Defence Secretary, did. Although Thatcher and Heseltine had initially got along well, Younger recognised that they had an 'incompatibility of temperament'. The so-called Westland affair – which concerned the relative merits of merging the ailing Westland helicopter manufacturer with a consortium of European or American companies – was an otherwise innocuous political spat which was exaggerated by this incompatibility of temperament and boiled over into a full-scale Cabinet battle.

Heseltine believed that as a matter of principle the government should favour a European consortium for the merger, and continued lobbying over the Christmas recess despite a Cabinet ruling that it was for Westland's shareholders to decide. When Cabinet met for the first time in 1986 on 9 January, Mrs Thatcher sensed that Heseltine was now completely isolated.

When the Defence Secretary tried to get clearance for another speech supporting a European consortium, Thatcher reminded him that the principle of collective Cabinet responsibility had to apply. Heseltine retorted that this was scarcely possible since she had not permitted a full Cabinet discussion and promptly slammed his Cabinet folder shut. As Younger recalled:

> He just said, 'I've got this speech that I'm making, but I haven't managed to get it cleared by your department.' She said, 'Well I'm not going to clear it as it is.' And he said, 'Well I'm not going to make it as it is.' She said, 'Well that's very difficult.' So then, he said, 'Well, are you prepared to approve me making this speech?' And she said, 'No, I'm not.' And he then said, 'Right, well there is no point in my carrying on,' bundled up his papers under his arm and walked out.[139]

A visibly shocked Prime Minister merely said 'Well, I'm very sorry' as Heseltine strode out of the room. Younger immediately knew this meant a mini Cabinet reshuffle. 'I was a lifelong specialist in defence', he later reflected, 'and I remembered thinking that if I wasn't appointed to succeed Michael, it would be a great blow to me.' The Prime Minister called an adjournment for coffee, and after a few moments Nigel Wicks, Thatcher's principal private secretary, summoned Younger to her private office where, 'to my great joy, Margaret offered me defence'.

George accepted, and when the Prime Minister asked him who should

---

[139] Autobiographical notes, GYP.

take over in Scotland, he cautiously suggested Malcolm Rifkind, suspecting she might reject him 'because I thought she felt he was too keen on devolution'. Mrs Thatcher, however, readily agreed and went through to a secretary's room to telephone Rifkind, who was at home suffering from flu. He also accepted; the Queen was contacted for approval, and the reconstituted Cabinet reconvened. Younger recalled:

> There then followed a farcical scene which can only happen when things go unexpectedly wrong. When Cabinet resumed, Margaret announced that she had appointed me Secretary of State for Defence and there were congratulations all round. But the next business was an important paper on the future poll tax which I had been due to introduce as Scottish Secretary. But with no Malcolm, I had to introduce it as defence secretary. As we always address each other by our titles, I was constantly referred to as Secretary of State for Scotland as everybody kept forgetting I was now Secretary of State for Defence.[140]

The 'important paper' was in fact Kenneth Baker's green paper, *Paying for Local Government*, which finally paved the way for Younger's long-standing demand that the Community Charge be introduced in Scotland ahead of legislation in England and Wales. Ironically, that turned out to be an even more serious dispute than the Westland affair, and neatly emphasised Younger's luck in having been promoted when he was. An historic Cabinet meeting ended at just after midday.

Instead of heading straight over to the MoD, however, Younger returned to Dover House. 'My already appointed successor,' recounted Heseltine in his memoirs, 'with great tact and understanding had telephoned to ask at what time it would be convenient for him to come and take over his job as Secretary of State. He made no protest when it was suggested that six o'clock would be a good time and no attempt was made to prevent me using the facilities of the Ministry for what turned out to be a momentous press conference.'[141] Diana, meanwhile, had only learned of Heseltine's dramatic resignation when one of her sons telephoned her, quickly followed by another call from George with even more dramatic news. Diana did not realise, and perhaps nor did her husband, that a meeting at Chequers the previous weekend had already identified Younger as Heseltine's successor.

Shortly before 6 p.m. Younger left the classical splendour of Dover House and strolled across Whitehall to the austerely modern building which was to be his new departmental home. After acquainting himself

[140] *Scotland on Sunday* 17/10/1993.
[141] Heseltine, *Life in the Jungle*, 311.

with his new staff, he left London on a late flight to Scotland. The following day was taken up with press interviews and moving out of Bute House, which had very much become home for the Younger family. 'In the midst of all of this George was doing his smooth act as Diana rushed around tidying up because they were moving out,' recalled Alex Pagett. Their furniture van was an elderly estate car, into which Diana was squeezing their household effects. 'Every now and again you'd be in the middle of talking to the defence editor of the *Observer*', added Pagett, 'and she would say, George, where did you put such and such. It was such a bizarre scene.'[142]

'In the past 6½ years the economy of Scotland has been literally transformed,'[143] Younger proudly proclaimed after bidding farewell to staff and reporters at St Andrew's House. It was understandable political hyperbole, yet there was much to justify it. Silicon Glen and North Sea oil industries were profitable and firmly established, the service sector was expanding, cities such as Glasgow had become textbook examples of urban regeneration, while Younger's push for inward investment was credited with creating nearly 19,000 jobs over the past four years. '[W]e had got through the agonies of 1980, 1981 with very good consensus and extremely good relations,' he recalled in 1993. '[R]elations between us [the Scottish Office] and the STUC . . . were superb . . . I also felt and still feel that that was when you first saw in reality the new Scottish economy.'[144]

But there had also been protracted battles over local authority expenditure, bitter disputes with teachers and difficult decisions over the future of the totemic Ravenscraig. Yet against all reasonable odds, Younger had survived a troublesome period without making any enemies. He remained popular, even respected by some of his political opponents, perhaps because deep down they realised that he had, as he once claimed, managed to 'temper the winds of the free market'[145] in Thatcher's Scotland.

---

[142] Interview with Alex Pagett.
[143] *Financial Times* 11/1/1986.
[144] Kemp, 181.
[145] *Question Time* (BBC) 23/5/1985.

Chapter 13

'THE ULTIMATE DETERRENT'

THE WESTLAND AFFAIR is one of those political rows which, in retrospect, becomes even more incomprehensible. At the time Younger summed it up well. Everyone involved, he said, 'had got overcooked'.[1] Michael Heseltine had reached boiling point, and his successor at the Ministry of Defence (MoD) needed to bring down the political temperature.

Ironically, George's European sympathies were not a million miles removed from Heseltine's, but while the outgoing Defence Secretary was a proselytiser his successor certainly was not. Younger's view was that the affair had damaged the government's 'moral standing',[2] and was bemused to find that few at the MoD were particularly exercised about it. In the long run, Westland carved out its own future free of foreign influence and continued to manufacture helicopters for sale at home and abroad.

Westland had been primarily a personal spat between Mrs Thatcher and one of her big beasts. At his first press conference as Defence Secretary, Younger simply reaffirmed the government's policy of leaving it to Westland shareholders to decide the company's fate. But the storm had yet to break. When it emerged that Leon Brittan, the Trade and Industry Secretary, had leaked legal counsel critical of Heseltine, he resigned on 24 January. Typically, Younger was careful to maintain good relations with Heseltine. 'How good of you to write,' he scrawled in reply to Younger following a stormy Commons debate. 'I[t] was quite lively with the inevitable [Dennis] Skinner interruption. But the need to stop others trying to exploit for their reasons what I had done for mine was all to[o] urgent!'[3]

Younger inherited a private office and permanent under-secretary

[1] Anderson, *John Major*, 33.
[2] *Scotland on Sunday* 17/10/1993.
[3] Michael Heseltine to GY, 30/1/1986, GYP.

(PUS) who had forged a close personal and professional relationship with his predecessor. Sir Clive Whitmore, the PUS, had been Thatcher's private secretary so he already knew George from his time at Downing Street and likened his laid-back style to that of another Tory Defence Secretary, Francis Pym. When it was leaked that Richard Mottram, Younger's private secretary, had helped draft Heseltine's resignation statement, it was dealt with maturely. 'George was very nice about it', recalled Mottram, 'although it could have been very awkward.'[4] Peter Levene, who had been controversially recruited to head up procurement at PUS level, was also regarded very much as Heseltine's man, but he too quickly hit it off with his replacement.

Heseltine had introduced what became known as MINIS (Ministerial Management Information System) to overhaul the MoD's clunky internal structure. This involved personal meetings between the Defence Secretary and the service chiefs, at which objectives would be set and progress assessed. It worked, to a point, although its logistical demands meant it had fallen into abeyance by the end of Heseltine's tenure. Officials noticed that the management flow-charts generated by MINIS held little interest for Younger, but instead of scrapping it he allowed it to drift on. Soon, however, MINIS fizzled out, and was not much missed.[5]

By contrast, Younger exercised a light touch, and Sir Clive found himself spending fewer hours massaging wounded egos among the chiefs of staff. 'The chiefs of staff liked him,' said Sir Clive, 'not because he wasn't his own man, but because of his style and approach. They thought he was a man they could do business with.'[6]

'Good choice, Younger,' a senior MoD official reportedly remarked. 'Father's a viscount.'[7] And indeed it seemed blue blood and a decent service record were enough to soothe the perennial twitchiness of service chiefs towards their political masters. Younger's affinity with the Army in general, and the regimental system in particular, was obvious. 'I had more military experience than all the staff,' Younger recalled. 'No other senior member of the team had seen active service, so when I gave an opinion they listened.'[8]

Younger's new department was, in 1986, little more than two decades old. The former autonomous positions of First Lord of the Admiralty,

[4] Interview with Sir Richard Mottram, 11/1/2007.
[5] Younger's second PUS, Sir Michael Quinlan, introduced the more systematic and less personality-dependent New Management Strategy.
[6] Interview with Sir Clive Whitmore, 9/1/2007.
[7] *Sunday Times* 12/1/1986.
[8] *Sunday Post* 25/6/2000.

Secretary of State for War and Secretary of State for Air had been consolidated along with the offices of the Admiralty, War Office and the Air Ministry in 1964. Having entered Parliament at the same time, George knew the Ministry of Defence well, first as a back-bencher fighting to save the Argylls, briefly as a minister in 1974 and again in opposition as Shadow Defence Secretary. Now, almost exactly ten years after being removed from that front-bench post, Younger had triumphantly secured the only Cabinet job, other than Scottish Secretary, he had ever coveted.

But there was more than just a row over helicopters to contend with during this second tour of duty. Younger had to resolve a rumpus over shipbuilding contracts, chiefly whether they should go to Swan Hunter or Cammell Laird at Merseyside, with which Heseltine had a long association. And even with a booming economy, if money was a perennial headache, then Younger had inherited an £18 billion migraine. That huge budget had to fund five main areas: NATO's commitment in Western Europe; the Southern (mainly the Falklands) and Eastern Atlantic, which needed £4.5bn a year to protect naval supply routes; rapid deployment outside the NATO zone, which cost £1bn annually; the defence of the British Isles against every conceivable enemy attack (another £4.5bn); and finally, the UK's controversial nuclear deterrent, the so-called last line of defence.

Yet despite all these pressures, Younger's £18bn Budget was not even keeping pace with inflation and financial pressures would be a recurring feature of his three-and-a-half years at the MoD. He also had a formidable eighteen inches of paperwork to shift each day, much of it highly classified. Richard Mottram gave Younger valuable continuity, having served every secretary of state since John Nott, and George amazed officials with his speed at processing briefs and letters. Nevertheless, if the Scottish Office of the mid-1980s had been a frying pan, the Ministry of Defence in 1986 was certainly a fire.

Soon, however, Younger got the department back on to an even keel. 'When George first took the job it was really quite striking how the atmosphere changed in the place,' recalled Mottram. 'With Heseltine it was quite a hyperactive environment as he had a very substantial agenda for change which he pursued and worked at. It was dynamic but slightly untidy; meetings didn't necessarily take place on time. When George came, he had different priorities.'[9] More interested in policy than internal restructuring, 'George was much less angular and noisy, strident if you like, than some of his predecessors in making decisions,' recalled Sir Clive

---

[9] Interview with Sir Richard Mottram.

Whitmore. 'So managing the relationship between him and the department for much of the time wasn't something I had to worry about. He got a lot of good out of people in the department, both military and civilian, in a much quieter way than Heseltine but equally as effectively.'[10]

After nearly seven years at the Scottish Office, Younger was in his element. He had always loved maps, although not the MINIS chart which hung behind Heseltine's old desk, and his childhood had been spent poring over copies of *Jane's Fighting Ships* and making models. George was also thrilled that his ministerial suite included furniture said to have been in the Admiralty during Lord Nelson's time, most notably his desk and octagonal globe.

There was also a Georgian bookcase which Winston Churchill was said to have kicked when he was Lloyd George's First Lord of the Admiralty. 'His way of letting off steam,' remarked Younger. 'My way is to keep one day a week completely clear and spend it outdoors. I am able to switch off totally.'[11] Indeed, private office staff were initially alarmed at his strict sense of work/life balance. It was said that on Younger's first day in the job he emerged from his office at 4 p.m. and announced that he was going home for some tea, or by another account a haircut. 'His permanent secretary wasn't quite quick enough to stop him,' recalled John Howe, one of George's private secretaries, 'but he came back half an hour later and was never allowed to do that again.'

Although he was diligent in tackling his red boxes, they rarely accompanied him home at night, and certainly not on weekends; he knew what to delegate and did not waste time with unnecessary details. Younger's private office adapted accordingly, particularly when it came to diary management. Officials sensed how important his family was and when Diana became unwell, diary commitments were juggled to allow ample time for him to see her. 'He was considerate; he was well-mannered; we never had sharp words,' said Howe. 'George put himself in the hands of the department and his private office in a way we were comfortable with. Nevertheless, there was a voice of authority there.'[12]

Younger struck up a particularly close relationship with Ian Andrews, his assistant private secretary, through a shared connection with the TA, while he would indulge in Old Wykehamist banter with older members of staff and his junior private secretary, David Ball. Unlike Heseltine, who had been selective in what he dealt with and difficult to get decisions from, Younger was brisk and decisive.

---

[10] Interview with Sir Clive Whitmore.
[11] *Sunday Express* 29/6/1986.
[12] Interview with John Howe, 11/12/2006.

As at the Scottish Office, Younger was not an innovative thinker, but an effective day-to-day leader of the MoD with shrewd judgement for people and problems. 'He had a very great ability without reading the papers in any detail of getting a sense of what the answer was,' said Andrews. 'His intelligence was very intuitive and if he got something slightly wrong, it didn't really matter.'[13]

George went with the grain of his department, implicitly assuming that officials were there to support, not work against, him. 'What was striking was that he was very, very shrewd,' said Mottram. 'You would have meetings which would roll along and he would say oh yes, I do appreciate your point. I would sit there thinking oh God, what they're saying doesn't stack up and they're getting completely the wrong impression. And afterwards he would say to me, you know, it's amazing, these people think I'm a fool, none of what they say makes any sense – what do you think?'[14]

Another technique of Younger's was patiently to hear a complaint, repeat the last half of what he had heard in response and then add, 'absolutely'. It was both disarming and non-committal. He also had superb political instincts. 'He could spot from a mile off a political banana skin,' recalled a former special adviser. 'LTCs – long-term costings – would come up and the department would churn through them with baskets marked A, B and C of potential savings. George was good at spotting any potential no-nos.'[15]

Relations with a large – and constantly changing – ministerial team were also good. Younger quickly identified individual ministers' strengths, so that effective use was even made of the occasionally difficult Armed Forces minister John (later Sir John) Stanley. Although different in temperament to himself, Younger knew that if Stanley had given something the once over then it was okay. Two junior ministers with Army experience had a particular rapport with George. Archie Hamilton, who handled the defence procurement and Armed Forces briefs, admired Younger's loyal support even when things went wrong, while Sir Timothy Sainsbury – the last National Serviceman appointed to the MoD – relished the autonomy he was given in defence procurement. The procurement brief was also handled by Lord Trefgarne in the House of Lords, while the future chancellor Norman Lamont served briefly under Younger, also in procurement.

The MP for Moray, Alex Pollock, who had served as Younger's PPS at

---

[13] Interview with Sir Ian Andrews, 11/1/2007.
[14] Interview with Sir Richard Mottram.
[15] Private information.

the Scottish Office, also remained in post. Weekly ministerial team meetings, known as 'prayers', were conducted in a calm, friendly, deceptively low-key way, again in sharp contrast to the Heseltine era. 'Business was always conducted as if at an Edwardian dining table over port in a large country house,' recalled Roger Freeman, who handled one of the Armed Forces briefs for a time, 'all the guests would be polite; the host would be polite, but everyone spoke very frankly.' Face-to-face meetings were similarly enchanting. 'It was rather like going to see your favourite history master, you felt as if it wasn't going to be an adversarial tutorial but more a genial chat; it was a pleasant experience.'[16]

A busy first year at the Ministry of Defence culminated with Younger's first speech as Defence Secretary at the Conservatives' annual conference in Bournemouth. Platform speeches had never been his forte, and Heseltine was a tough act to follow. Like his predecessor, George attacked Labour's non-nuclear stance as 'neutralist' and 'anti-American', while making fun of the SDP's divisions ('Dr Doolittle and Push me-pull you') over unilateralism. Yet in contrast to Heseltine's theatrics, Younger made a forceful yet unostentatious speech, declaring in conclusion that the Conservatives would never be 'soft on defence'.[17]

Heseltine was filmed joining in the standing ovation, but Younger's performance took many by surprise. 'He was, quite frankly, very much better than many had expected,' wrote one commentator. 'He was persuasive, unhistrionic and reasonable [and] if that is to be the party's message at the polls, then Younger is the man to sell it. In his twenties, he was the sales manager of Tennent Caledonian: the task of selling the Bomb to the British may be a little harder than selling spirits to the Scots.'[18]

In little more than nine months, Younger had steadied the ship and restored the government's credibility on defence issues. The Westland affair was a distant memory, and in just eight months' time, his record at the Ministry of Defence would be at the forefront of a battle to secure a third term for Margaret Thatcher's government.

'I DON'T THINK IT WORKED'

'The Nimrod affair constituted a unique – and uniquely costly – lesson in how not to monitor and manage defence procurement,' wrote Mrs Thatcher in her memoirs. 'A minister has to be prepared to work through

[16] Interview with Lord Freeman, 18/12/2006.
[17] Speech to Conservative Party conference, 8/10/1986.
[18] *Observer* 18/1/1987.

the details if he is going to come to the right decisions and this Michael [Heseltine] was always unwilling to do.'[19] To be fair, Heseltine had actually spent a lot of time on the detail before his resignation, while Younger had first learned of the Nimrod AEW (Airborne Early Warning) project as Shadow Defence Secretary in 1975.[20] The choice of replacement for the UK's fleet of Nimrod surveillance aircraft lay between US-manufactured Boeings, or a cheaper home-grown alternative. GEC pitched to produce the latter, and was awarded the contract by James Callaghan's government in 1977, beginning nearly a decade of rising costs, logistical difficulties and political posturing.

GEC undertook from day one to use the existing Nimrods and install new radar equipment, but the ageing aircraft simply could not be adapted using the technology then available. Heseltine had already introduced a series of plateaus, or targets, with a caveat that the plug would be pulled should any not be met. The whole project was also on a cost-plus contract, which meant that each further delay was accompanied by another bill for the MoD.[21] Younger bought himself time by negotiating a six-month fixed-price contract to assess whether the project could be salvaged, although it was already obvious it could not. 'We decided he [Younger] should fly in both the Boeing AWACs and the Nimrod AEW,' remembered Sir Ian Andrews, 'so we went up one week in an AWAC and the next week we flew in a Nimrod, and [George's] comment at the end of it was well, that's very interesting – either there's an airline strike we weren't told about, or I don't think it [the Nimrod] worked.'[22]

The future of Nimrod was, therefore, a foregone conclusion, but one that had to be managed. 'I said to George we've just to get on and do this,' remembered Peter Levene, 'and he said yes, I know, but we've got to do it my way.'[23] The main problem was handling Arnold Weinstock, the prickly managing director of GEC, and also Jim Prior, the former Cabinet minister-turned GEC chairman. While Thatcher was on good terms with Lord Weinstock, Younger remained friendly with Prior. Both exerted maximum pressure on the government to press on with Nimrod, often phoning and visiting Thatcher or Younger several times a day. At one meeting, the Defence Secretary was appalled when Weinstock asked him for a private word before ostentatiously asking Prior to leave the room, largely to demonstrate who was boss.[24]

---

[19] Thatcher, *The Downing Street Years*, 424.
[20] See pp. 124–125.
[21] Sir Peter Levene later banned cost-plus contracts and introduced competitive tendering.
[22] Interview with Sir Ian Andrews.
[23] Interview with Lord Levene, 15/3/2007.
[24] Private information.

'I remember the thoroughness with which George went into it,' recalled Sir Clive Whitmore. 'There were all sorts of studies around the central issue. George applied himself to all of that with great tenacity, and in a scrupulously balanced way to reach the final decision.'[25] That decision also needed careful presentation. Not only did it have uncomfortable echoes of the Westland affair in that the choice lay between a US and domestic solution, but the Conservatives had backed the scheme as approved by Callaghan. Nevertheless, remembers John Howe, 'he handled it with enormous skill. He had a tremendously strong instinct for where the political flak was going to come from and he went to enormous lengths to lobby and make sure the arguments were strong so that he could stand his ground.'[26] Younger also applied his charm to at first the Cabinet, then Conservative back-benchers, while the Prime Minister prepared Weinstock for the inevitable. 'It was going to be politically controversial but he did it so skilfully that by the time he actually announced the decision,' said Levene, 'he'd taken the sting out of it and it just went through. It was an extraordinary good piece of political management.'[27]

In December 1986 Younger told the House that the Nimrod scheme was to be scrapped, having already cost the government around £1bn. 'His pitch was that it's been an absolute bloody disaster', said Archie Hamilton, an MoD minister at the time, 'but we're now rectifying the situation and this is really the only way out.'[28] It was an assured and perfectly-pitched performance. Instead, announced Younger, the MoD would order six Boeing E-3As (or AWACs) with an option on a further two.[29] These had to be procured from the United States, but a unique deal was negotiated (and carried out) which provided for 120 per cent of the cost to be offset by work placed by, and through, Boeing in the UK. MPs could easily have reacted with hostility to the vision of British defence ministers going cap in hand to the United States, but, said Sir Clive, 'the very positive thing about George was that when he was dealing with an issue like that people had confidence in him to come to it with an open mind, whereas with Heseltine the Prime Minister always had a suspicion that there was another agenda. People trusted George and had a view of him, rightly, as a man of integrity.'[30]

Arnold Weinstock, predictably, was enraged. '[A]lthough years later I

---

[25] Interview with Sir Clive Whitmore.
[26] Interview with John Howe.
[27] Interview with Lord Levene.
[28] Interview with Lord Hamilton, 9/1/2007.
[29] The switch to the E-3As later caused financial problems in its own right.
[30] Interview with Sir Clive Whitmore.

tried very hard to assure him that I would almost certainly have taken the same decision', wrote Heseltine in his memoirs, 'he was never wholly convinced that it was anything other than a price that he paid for the remarkable support he gave me over Westland. In fairness to George Younger and to the military establishment in the Ministry of Defence, I don't believe that their judgement was influenced one way or the other by Westland.'[31]

Younger's stock was running high. 'There was a moment following Nimrod where everybody said that George is an absolute genius,' recalled Lord Hamilton, 'he's handled the biggest defence procurement cock-up in history very well, and as the hunt for a future leader of the Conservative Party got under way, people said – although it didn't last long – that he should be the next leader.'[32] 'If Younger were to emerge,' speculated the *Sunday Telegraph*, 'still the Member for Ayr, with the Conservatives, however diminished, still in power, he would be wearing garlands; a very high proportion of the credit would have accrued to him. He would have to disclaim the viscountcy . . . but blessedly he has no aristocratic ways to dispose of.'[33]

'SCIENTIFIC ORGIES'

The cost of shelving Nimrod, and also of funding its replacement, placed enormous pressure on an already tight defence budget. The military was well-known for its ability to dream up new ways of spending that budget, and one commentator warned that the MoD had to end its 'scientific orgies with taxpayers' money'.[34] There was also considerable press speculation about the need for another defence review, which Younger wanted to avoid, the word 'review' being synonymous with 'cut'. George, therefore, was conscious of the need to protect the defence budget from the Treasury, although the prospect of an election the following year was a political ace in an otherwise difficult hand.

In an effort to increase value for money, Younger had already cut back a generous system of giving defence contractors interim payments of up to 100 per cent of costs, but there were still money pressures. The MoD had to fight each year for its allocated budget, unlike the Scottish Office's block grant which was calculated using the Barnett Formula, so negotiat-

---

[31] Heseltine, *Life in the Jungle*, 270-71.
[32] Interview with Lord Hamilton.
[33] *Sunday Telegraph* 12/10/1986. Younger's PPS, Alex Pollock, remembers the senior Conservative backbencher and historian, Robert Rhodes James, expressing similar sentiments.
[34] *MOD* II (BBC) c4/1986.

ing an overall budget with the Chief Secretary to the Treasury was unfamiliar territory for George. Details of spending on individual projects remained a closely-guarded secret, although Armed Forces' pay was considered separately through the Pay Review Body. But, said the former chancellor Nigel Lawson in his memoirs, 'The sanctity of the defence block budget came to an end with the arrival of George Younger.'[35]

Robin Butler had recently become second PUS at the Treasury in charge of public spending, while Sir Clive Whitmore was still reasonably fresh in his more senior post at the MoD. These personnel changes paved the way for a little-publicised concordat between Younger and John MacGregor (the Chief Secretary to the Treasury) which opened the MoD's books for the first time and allowed expenditure negotiations to be conducted on an item-by-item basis. Lawson was delighted by the change, although it hardly made life easier for Younger, who also had the ordeal of presenting the defence estimates to Parliament each year. In doing so, he was fond of repeating his rather vague maxim, first aired in the 1960s and 1970s, that any defence policy had to include a provision for the unforeseen. The trouble was, planning for the unexpected could be very expensive.

Essentially, Younger wanted to extract as much money from the Treasury as possible, although he was acutely aware that seven years of relative affluence at the MoD were giving way to another seven of belt-tightening. Lord Whitelaw proved helpful in ensuring the Prime Minister supported George's aim, and although the financial pressure came to a head in 1987–88 he managed to secure an increase of one per cent per annum (compared with three per cent previously) in real terms over the next three years (starting in 1988–89), which equated to an extra £1bn a year in cash terms.[36]

But when negotiations moved on to individual expenditure areas, the Defence Secretary had a tougher fight in 'bilateral' discussions with John Major, the Chief Secretary to the Treasury for most of his period at the MoD. Although temperamentally similar, both were capable of being politely stubborn. The 1988–89 spending round was particularly lengthy, even spilling over into the autumn Conservative Party conference. 'I sat in my hotel bedroom as ministers trooped in and out, but decamped to a different hotel for especially long discussions with George Younger, who as ever fought politely but determinedly for every penny,' recalled Major

---

[35] Lawson, *The View From No. 11*, 313.

[36] John Howe, the second of Younger's private secretaries, said this success in extracting resources from the Treasury was 'a critical test, in the department's eyes, of the calibre of a Secretary of State' (*The Times* 31/1/2003).

in his memoirs. The future prime minister was on top of his brief and, more importantly, the statistics, and insisted there was room for improvement in certain areas. Younger was weaker on the detail but a skilled negotiator, insisting with equal force that his department was already operating at maximum efficiency.

The grindingly tedious negotiations took more than 24 hours over a period of four or five days. 'Gradually the deals were reached,' said Major, 'and eventually [George] accepted that if he pushed his case to an adjudication by the so-called "Star Chamber". . . he would get no more cash. George was a good Defence Secretary: he attacked in strength and retreated in good order.'[37]

Younger also knew when to attack or retreat on procurement issues. Peter Levene, who Heseltine had turned from poacher (he used to sell the MoD weapons) to gamekeeper (at the MoD he was in charge of buying them), remembered being amused at a volte-face by his new chief in early 1986. 'Just before George arrived he had been fighting like mad to have some of these built in Scotland [AORs – Auxiliary Replenishment vessels for the Royal Navy] and was sending us rude letters,' he recalled, 'so when he turned up I said what do you want to do about these? He said "well I'm not Secretary of State for Scotland any more, I'm at defence, and it's clear to me – as you say – that we shouldn't build them in Scotland." I thought that was a very professional response.'[38]

This did not mean, however, that he ignored Scottish considerations while at the MoD. Alex Pollock remembers that when the position of chaplain-general to the Armed Forces fell vacant, Younger was advised that it ought to be filled by an Anglican. 'This came up at one of the first ministerial meetings,' Pollock recalled, 'and he just turned to me and said "I don't think that would be very well received among the Scottish troops, would it Alex?" That was the end of it and the next appointment was a Church of Scotland man.'[39]

Procurement could, of course, also be subject to political considerations. Younger announced an order for three Type 23 frigates (the backbone of the Navy's anti-submarine force) in July 1986, two of which were to be built at Yarrow on the Clyde and the other at Swan Hunter on Tyneside. 'George was a Scottish MP and it was a good news story', recalled Sir Timothy Sainsbury, 'and normally the SoS would make that

---

[37] Major, *The Autobiography*, 108 & 105.
[38] Interview with Lord Levene. Younger had lobbied for some to be built at Scott Lithgow in Glasgow, but instead the contract was divided between Vickers at Barrow-in-Furness and Cammell Laird on Merseyside.
[39] Alex Pollock to the author, c11/2007.

announcement, but he left it to me and for days afterwards Scots MPs with accents I couldn't understand were coming up to me and thanking me for the orders.'[40]

The financial squeeze of 1987–88 led to the suspension of any further contracts, but back-bench pressure prompted Younger to announce orders for four additional vessels at the 1988 Conservative Party conference. Eventually, a total of six Type 23 frigates were ordered together with 19 new mine-hunters from yards in different parts of the country. Influenced by his experience as Scottish Secretary, this spread of naval orders to sustain several yards during a difficult period for the shipbuilding industry was a central part of Younger's procurement policy.

George also continued Heseltine's policy of privatisation, and applied it to the Royal Ordnance Factories (ROF). 'Again, hugely controversial', said Sir Ian Andrews, 'but people trusted him to make the right decision.'[41] Younger had announced in June 1986 that with the exception of one factory, the government intended to invite bids for ROF as a whole. The exception was a troubled tank-building business in Leeds, which was to be sold for £11m to Vickers, who would in turn build a major new facility to meet a new £100m order for 76 Challenger tanks. In April 1987 Younger informed Parliament that ROF was to be sold to British Aerospace for £190m.

Also controversial was the £500m Zircon satellite, details of which emerged in January 1987 when an investigative journalist called Duncan Campbell planned to broadcast them as part of a BBC Scotland series called *The Secret Society*. Younger was one of only four ministers who actually knew the satellite existed, and the government was sensitive enough to lean on the Defence Secretary's old chum Alasdair Milne (now director-general of the BBC), to ban the programme. When Campbell instead published an article in the *New Statesman*, Mrs Thatcher instructed Michael Havers, the Attorney General, to issue an injunction against him and every other newspaper.

Undeterred, Campbell arranged a private viewing of his film for MPs, and Younger also sanctioned a screening for members of the Defence Select Committee. 'In a somewhat unfortunate blaze of publicity,' recalled Nigel Lawson, 'the police raided the offices both of the BBC in Glasgow and of the *New Statesman* in London in an attempt to discover the source of this information.'[42] Even more unfortunate was the presence of Scotland's

---

[40] Interview with Sir Timothy Sainsbury, 23/1/2007. Sir Timothy represented the Hove constituency on the south coast of England.
[41] Interview with Sir Ian Andrews.
[42] Lawson, *The View from No. 11*, 313.

Lord Advocate, Lord Cameron of Lochbroom, who was being interviewed at the BBC on a separate matter while the raid took place. A few
weeks later Milne resigned as director-general.

THE SPECIAL RELATIONSHIP

In 1985 Margaret Thatcher became the first prime minister since Winston
Churchill to address both houses of the US Congress. Her much-parodied
'special relationship' with president Ronald Reagan was at its peak, and
Younger soon forged a similar relationship with the US defense secretary
Caspar, or 'Cap', Weinberger. Known as 'Cap the Knife' through his
reputation as an able administrator and cost cutter, at the US Department
of Defense he quickly earned the sobriquet 'Cap the Ladle' because of his
vigorous advocacy of huge increases in defence spending.

In that respect, Weinberger and Younger had much in common, and
although Cap's approach to defence matters was more intellectual, he was
a confirmed Anglophile and immediately hit it off with George. Cap
considered his UK counterpart 'an exceptionally able, intelligent, effective
Minister', with whom he 'worked closely and effectively together in all
defence matters, including carrying out the first of our SDI foreign
contracts, which were with Britain'.[43]

Weinberger shared President Reagan's conviction that the Soviet
Union posed a serious threat to the United States, whose defence
establishment needed to be strengthened and modernised. Consequently,
he was a strong advocate of the controversial Strategic Defense Initiative
(SDI), otherwise known as 'Star Wars', which proposed a space-based
missile defence shield. Good relations with Younger (and Heseltine before
his resignation) ensured that between October 1985 and December 1988
UK firms and research establishments received $55.8m in SDI con-
tracts.[44]

Weinberger resigned in November 1987 citing his wife's declining
health,[45] but Younger sustained good relations with his successors Dick
Cheney and Frank Carlucci. 'He was very congenial; very easy to get
along with,' recalled Carlucci, 'although that isn't to say that he didn't
have any convictions; he always represented the views of his country in a

---

[43] Weinberger, *Fighting for Peace*, 220.

[44] Both Younger and the Foreign Secretary, Sir Geoffrey Howe, however, were uncomfortable with
US zealousness in developing and deploying SDI, emphasising the need for consultation with the
allies.

[45] 'Anything I can say is inadequate', Cap wrote to Younger on leaving the Pentagon, 'you have been
great to work with & I do hope we can stay in touch. C' (Caspar Weinberger to GY, 17/11/1987,
GYP).

forthright way, but in a way which didn't offend anyone. He was also a very good ally; I can't remember a single issue we had with George which was at all acrimonious.'[46]

The special relationship had been put to the test when in the early hours of 5 April 1986 a bomb exploded at a disco frequented by US servicemen in West Berlin. Two people, one a US soldier, were killed and 200 others, including 60 Americans, were injured. Both US and UK intelligence suspected Libyan involvement. A few days later Reagan sent a message to Mrs Thatcher requesting support for the use of American F1-11s and support aircraft based in the UK in air strikes against Libya. He wanted an answer by noon on 9 April.

Conveniently, Sir Geoffrey Howe, the foreign secretary, and Younger were already at 10 Downing Street for a dinner with the president of South Korea, and the Prime Minister quickly convened a private meeting. France and Spain had already refused the US permission to fly over their territory, but after the Falklands Mrs Thatcher could not realistically withhold consent. But all the ministers present, including Lord Whitelaw, had reservations. Howe had already criticised the presence of a US Sixth Fleet exercise close to the Libyan coast, while Whitelaw wanted to make a clear distinction between acceding to a request from an ally and enthusing about every action the ally proposed to take. According to one account, Younger even went public with his anxieties the following day.[47]

Conscious of their doubts, Thatcher dispatched a holding message to Reagan asking for more details of the proposed raids, an initial reaction which she later felt was 'probably too negative'. 'The reply which came back the next day was okay on most of those issues, but there was then a further discussion in which both Geoffrey and George continued to be very reluctant,' recalled Thatcher's private secretary for foreign affairs, Charles Powell, who was also present. 'My recollection is that Geoffrey was still opposed and George was at the very least still wobbly on the subject but determined to go ahead anyway.'[48]

That day there were more ad hoc meetings with ministers, and also the Attorney General Sir Michael Havers. Gradually, most became convinced that the action proposed was consistent with the right of self-defence and Article 51 of the UN Charter. Younger had commitments in Scotland the following weekend, but Howe and the Prime Minister met Reagan's special envoy, Ambassador Vernon ('Dick') Walters, on the

---

[46] Interview with Frank Carlucci, 5/1/2007.

[47] Young, *One of Us*, 476. Young claims Younger voiced doubts when interviewed by a Scottish radio station.

[48] Interview with Lord Powell, 31/1/2007.

Saturday. He argued his case vigorously, and, recalled Howe, '[b]y the end of that weekend the Prime Minister and her key Secretaries of State (Foreign and Defence) were of one mind'.[49]

The US air strike took place on the evening of 14 April, coinciding with the government's shock defeat over a Bill to legalise Sunday opening. The proposed targets had been restricted to reflect UK concerns, and only some of the specified Libyan targets were actually hit. The bulk of European – including British – public and political opinion was hostile, and Cabinet meetings on 15 and 17 April were long and deeply uneasy. News of the death in Beirut of two British hostages added gloom to the proceedings, as did news that the television journalist John McCarthy had been kidnapped.

Terrorism was an unfortunate by-product of Younger's brief, both domestic and international. Libya was also implicated in the Lockerbie bombing just before Christmas in 1988, and the security aspect of Northern Ireland took up a sizeable portion of Younger's time and in-tray. He held monthly meetings with the Northern Ireland Secretary[50] and would often visit the province to inspect troops. The fragility of the situation was brought grimly home when, in March 1988, two British soldiers in civilian dress took a wrong turning and drove close to an IRA funeral. They were dragged from their vehicle and beaten before being fatally shot.

Although Younger was used to the presence of personal bodyguards (or 'heavies') from his seven years as Scottish Secretary, the security risk was even greater in his capacity as the political head of the UK's Armed Forces. His bodyguards even came on winter shoots carrying pistols under their Barbour jackets, but were also good company at New Year's Eve parties with Sir David Montgomery at Kinross (at which George would 'see in' the new year by playing 'Auld Lang Syne' on the piano). On one occasion Lady Montgomery put an explosive canister in the middle of the table filled with Quality Street chocolates. At the appropriate moment she surreptitiously lit the fuse; it exploded and showered the room with its contents as the heavies leapt to their feet and reached for their guns.

Fortunately, they had a sense of humour. In the summer, the bodyguards had to wear bullet-proof vests despite the seasonal warmth. When George's son, Andrew, asked why it was that they were fully protected while the minister and his son were clad only in casual summer clothes,

---

[49] Howe, *Conflict of Loyalty*, 505.
[50] The Secretary of State throughout Younger's time at the MoD was Tom King, who later succeeded him as Defence Secretary in 1989.

'the reply was that if anyone shot any of us then they would be able to shoot them back!'[51]

'FINE, I'LL GO BY CONCORDE'

Being Defence Secretary inevitably involved a lot of travelling, and although often gruelling, Younger's childlike curiosity ensured overseas trips were enjoyable as well as constructive. More often than not, Diana would accompany him and carry out her own programme of visits. George had expressed a desire to visit the Argylls in the Falklands on becoming Defence Secretary in early 1986, and a visit was duly arranged for early the following year.

On his first day in the islands, Younger formally inspected the 1st Battalion Argyll and Sutherland Highlanders, the garrison battalion in that remote outpost of the British Empire. The next day he encountered them again, but this time informally as a former officer, and the tone was markedly different. George chatted to all ranks with consummate ease, and the admiral who accompanied him quickly became aware that he was inside a club of which he was not a member. Younger encountered many soldiers whose fathers or uncles he had known, including the son of one of his old platoon sergeants. He ended his trip with a spot of fly-fishing on a stretch of river on West Falkland, and although George's luck was mixed, his catch travelled back to the UK in the tail of a Tristar.

International trips could also make for fraught diary management. Younger was due to witness a Polaris missile test in Florida the day after he was to greet the Queen at Holyrood in his new role as a brigadier in the Royal Company of Archers. 'It was a logistical nightmare,' recalled Sir Ian Andrews, 'and we said we would have to put him on Concorde or something, and he said "fine, I'll go by Concorde". He even changed out of his finery en route to the airport.'[52] The MoD was baffled by its Secretary of State's rank of brigadier, which was actually the lowest position of an officer in the Archers. Younger once joked that the bow and arrows he sported on ceremonial occasions were the 'ultimate deterrent'.[53]

Some jaunts also satisfied Younger's boyish love of military hardware. 'We were wondering about what tank should replace the Chieftain,' remembered Sir Timothy Sainsbury, 'So George and I went to the ranges in Germany and got into a Leopard, then an Abrams in the US, and then

---

[51] Andrew Younger to the author, 30/1/2008.
[52] Interview with Sir Ian Andrews.
[53] *Sunday Mail* 27/7/1986.

our own Challenger, and we had great fun firing the guns.'[54] The existing
Chieftain battle tank was long overdue for replacement, and although the
Challenger 2 Mk 2 alternative had been designed in the UK by Vickers
Defence Systems, the military was very keen for capability reasons on the
Abrams MI, manufactured by General Dynamics in the US. Younger
faced not only conflicting views within the MoD, but also from the Prime
Minister's policy advisers concerning the tanks' technical details. 'They
tended to come in with detailed technical data about the theoretical
superiority of the German tank over the British Challenger', recalled
Younger a few years later, 'but they did not always possess the complete
military picture. Unfortunately, Mrs Thatcher would listen to her own
people instead of the Ministry of Defence and we were left with the wrong
balance.'[55]

A former special adviser remembers watching Younger in action as a
Cabinet committee worked towards a decision. 'In one of them, George
played a very neutral role, giving the pros and cons of each without
coming down strongly one way or another', he recalled. 'But the Prime
Minister, for obvious defence industry and political reasons, was keen to
go down a "Buy British" route; George therefore trod a very careful line
that balanced the views of his department with the wider political
imperatives. By remaining neutral he enabled the strongest "Buy British" currents in the committee to prevail, even though this potentially
entailed more development risk.' But when a decision was taken to go for
the British option in principle, the committee met again. 'Suddenly he
came alive, flagging up much more strongly the development risk issues
associated with Challenger 2 so that should things subsequently go wrong,
he had successfully balanced political imperatives with protecting his
department's position.'[56]

On another trip to Germany with the Prime Minister, the Secretary of
State was delighted to be given an Army smock with a 'Younger' name-
badge attached to it. 'When he came back', remembered Sir Ian Andrews,
'he said "I shall wear this whenever I go somewhere, but I need a hat to go
with it". We said why can't you wear a trilby, and he said "no, I want a
beret"; we said well you can't have a beret without a badge, and he said
"well, get me a badge!"' This threw up protocol issues, as although
Younger was Secretary of State, he was not technically a member of the
Armed Forces. 'In the end we decided that as chairman of the defence
council it was appropriate to have a defence council badge. So we went to

---

[54] Interview with Sir Timothy Sainsbury.
[55] *Scotland on Sunday* 10/10/1993.
[56] Private information.

the manufacturers and commissioned two, one was a reserve, and my wife sewed it on to a beret. He was very happy with that.'[57] A photograph of Younger wearing both the smock and beret became a family favourite.

Perhaps the highlight among Younger's ministerial trips was that to Korea in 1988, the first time he had been back since the war. The resulting hospitality was generous. 'The Koreans understood I had been in the war and the speeches of welcome got more and more over-the-top,' recalled Younger. 'It was reassuring that they appreciated our efforts.'[58] The trip began in Hong Kong, where Diana was left to pursue her own itinerary – both social and formal – while Younger, accompanied by his private secretary Brian Hawtin, visited the Demilitarised Zone (DMZ) on the border between North and South Korea. He also made the symbolic gesture of crossing the demarcation line under the watchful eyes of armed South Korean and US escorts, thereby entering North Korean territory.

Younger was also escorted more than 200 feet below the DMZ, and walked almost a mile along a North Korean invasion tunnel discovered in 1978 to a small cavern where the South Koreans had installed a deadly maze of razor wire, mines, booby traps and machine-guns. 'On the last day we ended up in a helicopter with George in the co-pilot's seat,' recalled Hawtin, 'with a map on his knee plotting the course of his battalion and where he'd actually fought. It was obviously a life-forming experience.'[59] He later laid a wreath at the Commonwealth war memorial at Kapyong, thirty miles south of the DMZ. 'You can't help recalling colleagues who fell,' Younger reflected, 'but it is something to see the freedom they were fighting for very much alive.'[60]

A CLOSE SHAVE

Younger's stature within the Conservative Party had grown steadily over the past year-and-a-half. Party grandees even regarded him as a possible leadership contender, someone who might slip through almost unnoticed as a latter-day Sir Alec Douglas-Home, while his growing influence was recognised when he became president of the National Union of Conservative and Unionist Associations from 1987 to 1988. This was largely honorific, although Younger was pleased to follow, once again, in his

---

[57] Interview with Sir Ian Andrews.
[58] *Sunday Post* 25/6/2000.
[59] Interview with Brian Hawtin, 10/1/2007. When Younger visited Turkey as Defence Secretary, he took with him a pair of binoculars inherited from his grandfather, the 2nd Viscount, who had used them at Gallipoli.
[60] *The Times* 30/3/1988.

great-grandfather's footsteps, the other George Younger having held a similar position back in 1904.

As expected, defence policy played a prominent part in the general election of 1987, and Younger had the honour of hosting the first press conference of the campaign. Soon after the Libyan bombing raids George had signalled the start of an intensive ministerial and Conservative Party campaign to promote the government's defence policies while attacking those of the opposition parties.[61] This was political child's play. Not only was Labour back-pedalling on its unilateralist stance, but the SDP/Liberal Alliance was publicly squabbling over its joint defence policy. This twin-pronged approach reached its height during the election battle. Younger claimed Alliance policy amounted to unilateral nuclear disarmament by stealth which, combined with Labour's unilateralism, would produce a 'frightened and fellow-travelling Britain'[62] vulnerable to Soviet blackmail.

The MoD had recently acquired a special adviser called Andrew Dunlop to aide Younger with this sort of 'rough and tumble' politics. Although George performed well during the four-week campaign, there were difficulties with the Conservative strategy, culminating in a famous wobble by Mrs Thatcher as polling day approached. There was no such anxiety at the MoD, where officials used the election hiatus to have the office painted and re-carpeted, so inevitable did the outcome seem. 'I remember at about 2 a.m. on election night the television coverage flashed up "recount in Ayr", and then second recount,' remembered Sir Ian Andrews. 'I could just see a new Secretary of State turning up the following morning and us having no briefing whatsoever. John Howe and I aged a lot that night.'[63]

But despite having consistently increased his majorities in Ayr since the early 1970s, this time Younger's majority was just 182, a result of tactical voting and a general decline in Scottish Tory fortunes. 'George was very subdued and chastened, as I was as well,' remembered his agent Bill Taylor, who was present at the count, 'George was in a much busier job with foreign trips and he simply wasn't able to devote as much time to the constituency – we had lost his usual level of input.' The Ayr Conservative Association had also undergone a lot of recent personnel changes. 'I felt there wasn't the sharp combative edge in our organisation any more. There were a lot of lamentations and recriminations after that.'[64]

Although upset, Younger took the result on the chin. When challenged

---

[61] Labour's Shadow Defence Secretary was Denzil Davies, although the party's former Defence Secretary, Denis Healey, often went up against Younger in interviews. Healey would deliberately call George 'Kenneth', having known his uncle.

[62] Thatcher, *The Downing Street Years*, 424.

[63] Interview with Sir Ian Andrews.

[64] Interview with Bill Taylor, 2/8/2007.

about it on television, he replied with typical urbanity, 'well in this game one is enough and I've done considerably better than that'.[65] Sir Michael Quinlan, Younger's last PUS at the MoD, remembers him hosting a lunch for Marshall Akromeyev, the former head of Russia's armed forces. 'The Soviet Union was then going through the motions of democracy and he'd had to stand for election somewhere,' recalled Sir Michael. 'I remember him saying to George, rather glumly, I only got 78 per cent; and George said, "Oh, I've had to settle for 39.4." I remember him being very amused by that.'[66] Less amusing was the loss of ten Conservative seats in Scotland,[67] a result – although there was a minor revival in 1992 – from which the Scottish Conservatives never fully recovered.

Nevertheless, Younger's stock was still high following polling day. 'Personally popular and quietly persuasive,' commented *The Times*, singling him out for praise in its election analysis, 'he would be the obvious compromise choice in any succession struggle. He would offer a very different style of leadership: the chairman of the Cabinet, rather than a dominating force. But by that time the party and the country might want a little less domination.'[68]

When the new Parliament convened, Younger called John Howe and Ian Andrews into his office to talk about his priorities for the future. 'He had three of these,' recalled Howe. 'One was that he wanted a flat in town, so we revived occupancy of Admiralty House; number two was a personal flag for the car; and three was a personal cap badge, which had to be designed. That was rather charming in a way but indicative of him – he didn't come back and say I think we should invade Afghanistan.'[69]

THE BALANCE OF POWER

Throughout Younger's tenure as Defence Secretary, the North Atlantic Treaty Organisation (NATO) was the most important international forum in the context of the ongoing Cold War. Dominated by both European and North American members, Heseltine had considered the alliance to be lopsided and sought to defend British interests in relation to Europe by

---

[65] *Election 1987* (BBC) 12/6/1987.

[66] Interview with Sir Michael Quinlan, 13/3/2007. George also entertained the Liberal Democrat leader Paddy Ashdown with a similar story. 'He [Akromeyev] was standing against a young journalist who, he complained, "used some very misleading statements and slogans"' (Ashdown, *The Ashdown Diaries I*, 36).

[67] The losses included Alex Pollock in Moray, formerly Younger's PPS.

[68] *The Times* 10/6/1987.

[69] Interview with John Howe. Younger had also bought his first London home shortly after becoming Defence Secretary, a modest house on Cardigan Street in Kennington, which was within walking distance of both Parliament and the MoD.

awarding lucrative contracts to British Aerospace. Younger did not differ
greatly from his predecessor in this respect and continued to pursue
collaborative programmes with European allies, including a memoran-
dum of understanding with Italy. Importantly, Italy, the UK and West
Germany also collaborated on the production of the Tornado aircraft,
saving the MoD some much needed cash in the process.[70]

The UK was a major presence at regular NATO meetings, and
although Younger did not revel in the more intellectual discussions he
acquitted himself well with a measured but authoritative debating style. As
at the MoD, he derived kudos from his own Army service, something he
subtly reinforced through his practice of presenting antique prints of the
Argylls in routine exchanges of gifts.[71] A useful contact was his former
Cabinet colleague Lord Carrington, who served as secretary-general of
NATO from 1984 to 1988. Carrington actually asked Younger if he would
consider succeeding him, an offer he turned down chiefly because it would
have meant commuting to Brussels.

Below NATO in the diplomatic pecking order was Eurogroup (European members of NATO) and the Western European Union (WEU),
although the latter had limited membership and was more political in
purpose, Younger nevertheless saw it as a suitable vehicle for closer
defence co-operation alongside NATO, and backed Geoffrey Howe's plea
for an increasingly close partnership between Europe's two nuclear
powers, the UK and France. 'Pressure for this comes above all from
the United States itself,' commented Younger shortly after becoming
Defence Secretary, 'anxious that Europe pulls its weight within the
alliance to the maximum possible extent.'[72]

Another manifestation of continental co-operation was the so-called
European Fighter Aircraft (later known as the Eurofighter), a troubled and
expensive scheme which was still incomplete more than a decade after
Younger ceased to be Defence Secretary.[73] A collaborative project
between the UK, West Germany, Italy and Spain, Younger helped
convince Mrs Thatcher of its merits but struggled to grasp the detail
of its actual capability. 'I remember recommending he read Tom Clancy's
Red Storm Rising on his holiday,' said Sir Ian Andrews, 'passages of which

---

[70] Sir Donald Maclean, Younger's constituency chairman, remembered visiting Germany and
meeting a senior civil servant who had noticed that he was from the Defence Secretary's
constituency. 'Remarkable man,' he quipped, 'he is disarming even if his country isn't' (interview
with Sir Donald Maclean, 2/8/2007).

[71] This, remarked Brian Hawtin, 'must have left the print shops around Cecil Court well denuded of
stock' (Brian Hawtin to the author, 17/11/2007).

[72] *The Times* 26/2/1986.

[73] In 2007 the Eurofighter began to enter service with the RAF as the Typhoon.

described the capability of this sort of aircraft really quite well. He came back from holiday and said, "I've got it!" '[74]

But of even greater importance than good European – and even US/UK relations – was managing the ongoing East/West divide, otherwise known as the Cold War. Britain's first prime minister, Sir Robert Walpole, famously coined the phrase 'the balance of power', and it was as pertinent in 1986 as at any point in recent UK history. The latter period of Younger's time at the MoD (post-1987 election) witnessed profound changes in that balance, with resulting implications for UK defence policy. Although uncomfortable with the more intellectual aspects of the Cold War debate, Younger appeared more ostentatiously right wing than ever before. 'We have to show them that we're a tough nut,' he said early on in his tenure, 'if we do that they'll talk.'[75]

Talk they did, although the conversations were largely driven by the US and the Soviet Union. The culmination was a summit between Presidents Reagan and Gorbachev at Reykjavik in 1986, which in turn led to the historic INF treaty to eliminate certain kinds of ground-based nuclear missiles held by NATO countries. All of this, however, was not Younger's direct concern, although he was kept fully informed. 'I don't think George contributed in the architectural sense to the handling of East–West relations, he left the brainy bit to others,' judged John Howe, 'George wasn't interested in the deal struck at Reykjavik, he was completely non-ideological in that sense, but when it came to handling the human side he was very good.'[76]

The human side involved two historic visits by Soviet politicians to British soil. Gorbachev was the first, stopping off to see Mrs Thatcher at RAF Brize Norton en route from Iceland, while Younger personally invited the Soviet defence minister, Dimitri Yasov, to London and Scotland. It was a symbolic move in terms of détente, and a satisfying continuation of the good relations he had forged with Gorbachev during his truncated visit to Scotland in 1984. 'What I am most proud of having helped to achieve was the end of the Cold War,' Younger reflected towards the end of his life. 'It was a question of lots of people being tough and immovable with the Soviet Union until they ran out of money and the guts to go on with it. The whole thing was a huge leap of faith.'[77] Younger

---

[74] Interview with Sir Ian Andrews.

[75] *MOD* I (BBC) c4/1986.

[76] Interview with John Howe.

[77] *Soldier* 2/2002. 'We had sat there for years looking at 55,000 Soviet tanks lined up to sweep us across the north German plain,' Younger added. 'We had only about 15,000 in the whole of Nato. Then when the Berlin Wall came down we found out that a large proportion of their tanks didn't work or didn't even have crews. A 40-year bluff.'

may have had no burning desire to create a new world order, but he was content to help smooth its path.

The last line of defence in the Cold War was, of course, the nuclear deterrent. While Caspar Weinberger had pushed for dramatic increases in the US nuclear weapons arsenal, Younger grappled with a replacement for the UK's ageing Polaris submarines, eventually ordering four Trident-carrying submarines after a significant delay and fluctuating costs. And in the political war of words over deterrent, Younger consolidated Heseltine's success in tackling the CND. 'Don't let's forget that having our own deterrent has secured peace for us ever since the last war', he argued, 'Thank goodness for it and don't let us throw it away.'[78] Younger compared the nuclear weapons to the premium one paid on insuring a home: it might be cheaper not to pay it, but it would also be very foolish. And although expensive, it was the UK's insurance policy against the Soviet Union. It was also a policy that benefited Scotland. 'They intend to cut it,' he said of Labour's commitment to scrap it, 'and in doing this they will destroy almost overnight literally thousands of jobs, many of them in Scotland.'[79]

The government and the Royal Navy were both keen to push ahead with the Trident programme so that even were Labour to win the next election it would be too far advanced to cancel. So the tender and order for the first three Trident submarines had already been announced when Younger arrived at the MoD, while the fourth came up two years later. Sir Michael Quinlan, the Jesuit-educated intellectual who had replaced Sir Clive Whitmore as PUS in 1988, tried to convince him that three were enough at a time when the UK also had, and envisaged keeping, nuclear delivery systems of other kinds. 'George listened with immense politeness,' he remembered, 'and said, "well it's a very interesting idea but I think we'll shelve that Michael."'[80] Sir Michael did succeed, however, in articulating the moral justification for the nuclear deterrent, if not the case for one less submarine. Younger also faced questions over a disastrous US test of the Trident D5 missiles, which had ended up doing cartwheels. 'George said no, you don't understand,' recalled his private secretary Brian Hawtin, 'the whole point of the tests was to see if the missiles were working properly or not. On this occasion they clearly weren't, therefore the test wasn't a failure, it was a success. And he got away with it.'[81]

[78] *MOD* II (BBC) c4/1986.
[79] Undated speech, c1987, GYP.
[80] Interview with Sir Michael Quinlan.
[81] Interview with Brian Hawtin.

But while the Cold War was on the wane, another long-lasting conflict in the Middle East was on the rise. When an American supertanker struck an Iranian mine in mid-1987, Younger authorised the dispatch of two mine-sweepers to support the UK's own shipping in the Gulf, a response soon emulated by the French. 'We followed through a plan which George Younger had discussed earlier in the year with his French and Dutch opposite numbers,' recalled Geoffrey Howe. 'The whole European participation was now transformed into a Western European Union operation. The WEU Fleet would have a separate identity and a separate command from the United States.' The Prime Minister, however, saw things differently and promptly overruled her Foreign and Defence Secretaries. 'For her the notion that any Royal Navy ship should be under command of any "foreigner" – unless he were an Anglo-Saxon – was quite unthinkable,' judged Howe. 'We explained to her that this was no great novelty [but] it was another of those moments when the Thatcher touch was less sensitive than it could have been in a European context.'[82]

Younger frequently donned sunglasses to visit the region, most frequently Saudi Arabia, charming its absolute monarchs and, more importantly, encouraging them to buy British-made arms. Middle-Eastern leaders also regularly visited the UK. Geoffrey Howe remembered himself, Younger and Willie Whitelaw waving off Taha Ramadhan, Saddam Hussein's deputy prime minister, from the steps of the Foreign Secretary's official residence at Carlton Gardens. 'As we did so I realized that Ramadhan had enjoyed the privilege of being entertained by Margaret Thatcher's three Wykehamist ministers,' he wrote in his memoirs. 'None of us had a satisfactory answer when I posed the question: "What on earth would William of Wykeham have thought of such a villain being so fêted by three representatives of the Wykehamist tradition?" But in those days Iraq was still a potentially valuable export market.'[83] The Middle Eastern country was not only a valuable market, but a valuable counterweight to Iran, then considered the more immediate threat to Western security.

FAREWELL TO POLITICS

By the beginning of 1989 it was widely accepted within the upper echelons of the MoD that a defence review was inevitable if the shortfall between funding and capability was to be closed in the medium to long term.

---

[82] Howe, *Conflict of Loyalty*, 555–56.
[83] Ibid, 332–33.

Younger, however, continued to resist what Richard Mottram used to call the 'r word'.[84] Meanwhile, events in Berlin gathered pace and talk of German reunification was in the air. Mrs Thatcher, however, stood almost alone in opposing an event which would signify the beginning of the end of the Cold War. To many, the Prime Minister's dogmatism was a depressing manifestation of her declining political powers.

Younger's well-tuned political antennae could not fail to detect the shifting mood. His relations with the Prime Minister had been excellent in both his Cabinet jobs. Mrs Thatcher saw him as loyal, reliable and lacking in Heseltonian ambitions, while George handled the Prime Minister carefully and, realising she respected detailed arguments, diligently mastered his brief before confronting her over any potentially difficult policy position.

Although George's forte was not addressing the House of Commons or delivering major set-piece speeches, the Prime Minister particularly valued him as a media performer. 'As things were moving more towards television,' remembered a former aide, 'he was a very effective communicator, partly because he could put potentially dry policy issues in plain English, and I think that was a quality – certainly in the discussions I had with Number 10 as his special adviser – which was highly valued by the PM and the government in general. That was his great political skill.'[85]

The Prime Minister was full of praise when she unveiled a portrait of Younger at Dover House in May 1988,[86] and a year later she celebrated the tenth anniversary of her arrival at Downing Street. Yet around the Cabinet table there were only five survivors from the heady days of 1979 – Geoffrey Howe, Peter Walker, George Younger, Norman Fowler and of course Mrs Thatcher herself. Politically, the government was in the doldrums, and by the spring of 1989 George had resolved not to stand in Ayr at the next general election because of his hopeless majority. He was also conscious that inheriting a viscountcy might suddenly truncate his Cabinet career and, more to the point, the Royal Bank of Scotland was telling him that it was now or never.

The bank's chairman, Sir Michael Young-Herries, had first approached Younger about succeeding him back in 1984. A veteran of the King's Own Scottish Borderers who shared George's devotion to the regimental system, Sir Michael had been pestering the Scottish and

---

[84] A review did eventually take place under Younger's successor, Tom King, entitled *Options for Change*.

[85] Private information.

[86] Painted by Jane Robson, it was commissioned for the Scottish Office collection of paintings depicting former secretaries of state.

Defence Secretary ever since.[87] Finally, in the spring of 1989, Younger asked to see the Prime Minister to tell her that he was inclined to accept. 'Mrs Thatcher wasn't very pleased about it,' he recalled with a smile, 'but I explained to her that I had to decide what my future career really was; it was clearly going to be either in politics or in business and I had decided by that time that I had done all the major things I wanted to do in politics and that I better take this wonderful opportunity in business.'[88]

The Prime Minister even hinted at the Foreign Office in an effort to get him to reconsider. 'She may have raised the Foreign Office in conversation to be nice to him,' recalled Lord Powell, 'but there's no evidence that it was a serious proposition that had formed in her mind. She was genuinely sorry to lose him, although not wholly surprised I don't think.'[89] Lord Whitelaw was also unhappy when he heard the news, and perhaps disappointed that it removed Younger as his heir apparent.

Initially, only six people knew that Younger was planning to resign, including Diana. Sir Michael Quinlan and Brian Hawtin, his last private secretary, were another two of the six, and Younger's large ministerial team were only informed shortly before his decision was made public. Alan Clark, the colourful diarist and military historian, had coveted an MoD job for the last few years, and often speculated privately as to his prospects. 'I still think Defence is more likely,' he wrote on 24 July 1989. 'So many people have said that I am to go there first as M[inister] of S[tate] in order to be poised to slither upstairs if George inherits, or goes somewhere grander.'[90]

Coincidentally, Younger confirmed his resignation in writing that same day. 'Following our conversation some time ago when I explained that I wished to become involved again in business,' he wrote to the Prime Minister, 'I am writing to confirm that I think that this is the sensible time to make the change, and to leave the Government . . . I look forward to continuing to support you throughout the rest of this Parliament, and I will always be ready to help you in any way I can.'[91] Little did Younger realise just how quickly he would be called upon to provide that help.

By sheer coincidence, the Ministry of Defence was to have a special

---

[87] 'This obviously had to be kept very secret indeed', recalled Younger at Sir Michael's memorial service, 'and there were only six people who Michael told (most of them are here today). No 'leak' of any kind took place, before it was announced in 1989, and Michael was very proud of that. Perhaps he could have made a good head of MI5' (undated speaking notes, GYP).

[88] Autobiographical notes, GYP.

[89] Interview with Lord Powell.

[90] Clark, *Diaries*, 249. Younger disliked Clark, refused to read his books and told his wife that he would not work at the MoD for as long as he remained Secretary of State. Clark finally joined the department after Younger resigned.

[91] GY to MT, 24/7/1989, GYP (copy).

staff outing to the Royal Tournament at Earl's Court on the day it was announced that Younger was standing down as Secretary of State. 'George was going to take the salute anyway,' recalled Sir Michael, 'so I remember ringing up the band leader to ensure that at an appropriate moment when George went out into the arena, "Auld Lang Syne" would be played to mark the fact that he was going.'[92] It was a touching moment, but the news took most people by surprise. Unlike Norman Fowler, who would shortly resign in order to spend more time with his family, Younger was not frustrated politically, nor was he at risk of the sack. The RBS offer was simply too good to refuse and, more importantly, was from a major organisation headquartered in Edinburgh.

Younger attended his last meeting at 10 Downing Street three days later. 'It was sad to think of this morning as your last attendance at Cabinet', wrote Malcolm Rifkind later that day, 'and curious that you appeared to have metamorphosised into the Lord Chancellor for the occasion! [the seating arrangements had changed] In all seriousness, our counsels will be the poorer without you and it won't just be Margaret who misses your sage advice.'[93]

Rifkind had succeeded him as Scottish Secretary in 1986 and, fittingly, Younger's former Scottish Office private secretaries proposed a dinner to mark his retirement from the Cabinet. Held at Glasgow University, where his former PUS Sir William Kerr Fraser was principal, on 13 October, George and his wife Diana reminisced with all of his former under-secretaries and officials from not only his time as Secretary of State, but also from his earlier spell as minister for development. It was a tribute not only to Younger's ability to connect with civil servants on a professional level, but also to his very human capacity for forging lasting friendships.

---

[92] Interview with Sir Michael Quinlan.
[93] Malcolm Rifkind to GY, 27/7/1989, GYP.

Chapter 14

'THE BEGINNING OF THE END OF THE THATCHER ERA'

'ALL POLITICAL LIVES, unless they are cut off in midstream at a happy juncture, end in failure,' wrote Enoch Powell, 'because that is the nature of politics and of human affairs.'[1] George Younger's exit from the Cabinet, at a point of his own choosing, was a rare exception to Powell's oft-quoted maxim. While most Cabinet ministers aim for the top of the greasy pole, Younger had always been content to settle for a position about two-thirds of the way up. He had completed successful terms in both the departments he had coveted since becoming an MP in 1964, and that was enough for him.

For any other recently-retired Cabinet minister life would have been a little easier. Constituency commitments would be wound down, while rounds of golf would jostle for diary space with undemanding boardroom meetings. Not so for Younger. Within a year-and-a-half of his resignation he would move from deputy chairman to chairman of the Royal Bank of Scotland (RBS), continue at full throttle as the Member for Ayr and oversee two Conservative leadership elections.

By mid-1989 Margaret Thatcher had been Prime Minister for more than a decade. She, and her governments, had truly broken the mould of British politics, but unlike Younger – one of her longest-serving ministers – Mrs Thatcher did not choose to resign office at a happy juncture. Her trusted deputy, however, did. The wide-eyed Wykehamist, Willie White-law, had chosen to retire in January 1988 following a stroke, depriving the Prime Minister of a multi-purpose troubleshooter who was invaluable in neutralising what Whitelaw himself called 'trouble', of which there was an ever-growing amount.

Thatcher told Woodrow Wyatt that Whitelaw's successor would have

---

[1] Powell, *Joseph Chamberlain*, 151.

to combine 'bonhomie and steel'; someone whose diplomatic skills were not compromised by personal ambition. Younger fulfilled those criteria admirably. He was also close to Whitelaw, who may have suggested him to the Prime Minister as his replacement. But ultimately it was not to be. The main reason was Younger's commitment to RBS. The eventual occupation of the chairman's office was, after all, why he had left Cabinet in the first place. With Whitelaw gone, Mrs Thatcher increasingly retreated into a bunker where she listened to acolytes rather than clear-eyed friends.

It has been said that Mrs Thatcher tried to lure Younger back into government with an offer of the Foreign Office following Nigel Lawson's resignation in October 1989, but this seems unlikely to have gone beyond informal soundings.[2] Within months of his resignation, however, Younger did return to frontline politics – albeit in unwelcome circumstances – when a hitherto obscure Conservative back-bencher decided to challenge the Prime Minister for the Conservative leadership.

The Member for Clwyd North-West, Sir Anthony Meyer, of course, had no chance of winning and he knew it. The point was to make a statement, perhaps a rather vague statement, but a damaging one nevertheless. Dubbed 'Sir Nobody' by newspapers still flying the Thatcherite flag, Sir Anthony was deeply unhappy about Thatcher's hostility to Europe. 'There was talk of it,' Younger recalled, '[and] it's highly significant that his motivation was entirely European. That's why he did it. He was a passionate pro-European.'

Thatcher immediately turned to Younger to run her campaign. 'I think on the part of her advisors they were looking for somebody who was not a Thatcherite,' Younger reasoned, 'in order to maximise the non-Thatcherite votes. Someone who also wasn't a controversial left-wing figure.'[3] Ironically, as with the Westland affair, Younger was not ideologically far removed from the enemy of the moment, although loyalty to party and leader took precedence over any personal views.

Typically, Younger was charming to Sir Anthony throughout the rather surreal campaign. The contest was perfectly in order, he explained to reporters, but regrettable. 'I believe this should only be done under the rules when there are overwhelming and exceptional reasons and a very large demand for an election from the party as a whole. None of these

[2] 'An appeal was made to try to win him [Younger] back, to no avail,' recalled Lord Waddington when interviewed for a biography of John Major (Seldon, *Major: A Political Life*, 100).

[3] Interview with Lord Younger, 10/2/1993. '[I]f the Prime Minister wanted to minimise damage,' observed Sir Anthony Meyer, 'she could not have done better than to appoint George Younger to conduct her campaign for her' (Meyer, *Stand Up and Be Counted*, 165).

conditions exists.'[4] Nevertheless, George must have had misgivings. According to the BBC journalist John Cole he had advised Mrs Thatcher prior to the challenge to take a 'cool judgement as to whether or not she was likely to win the next election, and then to decide when to retire'. The Prime Minister, however, was not interested. 'Younger concluded gloom-ily that she was unlikely to follow the example of Harold Wilson, and go voluntarily,' wrote Cole. 'Wilson, he reasoned, was interested in holidays in the Scilly Isles and in golf, whereas the only subject which fascinated Margaret Thatcher was public affairs.'[5]

Younger became the main link man, channelling back-bench opinion to the Prime Minister. His management of the media was also masterly. Depicting the challenge as nothing more significant than 'typical mid-term blues', Younger even sought to downplay the European issue – despite his reservations – claiming it was a 'diminishing' issue among MPs. Writing in *The Times* the day before voting, he rubbished claims that Mrs Thatcher was personally anti-European, while damning Sir Anthony with faint praise. 'Sir Anthony Meyer is an honourable man and will, I have no doubt, come out of this contest with personal respect,' he wrote, 'but his decision to stand in this way is totally misguided. To try and change an incumbent prime minister in mid-term for such reasons shows a clear lack of perspective.'[6]

'There was no campaign to speak of,' wrote one observer of the contest, 'its ostensible leader, George Younger, merely let it be known that the Prime Minister expected all good Conservatives to do their duty.'[7] This, however, does not do the admittedly subtle campaign run by Younger and Ian Gow (yet another Wykehamist) justice. Back-benchers were contacted methodically and given the full Gentleman George treatment, his aim being to keep the total number of dissenters below 50; that is, a combination of those abstaining, spoiling their ballots or specifically voting for Meyer. He almost succeeded.

Younger spent the weekend of 2–3 December 1989 in the House of Commons quietly trying to win over waverers. He approached every Tory MP except those who were very ill, which included his friend Alick Buchanan-Smith, who was by then ailing from cancer.[8] Voting took place in Committee Room 12 throughout 5 December and the result was announced at 6.30 p.m. Mrs Thatcher had secured 314 votes and Sir

[4] Ibid.
[5] Cole, *As It Seemed To Me*, 354.
[6] *The Times* 4/12/1989.
[7] Watkins, *A Conservative Coup*, 177.
[8] Buchanan-Smith was thought to have voted for Sir Anthony.

Anthony a mere 33, but crucially another 24 MPs had spoilt their ballots, and three had not voted at all. Younger's target of no more than 50 antis had been broken by seven, yet the psychological 300 mark had been met.

George was on ebullient form at a victory press conference convened soon after. The outcome, he said, was a 'most remarkable achievement', while he claimed it would be 'stretching it' to interpret the result, with nearly 85 per cent of the Parliamentary party supporting Mrs Thatcher, as anything other than a resounding vote of confidence. Younger, however, also acknowledged that the 57 votes demonstrated that some MPs were 'not entirely happy with everything that is going on'.[9]

Armed with figures from the 1975 leadership contest, which Thatcher won with just 146 votes (less than half the 1989 figure), Younger was able to depict the result as a remarkable result for a party leader about to enter her 15th year. Bernard Ingham, meanwhile, plotted Thatcher's response. 'I think it would be a good idea', he suggested to her, 'for George Younger and Mark Lennox-Boyd to go outside with you to flank you as you say your piece.'[10] The Prime Minister was magnanimous as she did so. 'I would like to thank those who gave me their support,' she said, 'and particularly George Younger and his colleagues who have worked so splendidly for me in this election.'[11]

Opinions vary of exactly how many wavering MPs that splendid work managed to appease. In his memoirs, Michael Heseltine estimates that around 60 warned Younger they could not be relied on again should another challenge take place within a year. Another account puts the figure at 30,[12] while some press reports speculated that the campaign manager's 'hard man/soft man' approach had kept between 10 and 15 votes safe, preventing a dip below the critical figure of 300. 'Much credit for its prevention is being given to her campaign manager, George Younger, the former Defence Secretary,' observed the *Mail on Sunday*. 'He was open and conciliatory, listened patiently to criticisms and worries about the Prime Minister, and won universal trust as a channel of communication to her. But at the same time he made sure that constituency party chairmen were primed to help keep the waverers in line.'[13]

The actual figure, however, was actually much higher than 15. Younger's own notes recorded that at 'least 40 more voted for Mrs. T only v.

[9] *Financial Times* 6/12/1989.
[10] Downing Street briefing note, 5/12/1989, GYP.
[11] Downing Street speaking note, 5/12/1989, GYP.
[12] Shepherd, *The Power Brokers*, 9.
[13] *Mail on Sunday* 10/12/1989.

reluctantly'.[14] Those 40 were on everyone's minds when George convened a secret meeting of the campaign team on 6 December, the day after the result. 'We are talking about the beginning of the end of the Thatcher Era,' declared Tristan Garel-Jones. 'We have to try and ensure that that is managed in a way that enables her to go to the end of her Prime Ministership with dignity and honour.'

This set a rather downbeat tone for the 'post-mortem meeting', which began with a report from Ian Gow. 'If, in eleven months time,' he said,

> the economy is still in difficulties, with inflation still relatively high, interest rates high and the Balance of Payments responding slowly, with the opinion polls probably worse, all of which I predict, then I think the mood of the Party will be difficult and not least because MPs in marginal seats will be that much closer to the Election and more anxious about holding their seats. They may say to themselves we are doing badly enough to lose our seats under the present Leadership, might we do better under a different Leader?

For one of Mrs Thatcher's closest confidantes, this must have come as a difficult realisation. None of those attending the meeting, however, wanted a change of leader. Younger said a positive approach towards 'Dodgies' (or 'doubtfuls') – those who were doubtful that Thatcher should remain as leader – was needed, while Richard Ryder suggested making better use of the 'Apostles', those MPs who remained devoted to the Prime Minister.

Younger then asked Richard Ryder if he felt 'there had been a lot of moans about the ERM', observing that 'the Prime Minister believes she is totally in tune with the views of the country on Europe'. 'Yes,' Ryder replied emphatically. 'A lot of ignorant moans. Basically the Party is in favour of joining the ERM. The Prime Minister's words have not been believed.'

Everyone at the meeting was agreed on at least one thing, the future of the Prime Minister's two closest advisers, Charles Powell and Bernard Ingham. 'Charles must go,' declared Garel-Jones. '[But] Bernard is the one they all really hate. So Bernard has to go as well.' They, of course, were the many back-benchers, and in particular sacked ministers, who had experienced Ingham's effective yet often cruel practice of briefing the press off-the-record. He had famously described one soon-to-depart Cabinet minister as 'semi-detached'.

The Parliamentary Party viewed Powell and Ingham as sentries in a

---

[14] Hand-written note titled 'Things said', GYP.

bunker increasingly occupied by the party leader. Powell in particular was seen to have encouraged Mrs Thatcher to go on more frequent foreign trips, jaunts which enraged MPs in marginal seats who felt she should be playing to home crowds rather than grandstanding on the world stage. George, however, was realistic, pointing out that Powell was 'the nearest thing she has to a close confidante. She will feel lost without Charles.'

In terms of wider remedies, it was resolved that Mrs Thatcher should be relaunched for the 1990s, while more of her workload should be delegated ('All of this green stuff perhaps', suggested Garel-Jones) to either John Major or Douglas Hurd. There was also praise for Younger's role in the leadership campaign. 'I think the tone of what she should be doing was set by the way you conducted her campaign,' observed Garel-Jones. 'Meyer went out of his way to say how charming you had been to him.' And Gerry Neale added: 'I think the way you have led the campaign has been superb and the way that you have been promoting it in the media. [But w]e cannot do the same again next year. Some of the Apostles have been blown as well. We would have to be very wary of using the same people again.'

It was agreed that Younger should prepare a paper with observations and recommendations for the Prime Minister's weekend box, prior to his face-to-face meeting with her the following Monday. 'You should also speak to all Apostles because some of them are a bit depressed,' Lennox-Boyd told Younger. 'You should, on Monday, also suggest that you see her again in January.'[15]

'I cannot thank you enough for all you have done in the last two weeks,' wrote Mrs Thatcher to Younger the following day. 'I know the result would have been different had you not been in charge. You were calm and relaxed and struck exactly the right note to bring confidence to many of our colleagues who were not so assured. *I am so grateful.*'[16] Although drafting documents in long-hand was not usually George's style, he took particular care over his report on the leadership election, writing it out twice by hand before having the second version typed up for the Prime Minister's weekend box.

'The result is not as good as the figures,' Younger began bluntly. 'Many voted with varying degrees of reluctance for the Prime Minister. They cannot all be relied upon another time.' He said the discontent focused on three areas: the PM not being accessible enough; her not being prepared to listen to back-bench concerns; and a widespread feeling that Downing

---

[15] Undated minute titled 'Post Mortem Meeting Notes', GYP. According to Younger's pocket diary, a follow-up meeting with Mrs Thatcher in January 1990 never took place.

[16] MT to GY, 7/12/1989, GYP.

Street advisers had more influence than senior ministers. 'However unfairly,' observed Younger, 'there is great mistrust of them, and it is thought they "ring-fence" the PM from other advice.'

He also recommended that 'personality tensions within Cabinet . . . must be resolved if confidence is to be restored. In particular, Geoffrey Howe must be seen and treated as the PM's right-hand man.' Younger reiterated his campaign claim that many of these murmurings were typical mid-term policy concerns. 'However, the fact that the challenge took place has unearthed the significance of these problems. As there are likely to be economic and polls difficulties in a year's time, another challenge is not improbable. We feel everything possible must be done now to head this off.'

This, Younger told Mrs Thatcher, could be achieved by reducing her diary commitments. 'Space for thought and for unexpected requirements should be written into the programme.' Secondly, fewer 'foreign tours and more home ones', with the Foreign Secretary or Deputy Prime Minister doing 'what needs to be done abroad'. Thirdly, the 'passing of more business to Cabinet committees chaired by senior ministers'. This, he said, would constitute a clear 'rapprochement following recent tensions'. Fourth, more 'unplanned opportunities for chatting to backbenchers (e.g. casual visits to Smoking Room, etc. more invitations for Members of Parliament to No 10 lunches and dinners even at the expense of fewer ministers, particular efforts to chat with and listen to those known to be of different views).'

Then George came to the crunch: 'An early and visible change in Downing Street top advisors (this would be for their own good too).' And on Europe, he continued, while maintaining the existing policy, the Prime Minister had to make a 'major effort to sound positive about closer integration of the right sort. It is the *hearts* of the pro-Europeans that need to be reached, not their heads. Most of the new generation have grown up as pro-Europeans and have preached it as an ideal. They can be persuaded to be hard-headed on bad policy proposals, provided they believe our leadership passionately believes in Europe too.' And, he added, when 'we do join the ERM, we must do it with warmth and enthusiasm'.

Finally, suggested Younger, a 'new set of aims for the 1990s, different from the 1980s, will be needed. Perhaps a weekend seminar at Chequers with four or five ministers could set the tone for this. The PM and Government have been enormously successful in the 1980s. The 1990s will not be the same, but they can be equally successful. We must not let Labour seem new and different while we remain the same.'[17] Just five

[17] Memo headed 'Report and Recommendations from the Rt Hon George Younger MP', 8/12/1989, GYP. See Appendix, pp. 303–305.

years later, 'New' Labour would begin to do precisely that under the energetic leadership of Tony Blair.

The following Monday, Younger had a 'long and frank talk' with Mrs Thatcher over a glass of whisky, the Prime Minister's favoured tipple. 'As her campaign manager I had been in the unique position of feeling the party's pulse', recalled Younger of the meeting four years later, 'and it was only too clear that despite success in three elections, all was not well.'

Younger tried a different tack on the advice to ditch her two favourite advisers, saying that 'a change of advisers would be timely and would give a new lease of life to the image of a prime minister who had been at No 10 for as long as many people could remember'. And, he concluded, 'As the poll tax was emerging as a real political problem I suggested that something should be done to ease the burden, especially in the constituencies in the north-west of England.'

George later recalled that the potentially difficult meeting was both 'very frank and very friendly'. 'She said she would think about what I had said and would make a real effort to take the advice.'[18] His guidance, however, was largely ignored by Mrs Thatcher. 'Anthony [Meyer] had delivered a clear message,' recalled Michael Heseltine in his memoirs. 'No one appears to have taken it sufficiently seriously.'[19] Although Younger came to believe that the Prime Minister did come to the House more often, 'she did not change her tune on Europe and she refused to bring in a new team of advisers'.

And while Younger believed Mrs Thatcher had done well to see off Sir Anthony Meyer, 'she had missed the real point of his challenge. Meyer had conducted his campaign with considerable charm and style, readily admitting that he did not expect to win many votes and not attempting to conduct any high-profile campaigning. His object was to force a contest. In achieving that, he had done all he aimed to do.' Unfortunately, George observed, 'Margaret failed to realise this and her easy victory gave her a false sense of confidence.'[20]

Meanwhile, Younger was easing himself into his new role as a non-executive director of the Royal Bank of Scotland (RBS), and in January 1990 he was appointed deputy chairman. 'I've always thought of coming back into business,' he told an interviewer, 'but it became more difficult to envisage as one political thing led to another.' But, he added, if 'I can

[18] *Scotland on Sunday* 3/10/1993.
[19] Heseltine, *Life in the Jungle*, 351.
[20] *Scotland on Sunday* 3/10/1993.

make a contribution to this company for the next ten years I shall consider it an extremely worthwhile undertaking'.[21]

When George first arrived at RBS Sir Michael Young-Herries insisted that he share his room at head office in Edinburgh's St Andrew Square, and for nearly two years they worked side by side with no difficulty. And on 1 July 1990 Younger assumed the chair of the main RBS subsidiary (not the RBS Group) as Sir Michael prepared for retirement after more than a decade at the helm.

Younger obviously saw his involvement with RBS as yet another means of contributing to Scottish public life. As Scottish Secretary he had lobbied against two attempts either to take over, or merge with, the Edinburgh-based bank,[22] while towards the end of his time at Dover House a private Act of Parliament had merged the existing RBS and Williams & Glyn's under a newly-created banking group. The head office payroll in Edinburgh increased to 3,000, a jobs boost Younger naturally welcomed as Scotland's minister.

Now, as deputy chairman, Younger vowed to protect RBS from any future takeovers. Indeed, within a decade, RBS would itself be doing the taking over. His government contacts also proved immediately beneficial. George convinced the Treasury to allow representation for RBS and the Bank of Scotland on the Committee of Clearing Banks, which until then had merely tolerated their existence.[23]

Back at Westminster, Younger still did not think it was inevitable that there would have to be another leadership contest, despite continuing political difficulties for the Prime Minister. 'Not that the problems were not real enough,' he recalled. 'There was increased trouble over the poll tax (somewhat eased by local election success in Wandsworth and Westminster), there were by-election disasters and signs of economic trouble brewing.'[24]

But even more potent than any of those factors were the ructions caused by the recent appointment of the Thatcherite Michael Forsyth as chairman of the Scottish Conservative Party. Younger was horrified when the left-leaning Scottish Tory Reform Group told him of bullying, locks being changed and unpopular staffing changes at the party's Chester Street HQ in Edinburgh. George agreed to speak to the Prime Minister and told her in July 1990 that Forsyth should be removed from the chairmanship of the party in Scotland. 'This was not because of any

---

[21] *Scottish Banker* 2/1990.
[22] See pp. 201–202.
[23] Ironically, by 2001 RBS was the committee's largest member.
[24] *Scotland on Sunday* 3/10/1993.

doubts about his abilities,' he explained in 1993. 'I simply thought it was asking too much of him to carry out his ministerial duties, defend the marginal seat of Stirling and be chairman of the party ['I did the job, together with a front bench job, and discovered that,' he later told journalists] . . . Margaret listened patiently and kindly to what I had to say and said she would note what I said.'

Soon, Viscount Whitelaw had joined the so-called 'tweed-suit brigade' in calling for Forsyth to be sacked. Before the summer recess, Mrs Thatcher ordered a report on Forsyth's chairmanship from party whips, which uncovered a hotbed of discontent. 'Some of his acolytes probably thought they were helping him by surreptitiously leaking stories to the press that he was better . . . than Malcolm Rifkind, my successor as Scottish Secretary,' said Younger. 'I am sure Michael had nothing to do with the stories but some of his supporters, who were keen and enthusiastic, were [also] a bit naïve.'[25]

The Prime Minister now accepted the inevitable, albeit reluctantly. The beginning of the end came in early September when Younger confirmed that Mrs Thatcher was considering what he and others had to say. Shortly after, Forsyth was sacked and replaced with the more palatable Lord (Russell) Sanderson, who happened to be a long-standing friend of George and his wife Diana. Some newspaper reports suggested that Younger himself had been asked to succeed Forsyth.

Nevertheless, Mrs Thatcher asked Younger to keep an eye on the uneasy relationship between Rifkind and Forsyth, who remained a minister at the Scottish Office. Meanwhile, the Prime Minister was getting a little paranoid. 'This combination of the Left and the traditional establishment of the Party to rebuff Thatcherism in Scotland,' she later wrote of the Forsyth saga, 'was a prelude to the formation of the same alliance to oust me as leader of the Conservative Party a few weeks later – although I did not know it at the time.'[26] Writing in 1993, Younger said she was mistaken. 'It takes a flight of the imagination to suggest a plot,' he wrote. 'She may have felt there was one but there wasn't. We are not really big on plots of that kind. We are rather hard headed practical people who look at a situation and do the best we can with it.'[27]

Younger attended the traditional reception at 10 Downing Street on the eve of the new Parliamentary session on 6 November 1990. It was the day before the Queen's Speech, and he had been chosen by the whips to move the loyal address, an honour typically reserved for a senior Conservative

---

[25] Ibid., 17/10/1993.
[26] Thatcher, *The Downing Street Years*, 623.
[27] *Scotland on Sunday* 17/10/1993.

back-bencher. When the House of Commons convened the following morning, George delivered the usual combination of constituency descriptions, jokes (including one about his great-grandfather, Sir George Younger), commentary on current political issues and, of course, the year ahead.

As in his maiden speech twenty-six years earlier, Younger assessed the future of Prestwick Airport. British Aerospace was by then Ayr's biggest industry, manufacturing the successful Jetstream 31 commuter aircraft and exporting it all over the USA. In 1991, he said, it would be launching the Jetstream 41, the first aeroplane entirely designed and built in Scotland since the 1950s. Although George's presence in the Cabinet had ensured Prestwick remained Scotland's sole transatlantic gateway, it had finally lost that status in March 1990 under enormous pressure from the Scottish business community. Its future now hung in the balance following the government's decision to allow its transatlantic traffic to go to other airports. 'Most of it has now done so,' lamented Younger, 'leaving the best airport in Western Europe, from the environmental point of view, without any significant passenger traffic. I, and most of my constituents, disagreed strongly with that decision but we have accepted it, however reluctantly.'

Younger also welcomed a reference in the Queen's Speech to Europe. 'As a long-standing supporter of our full membership, I agree that we have a vital and constructive role to play in improving the way forward to the Single Market and other reforms . . . If my Right Honourable Friend, the Prime Minister, and all her Government continue to follow this course they can count on my full support.' And on defence, George said that despite the collapse of the Warsaw Pact, the UK still needed 'to keep a modern and balanced defence capability through the Nato Alliance. I include in this the essential need to make some provision to deal with the unexpected. Throughout history it has always been the unexpected that is most likely to happen.' It was a familiar refrain from Younger's two decades' experience of defence policy.

The speech was a triumph, perfectly combining humour, local, national and foreign affairs. 'It speaks volumes about his equable good humour that the only nickname he ever acquired from those who work for him was "Gentleman George", and it is a very good one,' said Mrs Thatcher in reply. 'He spoke of one of his ancestors who was Chief Whip under Lloyd George in 1922. That Chief Whip had the unique distinction for a holder of that office of bringing down his own Government. That was not as reprehensible as it sounds because he put a good Conservative Administration in place of the coalition that fell.'[28] Given the events that followed

---

[28] Hansard 180 c9–10, c22.

within a matter of weeks, the Prime Minister's historical analogy was uncomfortably poignant.

'Margaret Thatcher's fall from power in November 1990 was an extra-ordinary political disaster which remained unexpected right up to the day it happened,' recalled Younger in 1993. 'That it should have happened at all was due to a sorry sequence of mishaps which, as her campaign manager and long-time friend, I was able to witness at first hand.' The catalyst, as predicted by Younger the previous year, was Europe. The Prime Minister's increasing stridency against closer union sparked the resignation of Sir Geoffrey Howe as Leader of the House. His valedictory speech took place in the Commons on 13 November, just six days into the new session. 'In content and style it was vicious,' recalled Younger, 'not like Geoffrey at all, but it was a lethal stroke, for it gave Michael Heseltine the excuse he needed to say there was a new situation. He forthwith made his challenge and we were into a new leadership election.'

But unlike Meyer's stalking horse challenge of 1989, Younger felt this one came at a bad moment for the Prime Minister. Even apart from Europe, he believed Thatcher had allowed herself to become embattled over the Poll Tax. 'She seemed to be saying that as no one else in the government was putting the case strongly enough,' observed George, 'she had to show the way. By then I think she was not listening as much as lecturing.' But more seriously, she was now 'fundamentally out of agreement with the main political philosophy of a large and influential part of the party'.

Michael Heseltine announced his intention to stand against Mrs Thatcher the day after Howe's speech. The Prime Minister's PPS, Peter Morrison, immediately telephoned Younger to ask him to manage her campaign. Initially he refused, citing his commitments to RBS. Morrison assured George that most of the work would be done by a team of MPs closely resembling that of the previous year. 'Morrison also suggested that if I refused,' George recalled, 'it would be said that I was deserting her because I had lost the will to support her – a powerful argument which was difficult to refute.'

Reluctantly, Younger acquiesced, and went to see Mrs Thatcher at her rooms in the Commons. 'She was in determined mood but she was also intensely irritated by the challenge to her leadership,' he recalled. ' "I always knew that he was just looking for an opportunity. Geoffrey gave him it." To her way of thinking, Heseltine's decision was transparently self-serving and she made it clear to me that we had to "stop Heseltine".'[29]

---

[29] *Scotland on Sunday* 3/10/1993.

But, Younger later recalled, 'She reckoned that we could do the same the second year as we had done the first.'[30] If only it had been that simple. While Sir Anthony Meyer had been a barely credible stalking horse, Heseltine was a highly plausible big beast. In addition to that, a general election was a year closer and the government was at the height of its unpopularity.

A small office loaned by the Conservative treasurer Lord McAlpine was set up in Abbey Gardens, and the team met there frequently in the run-up to the first ballot. Tristan Garel-Jones, Gerry Neale, Richard Ryder and Mark Lennox-Boyd returned to the fray, while Michael Neubert (who had served under Younger at the Ministry of Defence), Ian Twinn, Norman Tebbit and John Moore comprised the rest of the team. Michael Jopling and George Gardiner also helped on a more informal basis.

Younger, however (and as agreed with Peter Morrison), was essentially a figurehead. RBS commitments meant he spent a lot of time shuttling between London and Edinburgh, although he kept in regular touch with the team by telephone. Later, he would be criticised for the campaign being less well organised than in 1989. 'I must refute that,' George wrote in 1993. 'Everyone who was remotely worth canvassing was covered; some several times. There were many more "no" voters, as this time we had a serious challenger in Michael Heseltine.'[31]

Neubert kept the 'tally' in Abbey Gardens, while Neale co-ordinated media interviews on College Green, although they quickly noticed that levels of moral and practical support from some ministers had ebbed since the previous campaign. Chance encounters in the House also established beyond any doubt that several MPs were promising to support both candidates. Some Cabinet ministers considered Younger's selection as campaign manager a little curious. Although the continuity from 1989 was considered valuable, his increasing preoccupation as chairman-designate of RBS had detached him from back-bench opinion, although it was not difficult to determine that it was increasingly hostile towards the Prime Minister.

Inevitably, accounts of Younger's involvement differ. Cecil Parkinson said he was 'discreet to the point of being invisible';[32] to Heseltine it 'did not appear to us that his heart was in it';[33] while even Sir Geoffrey Howe thought his role in 1990 was 'less committed'[34] than the year before. Ian

---

[30] Stark, *Choosing a Leader*, 110.
[31] *Scotland on Sunday* 3/10/1993.
[32] Parkinson, *Right at the Centre*, 25.
[33] Heseltine, *Life in the Jungle*, 366.
[34] Howe, *Conflict of Loyalty*, 670.

Lang, another old friend of George's, felt that neither campaign seemed to get off the ground. 'The overall effect was muffled and unreal . . . I was never sounded out by anybody on her behalf and saw no sign whatever of an active campaign.'[35]

Right-wing commentators were later openly scathing. 'Indeed, his main value to Mrs Thatcher was negative,' judged the Scottish journalist Bruce Anderson. 'If he had not been on the team, questions might have been raised as to why Gentleman George no longer supported her. That would have involved time-wasting explanations, denials and fuss. So it was important to have his name on the letterhead, as non-executive Chairman of the Thatcher campaign.'[36] The election, Alan Watkins wrote, had come at a most inconvenient time for Younger. 'It was the busiest time of year at the bank. There were numerous pressing matters that required his attention. Altogether, he seemed to suggest, securing the re-election of Mrs Thatcher was proving something of a nuisance.'[37]

Whatever the extent of Younger's involvement – and to be fair he had made his position *vis-à-vis* his RBS commitments perfectly clear – the political climate compared with 1989 made the task almost impossible. 'Some [MPs] had said that they felt Margaret's style was too abrasive, others were concerned about the effects of the poll tax,' recalled Younger. 'These were understandable. But much the deepest worry were those solid loyal back-benchers who said they did not like her attitude to Europe. Geoffrey Howe's speech had fired up all the pro-Europeans – he had described Margaret's interventions as "background noise" – and Michael's team were, of course, playing this up whenever they could.'

There was also criticism of the Prime Minister's decision to visit troops in Northern Ireland on 16 November before going to Paris for the Conference of Security and Co-operation in Europe. 'For myself I think that she had little choice but to go', judged Younger, 'her detractors would have seen it as a panic measure had she not gone – but it didn't help.'

Despite this ominous backdrop, Younger was reasonably confident that Mrs Thatcher would get more than 200 votes, possibly as many as 220; just enough (an overall majority plus fifteen per cent) to avoid a second ballot. 'In fact so certain were we of victory', remembered Younger, 'that no arrangements had been made for organising another stage.'[38] Accompanying this quiet confidence was the acute awareness that a victory

---

[35] Lang, *Blue Remembered Years*, 94.

[36] Anderson, *John Major*, 105–06.

[37] Watkins, *A Conservative Coup*, 179–80. 'I did do quite a lot myself,' Younger said in 1993. 'I didn't have as much time as I would have liked to have had and whether or not that would have made any difference, I don't know' (interview with Lord Younger).

[38] *Scotland on Sunday* 3/10/1993.

margin of only one or two votes could be as damaging as outright defeat.

On Saturday 17 November, the weekend before the vote, Mrs Thatcher's campaign team met at Chequers for dinner. All, that is, except George, who had a shooting engagement with friends. Later, this absence was used by his critics as evidence of his disengagement, although the Prime Minister does not appear to have minded.[39]

As polling day approached, the atmosphere in Parliament was electric. Heseltine's team oozed confidence, while worried loyalists passed Younger information about MPs who felt neglected. He recalled:

> The night before polling day, I had a chance conversation with Michael Heseltine in the Members' dining room, which is interesting in retrospect. His words were: 'Look, we all know what is going to happen tomorrow, I just want to assure you that as far as I am concerned, I will remain fully supportive of the party as I always have done.'
>
> These were not the words of a man who expected to win. No doubt his canvassing told him that he would get nowhere near as many votes as Margaret.

At 10.30 a.m. on Tuesday 20 November, Younger, Morrison, Wakeham, Kenneth Baker (the party chairman), Tebbit and John Whittingdale gathered, without Mrs Thatcher, in her room at the Commons. Voting was due to begin in Committee Room 12 in half an hour. Their task was to consider what the Prime Minister might say under each outcome scenario, the trickiest being her victory, but not with enough votes to avoid a second ballot. After much discussion, the crucial word 'intend' was inserted ('I intend to fight a second ballot') to cover both eventualities.

Peter Morrison left for Paris expecting Mrs Thatcher to avoid a second ballot by between ten and fifteen votes. She was already in the French capital to ratify the Conventional Forces in Europe treaty, an absence which disconcerted some back-benchers. Heseltine, meanwhile, was buttonholing MPs in the Members' Lobby as if it were an election to the Oxford Union.

After casting his vote Younger had flown north, so was in Edinburgh when the result was declared. The Prime Minister had secured 204 votes, four short of the number required to avoid a second ballot. George was shocked that just a handful more votes would have secured her the

---

[39] 'George Younger could not attend because he had another engagement in Norfolk,' recalled Thatcher in her memoirs (*The Downing Street Years*, 841). The shoot was in honour of his son Andrew's birthday on 19 November. Andrew remembers thinking it odd that his father had chosen to attend that instead of the meeting at Chequers.

leadership. 'Prudently, as it turned out, we had advised Margaret what to say from her meeting in Paris, whatever the result,' he remembered. 'It was clear to me and some others that if she did not win outright she had to say immediately that she would fight on. Anything less would have sealed her defeat then and there. It would have been a signal that she was totally wounded.'

The Prime Minister was at the British embassy when the news reached her at 6.30 p.m. Television cameras were already rolling when she emerged to say it was her intention to let her name go forward for a second ballot. But it was a hollow intention, and even her closest supporters knew the time had come for her to withdraw. Younger, too, urged her to resign when he saw her at Downing Street the following day. 'I, myself, was definitely out of the team after the final result was announced,' he recalled. 'I had always made it clear that I could only commit myself partially for a first ballot. Unfortunately, no plans seemed to have been made for who would take over, and there was much confusion about this on the final Wednesday.'[40]

Eventually, Norman Tebbit told the press that John Wakeham would replace Younger as campaign manager. But it was academic. Mrs Thatcher withdrew from the second ballot and, after nearly sixteen years as Conservative leader and more than eleven as Prime Minister, Margaret Thatcher left Downing Street for the last time. 'George', remembered Michael Neubert, 'just sort of faded from the scene more or less straight away.'[41]

'Although I felt desperately sorry to see Margaret go,' reflected Younger, 'I am quite clear that no fine tuning of the campaign could have altered the result. By the time the Heseltine challenge was launched, it was written into the political background that she would not win by a sufficient margin.'[42] Heseltine's team were jubilant, and believed Thatcher could easily have secured the required four extra votes. 'Looking back on it, of course, one feels that somehow we could have persuaded one or two more people,' conceded Younger. 'It is certainly the case that everybody who was remotely worth canvassing was canvassed, very thoroughly indeed. There were those, of course, who were not contacted at all. There's a matter of judgement there.'[43]

Norman Fowler, on the other hand, thought Mrs Thatcher could personally have altered the outcome. 'By deciding not to campaign

[40] *Scotland on Sunday* 3/10/1993.
[41] Interview with Sir Michael Neubert, 15/1/2007.
[42] *Scotland on Sunday* 3/10/1993.
[43] Stark, *Choosing a Leader*, 110.

personally, she discarded the most potent weapon at her disposal,' he wrote in his memoirs. 'Face to face Margaret could have won over some of the doubters . . . In the immediate aftermath of the vote it was the campaign team at Westminster, headed by George Younger, which took the blame. In truth, it is difficult to run a campaign without the presence of the candidate.'[44]

Within weeks John Major – as unassuming as Heseltine was flamboyant – was elected Conservative Party leader in the second ballot and became Prime Minister (George voted for him). Mrs Thatcher resigned on 22 November, a tumultuous day, not just for the departing premier, but also for Younger. Just hours after a Downing Street press release announced the Prime Minister's resignation, another press notice was issued by the Royal Bank of Scotland. It revealed that following its AGM on 10 January 1991, Younger would succeed Sir Michael Young-Herries as chairman of the RBS Group plc.

The 22 of November (the anniversary of Kennedy's assassination, a gruesome analogy for Thatcher's own political downfall) was also the date of Elizabeth Home's (Sir Alec's wife, who had died on 3 September) memorial service at Westminster Abbey, which both George and Diana attended. It was a day when Younger's past, present and future mingled with more than a hint of melancholy: the Homes had been friends since he stood aside in the 1963 Kinross and West Perthshire by-election; Margaret Thatcher had become a close political – and to a lesser extent personal – friend of George from the moment she appointed him Shadow Defence Secretary in 1975; and with her demise opened the next successful chapter in Younger's public life.

'What has happened is now in the past and – in line with your advice – I am seeing how best I can continue to have some influence on politics at home and overseas,' Mrs Thatcher wrote to Younger on 4 December. 'After 11 ½ years it seems very strange not to be making decisions day by day at No. 10. But that would have had to end sometime. And now we have the best hope in John Major of continuing the policies you and I believe in.'[45]

The timing was extraordinary, and perhaps more convenient than Younger at first realised. 'Mr Younger's elevation comes immediately after a period when his efforts on Mrs Thatcher's behalf upset some bank executives,' reported the *Glasgow Herald*, 'who were concerned at his re-emergence in a national political role.'[46] RBS, it seemed, would have

---

[44] Fowler, *Minister Decide*, 351.
[45] MT to GY, 4/12/1990, GYP.
[46] *Herald* 23/11/1990.

preferred its chairman-elect to campaign on behalf of Prestwick Airport rather than Mrs Thatcher.[47] But although Younger would eventually abandon political involvement altogether, for the time being he was determined to maintain a public role in two interconnected spheres – banking and politics.

Younger's appointment as chairman came as RBS was radically reshaped to cut costs and slim down the bank's operations to enable it to cope with growing competition. 'At that time the bank was really in bad shape,' recalled Sir George Mathewson.

> Eventually I went to Sir Michael and George as deputy chairman and said the bank's in serious trouble, we either lose our independence or I make some suggestions as to how we change it. And to be fair to Sir Michael, no doubt urged on by George, he accepted this and a small group of people then met once a week over a few months and redesigned the bank: myself and four or five executives. We put it to the board and there was an historic meeting, which happened the day Mrs Thatcher failed to win enough votes in her leadership contest. That meeting changed the bank forever: a large number of senior staff were fired and I became effectively chief executive. It was a dramatic day.[48]

Under the streamlining, all RBS's businesses were regrouped into six operating divisions of the clearing bank, known as the Royal Bank of Scotland. The bank itself was split into two parts: branch banking and corporate and institutional banking, bringing its structure more into line with other large UK banks. Charles Winter remained in post as chief executive, while George Mathewson – whom Younger had recruited as deputy chief executive – also remained in situ. George had already earmarked the SDA chief to succeed Winter when he finally retired.

RBS was then the seventh-largest bank in the UK, with pre-tax profits of £262m. 'Laughing all the way to the bank'[49] was one rather predictable newspaper headline, and indeed, with an annual salary of more than £110,000, Younger was certainly better paid than at any other stage in his career. He took great delight in kitting out his Lombard Street office with military mementoes, while he and Diana also made good use of an RBS flat in Edinburgh's Moray Place. George turned sixty that year and life was good. He had two new grandchildren to dote on – Emily (four months) and Katrina (nine months) – while another, Katrina's sister Arabella, was three

---

[47] Miller McLean, group company secretary at RBS, recalls that it was always understood Younger would only run Mrs Thatcher's campaign for the first ballot.

[48] Interview with Sir George Mathewson, 22/5/2007.

[49] *Daily Record* 10/1/1991.

years old. At an age when most men were thinking of retirement, Younger had embarked upon a new career.

'In the 1980s, the bank has been successful, steadily expanding its operations,' Younger told the *Observer*. 'What I want to tackle is how to make the next ten years as successful. This decade will be very different: competition is much more intense and banking is no longer automatically profitable; there is greater pressure on costs; and there is a need to change the emphasis of business from branches to a marketing and selling role.'[50] Consequently, RBS had recently encouraged its Spanish partner, Banco Santander, to boost its shareholding to 9.9 per cent and George was busy learning Spanish so he could hold his own on the Santander board.

The match – whereby each bank took a five per cent stake in the other – was made in banking heaven. Younger struck up a particularly close rapport with the Santander president, Emilio Botin, and every December he and Diana were invited to Botin's Spanish estate for two days' shooting. George also forged a lasting friendship with Larry Fish, the chief executive of Citizens Bank (or Financial Group) of Rhode Island, which RBS had acquired in 1988. On one trip to the US, Younger was delighted when the Boston Symphony Orchestra performed a favourite piece of French horn music at Fish's behest.

From the date of his appointment, Younger spent most of the following eighteen months in London – which allowed him regularly to attend the Commons – while he also found time for his other directorships. These included Murray Johnstone Investment Trusts (he became chairman in 1993), Scottish Equitable Life Assurance and, at the request of the Ministry of Defence, heading the small British board of Siemens Plessey.

George also pursued non-business interests. He joined the board of the Edinburgh International Festival and was appointed chairman of the Royal Anniversary Trust (TRAT), which had been conceived and created in 1990 by Robin Gill. As its first chairman, Gill wanted to provide a national expression of gratitude to the Queen to mark her fortieth anniversary as head of state. Five concepts, all educational in nature, were agreed: the School Awards scheme, a nationwide programme for schools to bring about long-term national or regional benefit; the 'Challenge', a similar scheme for adult organisations; a 'SovEIIReign' exhibition to demonstrate the myriad duties of the monarch; the creation of a Commonwealth Mace and goblets; and 'The Great Event', an ambitious televised celebration of the Queen's reign.

Each undertaking was financed by the private sector (Younger persuaded

[50] *Observer* 2/12/1990.

RBS to contribute to The Great Event), and as Gill had to concentrate on raising funds and designing the programme, a replacement as chairman of trust meetings was required. The trustees, Viscount Whitelaw, James Callaghan (the former prime minister) and John Major (the Prime Minister) were consulted, all of whom agreed that Younger was the natural choice. 'He was a wise and benign Chairman,' recalled Gill, 'and a hugely supportive role player in all that we did.'[51]

It took ten days and nearly 1,000 people working 24-hour days to prepare the arena at Earls Court for The Great Event. Younger grappled with various trials and tribulations as preparations gathered pace, but it finally took place on Monday 26 October 1992. The programme began on time, but ran later than planned, although nobody minded. The whole Royal Family was in attendance, and although the press noted that the Prince and Princess of Wales appeared to be on good terms, protocol dictated that they sat at opposite ends of one row of seats.

The Queen arrived in the middle of the arena in a Rolls-Royce lit by a spotlight. Younger escorted her to the Royal Box, and they watched as a who's who of British entertainers and personalities performed or spoke, each representing a different facet of the Queen's 40-year reign. Dame Vera Lynn and Cliff Richard sang; Roger Bannister talked about the four-minute mile; Sir Edmund Hillary about conquering Everest. The 1966 World Cup England team was reunited; Sir David Willcocks conducted a massed choir of 1,000; cannons fired and a Harrier Jump Jet roared overhead. Afterwards, the Queen mingled with 5,000 performers as the arena was cleared and tables covered so that more than 2,000 guests could tuck into a special menu created by the chef and restaurateur Anton Mosimann. Following her *annus horribilus* in 1992, the Queen praised TRAT's programme as the 'sunny interval' in an otherwise troubled year during an event at St James's Palace.

Always a staunch monarchist, Younger was in his element as chairman. TRAT was in surplus at the end of the Anniversary programme, and this funded the Queen's Anniversary Prizes for Higher and Further Education, which Robin Gill conceived as a long-term legacy of the Anniversary programme. George continued as chairman of a smaller board of trustees appointed to oversee the prizes, and the new national honour was subsequently approved by parliament.

Younger also began to accumulate honours at an astonishing rate. In 1992 he received an honorary law degree from the University of Glasgow, where his old Scottish Office permanent under-secretary, Sir William

---

[51] Robin Gill to the author, 9/11/2007.

Kerr Fraser, was principal. The occasion did not quite go to plan. The singer Pat Kane, also the university's rector, led a walkout of about twenty-five students in protest at George's anti-devolution stance. 'I didn't think he was at all out of order but I am not sure what he was protesting to me about,' Younger said breezily under questioning from reporters. 'I am very used to political protests – [and] delighted to take part in them.'[52]

A similar ceremony at Napier University the same year proved less eventful, and indeed Younger would soon become its first chancellor. The University of Edinburgh also summoned him to receive an honorary doctorate in November, while in 1994 Paisley University conferred the same honour at its Ayr campus, allowing Younger to reminisce about his battles to save Craigie College in the 1970s. English universities (such as, inexplicably, Middlesex) also sought him out, and at Liverpool University George implored graduates to pursue interests beyond their chosen careers. No one could accuse him of failing to practise what he preached.

Just as Younger had worked in the Scottish brewing industry as it adapted to the 1960s, he was preparing to help Scottish banking adapt to the 1990s. 'We are not proposing to make vast acquisitions and expand everywhere,' he told the *Scotsman*. 'Our objective in spreading out is not to get bigger per se but to show our customers that wherever they do business we can service them.' Within a decade, RBS would be pursuing a somewhat different expansion strategy.

On politics, George was unequivocal: 'I don't bring any party politics into this job. If there were to be a proposal for devolution, the bank would no doubt look at it and form a view. It has not got a political stance and will not have a political stance under my chairmanship.'[53] Yet over the next few years Younger would tread an increasingly thin line between his current and former careers, particularly over the thorny issue of devolution for Scotland.

At a session of the Scottish Grand Committee in February 1992, George made a considered speech in which he cautioned Scots against voting for a devolved system of government to express dissatisfaction with the status quo. A general election was imminent and with Labour confident of victory after thirteen years in the wilderness, Scottish devolution was again a realistic prospect. 'It does not follow that because Scotland is uncertain about its relationship [with the UK]', he told MPs, 'that anything is better than nothing.'[54] Younger claimed that financing a devolved parliament

---

[52] *Scotsman* 18/6/1992.
[53] Ibid., 15/1/1991.
[54] Ibid., 25/2/1992.

would lead to constant disputes with Westminster, where the influence of the Scottish Secretary would be seriously weakened.

Although Younger had once been an enthusiastic proponent of a Scottish Assembly, much like his friend Alick Buchanan-Smith (who had died from cancer in 1991), his feelings about devolution had long since hardened. George expanded upon his constitutional thinking in the first memorial Alick Buchanan-Smith Lecture, organised by the Scottish Tory Reform Group in 1992. He looked back on the high point of Scottish Unionism in the 1950s, when he and Alick first came into politics, and lamented its steady decline ever since.

But far from being a gentle tribute to a departed friend, Younger's speech was a robust defence of his pragmatic political beliefs. He dwelled in particular on the drive for inward investment while he was Scottish Secretary:

> We modernised the Scottish Development Agency and added 'Locate in Scotland' which has been enormously successful in attracting large numbers of entirely new, mostly high technology industries to Scotland. We can see the results now, as over the past few years Scotland's economic performance has been much better than most other parts of the UK. We have, of course, had the benefit of North Sea oil to help us, but the broadly based spread of industries we now have has kept Scotland going when many other parts of Britain were much worse affected.

'Add to all this', continued Younger, 'that successive Scottish Secretaries have secured for Scotland substantially greater amounts of money per head than what was provided for England, and it might be thought that this must be good government indeed.' So, why then, 'if all these splendid things were done, [were] the Scottish Conservatives . . . not returned to Parliament in ever increasing numbers, instead of becoming steadily fewer in number and less popular?' George answered that it seemed clear that electoral success in Scotland did not depend on producing tangible improvements in living standards. 'What we, as Scottish Conservatives have been failing to do in spite of all our successes is to win over the hearts and the emotions of the majority of Scots to our cause.'

Younger's solution was largely unchanged from what he himself had pursued as Scottish Secretary a decade before. The profile of the Scottish Office should be further enhanced, he suggested, and 'we must have as many national and international events in Scotland as possible. We must be as central to British life as any part of England or Wales is.' George also argued that the party's 'aims and political philosophy' needed to be better articulated, while on devolution, 'we do no service to the issue or to ourselves if we talk only from emotions and ignore facts that are staring us in the face'. He continued:

> The essential fact before us today is that no-one has so far produced a worthwhile scheme for running an Assembly in Scotland while at the same time having Scotland acceptably represented in Parliament. Even the so-called [Scottish Constitutional] Convention failed completely to tackle that problem . . . But, that said, Scottish Conservatives must continue to extend devolution of power wherever we can . . . We should aim to see that everything that can better be administered in Scotland is devolved to us up here. Let us have more UK ministries in Scotland. They will like it much better up here anyway!'[55]

Younger was at least consistent in that respect. He had campaigned for dispersal of government jobs throughout the 1970s; seen it implemented as a Cabinet minister in the 1980s; and now in the 1990s argued for its extension. George made this speech following the 1992 general election, in which he stood down as an MP after twenty-eight years in the House. The pugilistic Phil Gallie scraped home as his Conservative successor in Ayr, although it had widely been expected that most, if not all, Tory MPs in Scotland would lose their seats. As Scottish Secretary for most of the 1980s, perhaps Younger felt compelled to defend his legacy.

Inevitably, the House of Lords beckoned. 'I am most grateful to you for this proposal,' George replied to John Major, accepting his offer of a life peerage, 'and although I am now very much a full-time banker, I will do all I can to play a positive role in Parliament and to assist the Government's business in every way I can.'[56] Unusually, two generations of Youngers now sat together in the Upper House, although the 3rd Viscount Younger (Teddy) was a confirmed cross-bencher. 'I always expected that it would happen to me eventually,' quipped Younger during his maiden speech as Lord Younger of Prestwick, 'but my father and I are united in expressing the view that we are very happy that it has been made possible without the need for a death in the family first.'[57]

Although George was content to juggle the House of Lords with his duties at RBS, many could not help speculating as to what might have happened had he remained at the Ministry of Defence in 1989. Michael Jopling, the former Tory Chief Whip, was convinced that had Mrs Thatcher fallen on her sword at an earlier point in the late 1980s then

---

[55] Undated speaking notes, GYP.
[56] GY to John Major, 21/5/1992, GYP (copy).
[57] Hansard 539 c787–89. Younger was introduced to the Lords by his friends, the Lords Sanderson and Colnbrook (Humphrey Atkins). Another friend, Jeffrey Archer, was introduced the same day.

Younger would have been the choice of the Parliamentary party to succeed her. Certainly, in the wake of George's successful handling of the Nimrod issue, speculation of this sort extended well beyond Jopling.

'You cannot be a serious politician and answer no to that question, whoever you are,' said Younger when asked if he wanted to be prime minister in 1986, 'but I'm very happy where I am.'[58] It is an intriguing political 'what if?' Had George not committed himself to RBS and still been in the Cabinet when Mrs Thatcher fell, could MPs have turned to him as a proverbial safe pair of hands? After all, if John Major's selling point was that he represented Thatcherism with a human face, perhaps Younger's varied experience, sound judgement and innate charm could have made him an even more appealing option.

[58] *Three's Company* (BBC Scotland) c1986.

Chapter 15

'LORD HIGH EVERYTHING ELSE'

DESPITE ITS REORGANISATION, the Royal Bank of Scotland (RBS) was not a happy institution. As Younger got into his stride as chairman, Charles Winter, the outgoing chief executive, was increasingly dismayed at the rapidity and scope of the changes he had witnessed since December 1990. In July 1991 he wrote to George offering to resign as chief executive two years before he was due to retire. 'I have seen over the past few months the culture of the Royal Bank being quite destroyed by a series of radical and rapid changes', wrote Winter, 'all apparently generated by a feeling that the management of the Bank up to this point had been typified by total incompetence and that revolutionary rather than evolutionary change was necessary.'

Winter was also appalled at the compulsory redundancies of up to 200 managers as a result of the reorganisation, despite George Mathewson's assurances that there would be little 'pain' at branch level. But, he continued,

> I should put on record my appreciation of the support which I have had from you personally and, of course, from Sir Michael during all the years I served under his Chairmanship. From both of you, I experienced nothing but friendliness and understanding. It has been a privilege to work under you and I have greatly enjoyed the association. I do have feelings of sorrow now, of course, and some sense of failure, but absolutely none of bitterness. The Royal Bank is a great institution. It has been my whole life and my only concern is to see it continue to prosper. I am sure it still can prosper.[1]

In the event, Younger handled Winter with such diplomacy that he was still in place at the beginning of 1992. George had already identified

---

[1] Charles Winter to GY, 1/7/1991, GYP.

Mathewson as his replacement, and indeed the former Scottish Development Agency chief had essentially done the job since the end of 1990.
Some board members, however, were pushing a London-based candidate, although the chairman eventually charmed them into accepting
Mathewson.

'I think that was one of George's great things,' observed Mathewson,
later Sir George, 'to recognise ability and quality in people regardless of
background or personal politics, and also those who put the bank first. He
knew that I, Robin Duthie, Alastair Hamilton and Iain Robertson did
[put the bank first]. One or two others did not, and they soon faded from
view.' Mathewson and Younger were both Scots to the core, but while
one believed Scotland could only flourish through independence, the
other sought to achieve the same prosperity within the Union. Of course,
added Mathewson, 'he'd made a big thing of stepping out of politics to
come to the bank and it must have come as quite a shock to him to find
the bank in the state that it was'.[2]

Once again, the two Georges were a perfect match. While Mathewson
was perceived in the City as tough and aggressive, Younger was a perfect foil
in being seen as urbane and softly-spoken. Younger also proved to be an
effective chairman of the bank's regular (and very large) board meetings,
held every month or so at HQ in Edinburgh's St Andrew Square.

But Younger was not a trained businessman or number-cruncher; what
he brought to RBS was immense experience of public life, and perhaps
more importantly, an intuitive sense for people and tactics. In terms of
transferable skills, George's CV was impressive. As in politics, he lacked a
methodical grasp of detail, but then commercial acumen was Mathewson's job, and whenever the latter asked for the chairman's support he
generally got it. Younger's ability to master a brief also remained, while he
was in his element at the annual general meeting. 'It was a day you had to
get through,' remembered Sir George Mathewson, 'listening to concerns
while being patient and polite, and George did that very well. You get
asked the most obscure things, and you never know what might emerge
from the woodwork, so it's quite a tense thing to do.'[3] A sense of humour
was as useful in business as it was in politics, and George knew when to
apply a light touch.

Iain, later Lord, Vallance, served on the RBS board for most of
Younger's tenure as chairman and remembers meetings being informal
yet businesslike. 'He would not have claimed himself to be a commercial
businessman,' said Vallance, 'his strength was to preside, to be shrewd

² Interview with Sir George Mathewson, 22/5/2007.
³ Ibid.

about the people and make sure the business was done, and to be a great figurehead for the bank.'[4] Younger became a natural ambassador for RBS and relished the social and presentational aspects of his role. Glad-handing and witty speeches came naturally after a decade in the Cabinet. George deliberately did not interfere at an executive level, although he attended morning executive meetings as an observer. 'I meet people and introduce people,' said Younger, describing his role. 'Let's say I keep the machinery of the bank oiled.'[5]

Joining RBS at perhaps its lowest ebb arguably benefited Younger, for he caught the beginning of a tide – albeit one he had to harness and guide – which completely transformed the bank. In the early years of his chairmanship RBS refocused on its core business of retail banking, acquired the private bank Adam & Company in 1992, and launched Direct Banking two years later. It quickly became the UK's fastest-growing 24-hour telephone banking operation.

But there were also external events to contend with. Provisions for bad debt during the recession of 1991 had slashed profits and in October 1992, as Younger addressed a seminar at the European Parliament in Stras-bourg, the pound crashed on what became known as Black Wednesday. In early 1993 RBS announced job cuts totalling 3,500 over four years, around a third of which were to be compulsory redundancies. Younger was personally distressed, but said the move was 'essential for survival as a competitive retail bank'.[6]

In January 1993 it was announced that Younger was to be awarded the KCVO in the New Year's honours list, chiefly in recognition of his role in the Queen's fortieth anniversary celebrations. Typically, his friend Russell Sanderson congratulated him with some verse:

> Congrats to Lord Younger of Prestwick
> We're sure he's a nice man to know
> He's done very well for the monarch
> He deserves his K.C.V.O. . . .
>
> . . . Her Majesty looked up in wonder
> + pulled out her best silver sword
> 'Your advice is so good' she said wisely
> I'll make you a Knight now – my Lord.[7]

---

[4] Interview with Lord Vallance, 27/2/2007.
[5] *Scotsman* 7/2/1998.
[6] *Director* 7/1993.
[7] Lord Sanderson to GY, 31/12/1992, GYP.

The Queen's Anniversary Trust had not marked the end of Younger's extracurricular activities, even with the full-time job of chairing RBS. In 1991 he became chairman of the board of trustees of the Edinburgh Festival Theatre Trust (EFT), a project to restore Edinburgh's old Empire Theatre as a performing arts venue. George recruited Stephen Barry as general manager of the theatre soon after taking up the chair, and assiduously oversaw the renovation process.

The opening night concert took place on 18 June 1994 and boasted an all-star cast in an old-style music hall revue. A month later, the King and Queen of Norway attended an English National Ballet production of *Sleeping Beauty* at the venue, with Younger escorting the Queen, and Diana accompanying the Duke of Edinburgh (who once dubbed George 'Pooh Bah', 'Lord High Everything Else' in Gilbert and Sullivan's *The Mikado*). The arts had always been a keen interest of Younger's, and nothing gave him greater pleasure than seeing Scotland's capital acquire another state-of-the-art venue.

But, as ever in the arts, there were cash flow problems. Although the theatre broke even after 29 weeks of trading, by 1995 it was close to bankruptcy. Younger wrote to Edinburgh District Council suggesting the trust be allowed to go into liquidation. The theatre would then fall under control of the local authority, which could sell it on to a private operator. But shrewdly, Younger knew this would cause political uproar and gambled on the council coming up with a rescue package, which it duly did. 'The letter from George Younger pushed the district council into action,' commented a council source. 'Many people believe it was a serious, well-thought-out solution put forward by Lord Younger. Others see it as a wonderful piece of gamesmanship by a shrewd politician designed to shake people up. Whatever was in his mind, it certainly worked.'[8]

The EFT connection also proved useful when Napier University needed a temporary location for graduation ceremonies after the Usher Hall closed for repairs. Professor William (Bill) Turmeau, principal and vice-chancellor of Napier, had invited Younger to become its first chancellor in 1992. He readily accepted and was installed at the new university's inauguration in Edinburgh on 15 June 1993. Ayrshire-born Professor John Mavor, who succeeded Turmeau as principal in 1994, became deeply impressed by the extent of his interest in the university. As with so many of Younger's commitments, he turned out to be an inspired choice as the fledgling university's figurehead. He enjoyed greeting

---

[8] *Herald* 15/5/1995.

students at graduation ceremonies, at which he was always accompanied by Diana, and endured hundreds of handshakes. On one memorable occasion, he held an RBS £5 note a student had handed to him up to the light as if to check its authenticity.

Mavor, however, said Younger's true value lay in fundraising, particularly when it came to an estates strategy for a proposed development at Craiglockhart. George arranged access to the RBS executive suite at its offices in High Holborn, and hosted a series of luncheon meetings with potential benefactors. And when Craiglockhart was finally completed, he arranged for the Princess Royal officially to open the campus. 'When you had a resource,' said Mavor, 'such a willing, amiable, affable – but with a backbone of steel – resource, it was impossible to feel aggrieved when on the odd occasion he couldn't make a graduation ceremony.'[9] George remained chancellor until his death in early 2003.

Younger also remained actively engaged with two issues that had occupied him as a full-time politician – safeguarding the future of Prestwick Airport in his old constituency, and the Rosyth dockyard on the banks of the Forth.

When the government declared its 'Open Skies' policy in 1991, Prestwick lost its status as Scotland's only transatlantic gateway. The British Airports Authority (BAA), which owned Prestwick, quickly transferred existing transatlantic flights to Abbotsinch, otherwise known as Glasgow Airport (despite being in Paisley). Rumours spread that the airport was to be sold to a property developer.

Having first defended Prestwick against the development of Abbotsinch in his maiden speech a quarter of a century earlier, Younger was determined to save it. He had contacted Matthew Hudson, an ex-pat Canadian entrepreneur living on the west coast of Scotland, in early 1990 to ask for his help in forming a consortium to buy Prestwick, and with a little gentle cajoling Hudson became a key figure in what became known as PIK.[10]

By 1991 the airport was effectively defunct, with nothing beyond two FedEx DC-8s touching down weekly for night-time refuelling. Hudson agreed to look into whether or not the airport could be saved. He concluded that it could, despite BAA's argument that Prestwick was in the wrong place and operating within a market that was too small. 'I just can't imagine we'll find anyone to take this on,' George told Hudson,

---

[9] Interview with Professor John Mavor, 24/8/2007.
[10] PIK was the International Air Transport Association airport code, i.e. PIK – Prestwick; LHR – London Heathrow; STN – Stansted, etc.

'because they'd be bound to fail and couldn't raise the money, so would you do it?' He added that everyone else had turned him down. 'I said let me think on it,' recalled Hudson. 'I spoke to him the next day and said I would take it on, given one condition; George had to be chairman. I was an outsider and he wasn't. I needed the credibility he would bring and I needed to know where to deliver my message. George Younger knew where to go and could open the doors – all of them!' Younger served as chairman from 1991 to 1998.

There were a number of difficulties, both legal and commercial. Although British Aerospace needed a runway kept open for its flying school and Jetstream production, BAA simply did not want to sell the land and planned to destroy it. Hudson eventually tracked down an old legal document which obliged the government to retain the runway for 100 years after the taking of Scottish Aviation's property in the 1940s. BAA disputed the legal meaning of the obligation, but when a leading advocate supported Hudson's position, PIK's fortunes began to change.

BAA decided that it would sell the airport intact, but not to the troublesome Hudson. Undeterred, he rounded up influential local stakeholders, including the Labour-run local authority, to form a consortium called Ayrshire Community Airport Project (Acap) led by Younger. BAA remained hostile, but Younger eventually won them over. In early 1992 BAA sold everything to British Aerospace, which – as part of a continuous transaction – retained the runway and its manufacturing plant. It then sold Acap the balance of the airport (the land, terminal buildings and second runway) and leased it the main runway. Without George, said Hudson, 'it just would not, and could not, have happened'.

With Younger as chairman, PIK created what Hudson called a 'new paradigm'. Creative management, an enthusiastic workforce, refurbished buildings, and at long last a railway connection to the terminal building worked wonders. Yet the main feature of PIK's success was the emerging craze for low-cost airlines. By 1995 more passengers were passing through Prestwick than ever before, Ryanair having created a Dublin–Scotland service which was considerably cheaper than the competing route to Abbotsinch. The regulators did not, as expected, object, and because greater numbers were flying due to the reduced rates, overall market capacity actually increased.

'George had been involved in a high level of decision-making for a long time and so it was probably intuition,' said Hudson, who remained a friend of Younger's until his death. 'I would give him complex briefings and he would be letter perfect in meetings. But if I had a fact wrong or was pushing the boat too far out, George had a very subtle way of telling you.'[11] PIK was sold in 1998 to the Scottish businessman Brian Souter, and Younger, who had a minority interest, ended up with around £50,000 worth of shares in Souter's Stagecoach. It was a modest reward – although financial gain was never his aim – from perhaps George's most enduring political passion.

Younger's high-level lobbying over the future of Rosyth was, to his dismay, not as successful. At the end of 1992 speculation mounted that it would be closed and the job of refitting nuclear submarines transferred to Devonport on the south coast of England. George believed this contradicted assurances he had given as Scottish and Defence Secretary, and on 15 January 1993 he wrote to the Prime Minister, John Major. 'In both Offices I spent an enormous amount of time and effort in persuading the Scots to accept the nuclear submarine base,' he wrote, continuing:

> It was not easy but we succeeded by appealing over the heads of CND to their patriotism and by pointing out that any increased danger was counterbalanced by thousands of jobs in the high technology area for servicing and supporting the boats and dockyards. To take this away while leaving the base would be portrayed as a most cynical betrayal. It would leave your friends in Scotland, who argued the case, in an impossible position . . .

Crucially, continued Younger, 'if nuclear refitting was taken away from Rosyth I could not possibly support it, and there is no way I could avoid this being known publicly . . . I am very sorry to have to write like this, but only a real foreboding persuades me to do it.'[12]

Several weeks later Malcolm Rifkind, the Defence Secretary, made a statement guaranteeing that Rosyth would retain surface-ship refitting, but it did little to appease George's concerns. 'This would not conform with the assurances I and Michael Heseltine gave following the earlier Trident decisions,' he told Major on 18 March.

> Furthermore, it would enable Devonport, their future secure with the nuclear submarines programme, progressively to undercut Rosyth for surface work until the latter went out of business, thus driving a coach and horses through MOD competition policy. The inevitable closure of Rosyth will be obvious from the moment the decision is announced, and you will at once precipitate the 'damaging political row' which I know you want to avoid.[13]

---

[11] Interview with Matthew Hudson, 24/2/2007.
[12] GY to John Major, 15/1/1993, GYP.
[13] Ibid., 18/3/1993, GYP.

Younger was making himself perfectly – and perhaps uncharacteristically aggressively – clear. Disloyalty to the Conservative Party did not come easily to George, but integrity came first.

As with previous interventions of this sort, the Rosyth issue caused Younger problems at RBS. Viscount Weir was chairman of the Weir Group, which had interests at Devonport and was also a customer of the bank. He wrote to object, but George was not to be swayed. As a former Scottish and Defence Secretary, it was impossible for him not to have a view on Rosyth, and certainly not to keep it private.

In the event, nuclear refitting was transferred to Devonport. And although Rosyth's workforce was halved, it was guaranteed a high volume of surface-ship refitting (as Rifkind had promised) and remained open. That the choice of Devonport ultimately proved highly expensive, and its completion much delayed, was of little comfort to Younger.

Meanwhile, Younger continued to accrue honours with self-deprecating humour. Appropriately, on St Andrew's Day 1995 it was announced that he was to be installed as one of sixteen Knights of the Most Ancient and Most Noble Order of the Thistle (KT). Viscount Whitelaw and the Duke of Buccleuch – both former Commons colleagues and already KTs – led George into the Thistle Chapel at St Giles' Cathedral for his installation ceremony on 2 July 1996. Absent were two other former MPs and KTs, Sir Fitzroy Maclean – who had died just months before he was due to install George – and Lord Home, who had passed away the previous year. Alec had long been a sort of mentor to Younger, and at his memorial service, also in St Giles', he read movingly from Home's memoirs, *The Way the Wind Blows*.

It was also Home who had first articulated Conservative proposals for a Scottish Assembly in 1970. But when Younger expressed his views on Labour's pledge to establish a Scottish Parliament in the summer of 1996, he does not appear to have anticipated the reaction. In an unusual move for a financial institution, RBS issued a two-page statement just hours before George addressed a gathering of Eastwood Conservatives. 'The Royal Bank of Scotland will accept and operate within whatever con- stitutional arrangements are decided by Parliament,' the statement said. 'Our headquarters has remained in Edinburgh since our foundation in 1727 . . . and we do not see any diminution in our commitment to Scotland arising from the outcome of the current debate on the creation of a Scottish Assembly.'[14]

---

[14] 'We didn't have to be too obvious about it', said Sir George Mathewson, 'but George knew we weren't in favour of him speaking one way or the other' (interview with Sir George Mathewson).

Speaking in Eastwood, Younger was unabashed. 'Everything I say on this matter is my personal view,' he insisted. 'The Royal Bank does not have a view on Scottish devolution either for or against. Nor will it.' George went on to warn of the 'danger of a new parliament which relied for most of its money on another body, that is to say Westminster'. He also criticised Labour for not addressing the West Lothian Question and the over-representation of Scotland at Westminster. 'These problems must be taken seriously,' said Younger, 'for their effects if they are not solved will leave Scotland . . . saddled with an unworkable system of government that will do nobody any good.'

The SNP leader Alex Salmond, a former RBS oil economist, had a field day. He wrote to Younger claiming he had been barred from making political statements in the run-up to the 1987 election in which he contested, and won, Banff and Buchan. The chairman's response was less than convincing. Being chairman, said Younger, was not the same as being an oil economist:

> There was no suggestion that you should not speak as an individual, merely that, in view of your candidacy, it would be better that you did not speak for the bank in the very politically sensitive area of economics. Your freedom to speak as an individual was not curtailed, as it was the bank's policy to allow its staff to engage in political activity. That policy is unchanged and it is that freedom which I am now exercising in speaking as an individual on constitutional matters.

Labour also moved in for the kill. The opposition Chief Whip and future Scottish Secretary Donald Dewar said Younger's remarks were 'muddled and confused', while the MP Brian Wilson, a lifelong devolution-cynic, branded RBS the 'Tory bank' in reference to its overdraft facility for the Conservative Party.[15]

Whatever the subtleties of RBS policy, it was not Younger's finest hour. Judgement alone should have told him that such an ostentatious statement, delivered to a partisan audience, was bound to be interpreted – however wrongly – as the *de facto* view of the bank itself. His views soon became academic. At the 1997 general election every single Scottish Conservative MP lost their seat. Younger was appalled by the campaign, which bore little relation to those he had fought from the 1960s onwards. 'The Tory Party has behaved disgracefully and has come out decimated,' he wrote privately. 'They richly deserve it.' But, he added, 'Michael Forsyth fought

---

[15] *Scotsman* 6/8/1996.

a brilliant campaign in Scotland. He could not have put the anti-devolution case more strongly, and comes out with respect. Scotland had its full chance to vote it out and clearly did not take it. A Scottish Assembly will now happen.'[16]

As the resulting Scotland Bill was debated before the summer recess, Younger wrote in the *Herald* that he hoped all sides of the argument would be given an equal airing ahead of the referendum. 'My anxiety is that it may be portrayed as unacceptable even to discuss the arguments against,' he said, 'purely because it is thought that most people are in favour.' Again, George stressed that he spoke for himself and not RBS. 'The bank's position, which I fully support, is that it takes no part in party politics.' Although he was wrong in predicting bitter parliamentary debates and swift changes to Scotland's preferential public spending levels because of devolution, Younger was more prescient when it came to Tam Dalyell's favourite hobby-horse. 'The West Lothian Question is left hanging in the air without an answer,' he wrote, 'yet its effect would be seriously disruptive of relations between Scottish and English MPs.'[17]

The referendum, unlike that of 1979, produced a decisive vote in favour of a Scottish Parliament with tax-raising powers. Younger contributed financially to the Scottish Conservatives' ill-fated 'no' campaign, but gradually learned to love devolution. In 1999 he even agreed to sit for the artist Harry More-Gordon, who painted every surviving Scottish Secretary for a group portrait to commemorate the creation of a Scottish Parliament. George also resolved to refrain from political pronouncements. 'I think that as a former secretary of state, I ought to be able to express my own views,' he told the *Scotsman* in 1998 ('bristling' as he did so, claimed the reporter). 'But every time I said anything (the media) said it was the Royal Bank speaking . . . So I'll bide my time until I retire and then do a lot in the House of Lords.'[18]

Younger, however, did continue to make political pronouncements, although of a sort which attracted little media attention. His main outlet was an occasional column for the *Herald* newspaper during 1995 and 1996, while he also contributed infrequently to the *Sunday Times*. Europe was often a topic, and when John Major invited Tory MPs to 'put up or shut up' over his leadership, Younger applauded the Prime Minister's 'courage'. 'I sometimes wonder if more than 16 years in government has dulled the senses of Conservative back-benchers', he mused, 'as to what a

[16] Note titled 'General Election 1997 – First Thoughts', 2/5/1997, GYP.
[17] *Herald* c8/1997.
[18] *Scotsman* 7/2/1998.

privilege it is to provide the Prime Minister of the country, and also how extraordinarily difficult it is to get him or her there.'[19]

In October 1997 Younger called for the UK to enter the European single currency 'as soon as economic considerations permit'.[20] This time, he was directly stating the view of RBS, as well as his own. George also added his name to a letter in the *Independent* which urged the Conservatives to support the government in joining the Eurozone. 'I am a banker as well as an ex-politician', he explained, 'and as a banker I see great dangers in this thing going ahead for a long time and Britain being permanently out.'[21]

At the beginning of 1994 a row over the Malaysian Pergau Dam blew up as if from nowhere. The context was complex, and led to months of negative press coverage for Younger. As Defence Secretary in March 1988, he had visited Kuala Lumpur on seemingly routine MoD business. There, George signed an outline agreement that Malaysia would be eligible for UK aid 'alongside' a £1 billion-plus arms package involving Tornado jets. Crucially, the protocol directly linked the aid package to the arms deal, something which was of doubtful legality.

The Foreign Secretary, Sir Geoffrey Howe, and Chris Patten, the minister for overseas development, demanded that it be withdrawn, and in June 1988 Younger wrote formally to say that the link could not, after all, be made. But when Mrs Thatcher reiterated the civil aid pledge on another visit to Kuala Lumpur, the Malaysian government could be forgiven for thinking it was a done deal. The Malaysians were building a hydroelectric dam on the Pergau river, but as its estimated cost continued to rise, the Overseas Development Agency (ODA) repeatedly warned the UK government that the aid cash was not an economic use of taxpayers' money.

By the beginning of 1991 the Malaysian government was getting impatient. Having kept its side of the bargain by purchasing the Tornado jets, it now demanded funding for the dam. Finally, in July, Douglas Hurd (the then Foreign Secretary) overruled the ODA and, in consultation with the Prime Minister, authorised payment on the basis of Mrs Thatcher's prior commitment.

It was forgotten about until October 1993, when the National Audit Office published a report which revealed for the first time that Hurd had overruled ODA warnings and authorised payment of £234m

---

[19] *Herald* c6/1995.
[20] *Scotsman* 28/10/1997.
[21] Ibid., 6/1/1998.

towards the cost of the dam. The House of Commons Public Accounts Committee (PAC) also took evidence from Tim Lankester, permanent under-secretary at the ODA, who personally confirmed that his advice had been overruled.

Journalists smelled a rat, and the government whips' office began to get nervous. Alastair Goodlad, the Chief Whip, approached Younger in early 1994, a meeting swiftly followed by a letter from Hurd. 'Until now we have maintained the line taken in 1989 in a series of PQs [Parliamentary Questions] that there is no link between arms sales and aid,' he wrote. 'This is, of course, the strict position. We have, however, come under considerable pressure on Pergau in the wake of the PAC hearing and continuing allegations of linkage. We will come under more if, as seems likely, the FAC [Foreign Affairs Committee] decide to take up the issue.' Therefore, Hurd concluded, the government had to 'set the record straight' and acknowledge for the first time that the protocol signed by Younger included a reference to 'aid support of non-military aspects under this programme'.[22]

In February 1994 *The Economist* broke the Pergau story with an authoritative and detailed leading article. 'The consequences of this row are likely to be considerable', it asserted. 'Ministers continue to deny links between the arms deal and the aid package. But they will have difficulty explaining why, if they were not linked, they insisted on proceeding with such a dubious project.'[23] George was bombarded with interview requests but the timing could not have been worse. A few weeks later he underwent an operation for an enlarged prostate. Fortunately, it was discovered to be non-cancerous.

In early March, and as Hurd had suspected, the Commons' Foreign Affairs Committee (FAC) began an inquiry. The Foreign Secretary was the first to give evidence.

> The Malaysians told us in 1988 that they wanted as part of a deal to link an arms sales agreement to a set percentage of aid. The protocol which George Younger signed in March 1988 reflected the Malaysian wish. Having looked at it further and consulted his colleagues, George Younger wrote to the Malaysians in June 1988 – three months later – to say that a link was not possible. The memorandum of understanding or final agreement signed later in the year contained no such linkage. There was a temporary and incorrect entanglement . . . There is now no such link.[24]

---

[22] Douglas Hurd to GY, 26/1/1994, GYP.
[23] *The Economist* 5/2/1994.
[24] HC 271–i Q 1.

Younger, who also agreed to give verbal evidence at short notice, concurred with Hurd's use of the word 'entanglement'. He appeared alongside Sir Nicholas Spreckley (the former British High Commissioner in Kuala Lumpur) on 8 March, facing, among others, Sir John Stanley, a colleague from his MoD days. 'I do not remember there being . . . such a clear request from a customer to link aid with a defence sale in any other case,' he told the committee. 'All the briefing that I received was perfectly clear that there would be a request for a linkage and that linkage was out of the question.'[25]

Although the Pergau dam affair was stressful for Younger, he was confident of his record and approached the proceedings with typical good grace and minimum fuss, even appearing on *Newsnight* to defend himself against a string of hostile press reports. As he explained to a former constituent who had written offering support, 'there was nothing which occurred in March 1988 that wasn't absolutely normal in any negotiation of this kind'. He added: 'We are really remarkable in this country for managing to make failure out of success, but fortunately this deal is still, I think, going to be of enormous value to British industry.'[26]

The Foreign Office then tried to establish if Younger had been directly involved with the final decision to send two 'de-linking' letters to the Malaysian finance minister on 28 June 1988; that is, letters stressing that aid payments would not be directly linked to arms sales. George had attended a ministerial meeting on 23 June at which the text of both letters was agreed, although this had not yet been revealed publicly. Hurd was conscious that he would be asked about this, and warned Younger that the government would be forced to confirm his presence at the meeting:

> This is inconsistent [wrote Hurd] with your statement to the Committee that you did 'not know how the actual decision of the sending of those particular letters took place'. However, you went on to explain in your evidence that, although you did not remember having been responsible for the co-ordination, it was rather a long time ago and you would not have objected in any case. It is not unreasonable that you might have forgotten a point of detail after six years.

The inquiry also appeared to be taking its toll on Hurd. 'I hope we are nearing the end of this saga,' he scrawled at the end of his letter to George, 'but the Ctee is unpredictable, and I am likely to face judicial review of my decision of Feb. 1991.'[27]

---

[25] HC 271–iii Q 278 & 281.
[26] GY to John Kennedy, 8/3/1994, GYP.
[27] Douglas Hurd to GY, 4/5/1994, GYP.

The FAC's report, 'Public Expenditure: the Pergau Hydro-Electric Project in Malaysia, the Aid and Trade Provision and related matters',[28] was published on 20 July 1993. It concluded that in linking aid to arms sales, guidelines had been broken, and censured Younger's 'reprehensible' signing of the military protocol in March 1988. Remarkably, George took much of the blame and associated criticism on the chin. Having defended himself at the FAC hearings, he had nothing more to say.[29]

'I am sorry that you have been made to bear the worst of the criticism over the Pergau affair,' wrote Sir Nicholas Spreckley a few days later. 'It must be very galling to be made into a political football, when all one's efforts have been committed to getting the best possible deal for Britain . . . Nothing has happened to alter my view that I gave the right advice and you took the right decision, or to persuade me that anything that could be called a scandal took place.'[30]

Sir Raymond Lygo, chairman of the Rutland Trust, also penned a short note of sympathy. 'Having been involved in the preliminary discussions with the Malaysian authorities,' he wrote, 'I can only sympathise with all that subsequently transpired. The trouble is too many people believe that you can operate these affairs as if you were in a sanitised crystal palace! Knowing you as well as I do, I am sure it won't get you down.'[31]

Younger, of course, did not let it get him down, and while a Cabinet reshuffle quickly distracted the media gaze, he was amused to read *Private Eye*'s take on the affair. 'A man in a suit was today singled out in a shock report by MPs as the only person who was to blame for the appalling £450 million Pergau Dam scandal,' it read. 'The report concluded that it was very important for everyone to realise that Lord Younger bore sole responsibility for telling the Malaysians that we would build them a free dam if they were silly enough to buy some of our planes.' Younger, noted *Private Eye*, was 'now conveniently out of the way.'[32] Albeit irreverent, it summed up to many the unfairness of what had transpired.

George's father Teddy, the 3rd Viscount Younger of Leckie, died on 25 June 1997 aged 90. Despite gradual memory loss he had remained fit

[28] HC 271, 1993–94.
[29] 'The parliamentary committee got it completely wrong,' Younger told a reporter in 1998. 'The Pergau dam was absolutely nothing to do with me. I'd never heard of it until it appeared in the papers. They, or possibly the Malaysians, put together a link with civil aid that they apparently were negotiating with somebody. I don't know who it was, but it wasn't me' (*Scotsman* 7/2/1998).
[30] Sir Nicholas Spreckley to GY, 23/7/1994, GYP. 'All good wishes', he added, 'and make sure my investment in the Bank prospers, pronto!'
[31] Sir Raymond Lygo to GY, 28/7/1994, GYP.
[32] *Private Eye* 29/7/1994.

and cheerful into his old age but, as his son told a friend, 'Last Wednesday he had a major stroke after lunch and that was that.'[33] Teddy had sat in the House of Lords as a cross-bencher but, as his son was already a member of the Upper House as a political appointee, the new Viscount Younger made a rare switch from a life peerage to a hereditary viscountcy.

This proved harder than one might have thought. Producing his father's marriage and death certificates, as well as his own birth certificate, was not enough. 'They said they wanted to have a witness of my birth to prove that I hadn't been smuggled in with a bed pan,' George joked. 'As you can imagine this posed a bit of a problem.'[34] Fortunately, his sister Rosalind – by then long settled in Australia – came to the rescue by producing a sworn statement supporting his claim to the title. Her brother was thus summoned by writ on 11 February 1998 to sit in the House of Lords as the 4th Viscount Younger of Leckie, and took the oath on the 23rd. His youthful assertion that 'the hereditary principle should have no place in a modern constitution' was long forgotten.[35]

In a peculiar twist of fate, another aspect of the Younger family heritage also changed at around this time. The Church of Scotland's Board of Social Responsibility, which for the past half-century had run Watson House[36] – formerly the family seat of Leckie – as an old people's home, decided to put it up for sale. Younger, who had many happy childhood memories of the house, seriously considered buying it to convert into flats. The cost, sadly, was prohibitive and instead it was redeveloped and divided into private apartments.

George, however, had more than enough to occupy himself at RBS. In 1997 it launched the UK's first fully-fledged online banking service, as well as joint financial services ventures with Tesco and Virgin Direct. Aged 66, he showed no signs of easing his schedule of workload. Even after breaking his leg during a shoot in the Borders (he slipped on some ice), Younger bemused RBS directors by chairing the AGM from a wheelchair just a few days later. The year was 1999, and George was about to reach the peak of his chairmanship of what was about to become Europe's fourth-largest bank.

A new wave of consolidation had recently hit the financial services sector, and it inevitably reached Scotland. That summer there were 'friendly talks' between the Bank of Scotland (BoS) and RBS to discuss

---

[33] GY to Lord Milne, 2/7/1997, GYP.
[34] *The Times* 20/2/1998.
[35] See p. 78.
[36] As a condition of its sale in 1946, Teddy Younger had stipulated that it should cease to be called Leckie.

taking over the National Westminster Bank (known simply as NatWest)
with a joint bid. Peter Burt and Gavin Masterton at BoS wanted to press
ahead, but, said Younger, the 'problem was how we would divide up
NatWest between us. Would you take an arbitrary line and say you guys
can have everything north of the Wash? Peter thought it would be possible
but we were doubtful.'[37] Opinion at RBS was split, while George
personally opposed the scheme. Both sides quickly realised how difficult
it would be to implement such an arbitrary division of NatWest's branch
network, and the talks collapsed.

BoS quickly resolved to go it alone. On 24 September 1999 it launched
a £21bn hostile takeover bid for NatWest, which it intended to fund by
selling off NatWest subsidiaries like Ulster Bank and the upmarket Coutts
(chaired by Lord Home, Sir Alec's son David). That same day, Younger
met with Sir David Rowland, his opposite number at NatWest, to discuss
an alternative RBS deal. But despite having known Sir David since his
days as Defence Secretary, the NatWest chairman would not budge.

Publicly, however, RBS did nothing for the next two months, deliberately allowing BoS to make all the running. It was November before it
made a dramatic counter-offer of £26.5bn, trumping an increased bid of
£25bn from BoS. This allowed RBS to portray its bid as non-hostile
while, in contrast with BoS, it proposed to retain all of NatWest's
subsidiaries.

A veritable war of words quickly ensued. Significantly larger than both
its Scottish suitors, NatWest's David Rowland dismissed the BoS as a
'toytown treasury' business. In turn the BoS chief executive, Sir Peter
Burt, dubbed Fred Goodwin, deputy chief executive at RBS, 'Fred the
Impaler', a reference to his cost-cutting at the Clydesdale Bank, while the
epithet 'Fred the Shred' also did the rounds. Such puerile language did
nothing to disguise what was at stake in the largest hostile takeover battle
in UK corporate history.

Younger was fully behind the bid and soon became a positive driving
force, pressing investors to make a decision while Mathewson and Goodwin concentrated on the figures. George also ensured the banking
machinery back at HQ was well oiled, while entrusting day-to-day
management to the senior executives Iain Robertson and Norman
McLuskie. 'I said to them,' he recalled, 'at the other side of this bid
we want to see a smashing set of results from the Royal, and that is just
what they delivered.'[38] No stranger to high-stakes battles, Younger was in
his element.

---

[37] *Sunday Herald* 13/2/2000.
[38] Ibid., 5/8/2001.

'Put it like this,' said Sir George Mathewson in summing up Younger's contribution to the battle for NatWest, 'it may be hard to say exactly *why* he was important but he *was* important, and the Bank of Scotland suffered through not having someone with his breadth of experience.' George was responsible for most communications with Sir David Rowland, and through his connections with a few NatWest directors he kept the negotiations on a civilised footing. Rowland first approached George via Diana, asking her to emphasise that their initial meeting would merely involve 'cuddles', not hard negotiating.

Each morning there was a 'War Cabinet' at which the RBS executive and its advisers discussed tactics. Younger also attended, displaying great energy, commitment and an infectious determination to succeed. 'He went round with Fred and I and helped create the right atmosphere for our presentations,' recalled Sir George. 'He was always calm and made sure that Fred and I had exposed all the issues.' The intricate small print of the bid, however, was not his forte. 'George wasn't a detail man in that sense,' added Mathewson, 'but he did create the right climate for us to pull it off.'[39] Even more importantly, whereas Sir Peter Burt bored the Institute of Investors with a routine presentation, Younger charmed the pants off them. 'I think the handling of the senior figures involved was done with the kind of adroit expertise you'd expect from George,' recalled Lord Vallance, a member of the RBS board. 'You'd never get trading insults from George. The negotiations were edgy, because there was a lot to win and to lose . . . he was a key player in that, taking the broader view while leaving the commercial aspects to George Mathewson.'[40]

The battle continued over Christmas 1999 and into the New Year as the two banks fought for the crucial votes of institutional investors ahead of the February deadline. The first to go public declared for BoS, a chilling moment for RBS, although other big guns, including Standard Life, backed RBS. For Younger, the three days from 9 to 11 February proved to be tumultuous, and he kept brief diary notes as events unfolded.

It began with a phone call from Sir David Rowland to notify Younger of a NatWest board meeting at 11 a.m. on 9 April. 'Congratulations you have won,' Sir David told him. 'P[eter] Burt has rung me to say you have won.' Younger quickly phoned Iain Allan (RBS Group Director, Strategy) to pass on the good news before digesting it on a flight to London. But as George was driven from Heathrow to the City he took another call from Sir David. It was a dramatic turnaround. The board, he said, had met and 'was *not* satisfied that they believed we have enough votes to carry'.

[39] Interview with Sir George Mathewson.
[40] Interview with Lord Vallance.

Rowland added that NatWest had asked its broker, David Mayhew (a senior partner at Cazenove & Co), to investigate and give an opinion. 'I offered our brokers to talk to his,' noted Younger.

George had a busy day of meetings ahead, and constantly had to break off in order to answer frequent phone calls. During a lunch with Grosvenor Estates George Mathewson phoned to say that NatWest's brokers had no instructions to investigate. Younger called Rowland immediately 'to ask him to brief Mayhew & Co. He said he had just spoken to M[ayhew] & he is briefed.' A brokers' meeting followed at 2.45 p.m. but there was no progress. 'They don't believe we have signed up support,' recorded George, whose mind must have been on other things as he chaired fundraising meetings for Winchester's music school and the Royal Anniversary Trust at Waterhouse Square.

Sir David Rowland met him there at 6 p.m. '[He c]onfirmed they are not satisfied,' noted Younger. 'Went on to say he does *not* wish to accept my offer . . . of vice-chairmanship.[41] Wants to retire from this to family but will help in any way he can in transition.' Rowland obviously considered an RBS victory to be a foregone conclusion. '[He c]omplained about [Mathewson] saying . . . that he would not "ever" be in London.' George doubted that Mathewson had actually said this, but was conscious that Sir David had made much of the alleged remark with his staff. Rowland went on to suggest positions at RBS for certain NatWest figures and said 'he w[oul]d be holding a Board meeting (not clear whether full or Ctte) to assess position. *If* they are satisfied [they] will make statement that: "Board notes that shareholders have made their decision. Our duty now is to do all we can to help transition." Will ring tomorrow to let us know outcome.'[42] A dramatic day ended with the news that the investors MAM and Schroder had declared for RBS.

Newspaper headlines the following morning declared RBS to be headed for victory. Younger remained in London as RBS advisers worked hard on undecided investors, such as Prudential and PDFM, but 'All day more come aboard.' '[P]ercentage of committed investors up from 28% to 45% to 48%,' George noted. 'Pru came on board about 1645 but no statement.' There was another dramatic twist as a leaked internal BoS memo appeared to inform staff: 'we lost, but thanks for your support.'[43] Sir David phoned Younger at 4.25 p.m. as Ron Sandler, NatWest's chief operating officer, listened in.

[41] Younger had made the offer in writing ten days before.
[42] 'RBS/NatWest – Lord Younger's notes', 9/2/2000, GYP.
[43] Burt's internal memo actually said: 'You will have heard that we have lost our bid to NatWest. This saddens us, but we are far from downhearted.'

Complained contents of his conversations with me are public (viz his statement about waiting for Board to be satisfied we had won etc) . . . Accused us of hassling shareholders to switch to us & 'using our conversations as Brokerage'. Anyway, they are still not satisfied that we have the votes & [therefore] will not make a statement. He will let me hear if & when they are satisfied & will make a statement. If he does so, will still be as helpful as he can in transition etc.

Younger waited for a few minutes and then picked up the telephone. 'I rang again to say I had re-checked figures and they are now 55% going on 60%. He [Rowland] replied "Congratulations".' But still there was no formal confirmation, despite there being no evidence of any investors withdrawing support from RBS. 'Rowland making much in market about volatility of our shares,' wrote George as another dramatic day ended. 'They have fallen, but so have most exc[ept] BoS which is a little up.'[44]

At 8.45 a.m. the following morning Sir David contacted Younger with some good news. 'Phone call from Rowland conceding everything,' he recorded soon after. 'Statement going out now. He will do all he can to help. Meeting to discuss at NW on Monday confirmed.' Nearly three months of negotiations had finally paid off and ironically, BoS's second bid of £27.6bn and RBS's first bid of £26.5bn (both rejected by Rowland as 'inadequate') were substantially higher than the £20.9bn now accepted by NatWest, although a drop in share value during the offer period was largely the cause. Younger personally thanked staff involved in the bid ('plus those who kept RBS running') at a celebratory buffet luncheon that afternoon. 'N[orman]. McLuskie (as senior executive present) responded to my thanks. Morale high, but we still have to see if it works out on 14-2-00.'[45]

Some likened it to the St Valentine's Day massacre. 'It was the nearest run thing you ever saw in your life,' said a bruised Sir Peter Burt, paraphrasing the Duke of Wellington. 'It was certainly the nearest run thing I have ever seen in my life.'[46] Ironically, Younger's failure to persuade Rowland to recommend RBS's bid turned out to be in the bank's favour, as it could now take over NatWest without a single concession to honour. The long process of integrating the two banks began, and as it continued Fred Goodwin succeeded George Mathewson as chief executive in 2001, while Mathewson prepared to take over from Younger as chairman.

On the day the merger was announced, George rang the chairman of

[44] 'RBS/NatWest – Lord Younger's notes'.
[45] Ibid., 10/2/2000, GYP.
[46] *Scotsman* 18/4/2005.

Coutts, David Home, to offer him lunch. 'I thought he was going to sack me,' he joked. In fact, with a Scotsman as its founder, RBS was a natural home for the Queen's banker. 'He was so obviously honest, with such an open face,' added Lord Home. 'If he hadn't been chairman, some of the investors would have been doubtful about backing the bid.'[47]

Younger, however, firmly believed that RBS had succeeded due to the sheer credibility of Mathewson's management and his transformation of the bank since 1992. 'The one thing I was always anxious about as Secretary of State for Scotland was losing Scottish companies,' Younger later reflected. 'The Royal Bank of Scotland is now a permanent feature of life in Scotland. It is the seventh largest bank in the world and that is deeply satisfying.'[48]

'He told me that that marked the high point of his banking career,'[49] recalled Mathewson. And, as in 1989, it was therefore a suitable time for George to leave the chairman's office – on a personal high. Younger had almost become a fixture at RBS. He continued to legislate, guiding the Cheques (Scotland) Bill through the House of Lords to correct a long-standing anomaly between English and Scots Law in relation to the honouring of problematic cheques, while in his last year as chairman George had his company portrait painted by the Spanish artist Daniel Quintero.[50] Sir Peter Burt pointed out the irony of his leaving the bank 'twenty years after your predecessor sought to sell a demoralized and underperforming RBS to Standard Chartered!'[51]

Younger, however, faced one final challenge as RBS chairman, presiding over an AGM that was expected to be stormy. Shareholders were angry about £2.5m of bonus payouts to executives as a reward for the NatWest acquisition. George was bemused that something announced 15 months ago had only then created a fuss, although his assurance that four executives had taken at least half their award in shares, and Fred Goodwin all of his, deflected some of the ill will. After all, he argued, the acquisition of NatWest had trebled the size of RBS overnight and senior management had to be rewarded.

Before the AGM on 11 April 2001, Younger attended two farewell soirées, one in London and the other in Edinburgh. The first – and biggest – took place at the end of March in Inigo Jones' imposing Banqueting House on Whitehall. Friends and family sat alongside former private

---

[47] Interview with Lord Home, 13/2/2008. When Younger later toured Coutts, Home challenged his staff to spot George's physical defect. No one noticed his missing index finger.

[48] *Scotsman* 19/5/2001.

[49] Interview with Sir George Mathewson.

[50] 'It was quite exhausting standing for two hours at a time in that kit,' remarked Younger, having posed in his full Thistle Knight regalia. The full-length portrait is now on display at RBS's Gogarburn HQ.

[51] Sir Peter Burt to GY, 3/3/2001, GYP.

secretaries from the Scottish Office and MoD, while senior bankers wondered how to make conversation with Archers and former Argylls. The King's Singers cleverly mixed serious music with lighter numbers, and George Mathewson (who was to succeed George as chairman) followed Younger's witty speech by complimenting his achievements over the past decade. 'In a novel you wd. now renounce yr. peerage', wrote Douglas and Judy Hurd in thanks, 'and fight Perth & West Kinross to show how the wheel turns!'[52]

George's handling of the AGM two weeks later was masterly. Questions were handled with sensitivity and charm after he had given a lucid and comprehensive explanation of the issues before voting got under way. The feared shareholder rebellion was quelled, but through diplomacy rather than force, and instead they paid him warm tributes. After the final item on the agenda had been dealt with, Younger ceased to be chairman of RBS.

Tellingly, when Younger drafted subject headings for memoirs which were planned but never written, he put retirement in inverted commas, as if it were an abstract concept. Indeed, by early 2002 George was still using his old offices in Holborn and St Andrew Square, and had spent much of the previous ten months 'on safari', touring the RBS Group's nether regions and enjoying, as he put it, 'a last chance to say hello'. Despite no longer being chairman, he was yet to play a round of golf or pick up a tennis racket, although he had managed a few weeks' sailing in Argyllshire the previous summer.[53]

George also remained on the international board of Banco Santander, and flew regularly to Madrid on business. That, combined with frequent trips to London to satisfy his various commitments as chairman of the Fleming Mercantile investment trust, chairman of the Royal Armouries, Warden of Winchester and a peer, meant his schedule had changed little from his days as chairman. Friends marvelled at the breadth of his interests while Younger maintained that a good diet and regular exercise helped sustain his stamina. A pun on the family crest seemed apt: *Junior Labentibus Annis*, or 'Younger as the years go by'.

The first year of the new millennium was also Younger's seventieth birthday. His children organised a memorable evening at the recently-restored

---

[52] Douglas & Judy Hurd to GY, 31/3/2001, GYP.

[53] The Younger family used to decamp *en masse* to Melfort Village, Kilmelford, by Oban, each summer. They owned three boats; the first was an 11-foot Gull called *Smoky*, the second a Mirror named after Younger's daughter Joanna, and the third a 16-foot Norfolk Oyster called *Karmelia*, a composite of his granddaughters' initials. 'One thing I look forward enormously to when I retire is going sailing when I want to,' Younger told STV's *VIP* programme in 1998.

Great Hall at Stirling Castle, a venue with which their father had felt a special affinity since childhood. Brigadier Andrew Graham gave his blessing for the event, which culminated with George and Diana singing 'Bring me Sunshine' together. Younger was especially touched that the Argylls' Pipe-Major, Gordon Rowan, had composed a new tune for the occasion called, naturally, 'George Younger'. George's youngest son Andrew remembers listening to it that evening and feeling uncomfortable. The bagpipes can produce a melancholy sound and although the specially-composed tune was jolly, in retrospect he thought it sounded like a lament. Andrew, and the rest of the family, would hear it again just over a year later. Within months of the party Younger was diagnosed with prostate cancer. Although radiotherapy treatment appeared to be success-ful, by Easter 2002 signs of the cancer had reappeared.

The presence of so many Argylls at Younger's birthday party made it almost a regimental occasion, and indeed, the Argylls had been very much in George's mind throughout 2000 – the fiftieth anniversary of the Korean War. As well as taking part in commemorative events, George also began to write and speak about his experiences for the first time. In 1998 he had agreed to act as patron of the Scottish Korean War Memorial at Witchcraig, which became the focus for several anniversary events.

Younger reflected on the conflict in his speech as Lord High Commis-sioner to the General Assembly of the Church of Scotland in May 2001. 'Because of the regimental system and its local base,' he explained, 'I still meet frequently many of my comrades from Korea in 1950, particularly when I visit the supermarkets in Stirling. Like me, they look older (and less athletic) but they are the same people and the bond between us is as strong as ever, if unspoken.'[54] Another enduring link had been George's popular presidency of the UK Council of the Territorial Auxiliary and Volunteer Reserves Association (TAVRA), which provided a link between TA soldiers and their employers. He took over in 1996 just as the Reserve Forces Act became law, enabling those called up to return to protected employment. Three years later, Younger asked Roger Freeman – a former colleague at the MoD – to succeed him as president.[55]

Younger also remained active in the Queen's Body Guard for Scotland, otherwise known as the Royal Company of Archers. He had served on its Council as a brigadier, and latterly as a lieutenant, so George was naturally proud when his two eldest sons, James and Charlie, were

[54] Speech as Lord High Commissioner, 20/5/2001, GYP.
[55] 'The regional Tavres were in awe of George,' recalled Freeman (interview with Lord Freeman, 18/12/2006).

admitted as members in 1997.[56] Both were on duty at the 2001 Garden Party Parade, as was their father as an officer. He was also to have commanded the Argylls to mark the Queen's jubilee at Buckingham Palace that year but was simply too ill. Despite his absence, George was touched to receive the jubilee medal.

Another military pursuit which gave Younger enormous pleasure was his chairmanship of the Royal Armouries, to which he had been appointed in 1994. Essentially the state's collection of arms and armour, the Royal Armouries had originally been housed in the Tower of London until much of it moved to a purpose-built museum in Leeds in 1996.[57] There had been financial problems associated with the move, as well as internal management issues and unusually, parts of the collection going missing. Although George had a lot on his plate even in retirement, the Royal Armouries was a favourite distraction. Ann Green, whom he asked to become his deputy when he first became ill, remembers that he loved being able to wander around the massive reserve collection. 'He was a great listener, very diplomatic,' she recalled. 'He never handled anything contentious, because he didn't allow it to become contentious. It had been a very serious academic organisation but under George we moved beyond just being a lot of glass cases into something which would encourage people to get more involved.'[58]

The Royal Armouries board met six times a year either in Leeds or London, and once a year at Fort Nelson, where an artillery museum opened in 1995. Green shouldered more of the responsibility as Younger wound down his duties because of his illness, although he managed to attend an important meeting at the Department of Culture, Media and Sport to resolve ongoing accounting problems in early 2002.

One chairmanship he actually declined during his final years was that of the Scottish arm of the 'Britain in Europe' campaign. Younger remained passionately pro-European but despite his earlier enthusiasm for the single currency, was now not at all convinced that it was either practicable or desirable for the UK to join in the immediate future. The former Tory chancellor Ken Clarke approached him in July 2000 to head up the Scottish campaign, but Younger demurred, saying that his chairmanship of RBS, although coming to an end, made it impossible.

---

[56] Younger's youngest son, Andrew, was admitted to the Archers after his father's death. He was able to wear his father's old uniform with minor alterations.

[57] Younger is commemorated at the Royal Armouries by an eighteenth-century basket-hilted sword and scabbard representing his Anglo-Scottish career (although crafted in London, the sword's hilt is Scottish in style), as well as his connections with the Santander region of Spain (its blade is Spanish).

[58] Interview with Ann Green, 9/3/2007.

Besides, he replied to Clarke, 'I am doubtful if it is wise for us to give the impression of not being fully in support of the Conservative Party leadership during this period. We all have our differences of view from time to time but the chronic divisiveness which has characterised our activities in recent years is absolutely disastrous, and the same ailment is now afflicting the Labour Party.'[59]

Younger remained loyal to the Conservative Party, although he often despaired of its apparent death wish following the disastrous general election of 1997. He backed Clarke for the leadership when William Hague resigned following the 2001 poll, but doubted he would be able to carry the party's Eurosceptic minority with him. He was right.

Otherwise, George's political interventions diminished to a trickle. In July 2000 he submitted written evidence to the Scottish Parliament on its Bill to ban fox hunting in Scotland, but the general election of 2001 was the first in which Younger was not personally involved for nearly half a century. 'I'm not exactly broken hearted to watch from the sidelines,'[60] he said, although in 2002 he compared Tony Blair's 'strong' foreign policy with that of Mrs Thatcher.[61]

Younger ended his life occupied with two institutions which had had a profound influence near its beginning, Winchester College and the Church of Scotland. He had been appointed a Fellow at his old school in 1992, but was even more thrilled to become Warden in 1997, the highest accolade for any Wykehamist. Diana busied herself with upgrading the Warden's lodgings, just as she had done with Scottish Office buildings a decade before, while George set about trying to revive Old Wykehamist (OW) dinners at the House of Commons. These had waned due to the declining number of OW Members in the House, but Younger suggested boosting attendance by inviting non-OWs, such as the Tory MP James Gray, whose children were at Winchester. He also authorised construction of a £4m extension to the music school for which he personally provided generous financial backing.

'He was a benign, rational, and efficient chairman presiding over a distinguished governing body,' recalled Alan Ryan, the warden of New College, Oxford, 'but bringing the managerial habits of a very traditional school up to modern standards was a time-consuming business, and sometimes a painfully acrimonious one.'[62] Acrimonious was an apt

[59] GY to Kenneth Clarke, 28/7/2000, GYP.
[60] *Scotsman* 19/5/2001.
[61] *Soldier* 2/2002.
[62] *New College Record*, 1/2003.

way to describe the two-year tenure of Dr Nicholas Tate as headmaster. An historian and experienced educationalist, Tate was the choice of Younger and the school governors to take over in 2000. Many staff felt his sympathies did not naturally extend to a very old and prestigious boarding school, while his attempted modernisations were met with stiff opposition. Perhaps if Younger had been on peak form he could have sorted it out (Earl Ferrers, the Deputy Warden, dealt with much of the fallout), and although George ensured relations were not as strained as they might have been, Tate moved on in 2003.

The other institution was the Church of Scotland, or Kirk. Although Younger's first formal experience of regular worship had been daily Anglican chapel at Winchester, he belonged – like the Queen – to both established churches 'as a matter of principle'. Although not ostentatiously religious or pious, Younger's faith was steady and unquestioning. He shared his mother's view that it simply was not feasible that the creation of the earth had been an accident. 'It isn't provable any other way,' he reasoned in 1998, 'which is why I firmly believe that God has created us.'[63] He was ecumenical in outlook, but regretted moves away from traditional forms of worship.

Younger slipped naturally into the vice-regality required as Lord High Commissioner to the General Assembly of the Church of Scotland. He served for two consecutive years, at first in 2001 and again the following year, by which time he was already seriously ill. As the Queen's representative, the post included residency at the Palace of Holyrood-house, where George spread charm and goodwill at the garden party and numerous lunches and dinners he was required to host over a period of ten days. His daughter Joanna also acted as principal lady-in-waiting.

On the first day of the 2001 General Assembly, the *Scotsman* carried an in-depth interview with Younger in which he spoke of his personal doubts that Jesus had been the 'biological' son of God. 'I don't think you can be absolutely literal and say he was born without a father,'[64] he said, instead subscribing to the progressive view that Jesus was divinely inspired by God. His speech as Lord High Commissioner a few days later, however, avoided controversy. Instead it was reflective, examining the challenges facing the Kirk in the twenty-first century:

Making the public proceedings of the Church exciting, attractive and relevant must in some respects be more difficult for this new, more sophisticated and more worldly Congregation. However, there is a strong culture of innovation

[63] *VIP* (STV) 17/8/1998.
[64] *Scotsman* 19/5/2001.

and self-criticism which pervades your annual debates which is thoroughly
constructive and bodes well for the future. Our congregations are changing,
and you are changing with them, and this gives me great confidence that our
Church will continue to serve the nation outstandingly well, as it has done for
hundreds of years.[65]

Younger chose as his chaplain Mike Erskine, who remembers him
recounting an almost spiritual experience in Korea, when he heard
the psalm 'The Lord's My Shepherd' sung by hundreds of men in a
paddy-field. George also grew close to the Very Rev John Miller, who was
Moderator during his first stint as Lord High Commissioner, an unlikely
and unexpected friendship (Miller was left-leaning) which deepened as he
learned that his cancer was terminal. On one memorable day Younger
brought his entourage to Miller's Castlemilk (a deprived part of Glasgow)
parish to visit the Jeely Piece Club and the fledgling Churches-Together
Refugee Centre.

The following year – fifty years after she became Queen – the monarch
herself attended the opening day of the General Assembly, after which
Younger once more assumed the duties of Lord High Commissioner.
Assembly week could be gruelling and his social duties were scaled back to
allow him more time to rest, although he was determined to carry on as
normally as possible.

By July 2002 Younger was cancelling more and more of his engagements as he learned that his cancer was most likely terminal, and although
he managed a short holiday at Loch Melfort the following month, this was
cut short when he was forced to return to hospital in serious pain. Initially,
only close family and friends knew of George's prostate cancer, and in
September his children were even summoned home for seemingly final
farewells. But doctors were able to manage his pain and in November the
Edinburgh Evening News broke the news, his resignation from the Murray
International Trust on grounds of 'ill health' being the first public
confirmation of his condition.[66]

Shortly after, Younger was booked in to the Strathcarron Hospice at
Denny near his home in Stirlingshire. Diana encouraged friends and
family to visit, even keeping an appointment diary, and he particularly
enjoyed being able to spend more time with his grandchildren. Younger's
second cousin, the Tory MEP John Purvis, gave him a copy of their
shared family tree, while George's brother Bobby dispatched humorous
notes. 'I hear of many people who choose to lie in bed all day shooting

[65] Speech as Lord High Commissioner.
[66] *Edinburgh Evening News* 6/11/2002.

drugs and sniffing glue or some such substance,' he wrote. 'I'm a little surprised to hear that you are one of them.'[67]

Younger joked cheerfully with the nurses, who were amused by his habit of waving a torch around when he could not reach the assistance bell at night. Visitors to the hospice usually arrived between 11 and 12 a.m., and again from 3 to 4 p.m. after he had rested. John Mavor, who was about to stand down as principal at Napier, brought George up to speed with developments at the university. 'He said something like "We're both retiring together",' he recalled, 'which was rather sweet.'[68] Matthew Hudson and Larry Fish even left the United States specifically to visit him.

Well-wishers sent Younger videos and talking books to keep him occupied, while RBS board members and his successor as chairman, George Mathewson, dropped in. Political friends also came to say good-bye. Tam Dalyell, with whom Younger had sparred over Aden and devolution, found him to be 'brave and resilient',[69] while he received Sir Malcolm Rifkind in a 'robust and cheerful mood'. 'He was concerned, even then,' remembered Sir Malcolm, 'for his party, for his friends and for his country.'[70]

John Major wrote, wishing George well, while Baroness Thatcher contacted one of her favourite ministers to say that she and Sir Denis were 'thinking of you and recalling all the good (and even *great*) things we did during our time in politics'. 'And how much you *did* for Scotland especially,' she continued. 'I think we can rightly say that we *made a difference*. May I also say that I am *personally* grateful for all the advice and support you gave to me. They were unforgettable years both for us and for Britain.'[71]

It was a touching gesture from Younger's former chief. Her note arrived as Scotland, and the rest of the UK, was enduring a disruptive firemen's strike. 'I was amused the other day to be [told] by someone that it is all very well for you to criticise the failure of the Government to solve the strike but you had the same trouble with the miners,' George replied. He continued:

I gave them a brief account of how we planned, well in advance and very carefully, as to how the miners could be defeated . . . I do think that Tony Blair and his colleagues have been extremely remiss in failing to use the last nine months to prepare, as we did, for the strike that was so clearly coming up. I do

[67] Bobby Younger to GY, c2001, GYP.
[68] Interview with Professor John Mavor.
[69] *Scotsman* 27/1/2003.
[70] Sir Malcolm Rifkind's memorial service speech, 26/4/2003, GYP.
[71] MT to GY, 18/11/2002, GYP.

hope that one day somebody will come to recognise this. We did have a lot of luck, particularly that Arthur Scargill was such a bad strategist, but the fact is that we prepared every detail of how to keep the country supplied with coal even when both the mines and the railways were not working. It undoubtedly was one of the highlights of my political life that we worked together on that and I am very proud that we did that so successfully.

'Once more many thanks for writing,' concluded Younger. 'I am being well looked after although I doubt if I shall be able to return to the House of Lords before many months are out.'[72]

Despite his illness, George had a very clear view of how he wanted his funeral and memorial services to be conducted. In fact, he instructed Diana so closely that she teased him, saying it was a shame he would not be there to see it. 'Don't be so sure,' he joked, 'I might ask for a day ticket.' Always a practical politician as well as a human being, he even faced death in a constructive spirit. John Miller, whom Younger had recently requested take part in his memorial service, asked him if it caused him to question his faith. After a long pause George replied: 'I feel as though I've been preparing for this all my life.'[73]

Miller had also been writing regularly with guidance. 'At times, when the road seems very rough ahead,' Younger replied to one letter, 'I do hope that I may recover well enough to see something of you and others during next year's General Assembly but at the moment this does not look, by any means, a certainty.'[74] George also spoke at length to each of his children, conversations they found both comforting and uplifting.

In December 2002, Younger managed to attend the wedding of his niece Minty and found enough strength to spend Christmas at home with his family. But he became much weaker. With the help of Penny, a stalwart carer and strong Buddhist, George was able to spend the last month of his life at Leckie, where Penny and Diana used walkie-talkies to co-ordinate each day. Diana believed that George's determination to enjoy all that life still had to offer kept him alive well beyond what he described as his 'sell-by date', but on Sunday 26 January – shortly after losing consciousness – Younger died peacefully with Diana by his side.

He was cremated a week later at Falkirk Crematorium, and laid to rest following a private service at Gargunnock parish church. Although George's death was expected, it was a tragedy that his retirement with Diana, to which they had both looked forward for so long, had been

---

[72] GY to MT, 28/11/2002, GYP (copy).
[73] John Miller's memorial service speech.
[74] GY to John Miller, 28/11/2002, GYP (copy).

denied to him. Younger's life was later celebrated with two services of thanksgiving which aptly reflected his dual Scottish/UK existence, the first at St Giles' Cathedral in Edinburgh, and another at Winchester Cathedral almost two weeks later. Both services summed up the man. In attendance were politicians – government and opposition – Argylls, musicians, Kirk ministers, neighbours from the village, civil servants past and present, family, and even representatives of the Queen and Duke of Edinburgh, Prince Charles, the Princess Royal, Princess Alexandra and the Duke of Kent, whom George had first met at a TA camp in 1957.

James Younger delivered the first reading at the Edinburgh service; John Miller an eloquent address; and Sir Malcolm Rifkind a warm and witty eulogy. Rifkind even quoted the 1st Viscount Younger: 'Whatever faults I may have, and there are many, I have always tried to steer a straight and clean course in my political life. It does not always pay perhaps, but it leaves one in possession of a comfortable conscience.' It applied just as suitably to his great-grandson. 'He was a man for all seasons,' concluded Sir Malcolm, 'we salute him.'[75] Mike Erskine said prayers, including that of the Order of the Thistle, while George's favourite pieces by Mozart, Bach, Elgar and Handel reminded those present of his love for music.

Music also pervaded the memorial service at Winchester Cathedral two weeks later. The choir included members of the Winchester College Chapel Choir and Quiristers (the Winchester choristers), while the Dean took the service and Earl Ferrers gave the address. George's daughter Joanna, and two sons – Charlie and Andrew – also did readings. Those present at both services listened intently as Pipe-Major Rowan reprised his tune, 'George Younger', playing as he slowly walked the length of each Cathedral, his notes filling the air but growing fainter as he disappeared from sight.

---

[75] Sir Malcolm Rifkind's memorial service speech.

CODA

I valued his common sense, trusted his judgement and relied on his loyalty. His career is proof of the fact that, contrary to myth, gentlemen still have a place in politics.[1]

Margaret Thatcher

'Gentleman George' was just one of many epithets which came Younger's way during his long career. 'He's a classic old-time Tory paternalist,' remarked one colleague, 'with noblesse oblige to the poor.' Mrs Thatcher agreed, observing in her memoirs that 'for all his decency and common sense [George] was very much of the paternalist school of Scottish Tory politician.'[2] Others accused him of wielding an iron fist beneath a velvet glove.

All of these descriptions are true, yet at the same time they do not quite capture the essence of Younger, who is something of an enigma. His brand of Conservatism was certainly paternalistic, yet he was never a 'wet' (and certainly did not see himself as such) in the manner of Jim Prior or Sir Ian Gilmour. Rather he remained in Cabinet long after most wets had been banished to the backbenches. But nor was George a passionate Thatcherite. Instead, he steered a middle way between the wets and the dries and emerged without even a hint of what Lord Thorneycroft called 'rising damp'. Essentially, Younger succeeded in being part of Mrs Thatcher's Cabinet while simultaneously portraying the Scottish Office as if it were not part of central UK government.

In this sense, Mrs Thatcher had in Younger the perfect manager of change in Scotland, although the image of him repulsing Thatcherism at the border is almost absurdly overdone. As Andrew Marr says in his book, *The Battle for Scotland*, 'Thatcherism did happen in Scotland. George

---

[1] Thatcher, *The Downing Street Years*, 756.
[2] Ibid., 620.

Younger and Malcolm Rifkind, displaying skill, good humour and loyalty, were the men who made it happen.'[3] Younger, however, made it happen with important modifications, most significantly when it came to the economy. He won a reprieve of the totemic steelworks at Ravenscraig, preserved and improved the interventionist Scottish Development Agency, won a Whitehall battle to establish the inward-investment bureau Locate in Scotland, secured dispersal of civil service jobs to the west of Scotland and maintained a system of regional industrial grants despite pressure to scrap them completely. Crucially, all of this was achieved in spite of Mrs Thatcher's monetarist instincts, not to mention those of influential Cabinet colleagues.

And although uncomfortable with the spending cuts of the early 1980s, George accepted that the central thrust of Thatcherite economic policy – even though he wrapped it in the consensual language of the Macmillan era – was necessary. To these fiscal ends he proved a surprisingly tough opponent of high-spending Labour councils, whom he effectively by-passed with measures such as the Right to Buy and legislation enabling 'parental choice' in local authority schools. He also transformed the relationship between central and local government in Scotland, most notably in financial terms.

George, of course, was not perfect, and while his administration of Scotland from 1979 to 1986 was successful, when it came to forging a long-term strategy for the Tories in Scotland arguably he failed. The election results in 1979 and 1983 certainly provided an opportunity for him to do so, but instead Younger spent much of his tenure simply responding to events, many of them traumatic and therefore deeply damaging to the Scottish Conservatives in electoral terms.

The main reason was Younger's lack of interest in political ideology. 'It is never wise to appear cleverer than you are,' Willie Whitelaw is said to have remarked. 'It is sometimes wise to appear slightly less so.' George would have agreed, and although he was renowned for his engaging ability to sell individual policies to the Scottish electorate, somehow he never quite managed to become an evangelist for the Scottish Conservative Party's broader view of life. And when he did take the lead with a bold new policy, the so-called Poll Tax, the result was disastrous. 'Irrespective of party allegiance,' Younger wrote prophetically in 1968, 'no government and no Prime Minister could go against the wishes of the united opposition of . . . Scottish M.P.s, and if it were the case they did not act in the best interests of Scotland, the Scottish people would not vote for them.'[4]

---

[3] Marr, *The Battle for Scotland*, 172.
[4] The *Scotsman* 15/12/1967.

Those words came back to haunt Younger as political ground was steadily lost. There were warning signs in 1983 when a Conservative landslide rested more in the south of England than to the north of the British Isles, and in 1987 George even came close to losing his own constituency, a fate that did befall nearly a dozen of his colleagues. It has been said that a combination of the Poll Tax and intransigence over constitutional reform were to blame for the 1987 result, but the reality is less clear cut. The Poll Tax played, in fact, no large part in that election campaign while on devolution George was lucky, as his successors were not, in being able to dismiss the question of whether there should be a Scottish Assembly as no longer of interest to the majority of Scots.

After 1987, however, demands for devolution gradually revived, as did cries that the Conservative government lacked a mandate in Scotland. Younger had, of course, supported a Scottish Assembly from Ted Heath's Declaration of Perth in 1968 until (privately, at least) the referendum of 1979. Office, however, was an adequate corrective for his pro-devolution instinct, as was – not unreasonably – the inconclusive result of that referendum. An intriguing political 'what if' surrounds the Scottish Assembly that never was. Some believe it would have acted as a focus for opposition to Mrs Thatcher and hastened independence. But perhaps the Conservatives could have carved out a niche for themselves on Calton Hill. And perhaps George could have led them.

But although Younger's balance sheet in Scotland is lopsided, the Scotland of the early twenty-first century is largely that created during his seven years as its Secretary of State. Council housing has all but gone through a related increase in owner-occupancy, local government remains largely under central government control, while – most significantly – heavy industries were long ago replaced by thriving electronics and service sectors. And even when Silicon Glen began to decline sharply in the late 1990s, the resulting job losses were quickly absorbed. Not a bad legacy of what George proudly called 'the new Scottish economy'.[5]

Younger's political career always included an element of luck, and his move to the Ministry of Defence in early 1986 was certainly lucky, coming as it did at the height of a bitter teachers' strike and just before the furore over the Poll Tax really took off. But even if Michael Heseltine had not resigned, it seems likely that George would eventually have moved to the MoD anyhow. There, he steadied the ship, skilfully resisted both spending cuts (relatively speaking) and a dreaded defence review, while capitalising on the victory won by Heseltine in the debate over nuclear weapons.

[5] Kemp, *The Hollow Drum*, 181.

More to the point, George managed to avoid the pitfalls of a particularly accident-prone portfolio while keeping defence issues centre-stage,
most notably during the 1987 election campaign. He was also the last
Defence Secretary with direct experience of a war zone, in Younger's case
Korea. It was therefore fitting that having fought in what has often been
described as the forgotten war, George ended his political career at the
MoD as the Cold War drew to a close.

In policy terms, being Defence Secretary was also ideally suited to
Younger. Always more concerned with day-to-day management rather
than innovative policy-making, the defence brief played to all of his
strengths. If there was a blot on those three years at the MoD it was the
so-called Pergau Dam affair, even though it only emerged several years
after George had retired from the Cabinet. Nevertheless, he endured a
rather unjustified scapegoating with typical good humour.

Good humour also accompanied Younger's accruement of honours
after he left political office. And as chairman of the Royal Bank of
Scotland (RBS) during a decade which saw unparalleled growth for one of
Scotland's oldest financial institutions, he also proved that there was life
after the Cabinet, bucking Enoch Powell's maxim that all political careers
end in failure. During George's tenure, RBS became the most successful
banking group in Europe, increasing its profits from £58m in 1991, the
year he became chairman, to £5,800m in 2001, the year he retired.

The warmth of George's relationships with staff at all levels throughout
RBS – relationships he cemented through hundreds of visits to offices and
branches – was a major contributor to building a high morale which Sir
George Mathewson, Younger's successor as chairman, believes was a
major factor in the success of RBS. Another colleague thought George
had created at RBS 'a wonderful blend of family and efficiency, which
seems to be what gives the team their self-confidence to dare and to
achieve'.[6]

That daring reached its height with the successful hostile takeover of
NatWest in 2000, transforming RBS into a truly global bank but one that
remained firmly headquartered in Scotland – always one of Younger's
key objectives. In 2005 the bank moved to its new international headquarters at Gogarburn on the outskirts of Edinburgh, while its old Gyle
site boasted a commemorative 'Younger building'. There was also some
family continuity. George's only daughter Joanna, who had started work
at RBS after her father retired, rose to become Head of Corporate
Responsibility.

---

[6] Jim Currie to GY, 31/10/2002, GYP.

But despite the rich tradition of political service in Younger's family, George was to be the last in his line to devote most of his life to the public good.[7] In that sense, political clans like the Youngers of Leckie are now very much part of Scotland's past. George represented a generation which believed it important to have done something in life before entering politics, a belief which now holds little sway in a country dominated by career politicians. So although George bridged two political generations in terms of style and outlook, he was to be one of the last representatives of a rapidly fading Tory era.

In evaluating Younger's life it should not be considered frivolous to point out that he was almost universally well liked. Considering that he was one of Mrs Thatcher's longest-serving Cabinet ministers, six years of which were spent in a largely hostile Scotland, it is no mean feat that he left Dover House with few critics and even fewer personal enemies. His life, therefore, is not only a testament to public service but also to simple humanity. 'What a nice man,' he used to say of the US defense secretary Cap Weinberger; following encounters with George – however brief – many people remarked the same of him.

Younger would have agreed with Rab Butler that politics was the art of the possible, although the US economist John Kenneth Galbraith – with whom George occasionally lunched as chairman of RBS – would not. Politics, said Galbraith, came down to a choice between the disastrous and the unpalatable. Throughout his career, be it in the TA, politics or business, Younger was always adept at fighting against the former, while ensuring that even the latter was expounded in a sensitive, and more often than not charming, manner. Moreover, he always enjoyed what Stanley Baldwin called the endless adventure of ruling men without ever considering it a burden.

---

[7] The present Viscount Younger, George's eldest son James, never sat in the House of Lords following the removal of most hereditary peers in 1999. He did, however, come a close second in a March 2007 by-election caused by the death of one remaining Conservative hereditary.

Appendices

Report and Recommendations

From the Rt Hon George Younger MP

Friday, 8ᵗʰ December [1989]

1. The result is not as good as the figures. Many voted with varying degrees of reluctance for the Prime Minister. They cannot all be relied upon another time.

2. Many worries expressed were typical mid-term policy concerns (e.g. inflation, mortgage interest, ambulance dispute, water privatisation). If these problems did not exist, there would probably have been no challenge. However, the fact that the challenge took place has unearthed the significance of these problems. As there are likely to be economic and polls difficulties in a year's time, another challenge is not improbable. We feel everything possible must be done now to head this off.

3. Apart from these current issues, the following points were made by many of the 'doubtfuls':

   a) Members feel the PM is not accessible enough. It is not clear why (she is often in the Lobby), but they clearly feel this.

   b) They also feel the PM is not prepared to listen receptively to their concerns.

   c) It is strongly felt (even amongst the greatest supporters) that the reshuffle in the summer went badly wrong and that Nigel Lawson's resignation could have been avoided. It is felt that not enough time was taken to plan how best to approach those being moved.

   d) There is a widespread feeling that Downing Street advisors are too prominent and have more influence than senior ministers.

However unfairly, there is great mistrust of them, and it is thought they 'ring fence' the PM from other advice.

e) It is felt that there are personality tensions within Cabinet and that these must be resolved if confidence is to be restored. In particular, Geoffrey Howe must be seen and treated as the PM's right-hand man.

f) The PM is marvellous in paying visits to constituencies. It is felt they would like her to do more, even if it means doing less of other things (e.g. foreign tours).

4. The following are some suggestions for major changes in style which might convince the Party that these complaints have been understood and dealt with.

a) A major effort by the PM to reduce her diary commitments. Space for thought and for unexpected requirements should be written into the programme.

b) Fewer foreign tours and more home ones. Foreign Secretary should do *most* of what needs to be done abroad. Failing him, could the Deputy PM perhaps do some of these?

c) The passing of more business to Cabinet committees chaired by senior ministers. This would contribute to a).

d) Clear rapprochement following recent tensions. Perhaps the Cabinet and wives should dine together socially at least twice a year.

e) More unplanned opportunities for chatting to backbenchers (e.g. casual visits to Smoking Room, etc. more invitations for Members of Parliament to No 10 lunches and dinners even at the expense of fewer ministers, particular efforts to chat with and listen to those known to be of different views).

f) An early and visible change in Downing Street top advisors (this would be for their own good too).

g) While maintaining existing policy over Europe, a major effort to sound positive about closer integration of the right sort. It is the *hearts* of the pro-Europeans that need to be reached, not their heads. Most of the new generation have grown up as pro-Europeans and have preached it as an ideal. They can be persuaded to be hard-headed on bad policy proposals, provided they believe our leadership passionately believes in Europe too.

h) When we do join the ERM, we must do it with warmth and enthusiasm.

i) A new set of aims for the 1990s, different from the 1980s, will be needed. Perhaps a weekend seminar at Chequers with four or five ministers could set the tone for this. The PM and Government have been enormously successful in the 1980s. The 1990s will not be the same, but they can be equally successful. We must not let Labour seem new and different while we remain the same.

'GEORGE YOUNGER'
BY PIPE-MAJOR GORDON ROWAN

BIBLIOGRAPHY

ARCHIVES

Conservative Party Archive (Bodleian Library, University of Oxford)
Scottish Conservative and Unionist Association Papers (National Library of Scotland)
Winchester College Archives (Winchester College)
Younger, 4th Viscount (George K. H. Younger) (Private Collection)
Margaret Thatcher Foundation (www.margaretthatcher.org)

PUBLISHED SOURCES

Anderson, Bruce, *John Major: The Making of the Prime Minister* (London 1991)
Ashdown, Paddy, *The Ashdown Diaries I: 1988–1997* (London 2000)
Baker, Kenneth, *The Turbulent Years: My Life in Politics* (London 1993)
Benn, Tony, *Conflicts of Interest: Diaries 1977–80* (London 1991)
Betjeman, John, *Summoned by Bells* (London 1960)
Birkenhead, 2nd Earl of, *The Life of F. E. Smith* (London 1965)
Butler, David, Adonis, Andrew and Travers, Tony, *Failure in British Government: The Politics of the Poll Tax* (Oxford 1994)
Campbell, John, *Margaret Thatcher I: The Grocer's Daughter* (London 2000)
— *Margaret Thatcher II: The Iron Lady* (London 2003)
Catchpole, Brian, *The Korean War* (London 2000)
Churchill, Randolph S., *The Fight for the Tory Leadership* (London 1964)
Clark, Alan, *Diaries* (London 1993)
— *Diaries: Into Politics* (London 2000)
Cole, John, *As It Seemed To Me* (London 1995)
Cosgrave, Patrick, *Thatcher: The First Term* (London 1987)
Crickhowell, Nicholas, *Westminster, Wales and Water* (Cardiff 1999)
Critchley, Julian, *Heseltine* (London 1987)
Crossman, R. H. S., *The Diaries of a Cabinet Minister II* (London 1976)
Currie, Edwina, *Diaries 1987–1992* (London 2002)

Dalyell, Tam, *Devolution: The End of Britain?* (London 1977)

D'e Firth, J., *Winchester* (London 1936)

Donnachie, Ian, *A History of the Brewing Industry in Scotland* (Edinburgh 1979)

Donoughue, Bernard, *Prime Minister* (London 1987)

Fowler, Norman, *Ministers Decide* (London 1991)

Galbraith, Russell, *Inside Outside: A Biography of Tam Dalyell* (Edinburgh 2000)

Garnet, Mark and Aitken, Ian, *Splendid! Splendid! The Authorized Biography of Willie Whitelaw* (London 2002)

Gibson, John S., *The Thistle and the Crown: A History of the Scottish Office* (Edinburgh 1985)

Heath, Edward, *The Course of My Life* (London 1998)

Heseltine, Michael, *Life in the Jungle* (London 2000)

How Scotland Should be Governed (Edinburgh 1968)

Howard, Anthony and West, Richard, *The Making of the Prime Minister* (London 1965)

Howe, Geoffrey, *Conflict of Loyalty* (London 1994)

Kemp, Arnold, *The Hollow Drum: Scotland Since the War* (Edinburgh 1993)

Lang, Ian, *Blue Remembered Years* (London 2002)

Lawson, Nigel, *The View From No. 11* (London 1992)

Linklater, Magnus and Denniston, Robin, eds, *Anatomy of Scotland: How Scotland Works* (Edinburgh 1992)

Malcolm, George I., *The Argylls in Korea* (London 1952)

Major, John, *The Autobiography* (London 1999)

McMaster, Charles, *Alloa Ale: A History of the Brewing Industry in Alloa* (Edinburgh 1985)

Marr, Andrew, *The Battle for Scotland* (London 1992)

Meyer, Sir Anthony, *Stand Up and Be Counted* (London 1990)

Mitchell, Colin, *Having Been a Soldier* (London 1969)

Mitchell, James, *Conservatives and the Union* (Edinburgh 1990)

Onward to Victory: A Statement of the Conservative Approach for Scotland (Edinburgh 1978)

Parkinson, Cecil, *Right at the Centre* (London 1992)

Powell, Enoch, *Joseph Chamberlain* (London 1977)

Ramsden, John, *The Making of Conservative Party Policy* (London 1980)

Roy, Kenneth, *Conversations in a Small Country* (Ayr 1989)

Schofield, Charles and Kamm, Antony, *Lager Lovelies: The Story Behind the Glamour* (Glasgow 1984)

Scotland's Government (Edinburgh 1970)

Seldon, Anthony, *Major: A Political Life* (London 1997)

Shepherd, Robert, *The Power Brokers: The Tory Party and Its Leaders* (London 1991)

Slaven, Anthony, *Dictionary of Scottish Business Biography* (Aberdeen 1986)

Stark, Leonard P., *Choosing a Leader: Party Leadership Contests in Britain from Macmillan to Blair* (London 1996)

Tebbit, Norman, *Upwardly Mobile* (London 1988)

Thatcher, Margaret, *The Downing Street Years* (London 1993)

— *The Path to Power* (London 1995)

Thorpe, D. R., *Alec Douglas-Home* (London 1996)

Torrance, David, *The Scottish Secretaries* (Edinburgh 2006)

Tosh, Murray, *Keep Right On . . . The Story of the Conservative Party in the Ayr Burghs and Ayr Constituencies* (Ayr 1992)

Walker, Adrian, *A Barren Place: National Servicemen in Korea 1950–1954* (1994)

Walker, Peter, *Staying Power* (London 1991)

Ward, J. T., *The First Century: A History of Scottish Tory Organisation 1882–1982* (Edinburgh 1982)

Warner, Geoffrey, ed., *In the Midst of Events: The Foreign Office Diaries and Papers of Kenneth Younger February 1950–October 1951* (London 2005)

Watkins, Alan, *A Conservative Coup: The Fall of Margaret Thatcher* (London 1991)

Weinberger, Caspar, *Fighting for Peace: Seven Critical Years at the Pentagon* (London 1990)

Winchester College Notions (Winchester c1940)

Young, Hugo, *One of Us* (London 1989)

Younger, Kenneth G., *Britain's Point of No Return* (London 1968)

INDEX

HARRIER